FACES OF MADISON

A Photographic Journal of the Madison, Indiana, Bicentennial Celebration

1809 - 2009

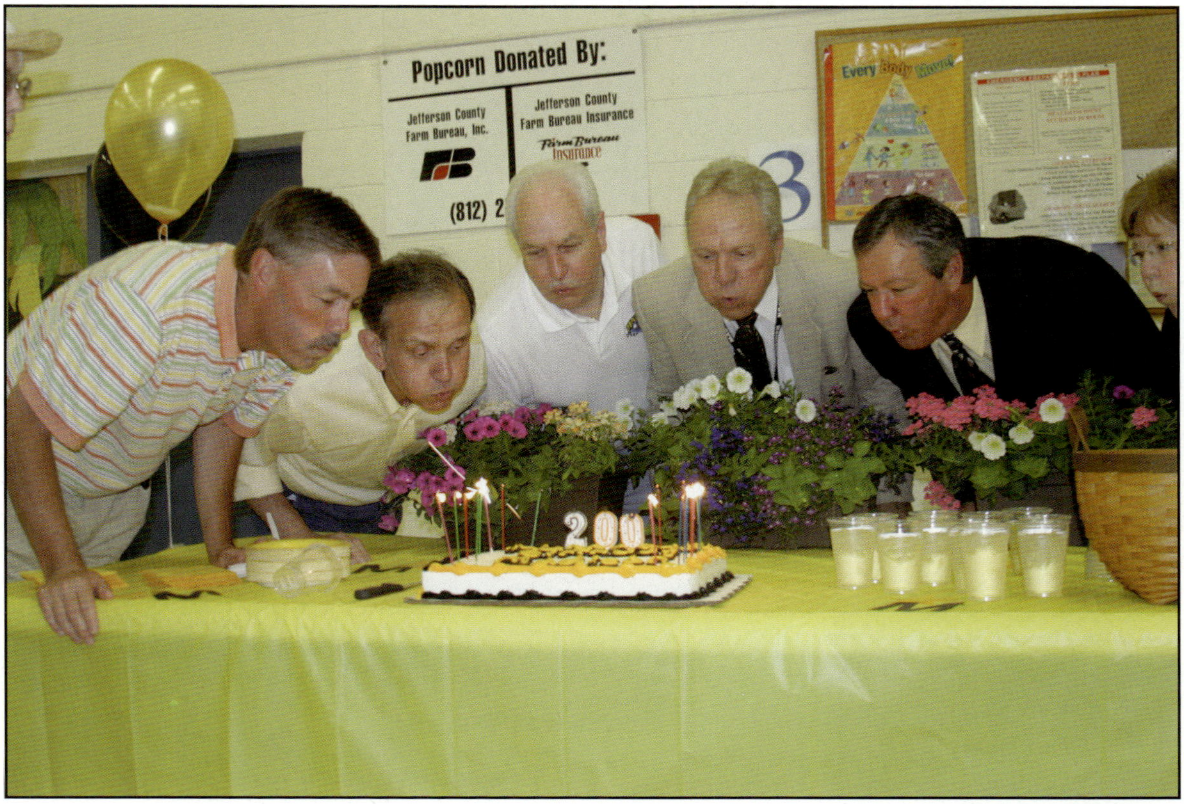

Photo by Don Ward

Madison city officials blow out a specially prepared Bicentennial birthday cake May 1, 2009, at Anderson Elementary School. From left they are Madison City Council members Rick Berry, Bob Schoenstein and Pete Backus, Madison Consolidated School Superintendent Tom Patterson, Madison Mayor Tim Armstrong and Council member Laura Hodges. The entire school participated in a balloon release outside the building prior to cutting the cake.

Produced by RoundAbout Madison
as an Official Publication of the Madison Bicentennial

RoundAbout MADISON

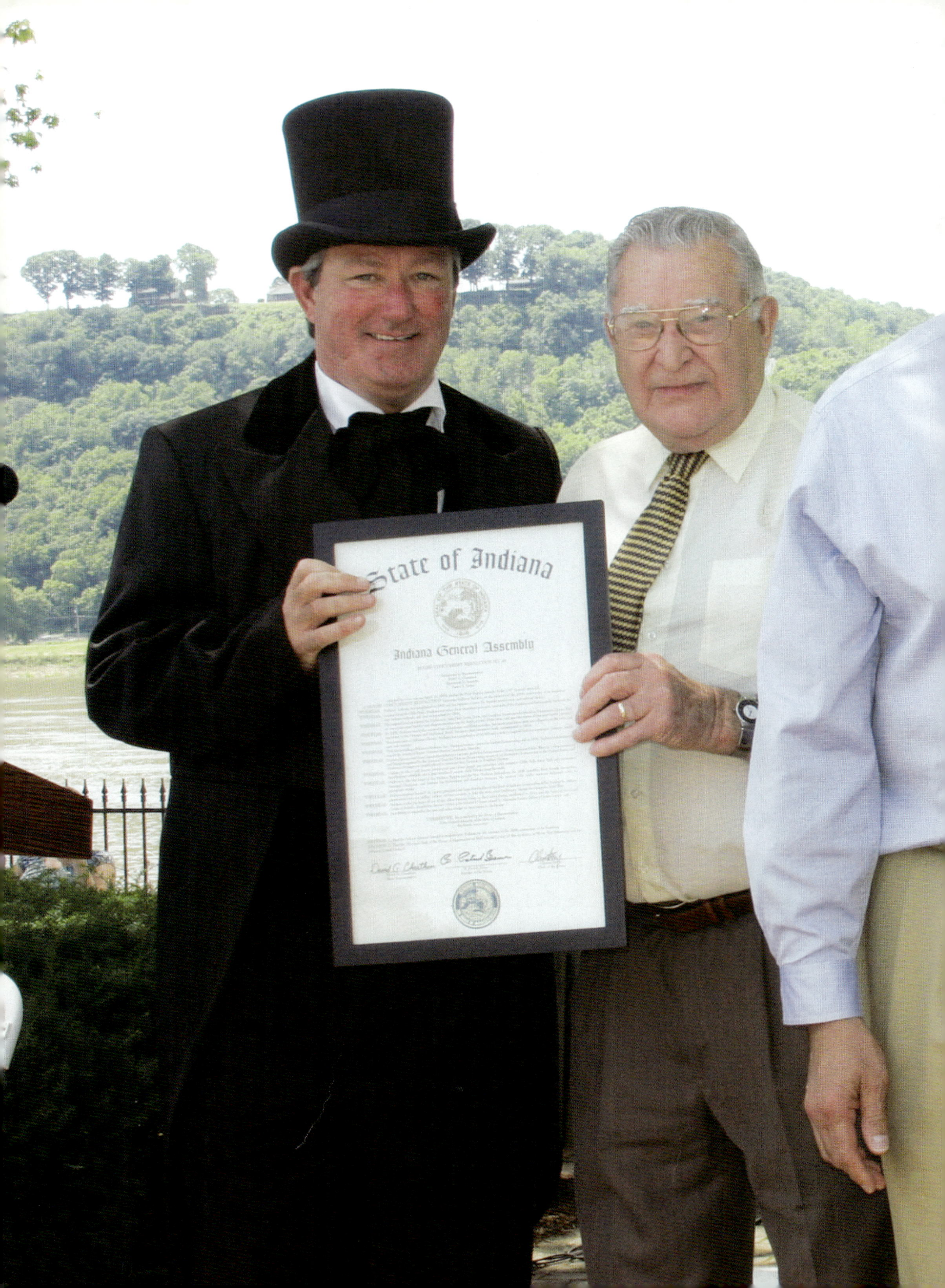
State of Indiana
Indiana General Assembly

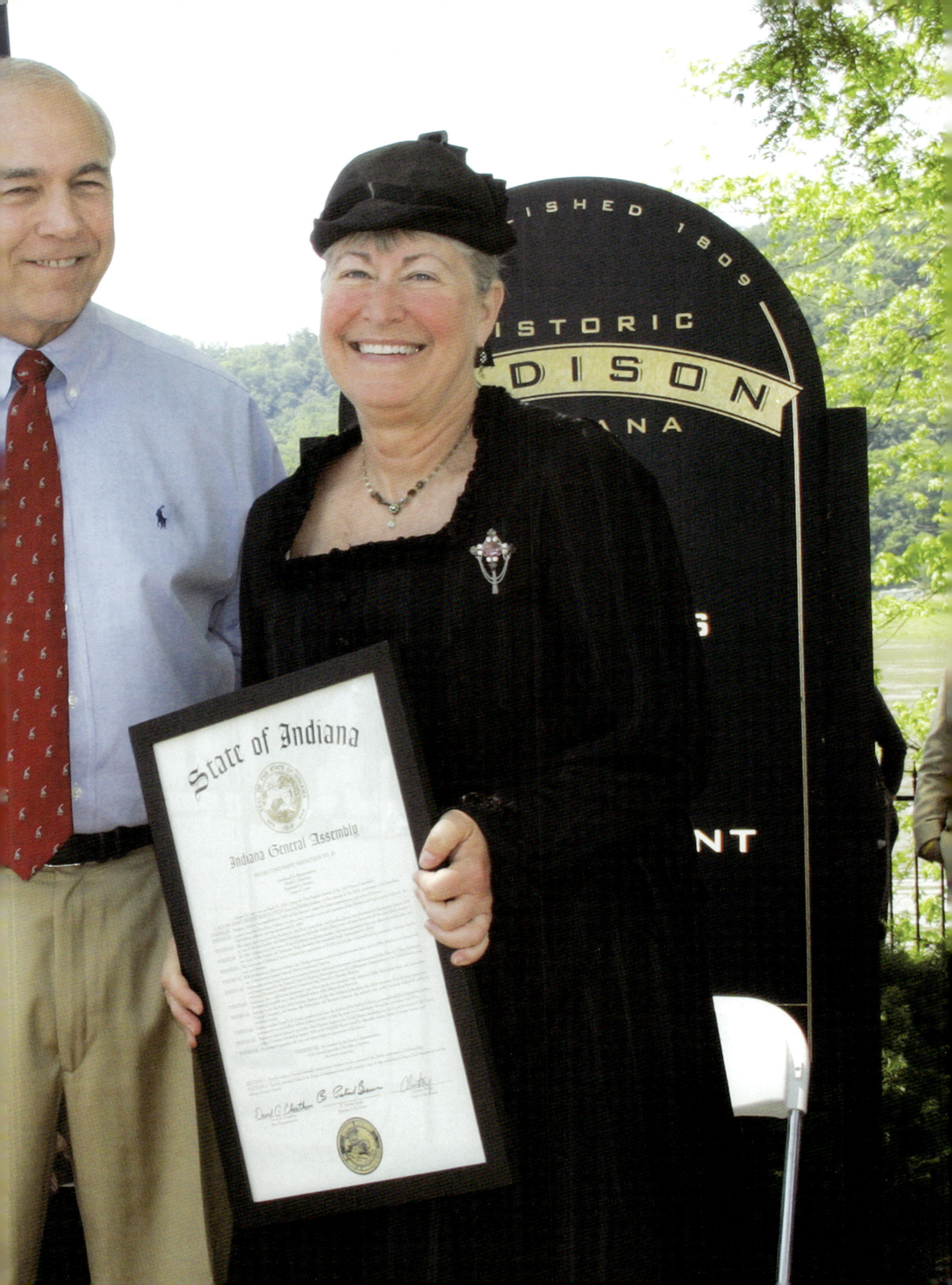
ISHED 1809
ISTORIC
DISON
ANA
NT
State of Indiana
Indiana General Assembly

Blue River Press
2402 N. Shadeland Ave., Suite A
Indianapolis, IN 46219
(317) 352-8200
Fax: (317) 352-8202
1-800-296-0481 (toll free)

This book is available in quantity at special discounts for your group or organization. For more information, contact:

RoundAbout Madison
314 Jefferson St., Suite 201
Madison, IN 47250
(812) 273-2259
1-800-343-3005 (toll free)
Fax: (812) 273-5490
Email: info@RoundAboutMadison.com
Online at: www.RoundAboutMadison.com

ISBN-13: 9780981928951
Printed in the U.S.A.

Produced by RoundAbout Madison

Book and Photo Editor: Donald L. Ward

Cover Design: Donald L. Ward

Photographers: Donald L. Ward, Matt Griffith, Randy Porter, Kathy Chandler, John Palmer Gregg

Photo Contributors: Laura Hodges, Dan Hodges, Emily Ward, Darrel Taylor, Konnie McCollum, Stephanie Hellmann, Bernie Kasper, Cristina Evans, Tara Gentile. Community group photo on back cover courtesy of Michael Heitz.

This book is an official publication of the Madison Bicentennial.

Faces on the Front Cover: (From left) Jim Grant, Nancy Gruner, Bill Demaree, Musical Resource dancer Erin Laufer, Jan Vetrhus as Charlotte Sullivan, Madison Mayor Tim Armstrong, "Rivertown" singer Kate McKay, Gerry Reilly, Bob Schafer, Laura Hodges.

Faces on the Back Cover: (From left) Andrew Forrester, Lisa Croxton, Harry Dobbins, Janice Stanley, Tammy Boldery, Susan Walters, Chris Ginn, Emily Kugler, Fred Koehler, Susan Ohlendorf.

Previous page photo of the presentation held during the June 6, 2009, Madison Bicentennial Opening Ceremony was taken by Don Ward. In the photo, Madison Mayor Tim Armstrong (far left) and Bicentennial Committee Chairwoman Jan Vetrhus (far right) receive framed certificates of concurrent resolutions from the Indiana General Assembly. Presenting the resolutions are Indiana State. Sen. Jim Lewis (second from left) and Indiana State Rep. Dave Cheatham.

Contents

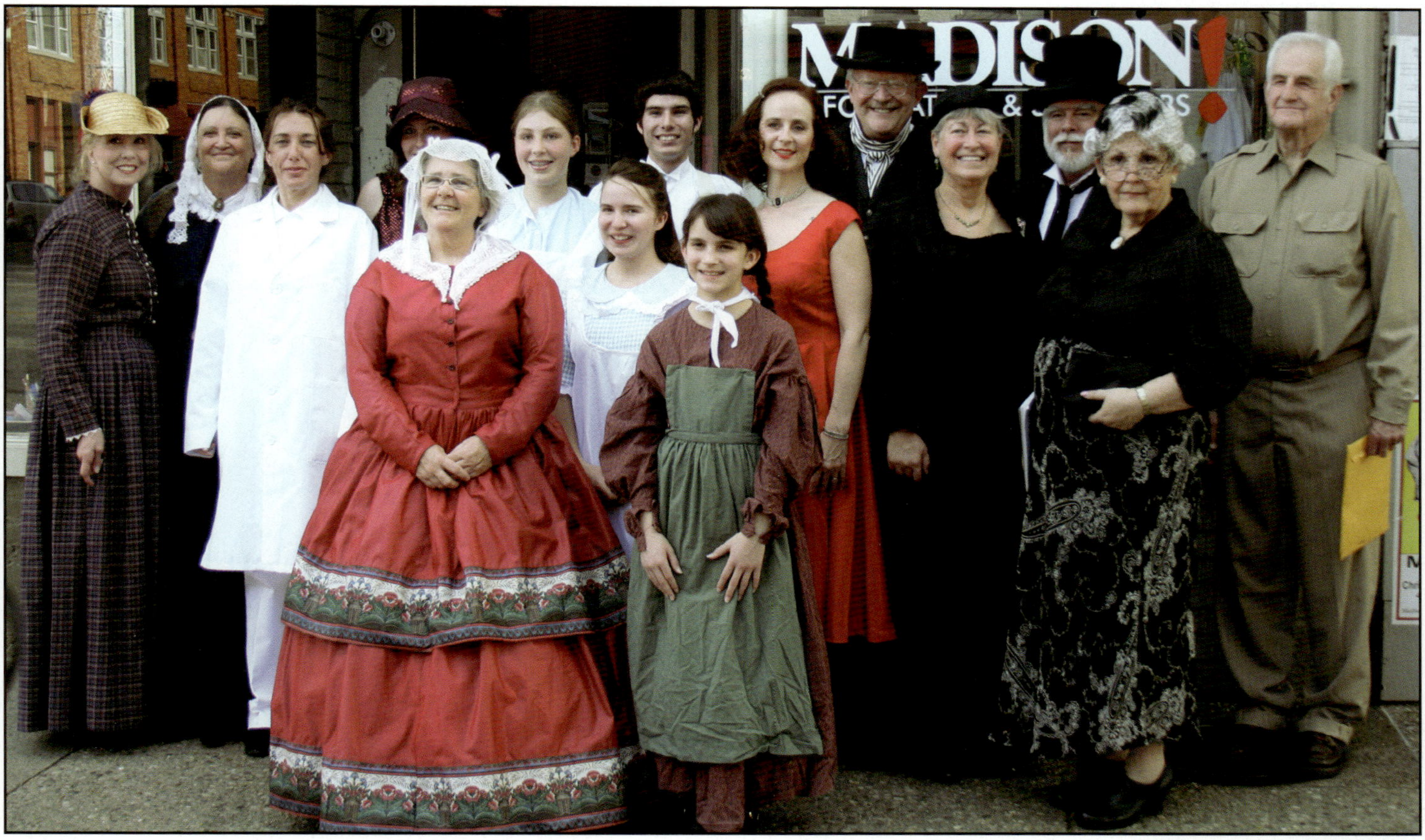

Photo by Kathy Chandler

Several Madison, Ind., residents portrayed famous people of the city's past during the Madison Bicentennial celebration. They are (from left) Joyce Randles (as teacher Lydia Middleton), Connie Partington (as poet Sarah Bolton), Sandie Gooden (as Helen Spry), Ashley Roberts (partially hidden in back as the fictional Betty Roberts), Stephanie Hellmann (in front as Delia Webster), Emily Roberts (as Sadie Lankford), Bryce Worrell (as Lt. Col. Alois Bachman), Brianna Worrell (in front of Bryce as Harriet McGlasson), Brandilyn Worrell (in the gray pinafore in the front row as Lillian Williams), Margo Watkins (in the red dress as actress Irene Dunne) Wayne Engle (as newspaper publisher Michael Garber), Jan Vetrhus (as Charlotte Sullivan), Bob Fourhman (as Ohio Gov. John Brough), Betsey Vonderheide (as Drusilla Lanier Cravens) and Bill Demaree (as Gen. Walter Krueger).

7 Foreword

10 Preliminary Events Related to the Bicentenntial

22 Jefferson Co. Courthouse Fire May 20

28 Bicentennial 5K Walk-Run June 6

32 Opening Ceremony, Founder's Parade, Boat Parade June 6

48 Cincinnati Symphony Orchestra Concert June 7

52 1920s-1930s Gala June 7

58 Arts Day and Rogers Corner Mural Unveiling June 8

67 Pie-Baking Contest, Community Picnic June 9

70 Historic Sites Day, Ice Cream Social, The Lincolns June 10

72 Hilltop Day, Cruisin' Clifty and Teen Concert June 11

79 Car Show, Talent Show, Block Party on Main Street June 12

88 Lanier Days & Trades Fair, Concert and Laser Light Show June 13

96 Closing Ceremony June 14

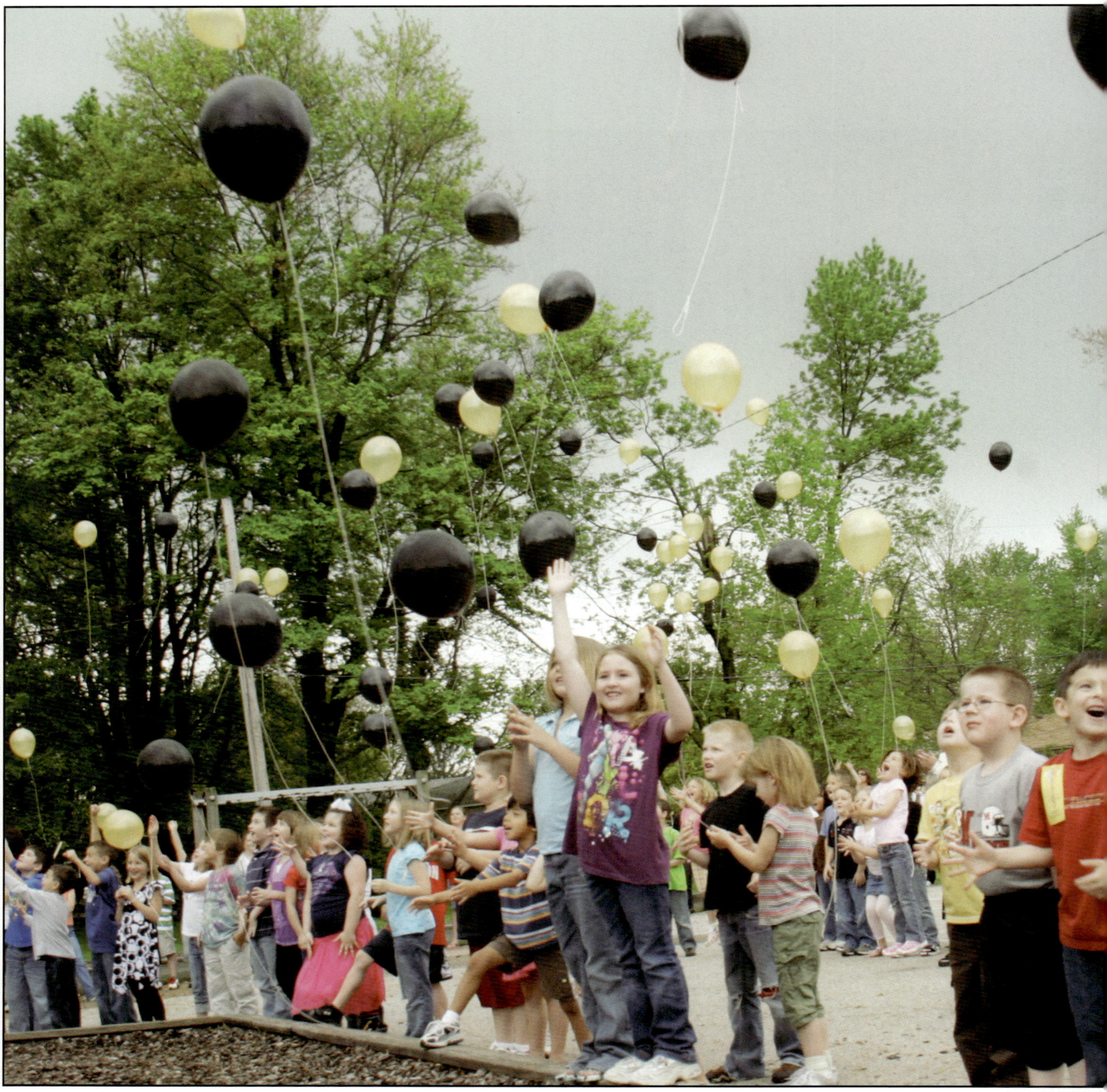

Photos by Don Ward

Anderson Elementary School students release hundreds of balloons into the air May 1 during a school-wide celebration of the upcoming Madison Bicentennial. They then went into the gymnasium, where they sang "Happy Birthday" to Madison and cut the cake (below).

FAR RIGHT: Madison Mayor Tim Armstrong and Hanover Town Council President Margaret Seifert helped kick off the 2009 Madison Bicentennial year Jan. 22 with a champagne toast at the conclusion of the Madison Area Chamber of Commerce's Annual Dinner. The event, held at Hanover College's Brown Campus Center, featured an Academy Awards-style party atmosphere, complete with live music and dancing.

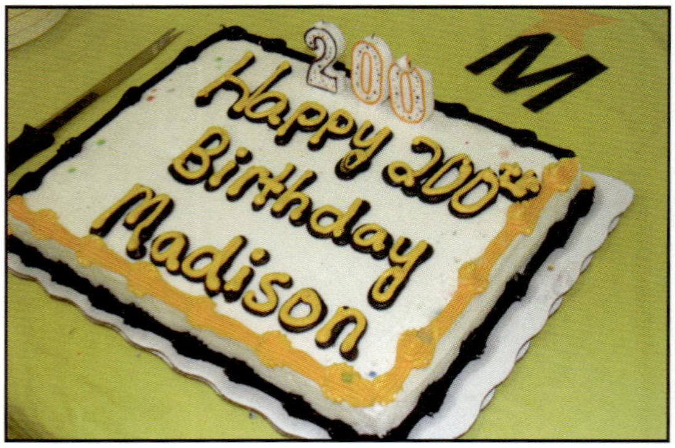

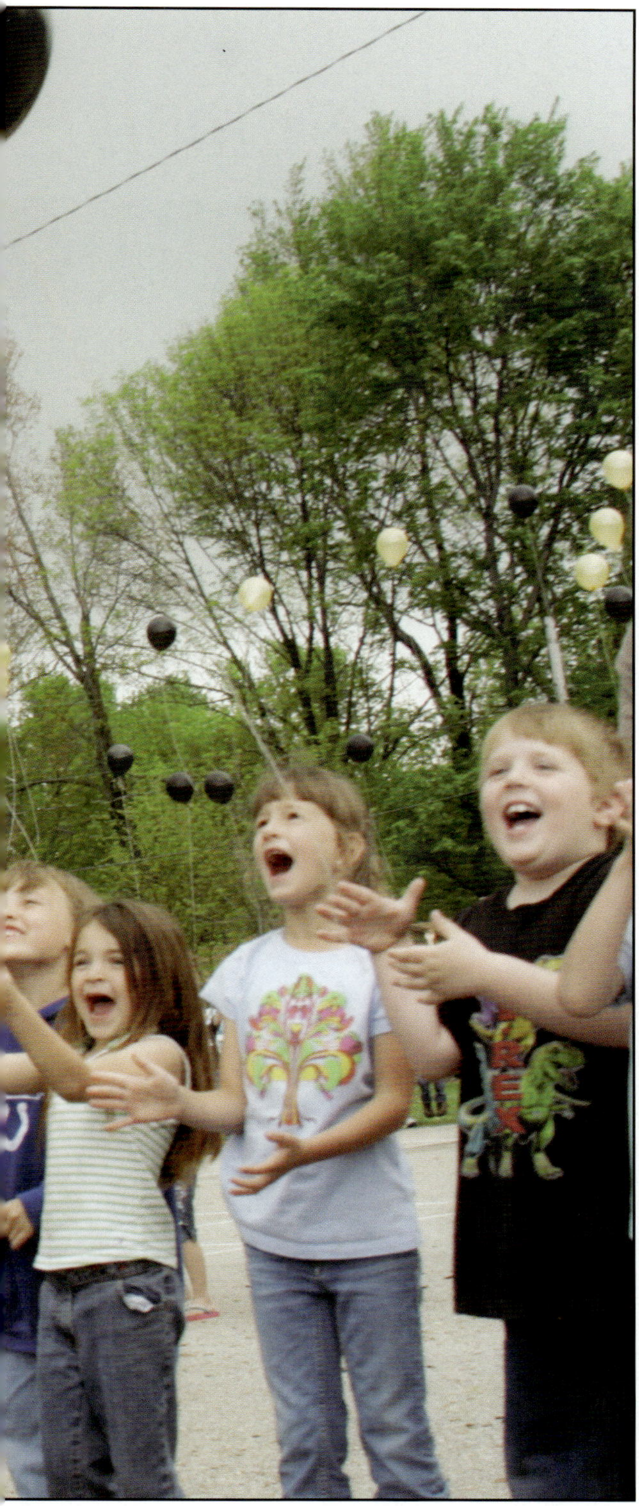

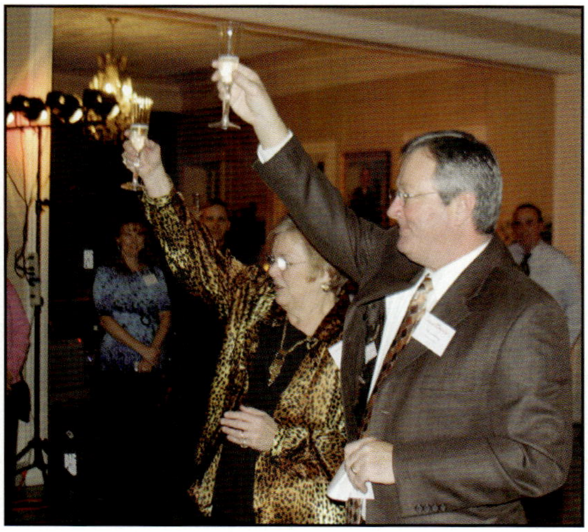

Foreword

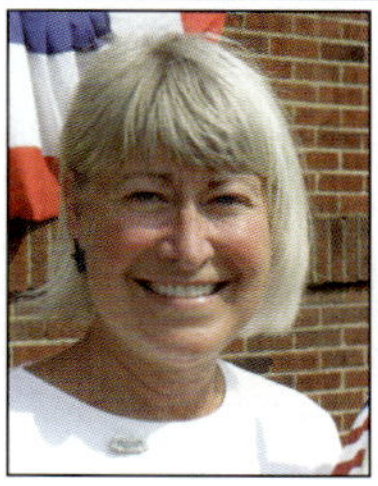

JAN VETRHUS

Bicentennial Committee Chairwoman

When we began planning Madison's Bicentennial in fall 2006, we had a few basic principles. We are an amazing community. We wanted the stories of the past to inspire the future. We wanted to celebrate all 200 years, not just one time period. We wanted to include all ages, groups, industries and traditions – to celebrate the diversity in our community. We wanted to celebrate throughout 2009, have one great party and leave a lasting gift.

The great party needed to be a unique celebration that would build on Madison's traditional festivals but offer something above and beyond the annual events.

In a town known for our decades-old Madison Regatta Unlimited hydroplane races and Madison Chautauqua Festival of Art, and already developing a tradition with newer festivals such as the Ohio River Valley Folk Festival and the Madison Ribberfest, this was no small undertaking. Just choosing a date that would not conflict was difficult. How fitting that we eventually chose to start the 200-hour party the day after Madison Consolidated High School's graduation and end it on Flag Day.

A special "Thank You!" to Nancy Gruner and the Madison Main Street Program for developing the concept of a 200-hour birthday party and coordinating the entire nine days. Thanks to Laura Hodges and the Madison Area Chamber of Commerce for incorporating the hilltop events and managing the publicity. And a big "Thank You!" to Madison Mayor Tim Armstrong and the city police, streets, parks and fire departments for their total support and competence. It has been a pleasure to work with all of them and the hundreds of artists, musicians, organizations and individuals who made this such a great party.

What started as a wish list of "wouldn't it be great if we could…" became a reality as committees formed, leaders emerged and events were added to the calendar. Thanks to the generosity of our corporate sponsors and the work of our tireless volunteers we were able to offer most events free.

The comments we heard over and over from neighbors and visitors alike – there is so much to do; our whole family got involved; we didn't know Madison had so much talent; this is fun, let's do it again! – are the measure of our success. We have left memories and planted seeds for generations to come. We have no doubt that the historic buildings and lush hillsides of Madison, Indiana, will continue to provide the stage for the talent and creativity of our people. Our youngsters will go on to do amazing things that we will celebrate in another 50 or 100 years.

This book is our official photo album of the 200-hour party. As you look through its pages, you will see that we had a great celebration worthy of Madison's finest traditions. We can continue to say with pride that this is an amazing community.

Getting the Party Started...

Pre-Bicentennial events set the mood

Several E.O. Muncie Elementary School students wrote a history book about their city for the Bicentennial. More than 500 students, grades kindergarten through fifth grade, contributed to the book. A few of the students who took part in the project are (front row from left) Brick Boldery, Arial Hall, Brienna Miller, Tucker Adams; (back row from left) Vance Neace, Caitlyn Brooks, Lesley Reverman and Kristen Garrett. The collection of writings and student poems has been published and is being sold for $13 at Madison area stores. Principal Joyce Imel came up with the idea for the book.

Photo by Don Ward

FAR RIGHT: Indiana Department of Corrections female inmates spent several days creating bunting and street banners for the Bicentennial celebration.

Photo by Konnie McCollum

RIGHT: (From left) Mary Elizabeth Goldsmith, Vivian Shatley, Louise Anthony and Anna Bell work on a Bicentennial quilt. It hung in the window of Madison City Hall during May and June 2009.

Photo by Laura Hodges

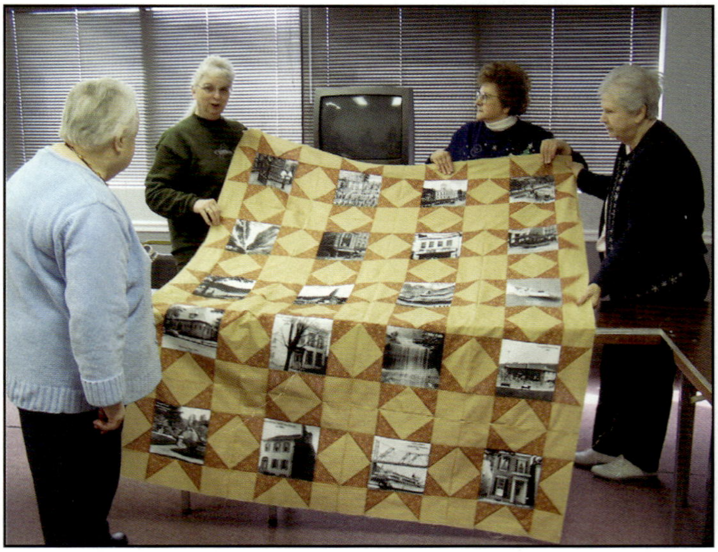

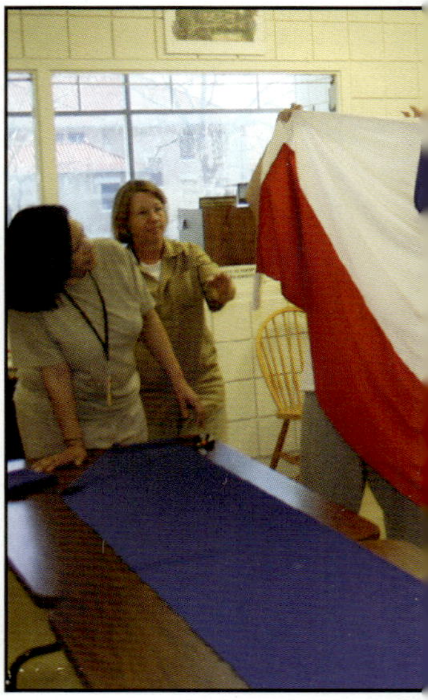

A time for us

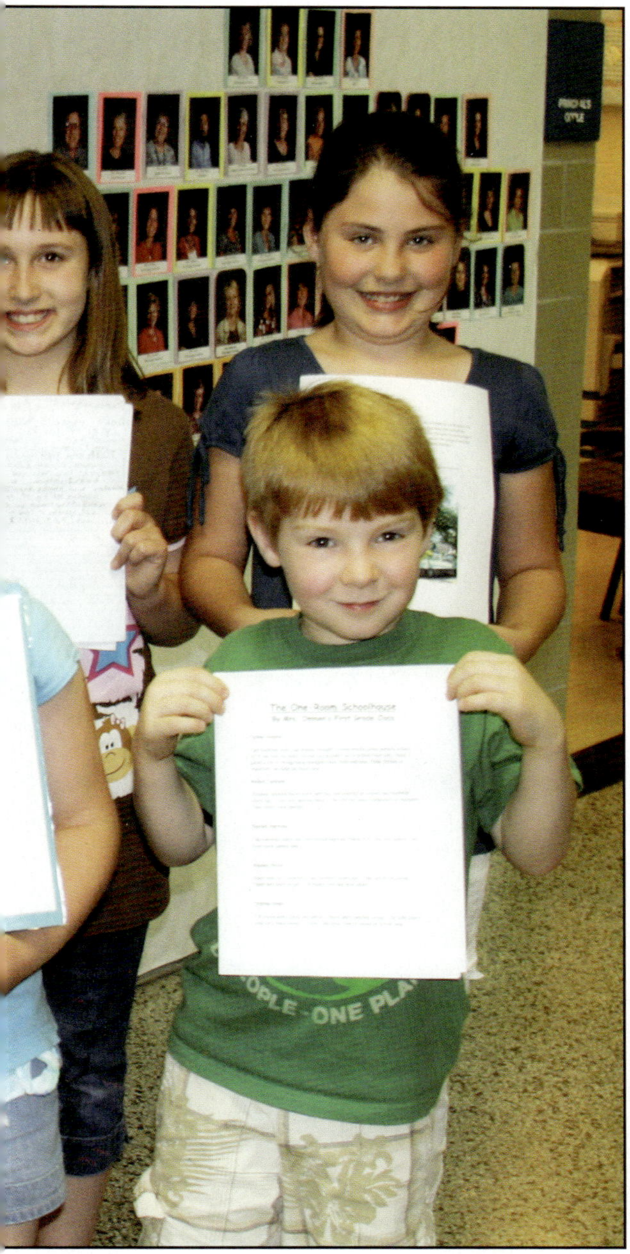

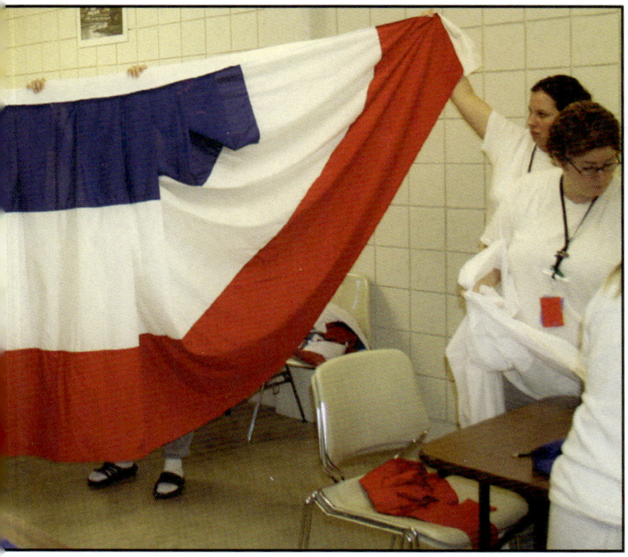

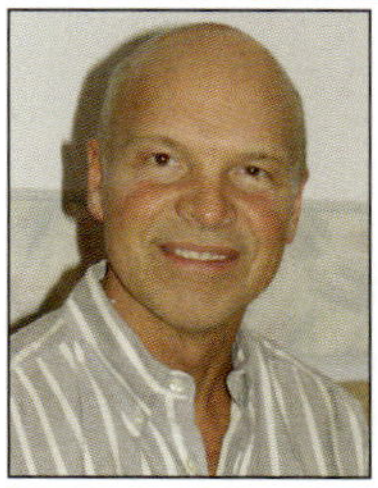

DON WARD

RoundAbout Madison Publisher

It took more than a year to plan, but when it finally arrived, those attending agree it was worth it. Madison, Ind., residents and visitors "partied like it was 1809" during the nine-day Madison Bicentennial celebration that ran from June 6-14, 2009.

Bicentennial Committee Chairwoman Jan Vetrhus led the year-long planning sessions, marshaling dozens of volunteers to head subcommittees and pull off the massive event. All the while, she insisted on having "something for everyone." One look at the 12-page color brochure and schedule, and it appears she accomplished her goal.

From classic cars, music and art to nature hikes and historical re-enactments, the Madison Bicentennial truly was a experience like no other. Additional events are planned throughout the rest of the year, including an original musical, "Rivertown," that will be performed by local high school students in October.

Vetrhus achieved another monumental goal by involving many businesses, large and small, non-profit groups and individuals in both sponsoring and taking part in the varied events.

Madison Bicentennial souvenirs are still available for sale around town, and several publications, a quilt, an afghan and a CD of church music have been created in honor of the event.

Now with the memories of these festive events slowly fading, *RoundAbout Madison*, the area's free, monthly arts and entertainment newspaper, has captured much of the week in photos. Several photographers covered daily events for this special commemorative book so Madison citizens can look back and recall the time we had in marking Madison's "200-Hour Party."

The result, "Faces of Madison," was designed to focus on the *people* who took part in the celebration. For after all, it is the people who have made Madison what it is today – a quaint, historic, rivertown that has both endured and thrived throughout its history.

So enjoy this book and share it with your friends and be sure to tell them what a wonderful time we had in June 2009 at the Madison Bicentennial.

Ryker's Ridge Elementary School teacher Katie Clark (white shirt with sunglasses), schoolchildren and other teachers (right and far right) take part in a balloon release May 21 on the North Lawn of the Lanier Mansion State Historic Site in downtown Madison. The event was part of the preliminary activities leading up to the Bicentennial.

Photos by Darrel Taylor

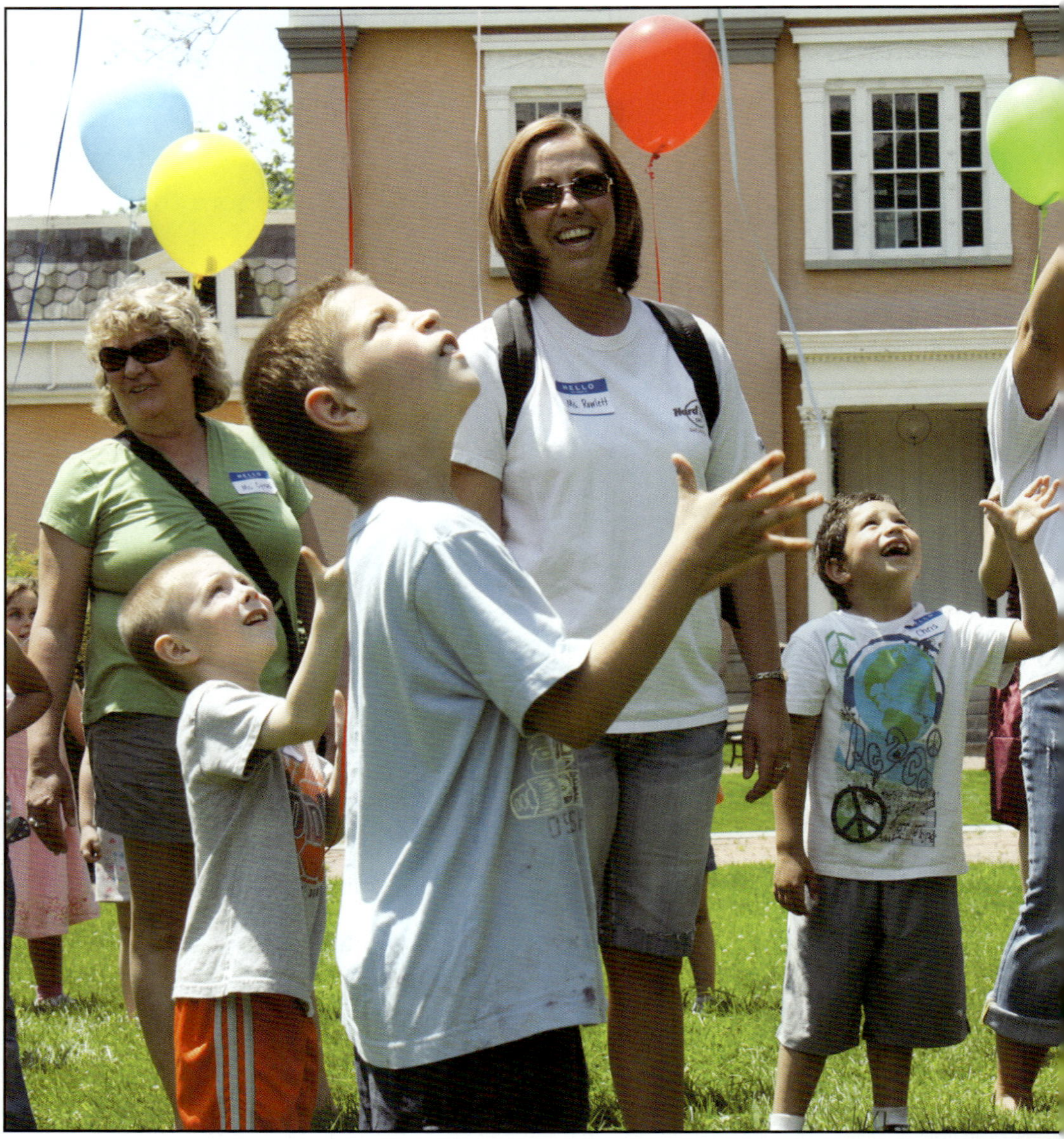

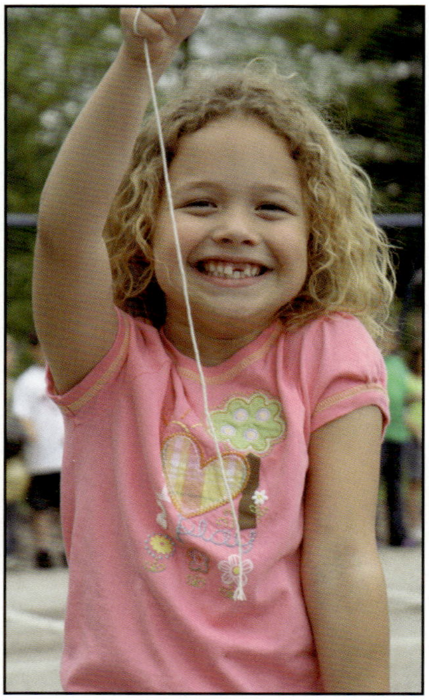

ABOVE: Jordyn Bilz, 6, smiles as she releases her balloon into the air.

RIGHT: Anderson Elementary School Fifth Grade Student Council members greet visitors arriving for the school's May 1 balloon release celebration. They are (from left) Jamie Smith, LeAnn Fox, Lydia Arney, Matthew Sedam and Katie Hartman.

Photos by Don Ward

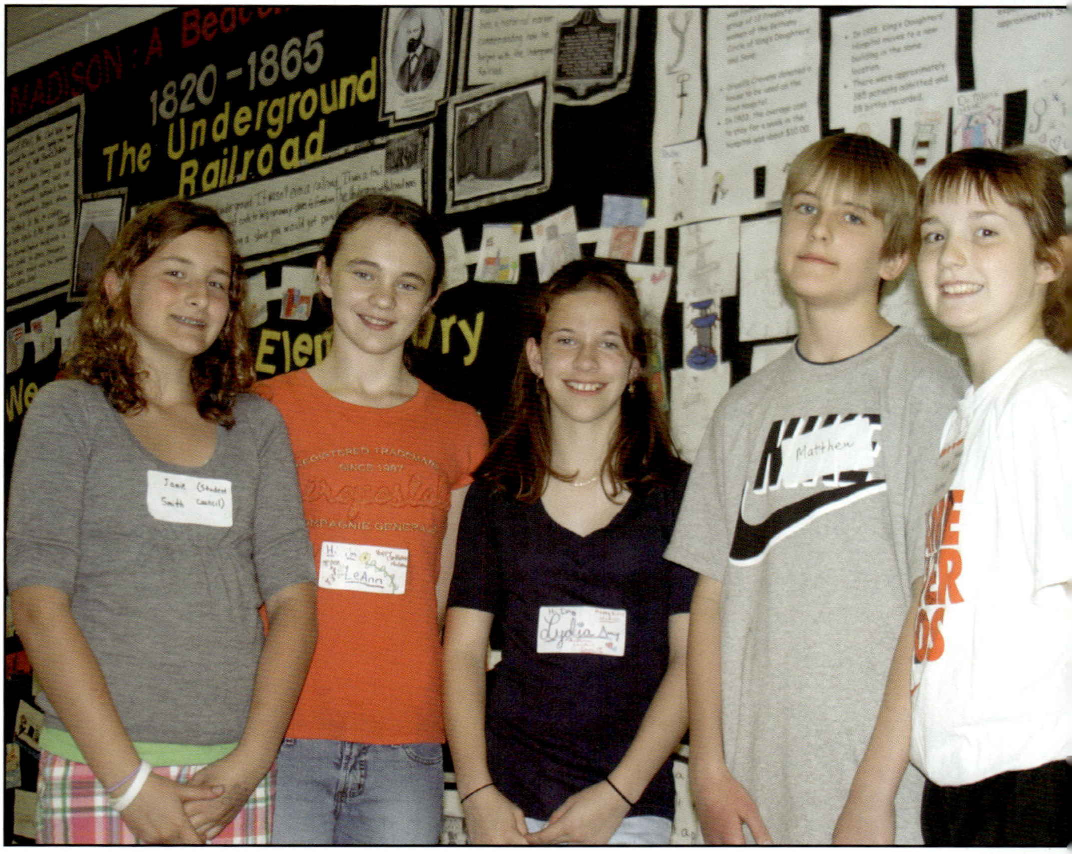

Anderson, Ryker's Ridge Elementary Schools' Balloon Releases

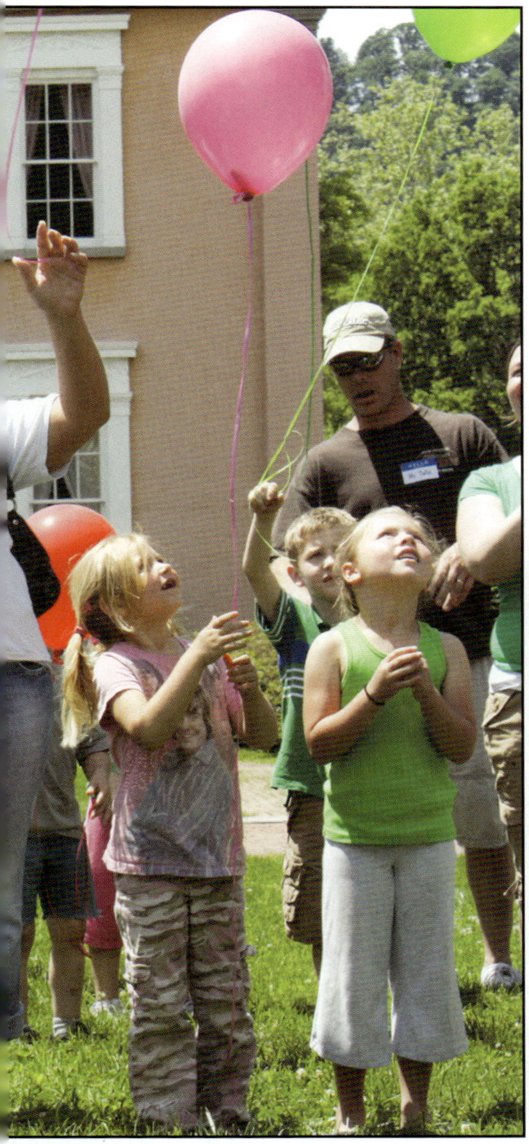

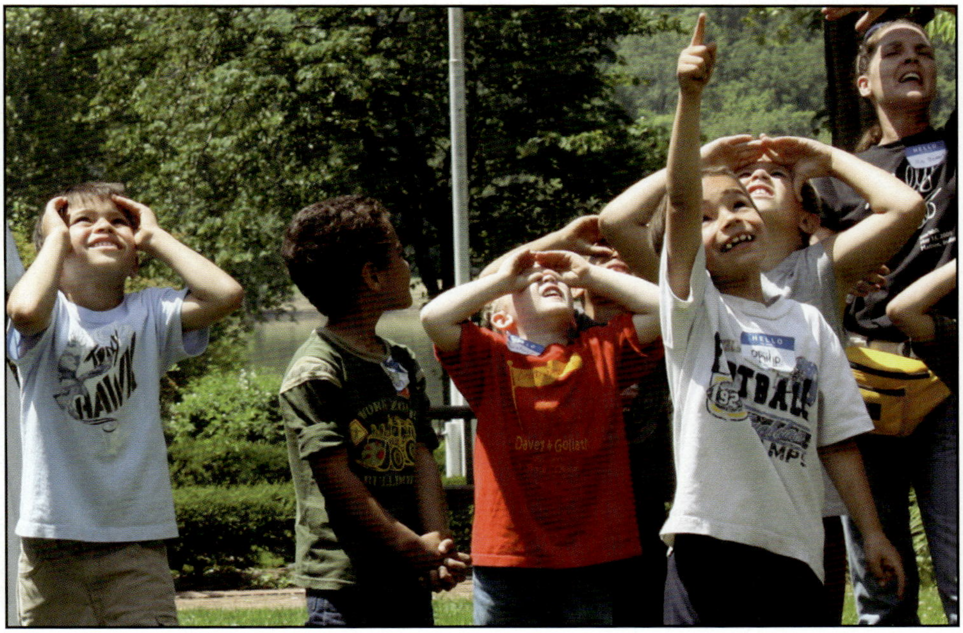

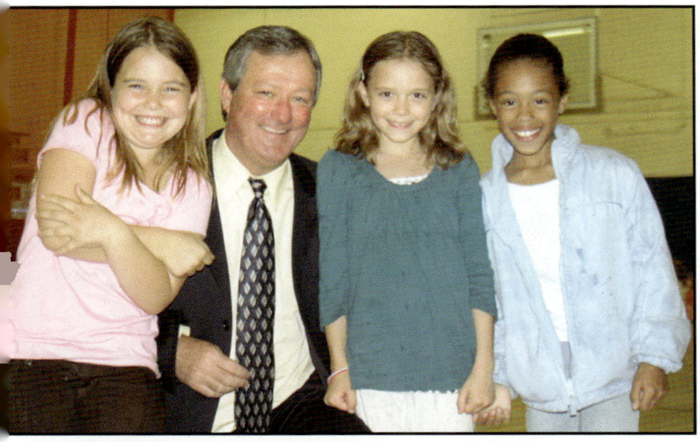

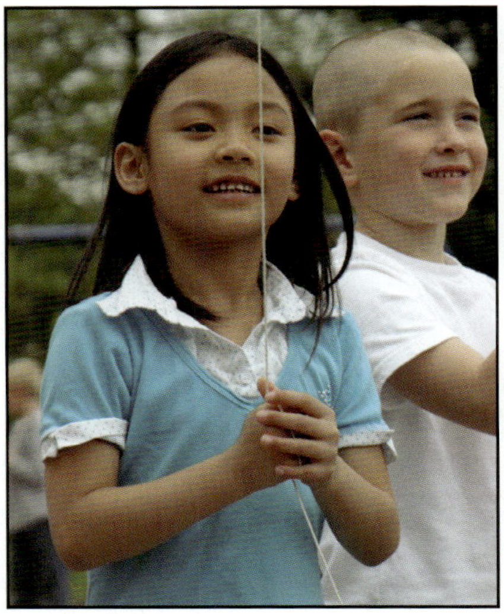

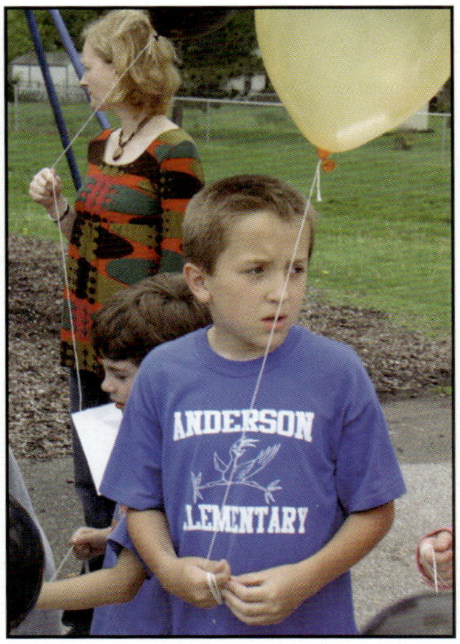

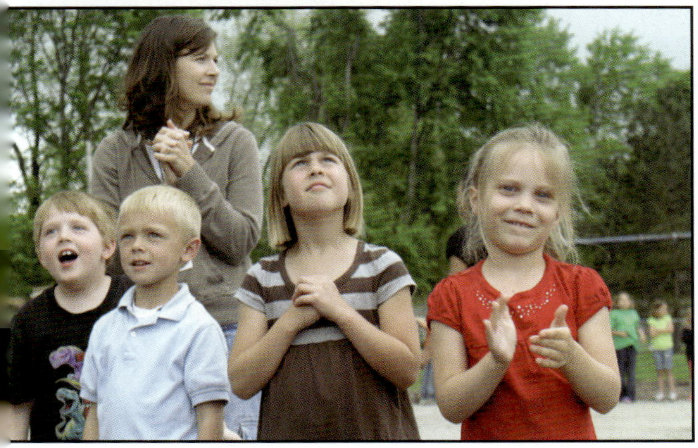

Madison Mayor Tim Armstrong (above left) poses with Anderson Elementary School third-graders (from left) Riley Chisholm, Brianna Humphrey and Tatiana Buckner.

Above left are Vy Huynh and Dalton Bowen with their balloons.

Above right, Aaron Blades prepares to release his balloon.

LEFT: Kindergarten teacher Amanda Asher with (from left) Zeb O'Neal, Gavin Wendel, Abby Hanson and Gracie True.

Photos by Don Ward

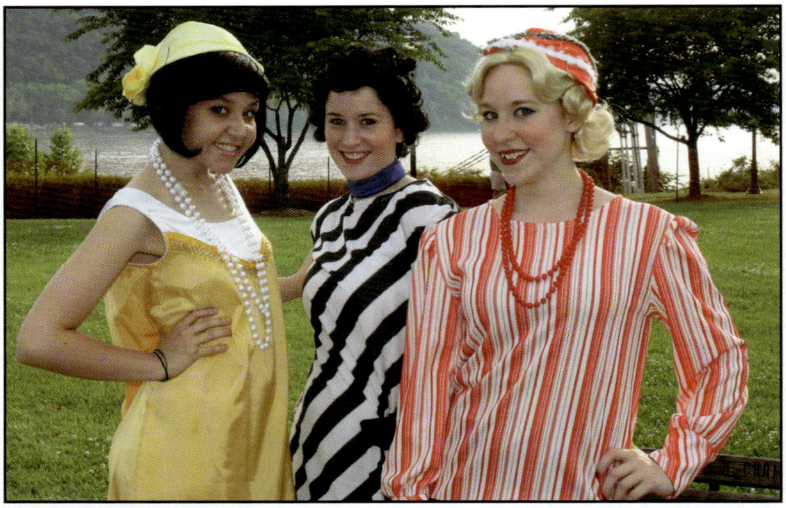

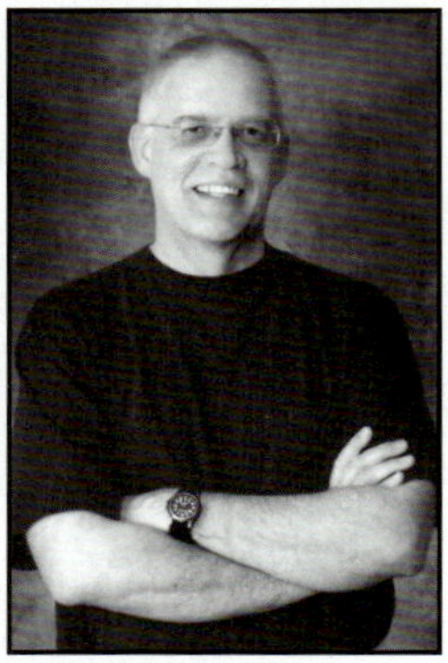

Charles Moman

Above photo by Randy Porter
Right photo of group by Matt Griffith

"Rivertown the Musical:" In honor of Madison's Bicentennial, an original, two-act Broadway style musical "Rivertown" has been commissioned by Seymour, Ind., composer Charles Moman to be a part of the city's year-long celebration. The show will run for two weekends, Oct. 9-11, and Oct. 16-18, and will be performed by a cast of high schools students, who auditioned in May 2009 for parts in the production. Pictured above (from left) are Sadie Courtney, Nichole Waldon and Kate McKay. The group (right) performed songs at the Opening Ceremony.

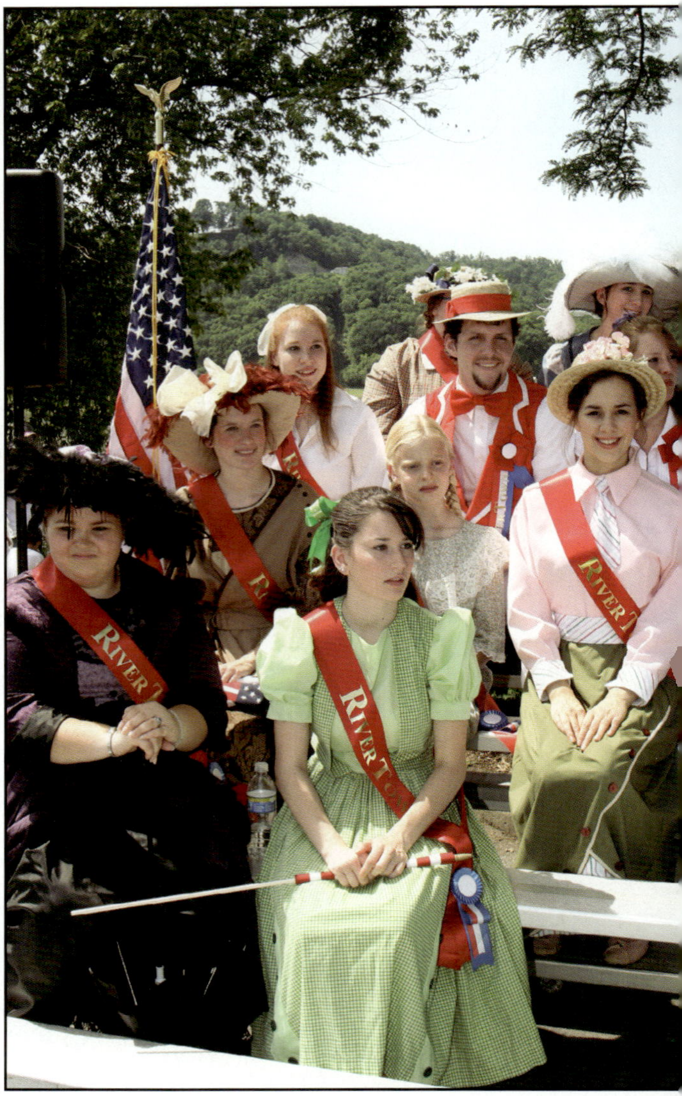

Bicentennial Postmark: Madison Postmaster Mike Bowen shows off the Bicentennial Postmark that was created for the city celebration and released during Arts Day, June 8. Upon request, post office patrons could request that the postmark be stamped on their letters for up to 30 days from its release.

Photo by Don Ward

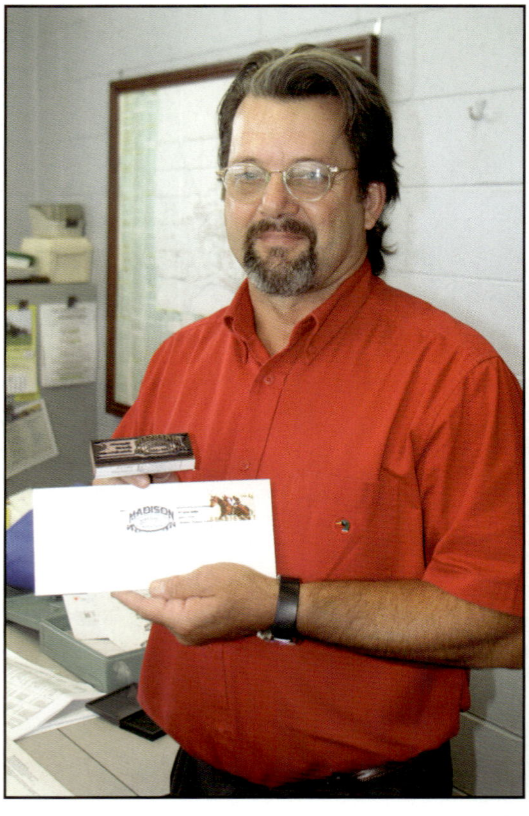

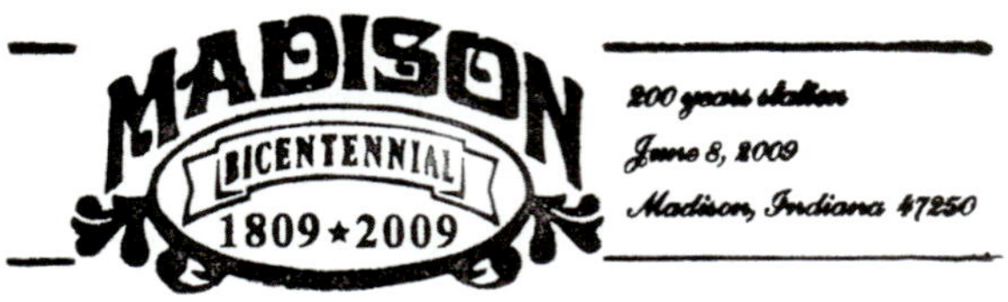

Madison Bicentennial Primary Sponsors:

Community Foundation of Madison-Jefferson County

King's Daughters' Hospital & Health Services

Arvin Sango Inc.

Grote Industries

City of Madison

Jefferson County

Madison Precision Products

Rotary Lift

Indiana-Kentucky Electric Corp.

River Valley Financial Bank

Madison Area Chamber of Commerce

Madison Main Street Program

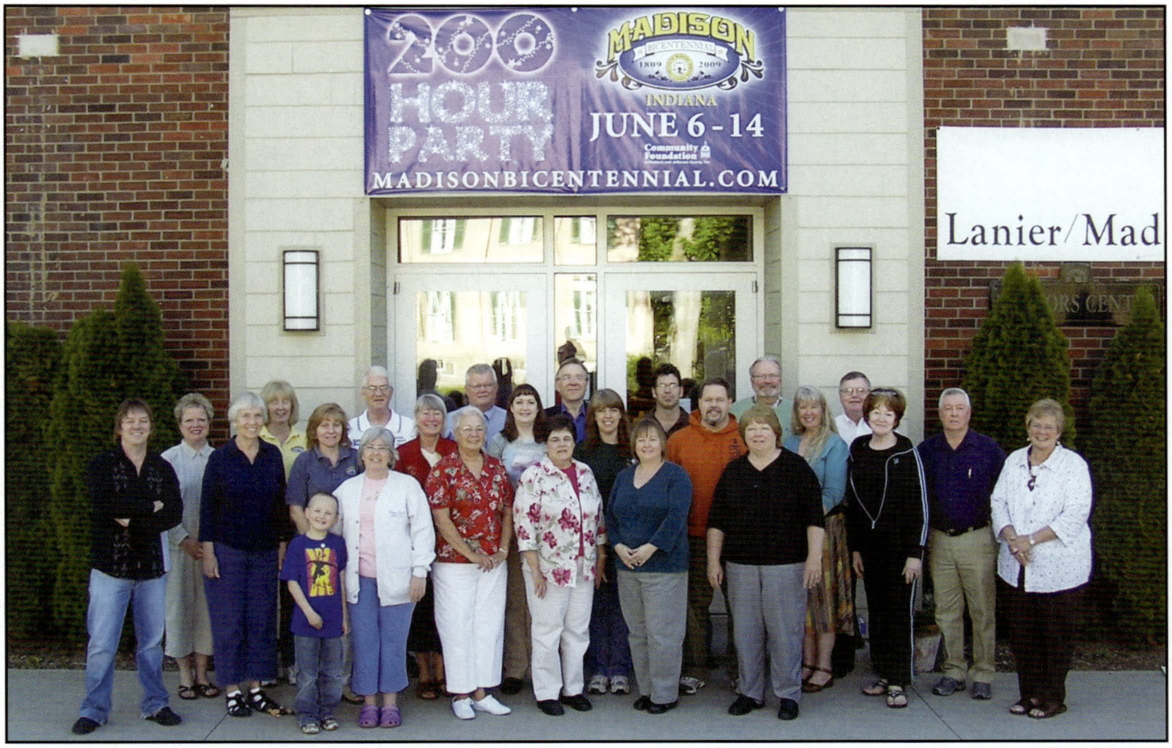

Bicentennial Committee: The Madison Bicentennial Committee was photographed in May 2009. They are (front row starting with child) Mathys Cutter (grandson of Stephanie Hellmann), Stephanie Hellmann, Janice Barnes, Carolyn Stutler, Lisa Smitley, Laura Hodges; (middle row) Rusty Bladen, Charlotte Hubbs, Rhonda Deeg, Jan Vetrhus, Amy Christner, Laura Ratcliff, Kevin Snyder, Nancy Gruner, Camille Fife, Harold Lakeman, Margaret Seifert; (back row) Susan Ohlendorf, Terrie Waller, Frank Taff, Matt Forrester, Alva Tripp, Chip Binzer, Jim Grant and Gerry Reilly.

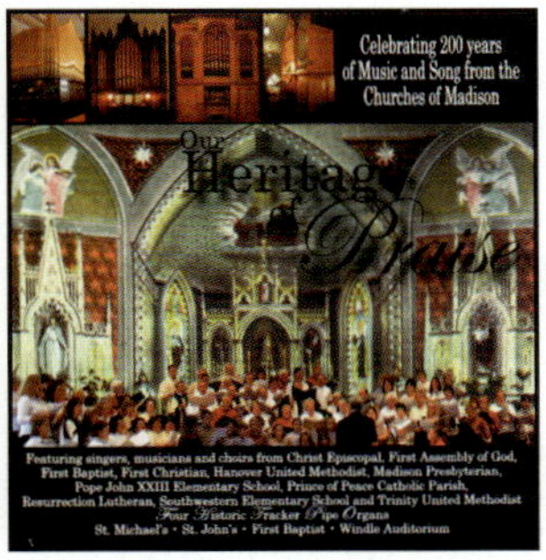

Madison Bicentennial Recipe Book: Madison, Ind., resident and cookbook collector Anne Saxe (right) has organized a recipe book for the Bicentennial that is for sale at Madison area retailers. The result is the 120-page book, "200 Years of Hoosier Cooking and Stories from Madison, Indiana, and the Ohio River Region." It sells for $10 and proceeds will benefit local nursing home facilities.

Churches of Madison CD: A new recording of music and song from 11 area churches is for sale at area retailers. It was organized by Larry Wickersham for the Bicentennial.

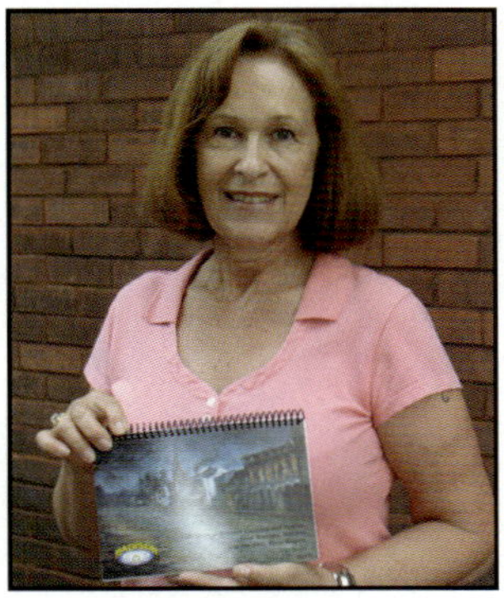

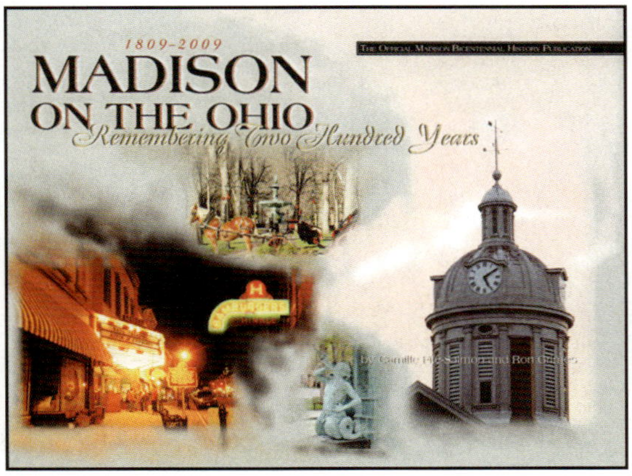

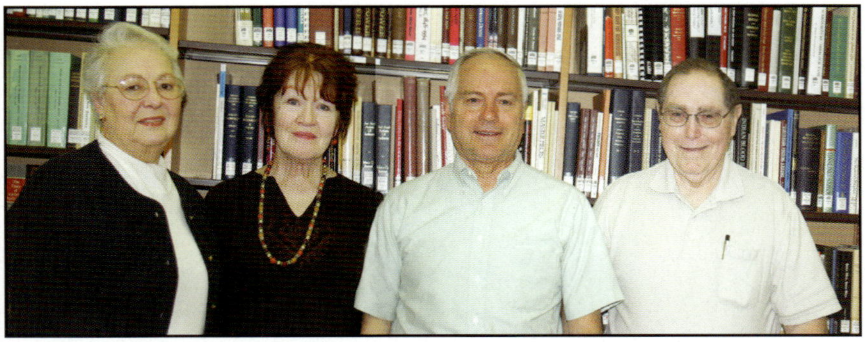

Bicentennial History Book: From left, Janice Barnes, Camille Fife-Salmon, Ron Grimes and Bob Thomas helped co-author the official Madison Bicentennial history book, "Madison on the Ohio," on sale at Madison area retailers for $34.95. The 136-page book contains many historical photos.

Twelve contestants advanced from four preliminary contests that began in January 2009 to compete in the June 12 "Madison's Got Talent" finale at the Ohio Theatre in Madison.

The overall winner, singer Drew Geerts, performed at the June 13 Bicentennial concert and Laser Light Fireworks Show. He also earned a trophy and $250. During each of the preliminaries, finalists received $50. Geerts won by singing "Summertime" from "Porgy and Bess."

Kyle Clerkin, who played "Cotton-Eye Joe" on the banjo, was judged as first runner-up. Second runner-up was soloist drummer Chris Croxton.

Other finalists included Sarah Perkins and Haley Bare, a vocal duet singing "The Climb;" Mariah Scott, a vocalist singing "Broken;" Sadie Courtney, a vocalist singing "Let It Be" by the Beatles; Kate McKay, dancing to "Better Days;" Tevis and Melissa West, a duet singing "Only You;" Samantha Buchanan, a vocalist and guitarist performing "Decode" by Paramore; Rockbox (a father-sons trio of Bob, Mitch and Matt Marsh) performing "America;" Hearts of Joy, a vocal trio singing "Redeemed;" and Flyers, a dance trio performing "Saturday Night."

Photos by John Palmer Gregg

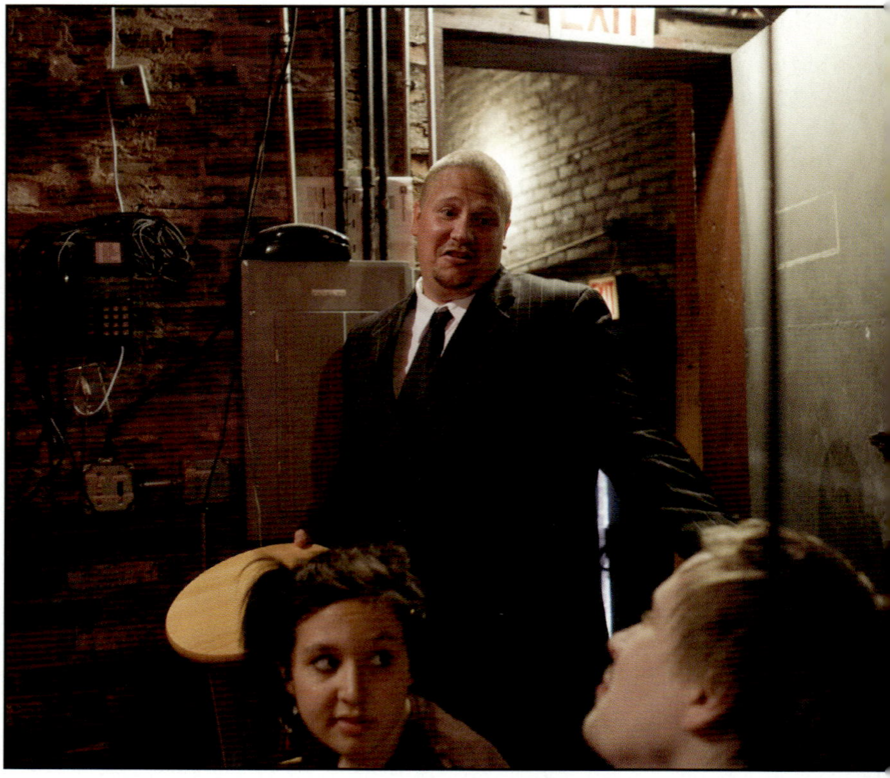

Singer Drew Geerts (standing) of Madison won the "Madison's Got Talent" contest, which took place over several months leading up to the Bicentennial. At right, 16-year-old banjo player Kyle Clerkin tunes up for his performance, which earned him second place.

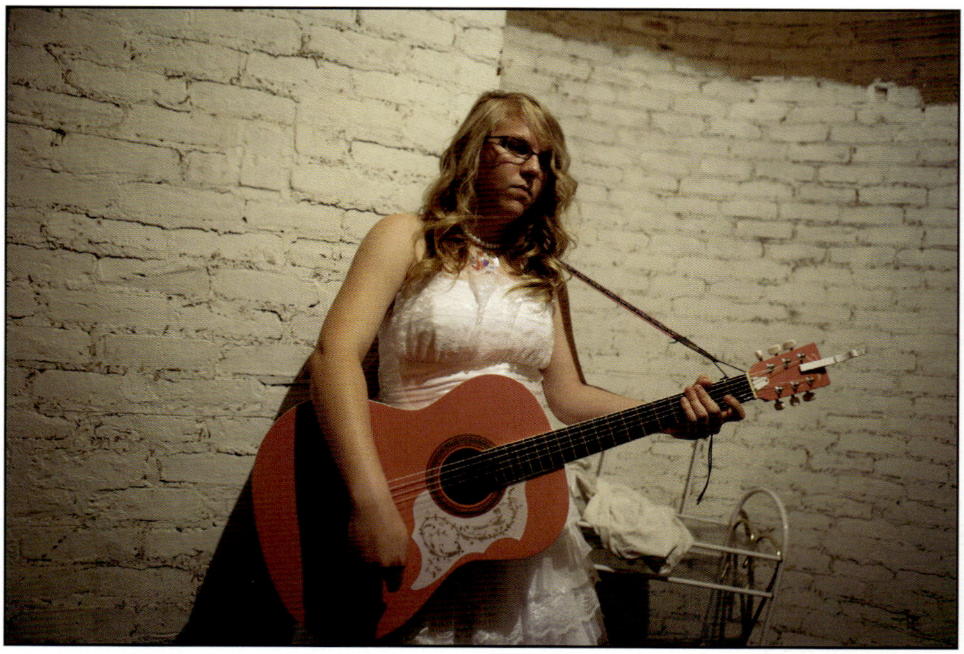

Singer-guitarist Samantha Buchanan warms up backstage prior to her competition performance at the June 12 finale.

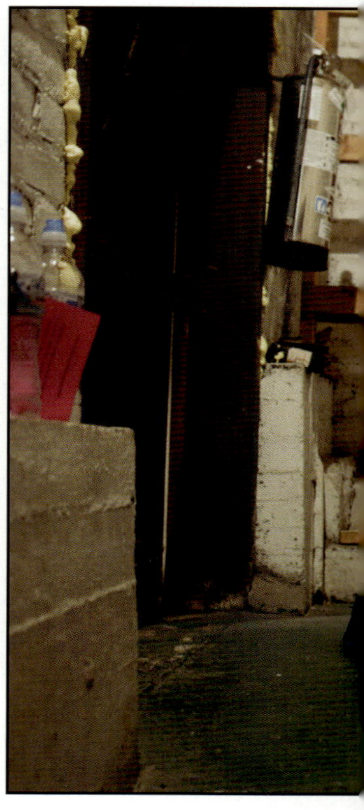

Madison's Got Talent

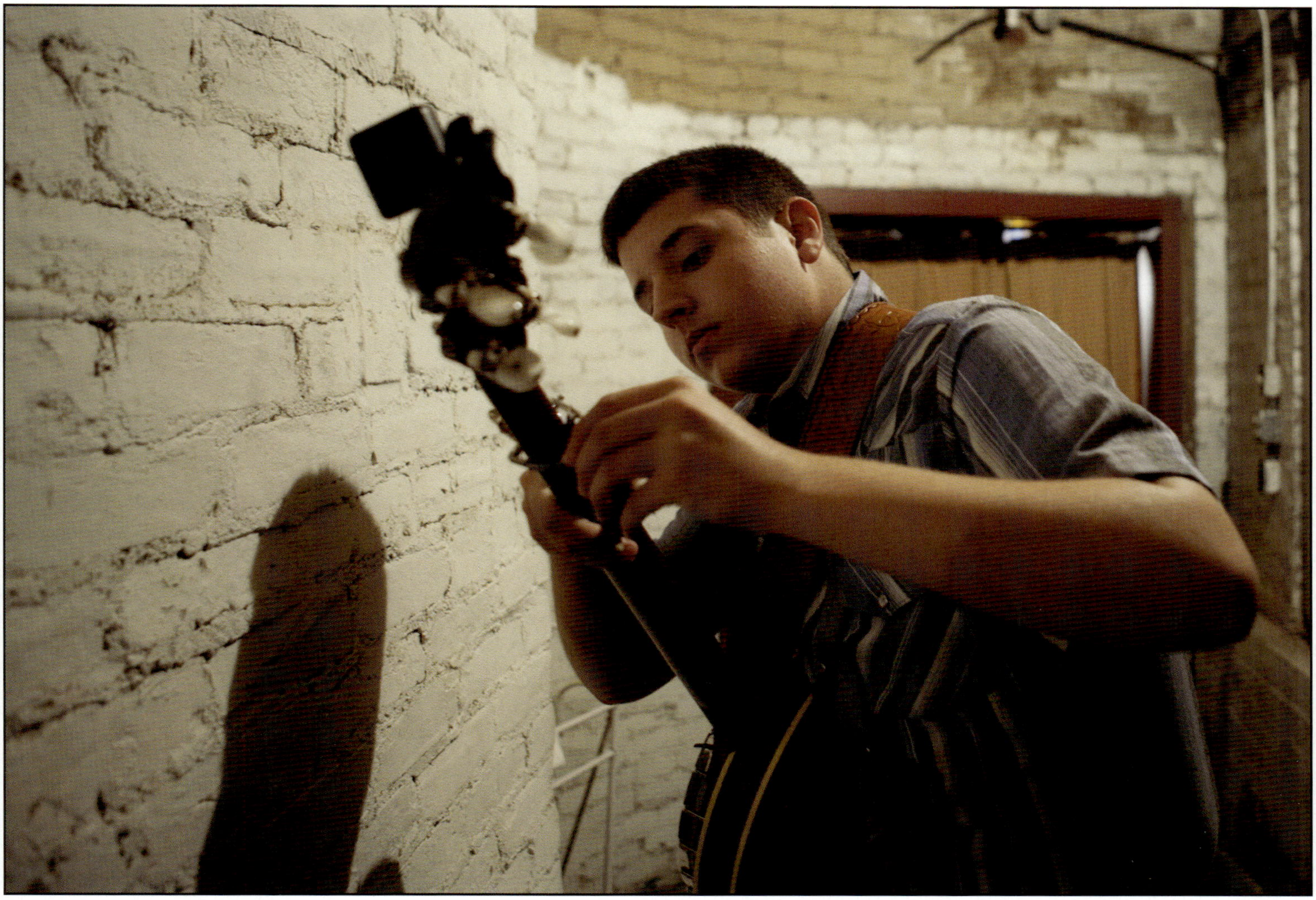

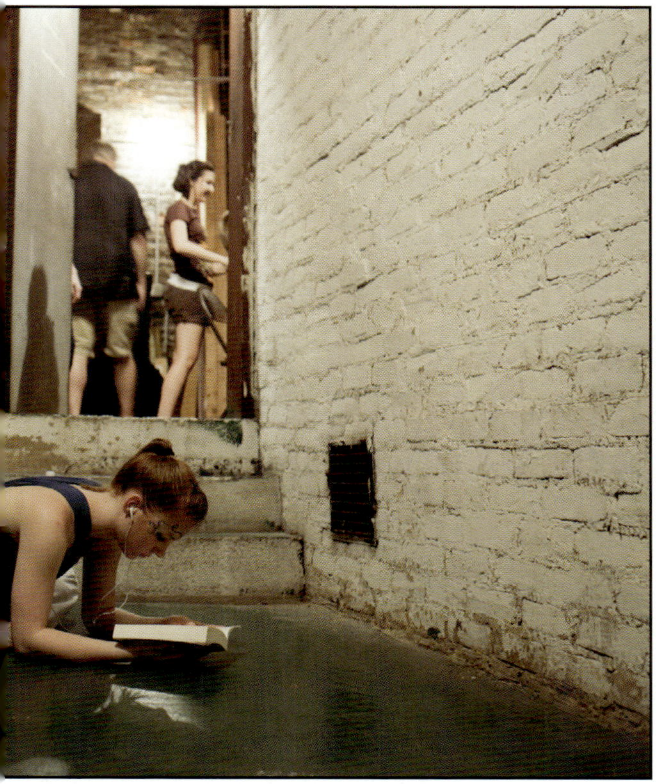

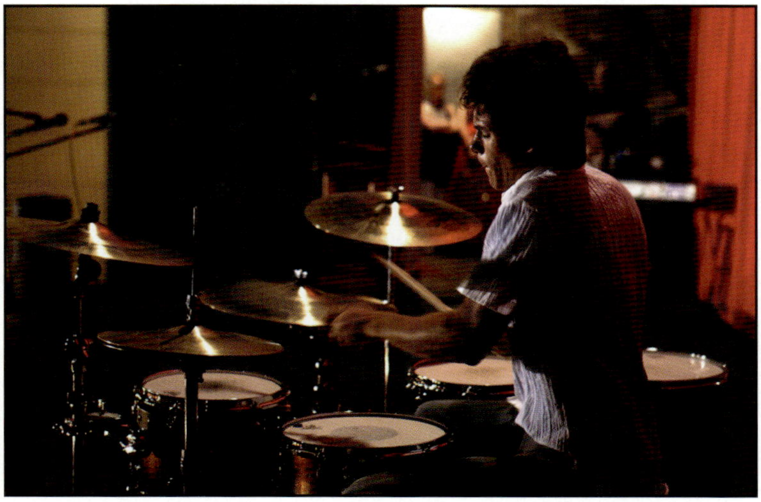

Drummer Chris Croxton plays a solo original piece during the June 12 competition. He placed third. At left, dancer Kate McKay reads a book while stretching backstage in preparation for her routine.

Meet the Bicentennial Characters!

Portraits by Don Ward

Drusilla Lanier Cravens
1864-1956
(Portrayed by Betsey Vonderheide)

The granddaughter of J.F.D. Lanier (and great-granddaughter of John Paul on her father's side of the family) was named for her mother. To avoid confusion, the younger Drusilla was nicknamed "Doot." She was the 10th of 12 children. Her childhood home was Cravenhurst, located on the site of the Moose Lodge on Madison, Ind.'s hilltop.

She received early private instruction and was sent east for further education, as well as to Europe, where she travelled extensively. Always interested in history and the arts, she studied piano with the famed Franz Liszt and voice with Lili Lehmen.

Her mother was a great benefactor in Madison, having donated the properties for the original King's Daughters' Hospital and the Old Ladies' Home, both located on Presbyterian Avenue. It was expected of privileged folks to spread the wealth, so to speak, so young Doot took her responsibility to heart. In her years, she provided funds for the education of many children, and supported charitable organizations.

She was a member of the DAR

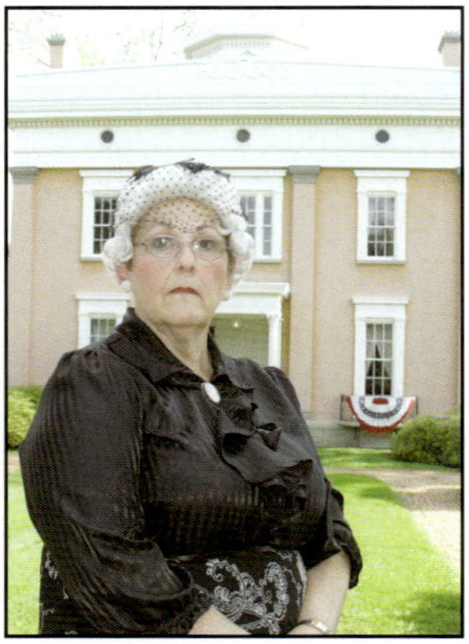

and many other societies for ladies and worked hard to preserve and promote Madison's heritage.

Miss Doot never married nor had children of her own. It is said a childhood illness left her unable to bear children. However, she was quite involved in the lives of her many nieces and nephews.

She injured a hip late in life and was unable to get around very well. During the 1947 construction of her home "Old Stones" next to Cliff House, she supervised from wheelchair and often brought the workers coffee and sweet treats.

Gen. Walter Krueger
1881-1967
(Portrayed by Bill Demaree)

Walter Krueger was a German-American soldier and U.S. Army general who grew up in Madison before moving away at age 18 to join the military, where he served for 69 years in five wars. The 10-acre Krueger Lake located just inside the gates of the Jefferson Proving Ground is named for the former Madison resident.

Krueger became the only private to rise all the way to general, playing a major role in World War II by commanding the 6th Army under Douglas MacArthur. He was on board the U.S.S. Missouri during the Japanese signing of the surrender treaty at the end of World War II.

He was born in Flatow, West Prussia (now Poland), the son of a Prussian landowner and former military officer. After his father died, his mother, Anna, and her three children emigrated to the United States. Walter was 8 years old at the time.

After his mother remarried, the family settled in Madison. Walter spent much of his life in military service, enlisting for service in the Spanish-American War right our of

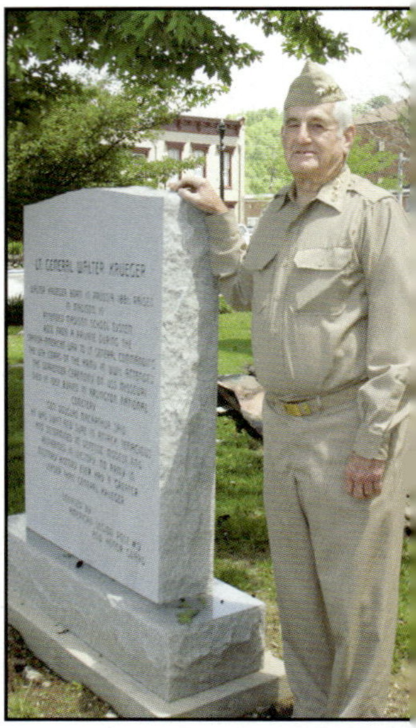

high school. He later re-enlisted and served in the Philippine-American War, and World Wars I and II.

He rose up the ranks to four-st general and served in different po during World War II, retiring as a general in July 1946. Krueger die in Valley Forge, Pa., at age 86 an is buried in Arlington Cemetery in Washington, D.C.

John Brough
1811-1865
(Portrayed by Bob Fourhman)

John Brough was born in 1811 in Marietta, Ohio, and rose to fame as a newspaper publisher and state politician in Ohio. In 1841, he and his brother bought the Cincinnati Advertiser newspaper and renamed it the Cincinnati Enquirer. He later moved to Indiana where he became involved in the railroad business.

In Madison, Brough operated the Madison and Indianapolis Railroad as president from 1848 to 1854. During that time, the railroad installed a more efficient cog system and acquired a more powerful engine to reduce the difficult haul up the 5.89 percent grade traveling through the cut to the hilltop. The efficient operation resulted in great prosperity.

Brough attempted to build two railroad tunnels to try and avoid the steep incline. The company spent $300,000 over two years before the effort was stopped in 1855. The project was known as "Bough's Folly."

Brough, a large man, left Madison in 1854 to become the president of the Bellefontaine and Indianapolis

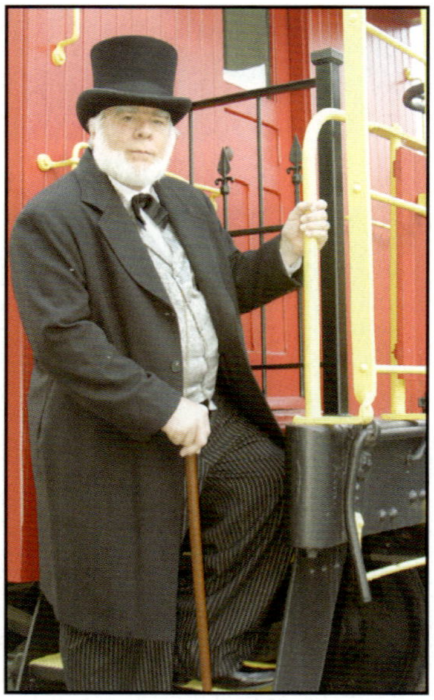

Railroad, a position he held through his tenure as the 26th (Democratic) governor of Ohio and until his death in Cleveland, Ohio, on Aug. 29, 1865.

He died in office at age 53 from gangrene that resulted from an injury he suffered in a fall in the Statehouse yard.

Lt. Col. Alois O. Bachman
1839-1862
(Portrayed by Bryce Worrell)

Born in 1839 to prosperous Swiss immigrants, Alois Bachman grew up in Madison, Ind. His parents ran a hotel and bakery in town. He attended Hanover College, where he studied law. Active, energetic and social, Bachman was skilled in debate and public speaking.

In 1858, he organized the Madison City Greys, which served three months as part of the 6th Regiment. Bachman was captain in the regiment and was later appointed major in the 19th Indiana, which became one of the four regiments in the Iron Brigade.

In July 1861, the 19th was put into service, and Maj. Bachman excelled as a soldier in battle. In February 1862, he received the rank of lieutenant colonel.

On Sept. 16, 1862, he was promoted to commander over the 19th Indiana due to injuries sustained by his superior officer. The next day, Bachman led a charge against the Confederate Army in the Battle of Antietam. The Confederates fired a volley, and Bachman was instantly killed. He was only 23.

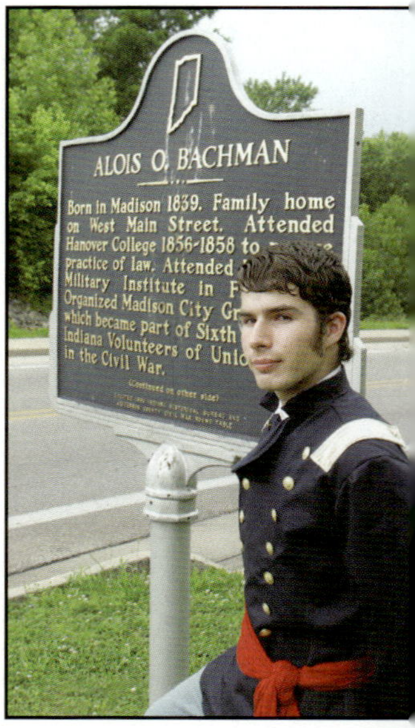

Although the charge was repel by the Confederates, it significar impacted the overall battle. Bachm died a hero, an officer in battle lo by his men. He is buried Springdale Cemetery in Madison.

Meet the Bicentennial Characters!

Portraits by Don Ward

Sarah T. Bolton
1814-1893
(Portrayed by Connie Partington)

Sarah Bolton was born in 1814 in Newport, Ky. Her parents are Esther Pendleton and Jonathan ɛlcher, and she was the oldest of six ildren. The family moved to a frontier m, near Six-Mile Creek, in Madison, d., when she was still a child.

In 1831, she married the editor of adison's newspaper, Nathaniel olton. Their marriage was no accint since Sarah's poetry had been nted in the Madison paper since e was 13. A year after their marge, they moved to Indianapolis, ere Nathaniel was editor of the diana Democrat and later a tavern vner. While he was busy running e tavern, she found herself being a usekeeper and cook, along with nning a large dairy farm. During s time, she wrote her first collecn of poems, titled, "Paddle Your wn Canoe."

Throughout the 1840s and '50s, e was considered the unofficial et laureate of Indiana. She contind to write poetry and be published newspapers and home journals.

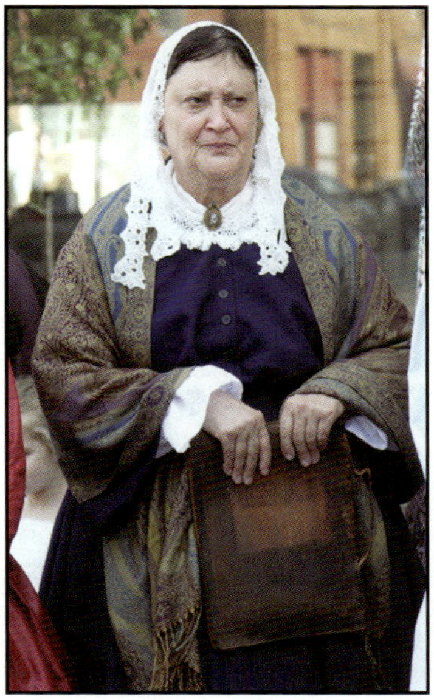

Later, Nathaniel became a U.S. councilman in Geneva, Switzerland, where he died. Five years after her husband's death, Sarah remarried. Her second husband wanted to live in Montana, but Bolton found it to be disagreeable, and so they moved back to Indianapolis, where she died in 1893.

Emilie Todd Helm
1836-1930
(Portrayed by Dorothy Jones)

In 1866, a Confederate Army General's widow, Emilie Todd Helm, moved to Madison, Ind., with her mother and three children in an effort to escape the harsh post-American Civil War conditions in her beloved state of Kentucky.

The family had survived the chaos and near poverty of war in the South and the deaths of many of their male relatives who had fought for the Confederacy. Madison, with its flourishing community, offered a quiet opportunity for the family to have a new beginning.

The Helm family at one time was a prominent family in the communities of Lexington and Elizabethtown, Ky. The war widow, rumored to have at one point committed treasonable acts against the government, was the half-sister to Mary Todd Lincoln, wife of President Abraham Lincoln.

When the Civil War began, Lincoln offered her husband, Benjamin Hardin Helm, the job of army paymaster in the Union Army, but he declined. Instead, he became a Confederate general and was killed

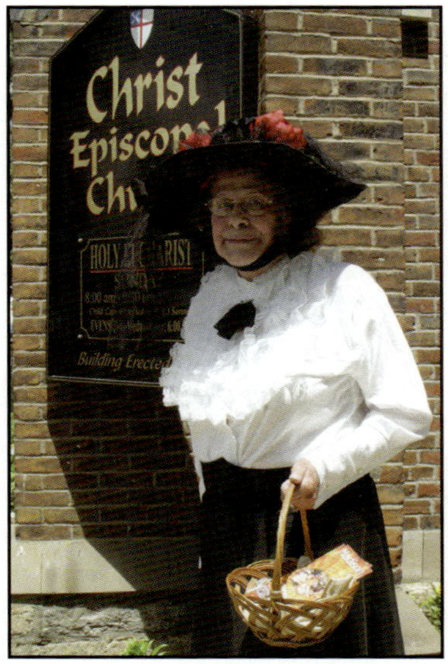

in the battle at Chickamauga, Ga., in 1863.

Emilie Todd Helm, as a war widow, lived for a time at 610 W. Main St., in Madison. After leaving Madison, she moved to Louisville, Ky., where she taught piano lessons. She never remarried and lived to age 93. She is buried in Lexington, Ky. City Cemetery.

Lydia Middleton
1854-1939
(Portrayed by Joyce Randles)

ydia Middleton was born in Madison, Ind., in 1854. She began teaching in the oneom country schools in 1873.

She then taught at the Lower eminary School on Main Street in 379.

She became principal of Lower eminary School in 1896. She was a ember of Trinity Church and taught omen's Bible class. She never arried.

She retired in 1917. She died in 939.

"Miss Lydia," as the students lled her, recalled in a newspaper terview of being paid $2 a day for e six-month school term. She called paying $1 a week to board th families as close to the school as ossible. And she remembered aching all of the classes (reading, riting, arithmetic and spelling).

But mostly she remembered how ger the students were to learn and w polite and respectful they were.

Middleton was considered smart d modest, and she truly loved

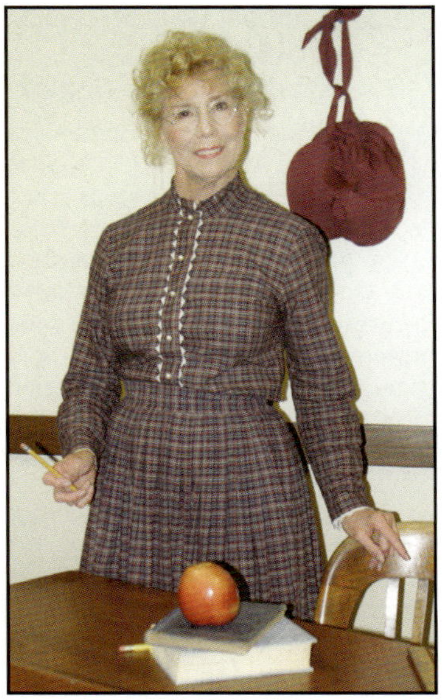

helping young people learn.

Today, Lydia Middleton Elementary School is named after her. The school, located in Madison's historic district, was recently remodeled and stands today as a lively and beautiful tribute to this woman who loved her students and loved to teach.

Charlotte E. Sullivan
1829-1907
(Portrayed by Jan Vetrhus)

Charlotte E. Sullivan was the fifth child of Judge Jeremiah Sullivan and his wife, Charlotte. She was born and raised in the house on the corner of Second and Poplar streets in Madison. In 1849 she married John Henderson Sullivan, whose family farmed in Saluda Township.

Sullivan, a lawyer and politician, merchant and railroad speculator, moved his young family west to Keokuk, Iowa, in 1855. After the Civil War, they moved to Louisville, Ky., where he joined his brother in the milling business. When Charlotte's mother died in 1875, they returned to her family home in Madison for many years. She was a popular hostess.

In 1882, John Sullivan was appointed Indiana Agent in New Mexico, and Charlotte and the children followed him to Albuquerque. There, she opened a finishing school. She buried her husband there and spent the rest of her life living with each of her children in Idaho, Louisville, New York and Arkansas. When she died in 1907, her body was brought back to Madison for burial in Springdale Cemetery.

Jeremiah Sullivan served on the first

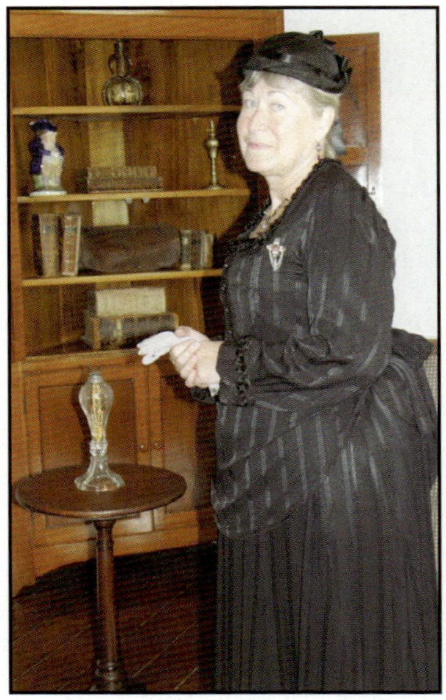

Supreme Court of the State of Indiana. The judge and his wife insisted that all their children were educated, including the girls. His library was one of the finest in the state of Indiana. He was a strong supporter of Hanover College and an elder at the Second Presbyterian Church.

The house is a museum, owned and operated by Historic Madison Inc.

Meet the Bicentennial Characters!

Portraits by Don Ward

Delia Webster
1817-1904
(Portrayed by Stephanie Hellmann)

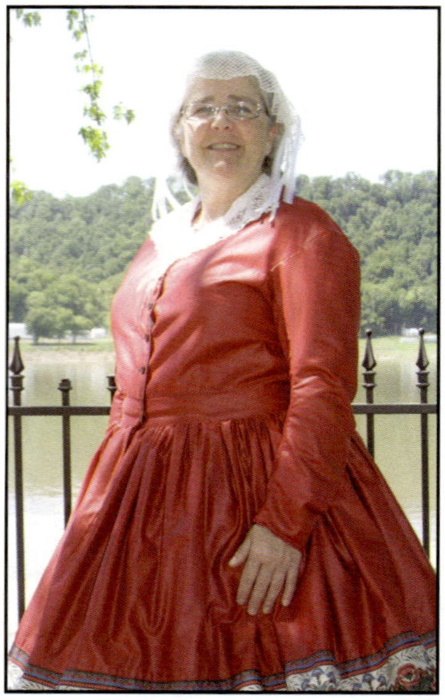

Delia Webster was born on Dec. 17, 1817, in Vergennes, Vt., and eventually found herself in Oberlin, Ohio, as a student. Oberlin at the time was a location where abolitionists gathered. She subsequently came to Lexington, Ky., where she started a girl's school – The Lexington Female Missionary Society – and was quite successful, until she and Calvin Fairbank, in the fall of 1844, rented a carriage to take Lewis Hyden and family to Maysville, and across the Ohio River to Ripley, Ohio, to put them on the Underground Railroad. Fairbank and Webster were caught, tried and convicted.

Delia was tried and sentenced first, and was imprisoned until Fairbank's trial was over. The warden, one Newton Craig, would lobby for her release, and would later board his children with her for their education, in Madison, Ind. She was soon pardoned. She returned to Vermont and wrote a book about her ordeal.

She later return to Madison near the time Fairbank was released from prison. In 1852, she bought a large farm on the Ohio River in Trimble County, Ky. She believed to have taken part in the Underground Railroad, She was put on trial in Bedford in November 1853 but it ended in a hung jury.

She was later jailed, and the Bedford citizenry eventually forced her to leave the county after threatening to destroy her property.

After several cold nights in jail, Webster decided to move to Madison and sell her farm.

Irene Dunne
1898-1990
(Portrayed by Margo Watkins)

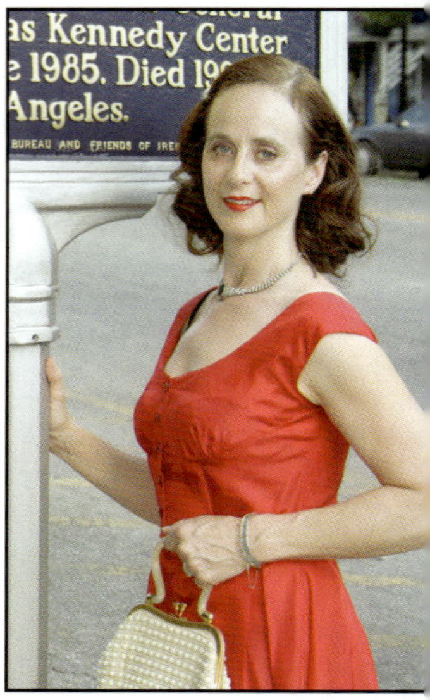

Irene Dunne was an American film actress and singer of the 1930s and 1940s. She was nominated five times for the Academy Award for Best Actress but never won.

Born Irene Marie Dunne in Louisville, Ky., she was the daughter of a steamboat inspector for the U.S. government. Her mother, Adelaide Henry, was a concert pianist and music teacher from Newport, Ky. She was only 11 when her father died in 1909.

After his death, her mother and younger brother, Charles, moved to her grandmother's hometown of Madison, Ind. She attended high school there and learned to play the piano and sing. She acted in dramatic plays at school and church before her graduation in 1916.

She earned a diploma to teach art but entered a contest and won a scholarship to the Chicago Musical College. She wanted to be an opera singer but failed an audition.

She turned to musical theater, making her Broadway debut in 1922 in Zelda Sear's "The Clinging Vine." She went on to earn many roles with major male theater and screen stars, such as Cary Grant. She became a major star herself in the 1930s, re ing in 1952.

Later in life, she served as one five alternative delegates to t United Nations in recognition of h many charitable causes and intere in Roman Catholic and Republic causes. She lived her last years Los Angeles following her husband death in 1965. The couple raised o adopted daughter. She was know as the best actress never to ha won the Academy Award.

Patsy Ann Harris
1821-1881
(Portrayed by Sue Livers)

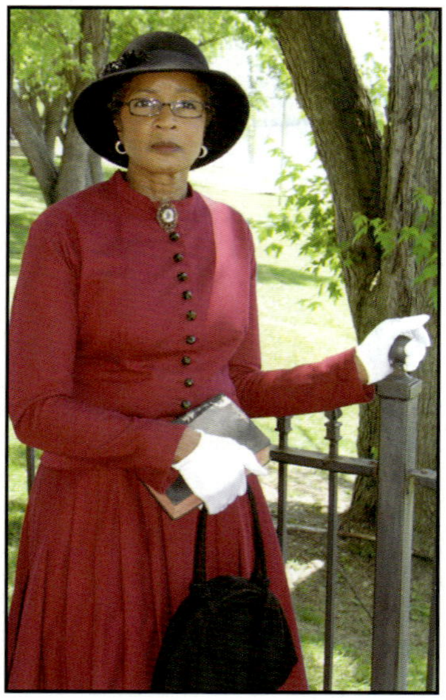

Patsy Ann Harris was the wife of the Rev. Chapman Harris, better known as the "Colored Apostle of Freedom." He was a free Black leader of the Underground Railroad and pastor of the St. Paul's Second Baptist Church at Madison, Ind.

Patsy along with her two oldest sons, Henry and Charles, assisted her husband in his efforts for the liberation of the colored people. Married in 1841, the couple settled at Eagle Hollow, where Patsy and Chapman raised their family on a 21-acre site. Together, the two of them worked in the Madison area.

The Rev. Chapman Harris, her husband, had become a character in history from his efforts for the freedom of his race. He was an Underground Railroad conductor, living with his family at Eagle Hollow.

She in her quiet way, greatly assisted her husband in his efforts for the liberation of the colored people and many a night she prepared food for fugitives and then rocked the cradle in loneliness while her intrepid husband led them through the dark ravines and thickets to the broad highway of Liberty. She was born on April 12, 1821, in Kentucky between Spencer and Shelbyville.

She married Harris in 1841. Together, they help many slaves to freedom. Additionally, they founded the St. Paul's Baptist Church, which later became the Broadway Second Baptist Church.

Michael Garber
1813-1881
(Portrayed by Wayne Engle)

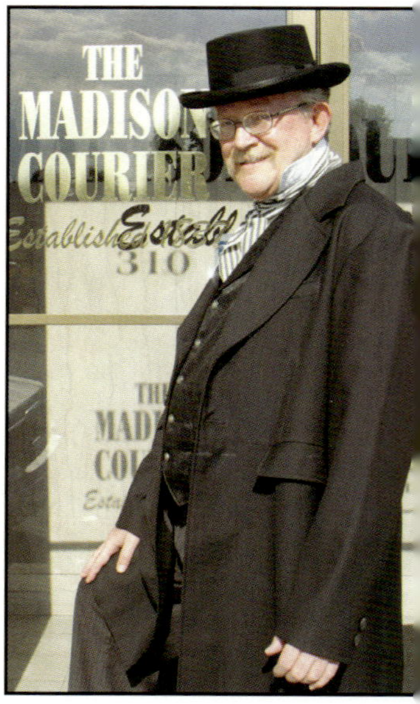

Michael Christian Garber was born April 7, 1813, in Augusta County, Va.. He was a fourth-generation American of German descent. During his life he bought The Madison Daily Courier in 1849 and operated it for many years, was a leader of the movement to keep slavery from spreading to the territories, and helped found the Republican Party.

Garber grew up in a family where his father owned several slaves, but he always felt a revulsion at the institution of slavery. He married a girl named Ellen Schell, a Pennsylvania German. In their middle 30s, the couple moved to Missouri to make a new start. But during a trip down the Ohio River, they were convinced by relatives to move to the Florence, Ky., area, where they lived for two years. They then moved to Rising Sun, Ind., in 1847, opening a store there that Garber and his brother, Christian, operated.

In spring 1849, Garber bought the Madison Daily Courier from Samuel Covington and served as its editor.

When the Civil War broke out, Secretary of War Simon Cameron appointed Garber a quartermaster in the Union Army. He served in th capacity throughout the war. Garb continued as editor of the Dai Courier throughout the rest of th 1860s and early 1870s. In 187 President Ulysses Grant appointe him Madison's postmaster, and h turned the newspaper over to h son, Michael Jr.

Michael Christian Garber Sr. w still postmaster when he died in 18 at the age of 68.

Bicentennial Characters

Photos by Don Ward

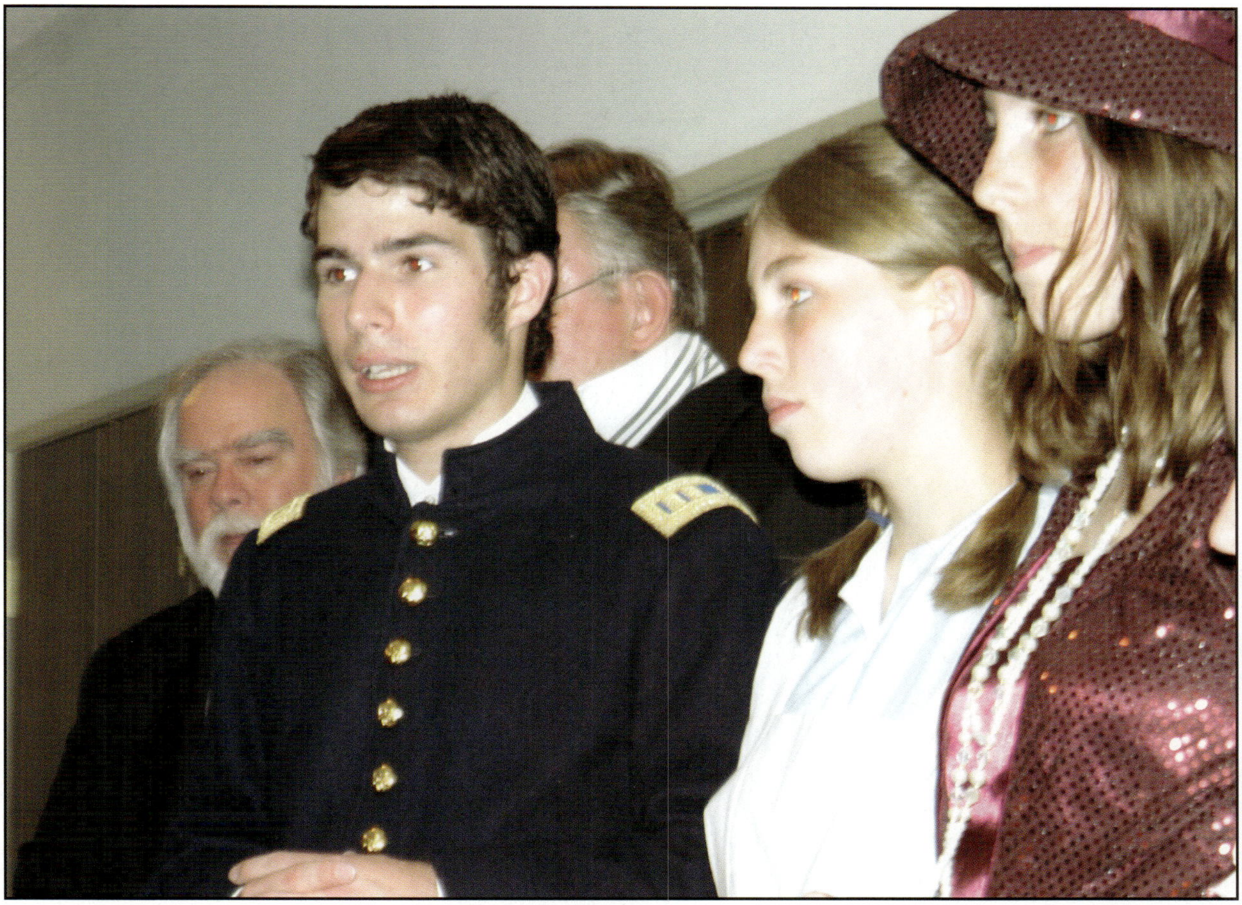

Several Madison Bicentennial characters talked about the people they portrayed during a pre-Bicentennial event held May 27 at the Jefferson County Historical Society. Above, Bryce Worrell, who portrays Lt. Col. Alois O. Bachman, discusses his character. Below, Wayne Engle, who portrays Madison Courier publisher Michael Garber, speaks as Bob Fourhman (far left) listens.

Joyce Randles of anover, Ind., portrays ` school eacher Lydia iddleton, for which the downtown elementary school was named.

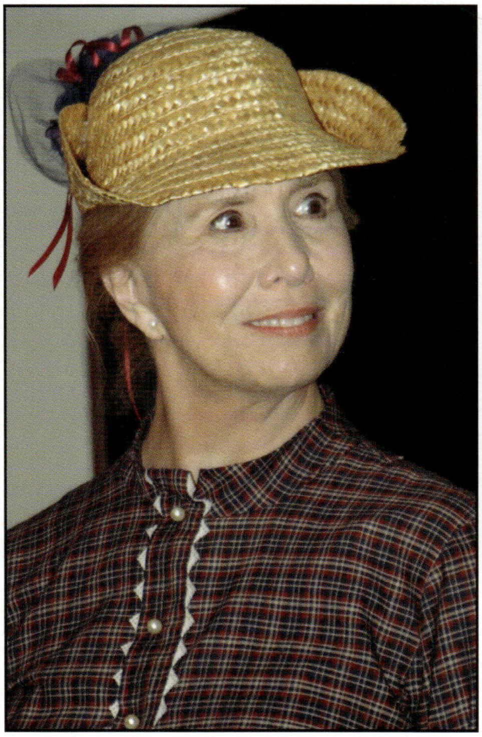

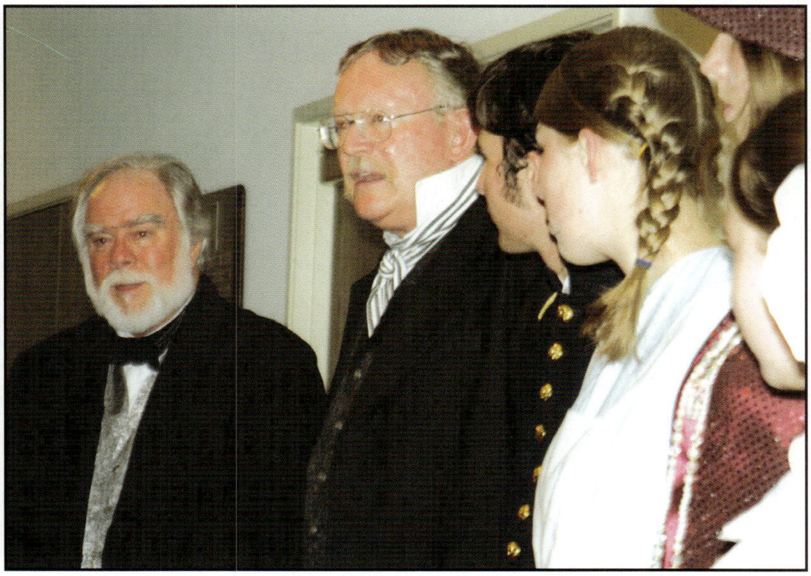

RoundAbout Madison, the area's free, monthly arts and entertainment newspaper, sponsored a Madison Bicentennial Photo Contest that ran from September through December 2008. Entries were judged and the winners announced in March 2009.

Chad of Seymour, Ind., collected the $200 first prize with a night time exposure shot of Madison's Main Street.

David Campbell of Madison took second place with an unusual angled shot of the Lanier Mansion State Historic Site. He collected $100.

Campbell's wife, Nina, placed third with an nighttime photo of the Broadway Fountain. She won $50 and also earned Honorable Mentions for a photo of a riverfront bench.

Other Honorable Mentions went to Laura Hodges (Delta Queen), Jill DeAtley (Clifty Falls Trail), and two photos by Carol Wilhelm (Crystal Beach, Regatta Parade Float).

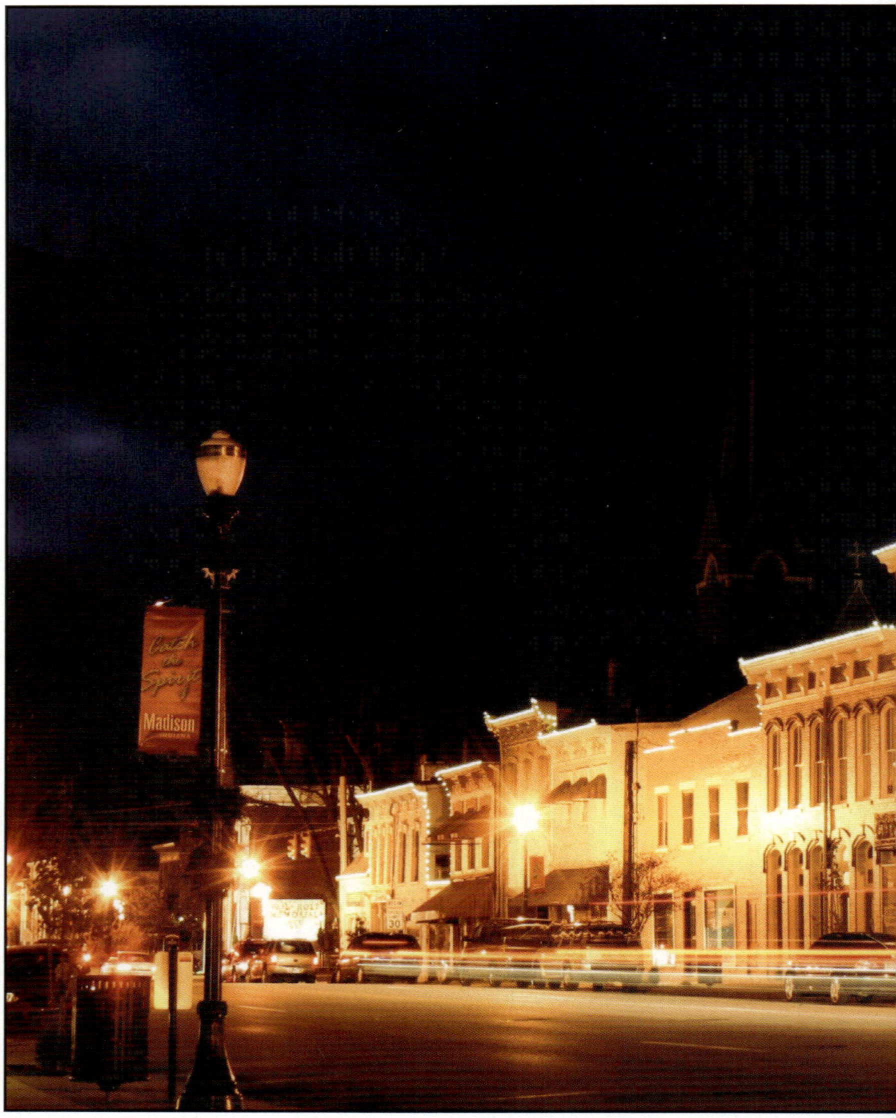

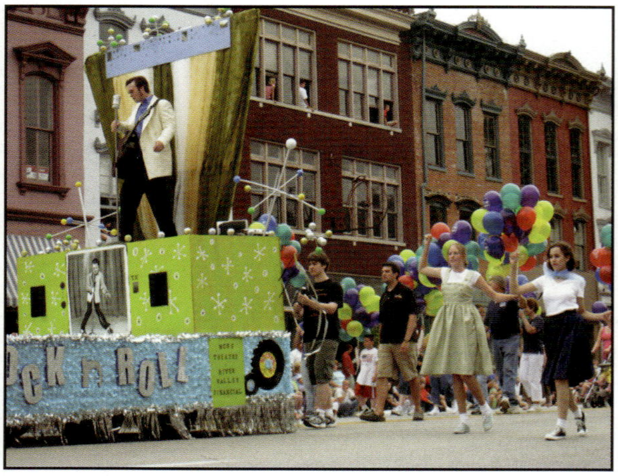

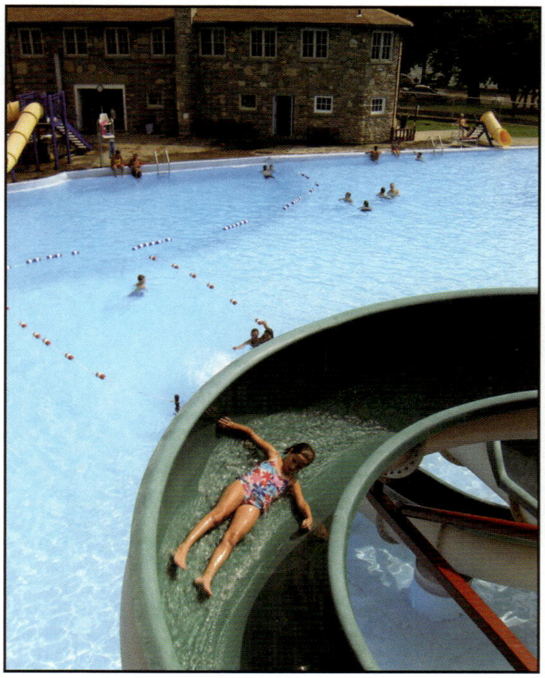

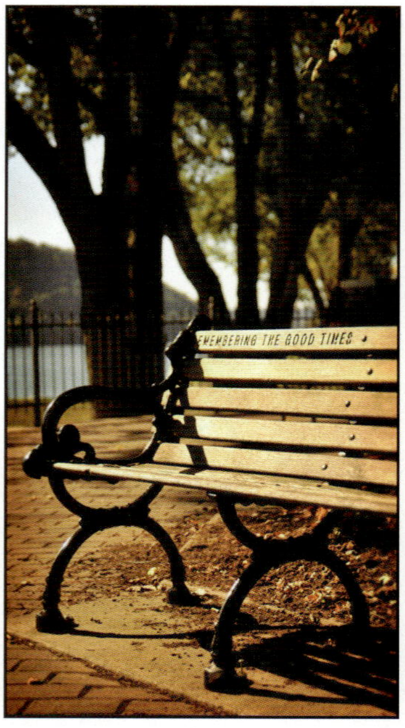

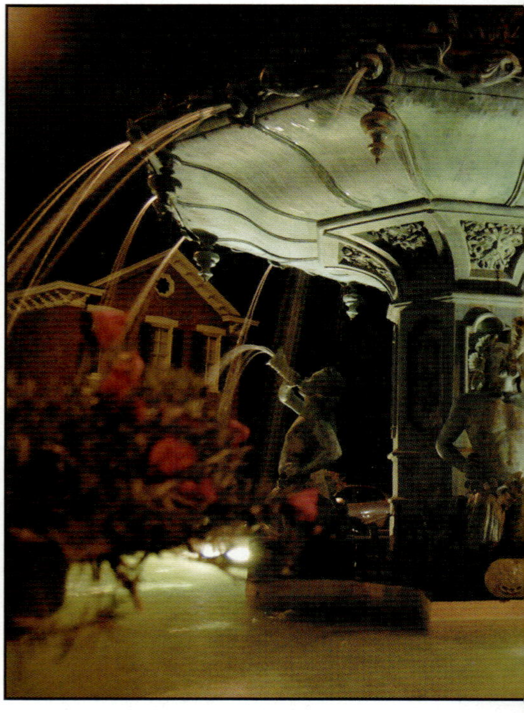

Photo Contest

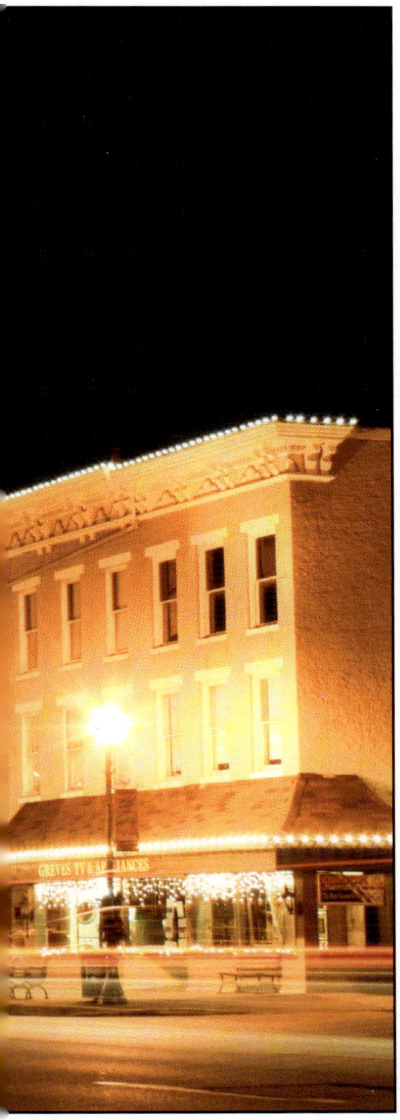

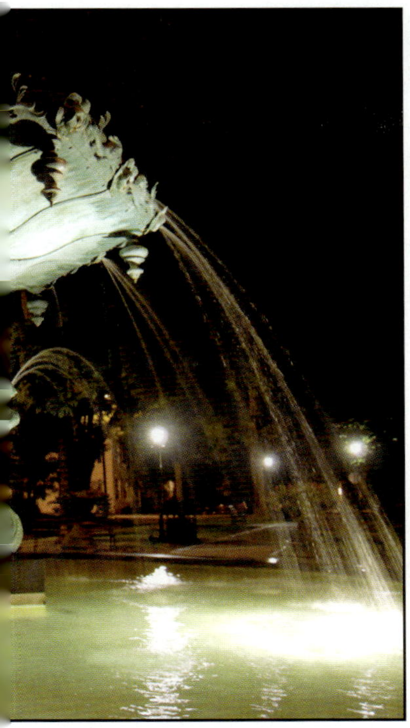

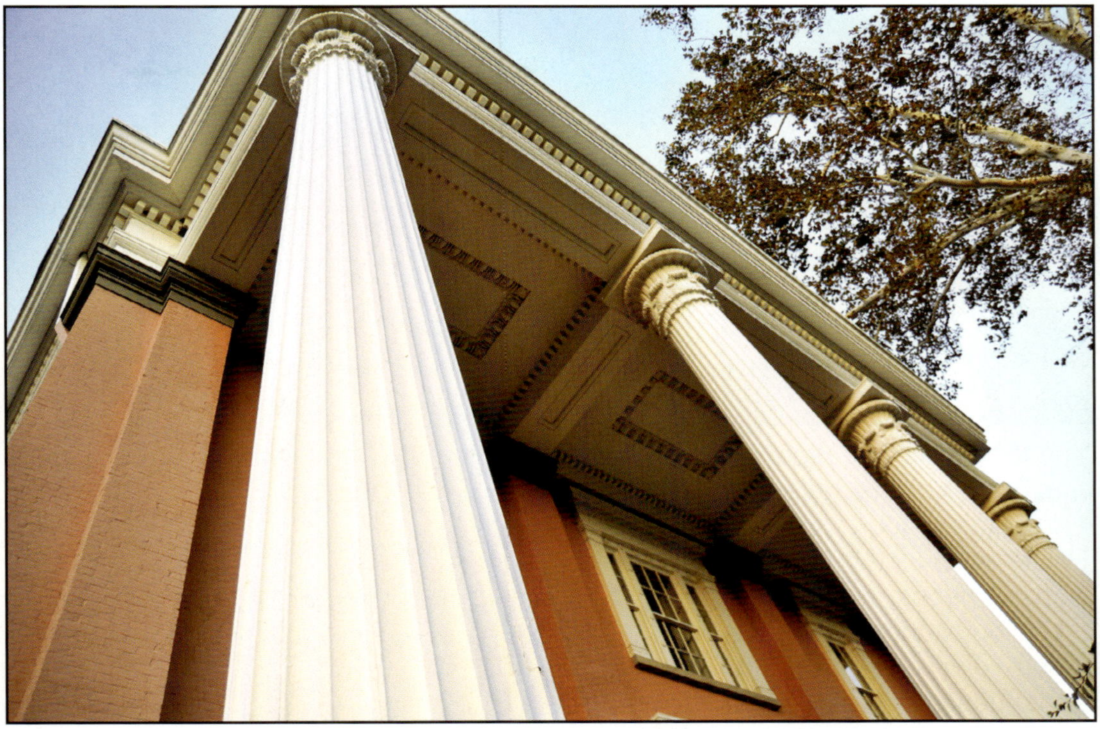

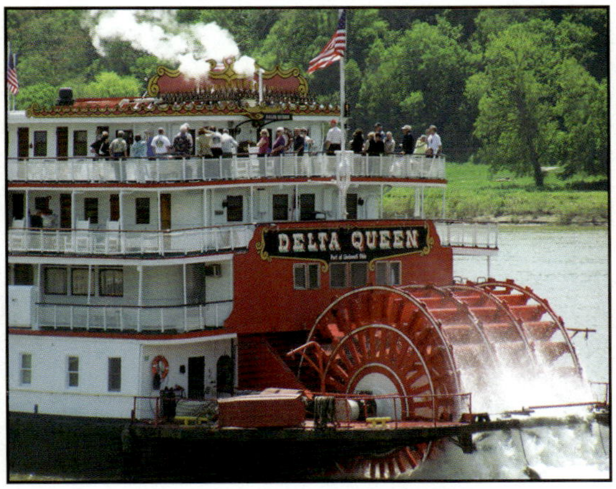

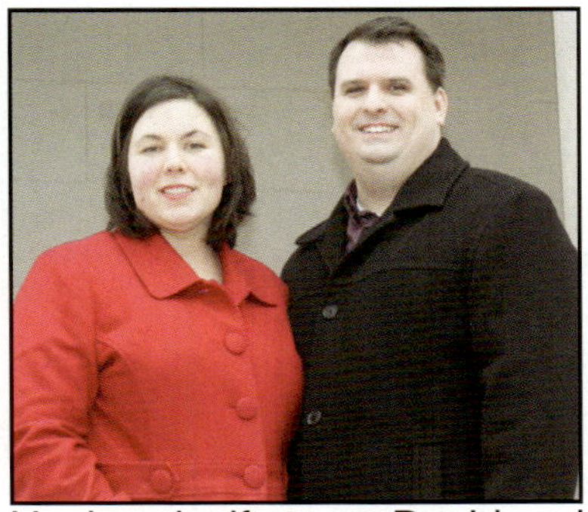

Husband-wife team David and Nina Campbell won second and third place, respectively.

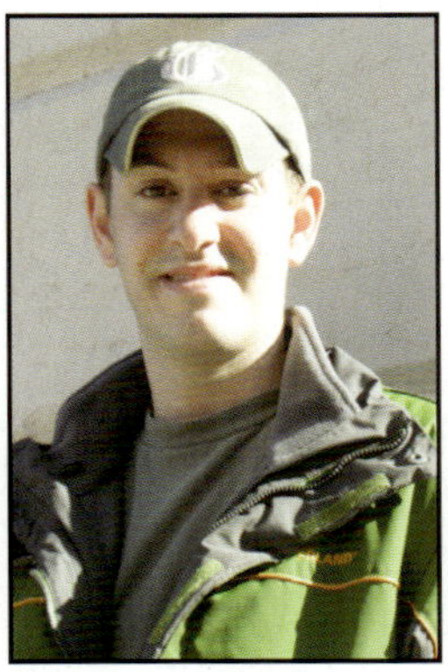

Contest winner Chad Schafer won $200 for his night-time photo of Madison's Main Street (above left).

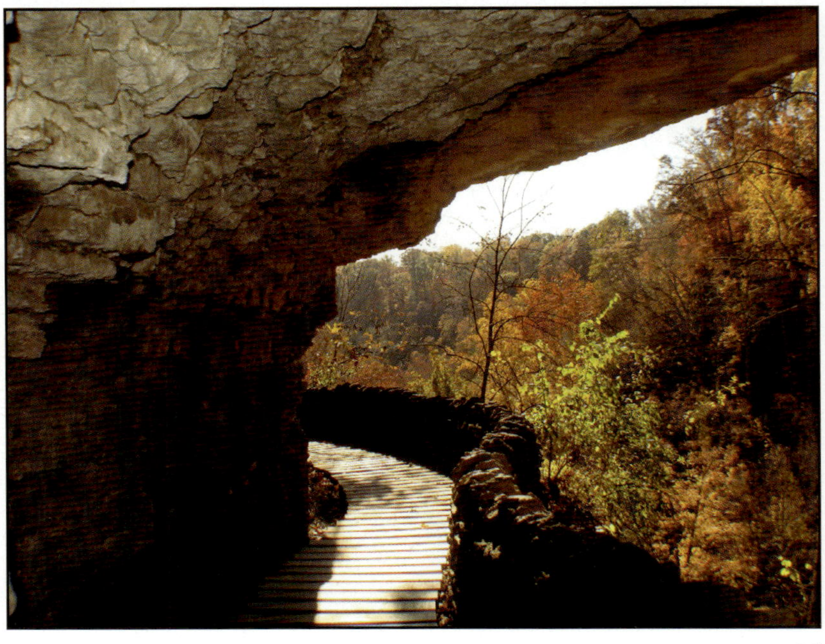

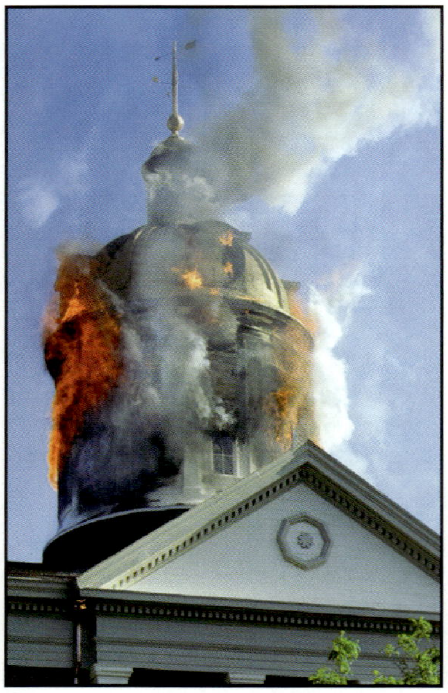

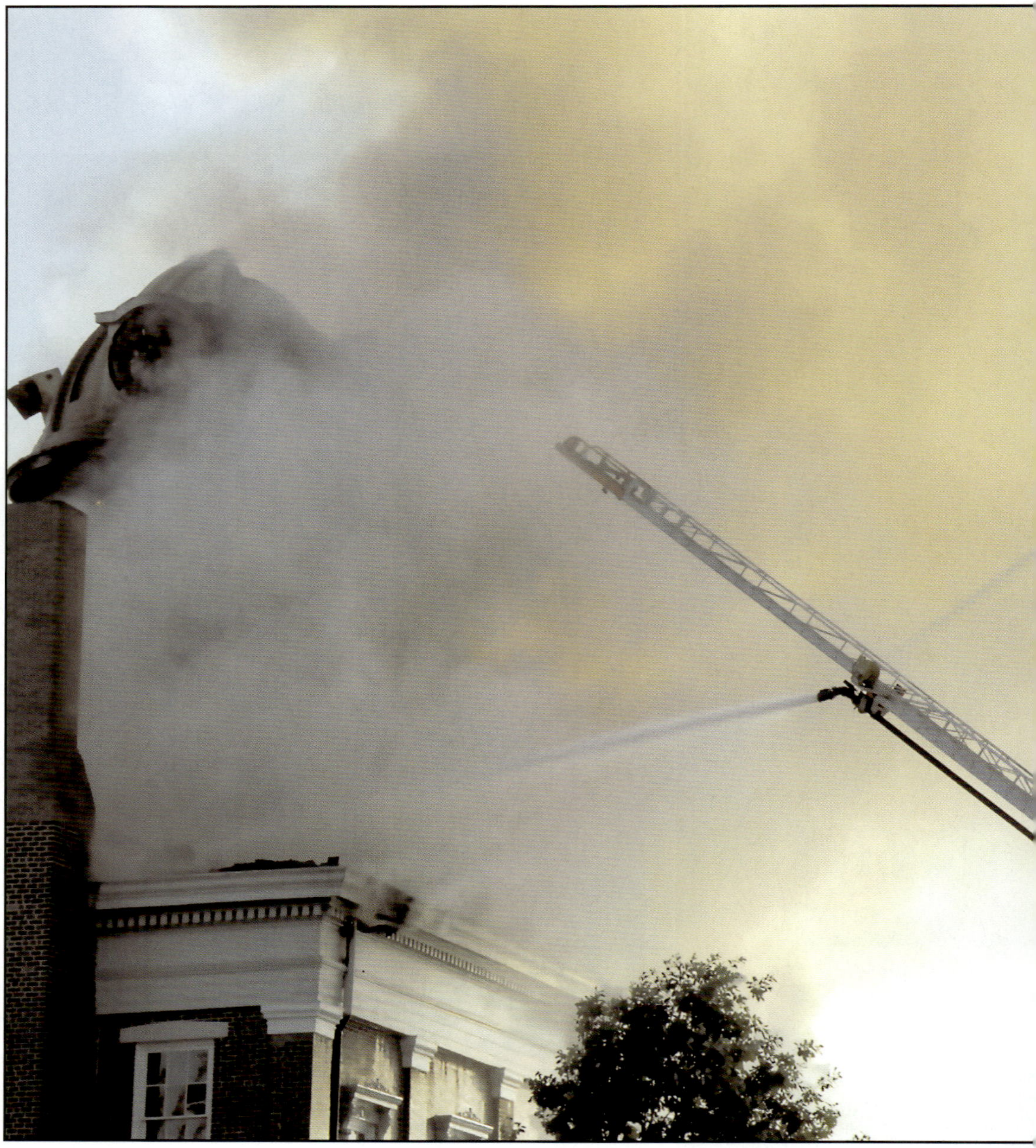

When fire engulfed the belltower of the Jefferson County Courthouse on Wednesday, May 20, hundreds of people watched as 17 city, county and neighboring volunteer fire departments battled the blaze into the night and the next day. Firefighters stayed on duty dousing small flames that kept erupting into Sunday. Thanks for their heroism and hard work, the historic 1854 building, one of the oldest courthouses in Indiana, was saved.

Photos by Bernie Kasper

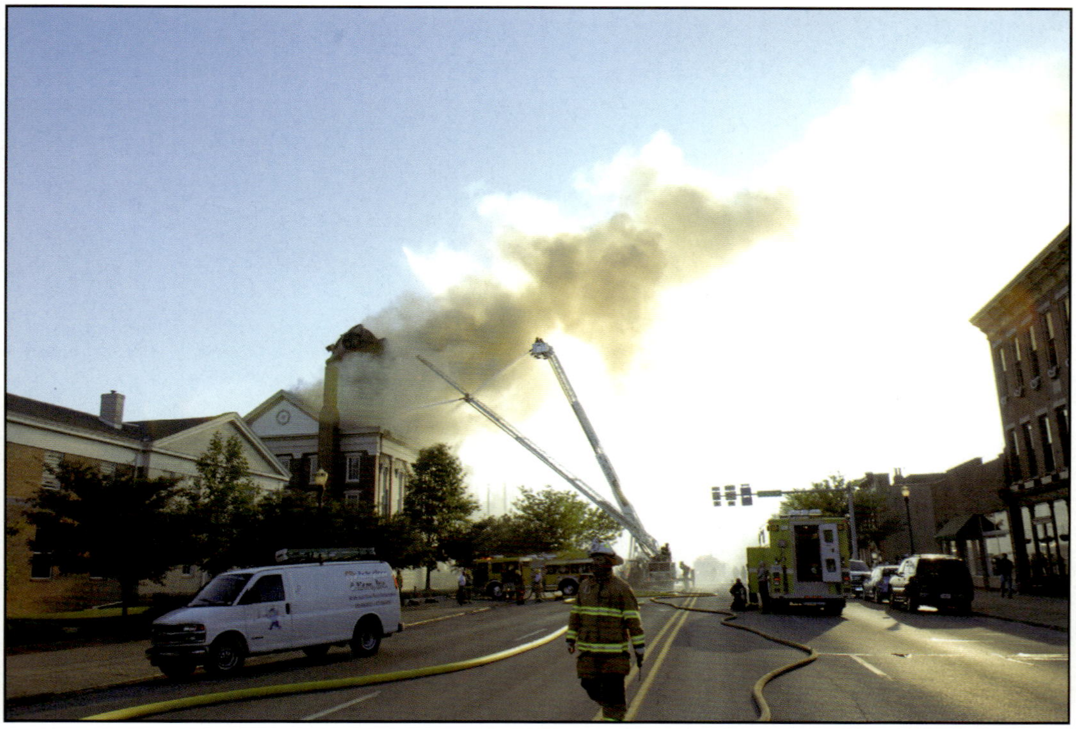

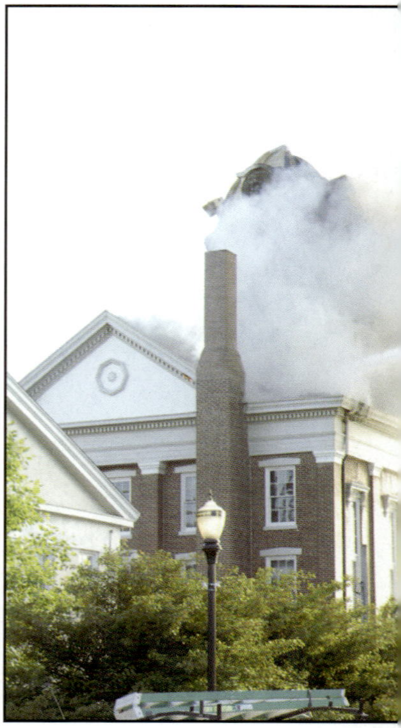

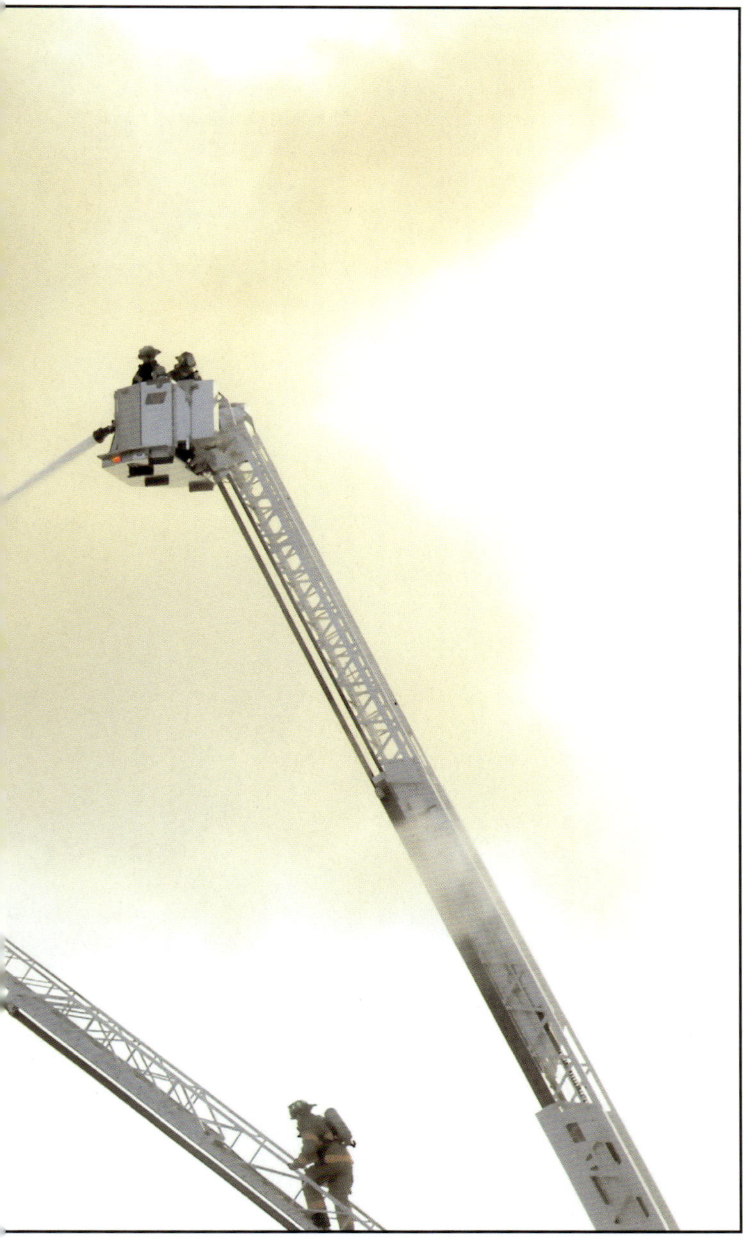

Fire at the Courthouse!

Just 2 1/2 weeks before the kickoff of the Madison Bicentennial, fire broke out the evening of May 20 at the Jefferson County Courthouse. The courthouse had been undergoing a renovation that was nearing completion in time for the Bicentennial. The renovation included painting the cupola and dome a bright colored gold.

The courthouse was to have been the centerpiece of the Bicentennial but instead became the focal point for bringing the community together in the aftermath of the fire.

The fire destroyed the roof but not the structure. The third floor sustained considerable water and smoke damage. Workers spent several days removing the 28,000-pound belltower, in two sections, and then the 3,000-pound steel bell located inside as people gathered each day to watch.

Several days later, the cause of the fire was determined to be accidental and caused when a worker was torching copper downspouts near the north door eaves.

The Jefferson County Commission has been working with insurance adjusters and construction companies to stabilize the structure, remove and salvage important documents, relocate the courts and county offices, and plan the long rebuilding process that could take more than two years.

Meantime, the Bicentennial Committee and the community has volunteered time and money to help the courthouse employees through the transition.

A banner was created from a photo taken May 19 – the day before the fire – by resident Andrew Forrester of the freshly renovated courthouse. It was hung from the flag poles in front of the building just prior to the Bicentennial kickoff. It still stands as a reminder of what was to be but the centerpiece of the city's celebration but instead became a symbol of something much more powerful – Madison's enduring strength to join together as a community to overcome any obstacle, as it has for the past 200 years.

– Don Ward, Publisher

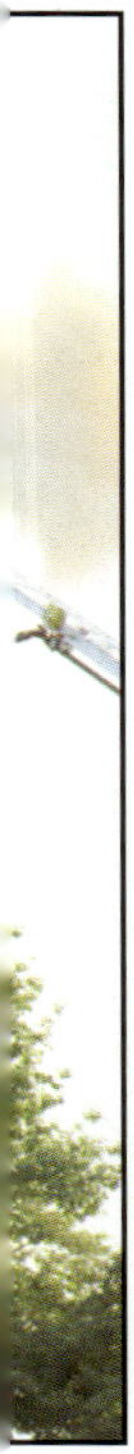

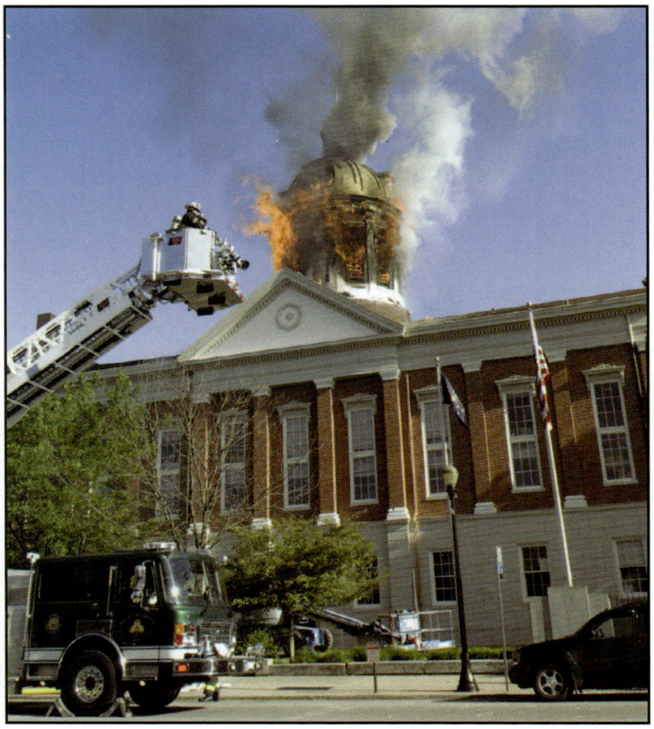

The Jefferson County Courthouse belltower (right) dissolved into a faint, ghostly image when smoke billowed from the scene as firefighters poured water onto the roof for several hours throughout the evening of May 20. Firefighters battled the blaze the night of May 20, then slept on Main Street in the early morning hours of May 21. Below, residents woke up to an eerie scene the day after the fire as the charred belltower clung to the burnt roof timbers, illuminated only by a solitary street light.

Photos by Don Ward

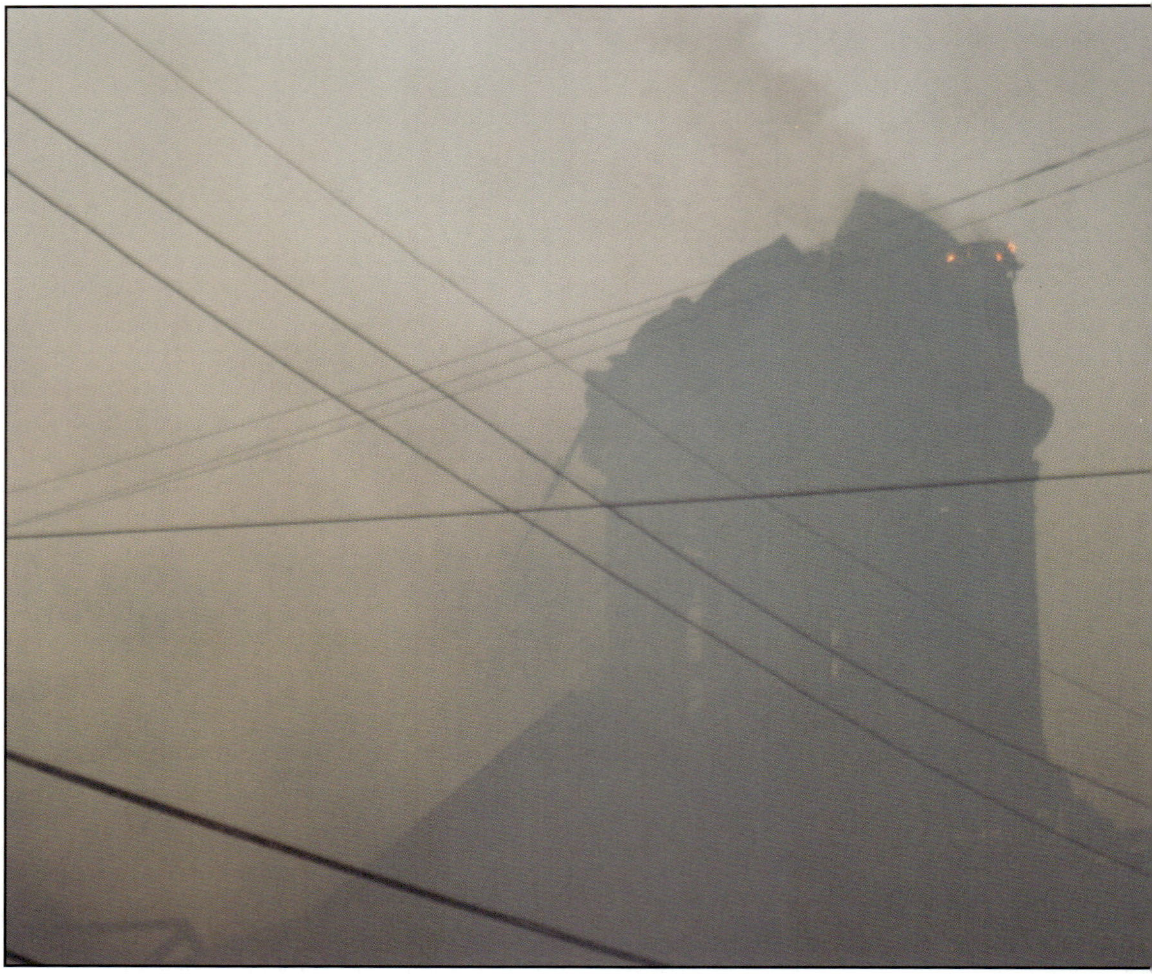

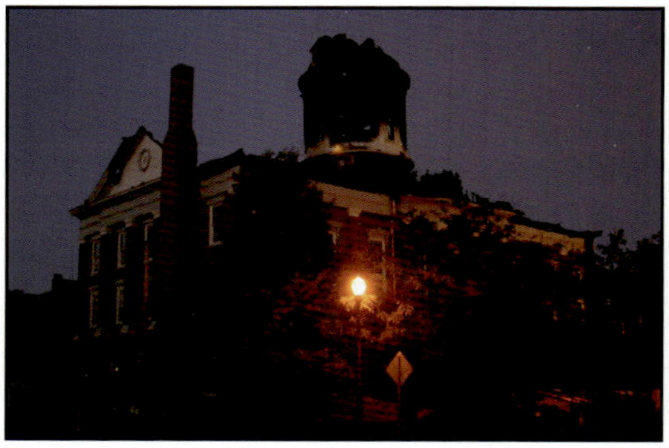

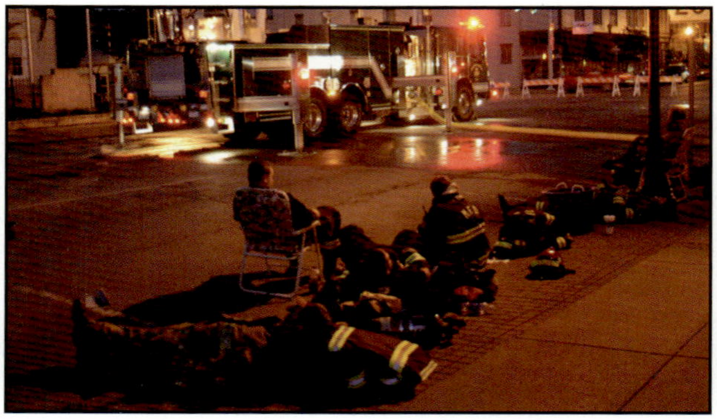

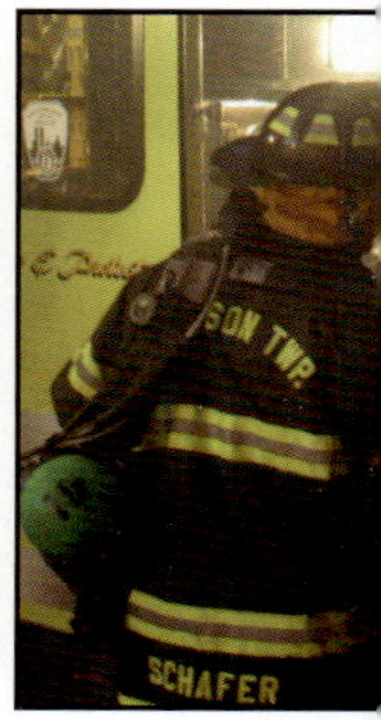

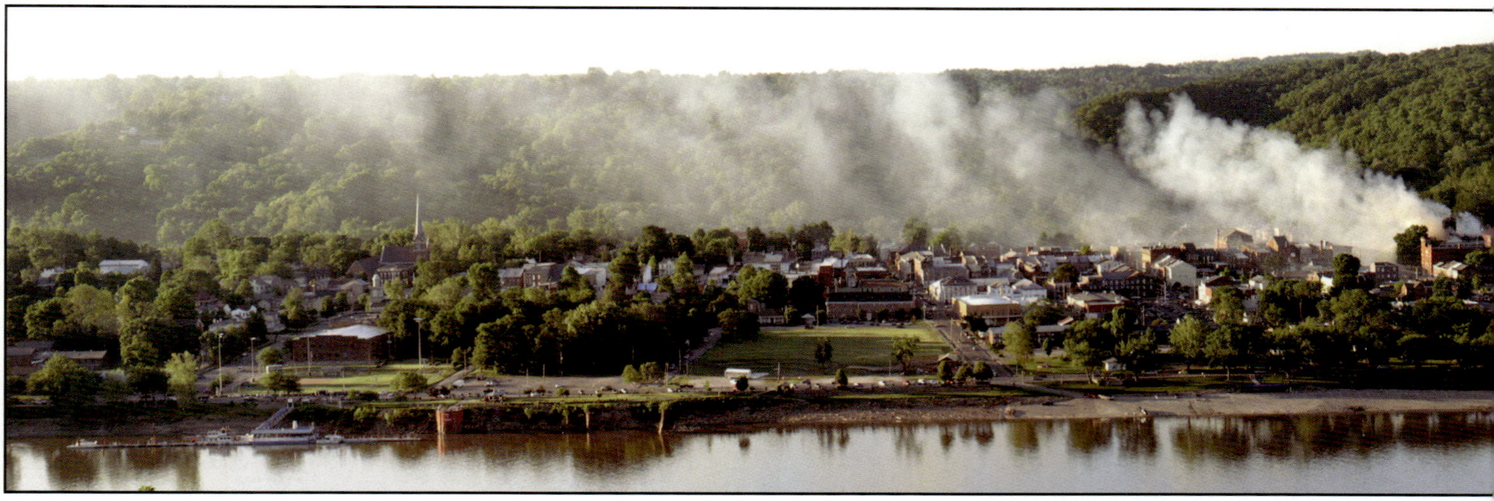

This series of photographs of the Jefferson County Courthouse fire were taken by Don Ward from the Milton, Ky., hilltop on the evening of May 20 and then merged into a panorama of the Madison cityscape. At right, Andrew Forrester poses in front of the banner created from a photograph he took the day before the fire showing the newly renovated courthouse. The banner cost $3,000 to create and was paid for by the Jefferson Co. Bar Association and local attorneys.

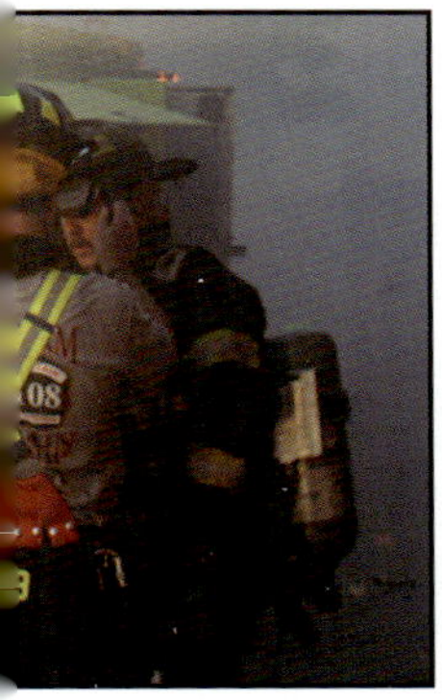

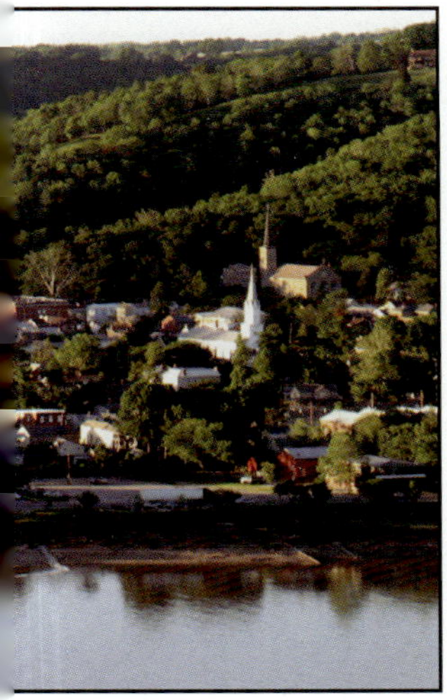

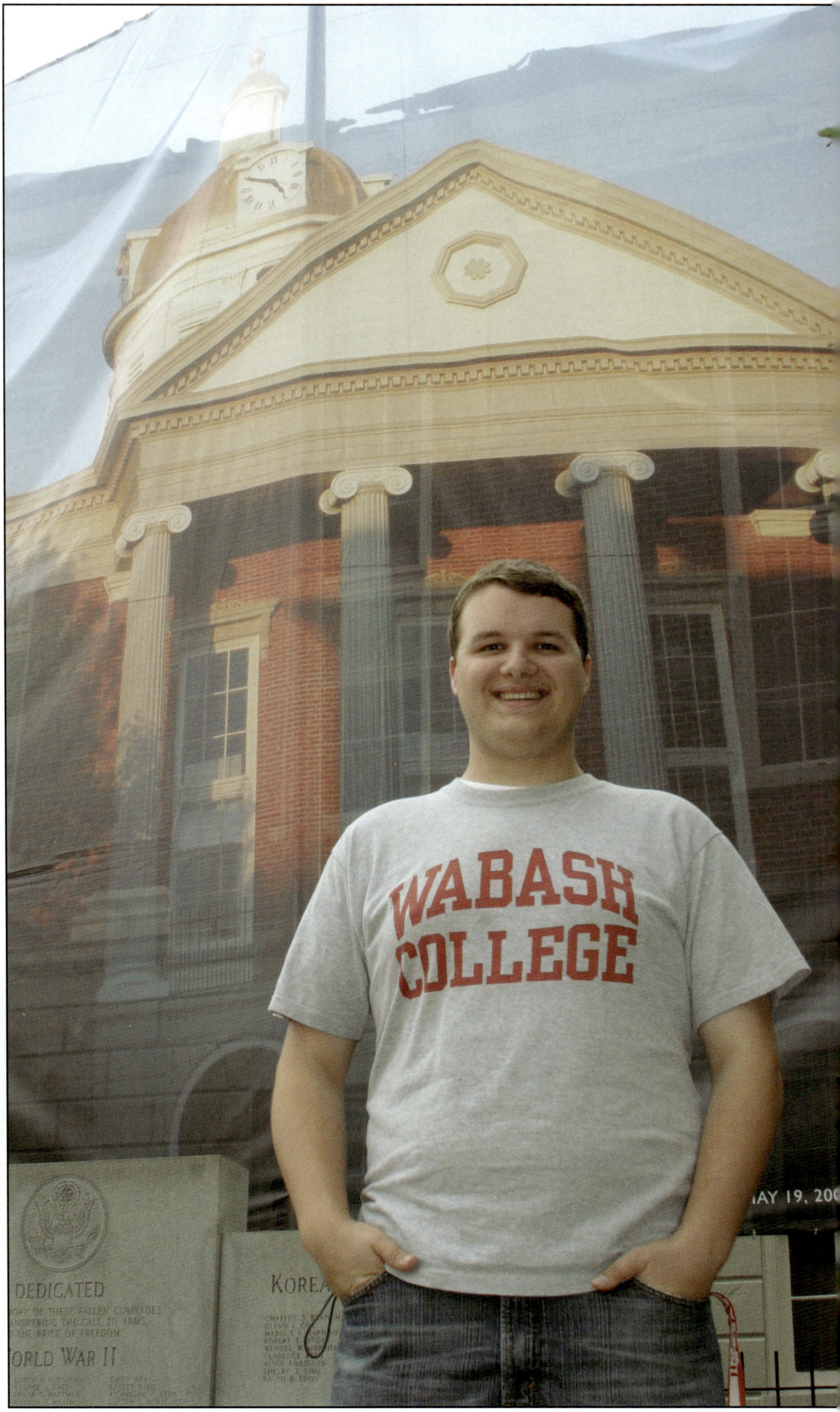
WABASH
COLLEGE
DEDICATED

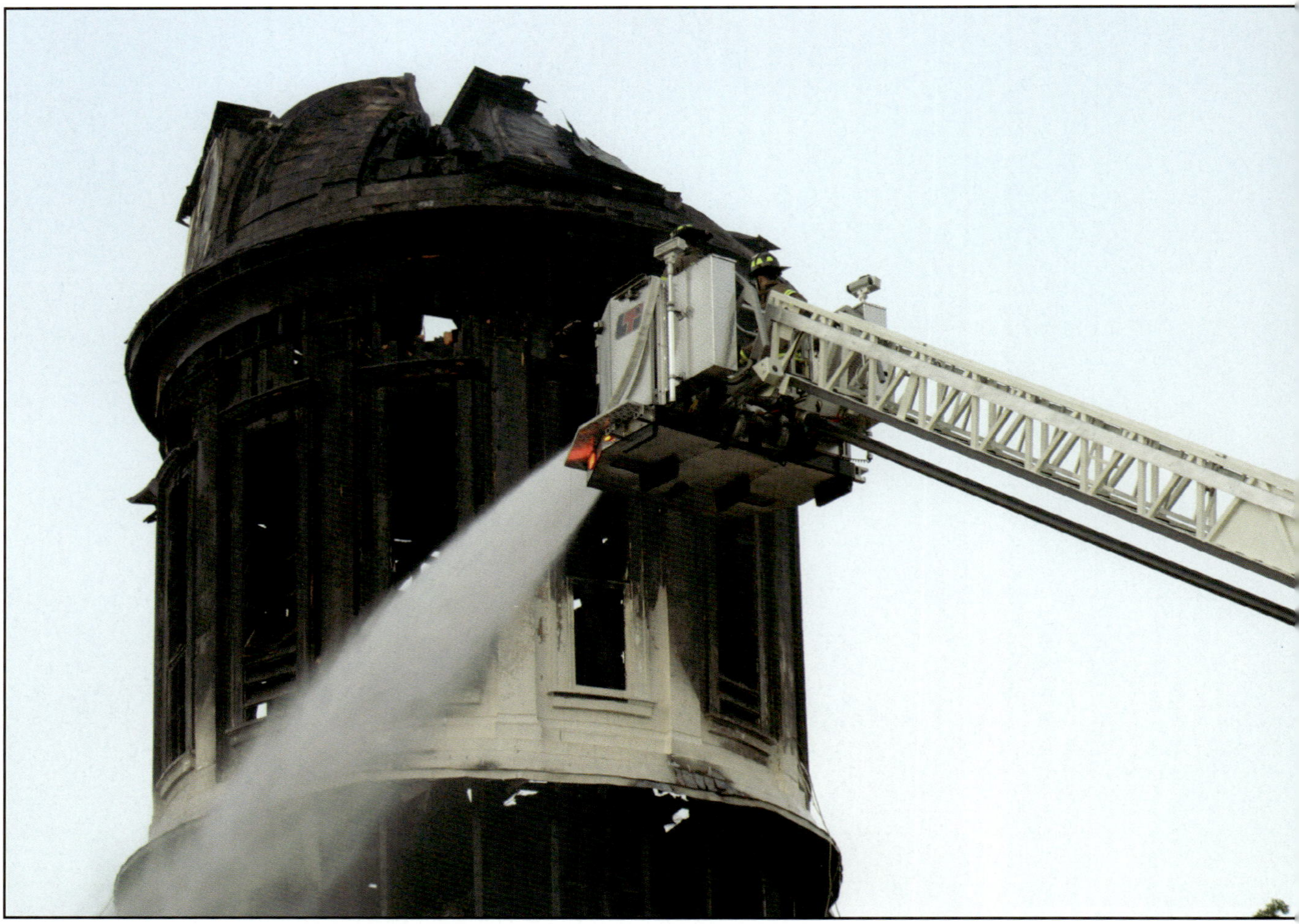

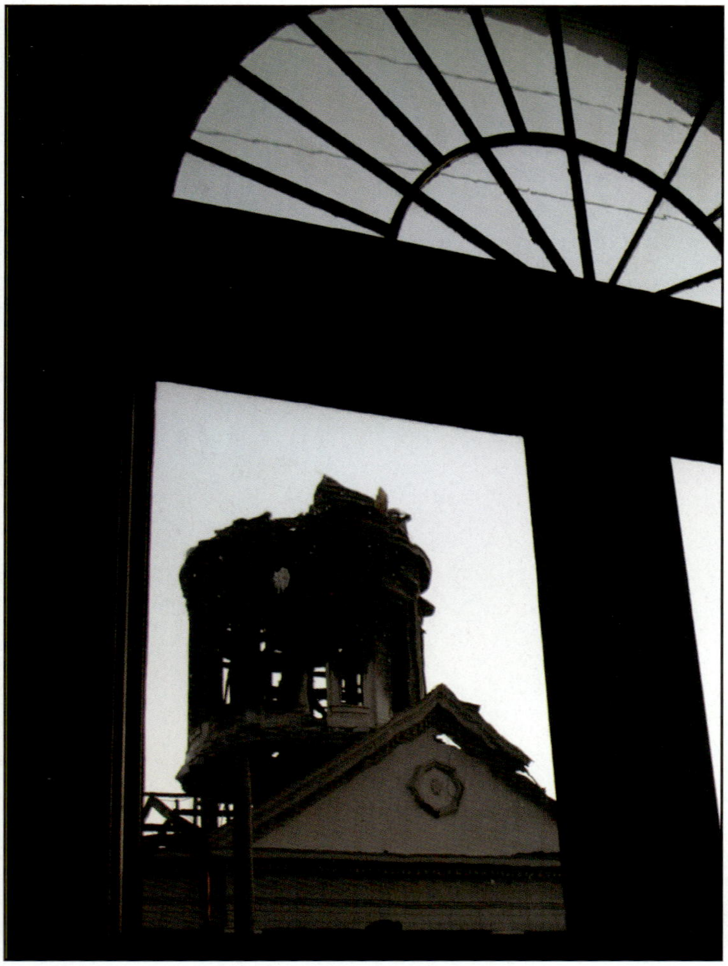

ABOVE: Firefighters spray water onto lingering flames early Thursday morning, May 21, onto the Jefferson County Courthouse belltower.

LEFT: The charred belltower hangs vicariously to the damaged roof of the courthouse the day after the fire.

BELOW: Jefferson County Commissioners Julie Berry and Tom Pietrykowski watch as the belltower is cut in half and then removed (above right) during a driving rainstorm on May 28, a week after the fire.

Photos by Don Ward

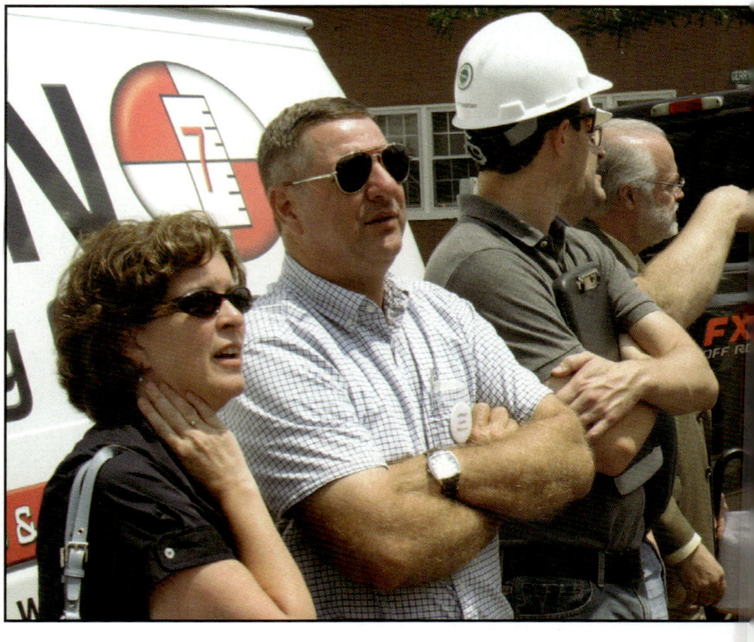

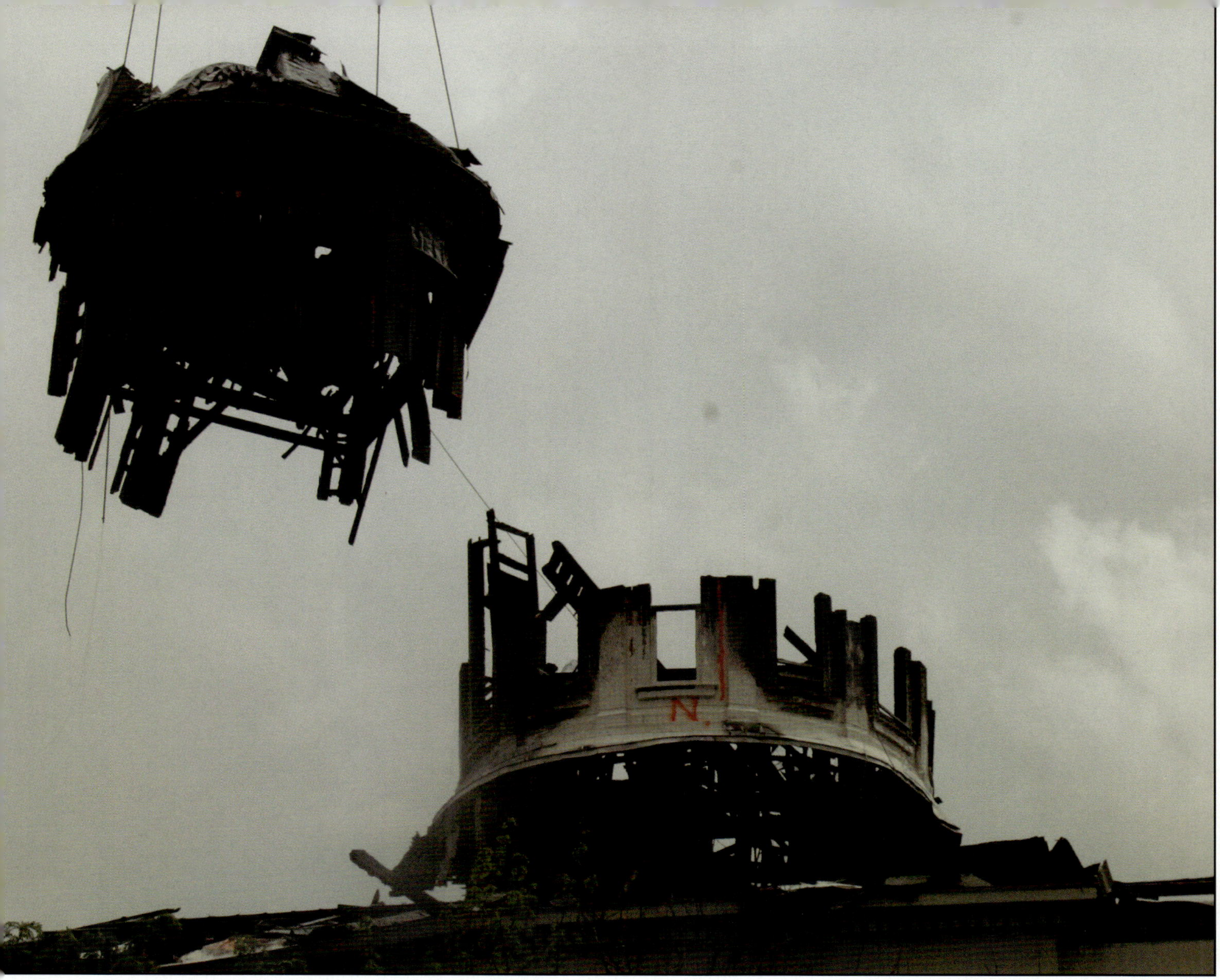

Once the 14,000-pound top half of the belltower was removed, workers removed the 3,100-pound bell (below right) and sat it down on Main Street, where spectators photographed it. The bell, which was made at a Cincinnati foundry, had not been seen in public since it was installed in 1864. Then workers cautiously removed the 10,000-pound bottom half of the belltower and sat it on the courthouse lawn (below) for fire investigators to inspect. The belltower sections remained on the lawn for nearly a month while the County Commissioners planned their post-fire recovery efforts.

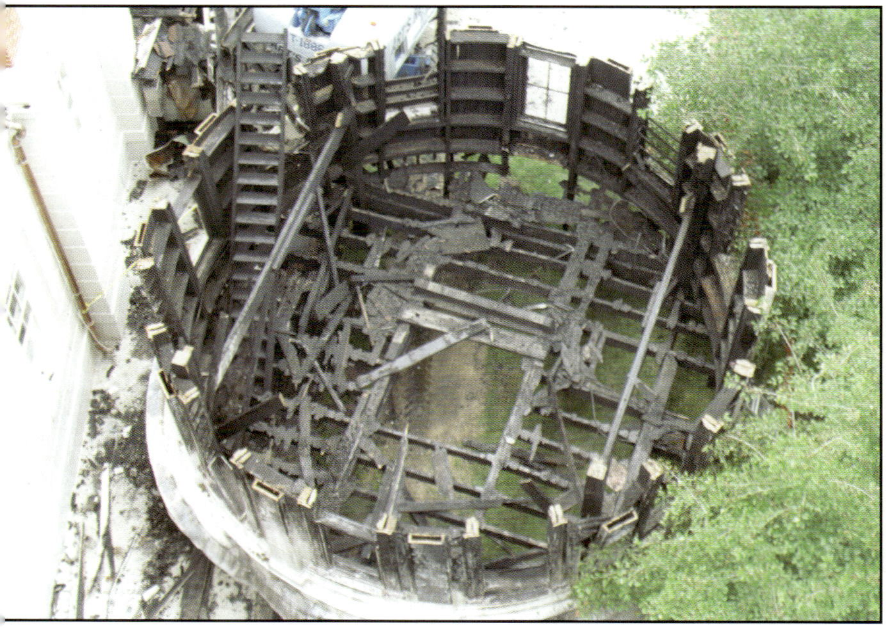

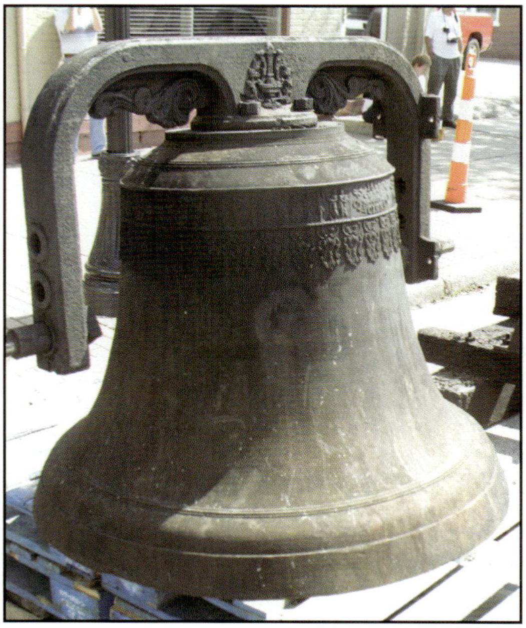

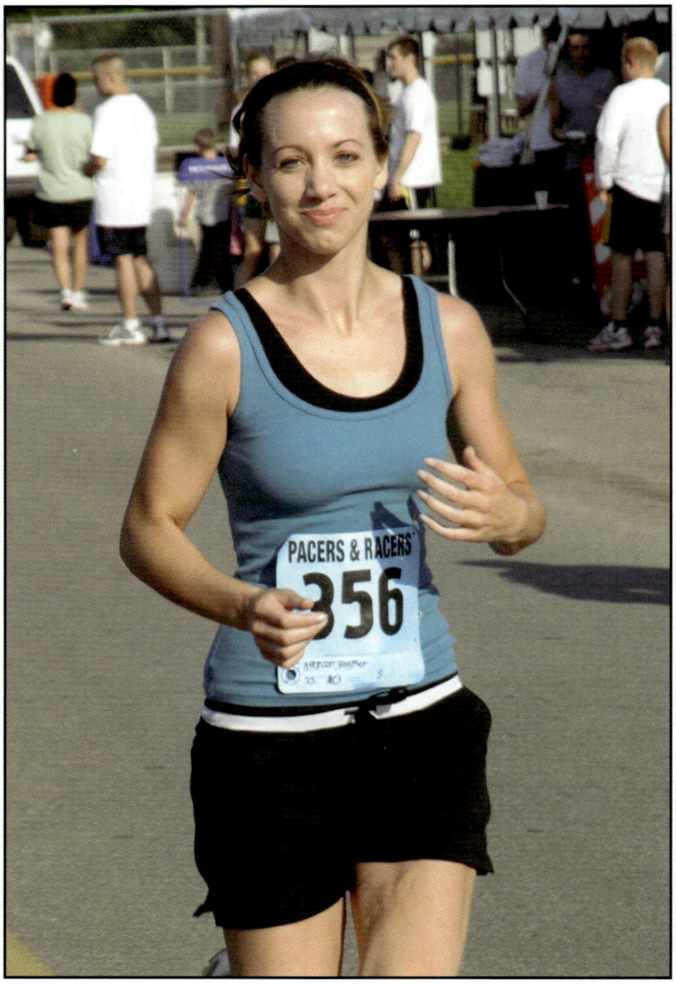

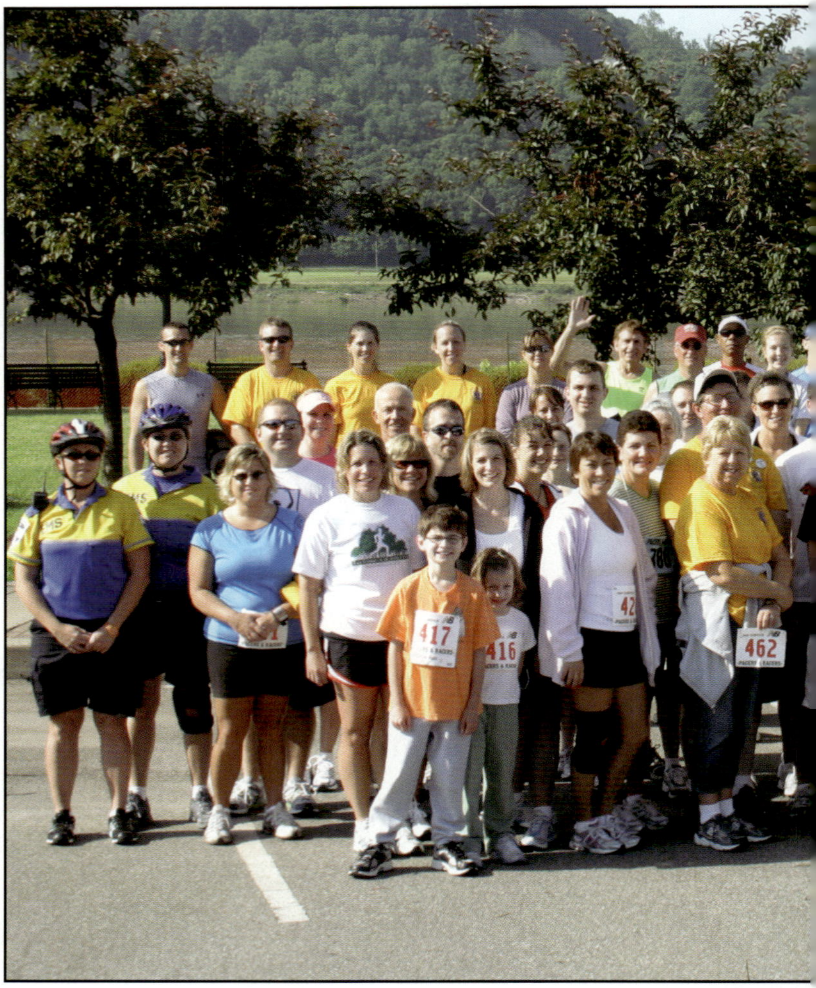

Heather Atkinson (above) of Madison crosses the finish line with a big smile. Many of the 240 runners and walkers pose for a group shot (above right) after the awards ceremony.

Mayor Tim Armstrong (right) poses with the women's overall winner, Catherine Graham of Hanover, Ind.

Trophies and Bicentennial T-shirts await the winners of each age group category and overall men's and women's winners.

Tonya Schmidt (far right) finishes strong in the women's 5K.

Photos by Don Ward

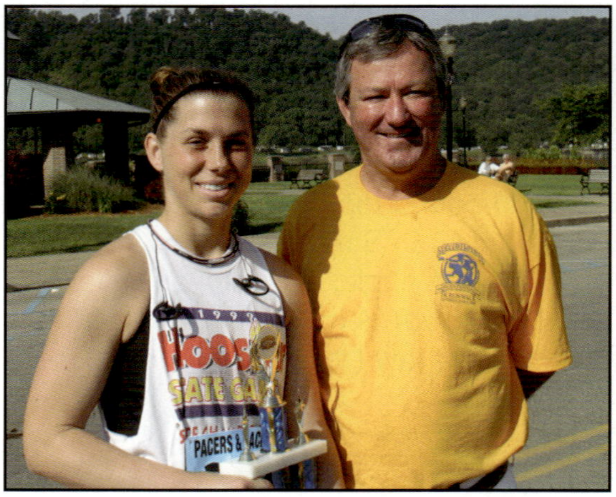

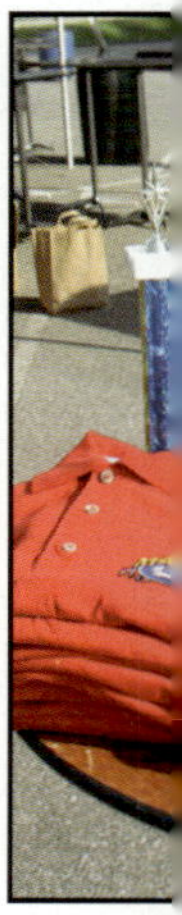

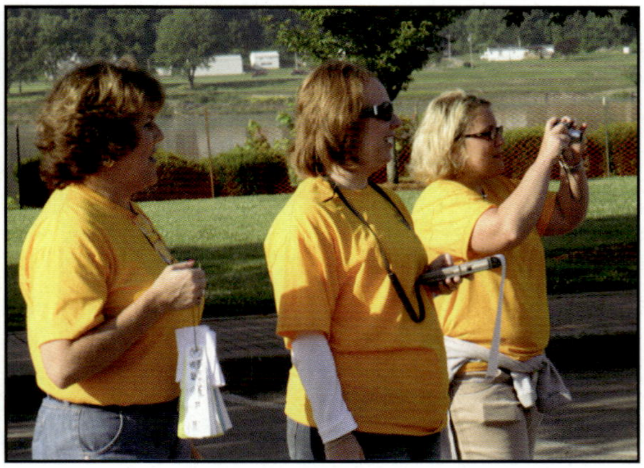

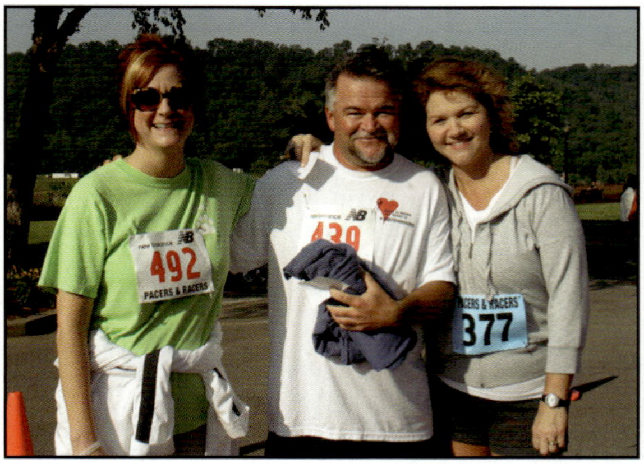

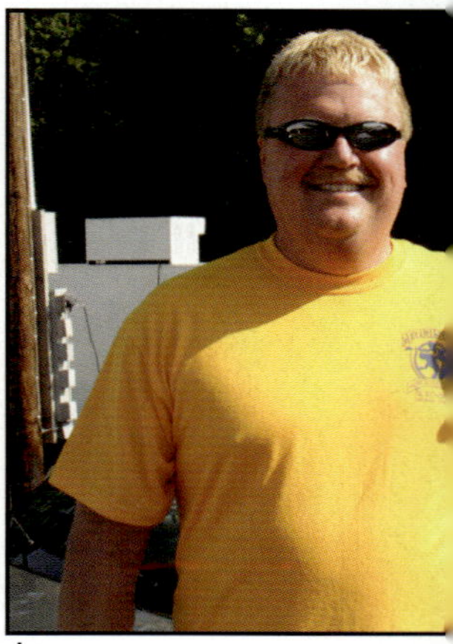

City of Madison staff members (from left) Lisa Konkle, Jenny Eggenspiller and Gina Center help check in the runners and walkers as they cross the finish line. Walkers (above from left) Linda Zapp, Jeff Melton and Tammy Courtney are all smiles afterward.

5K Run & Walk

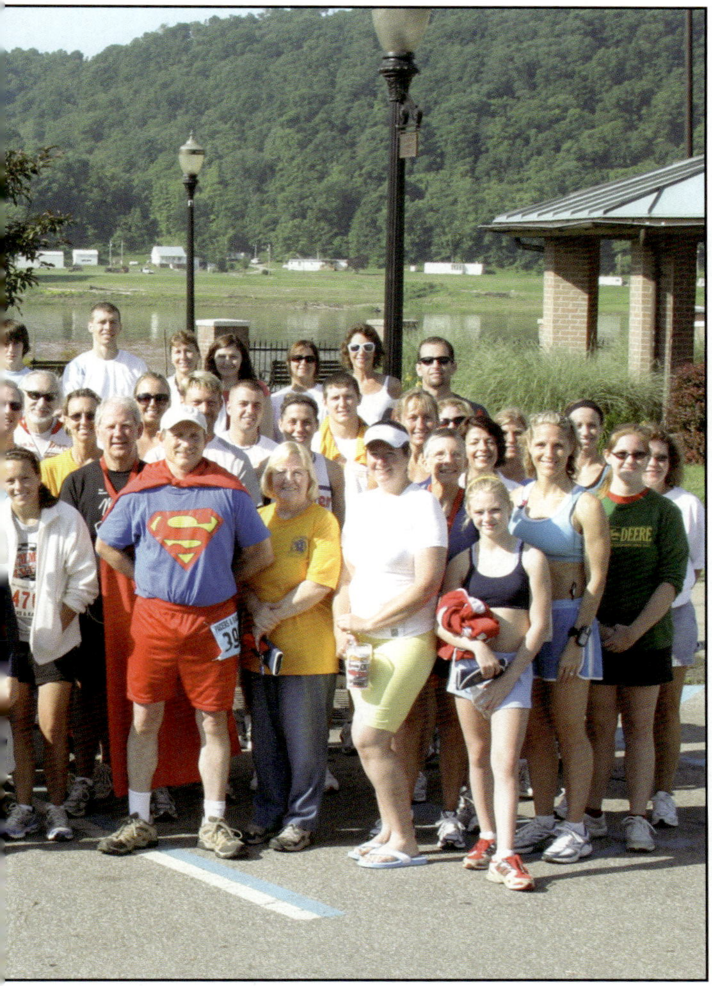

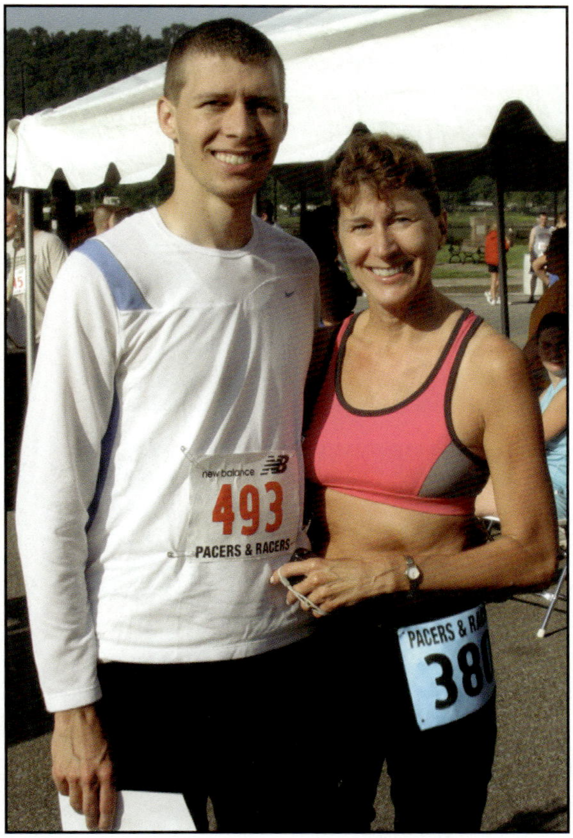

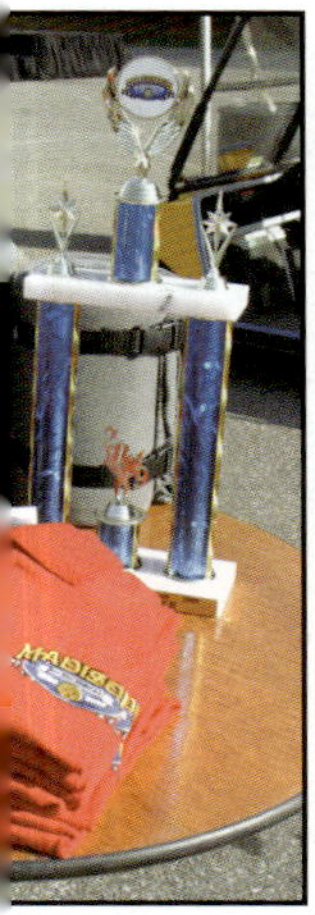

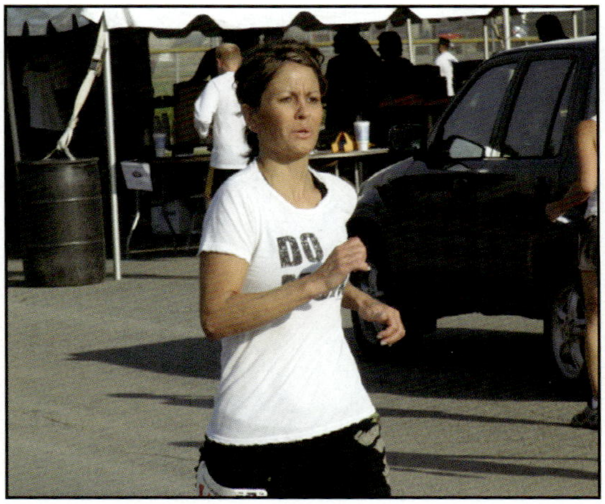

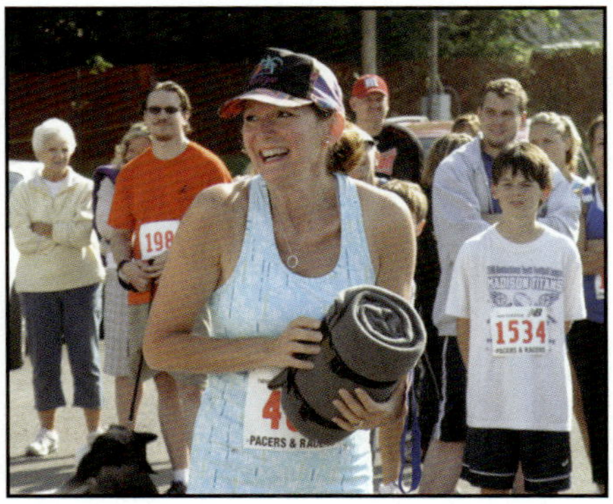

Leslie Cutshaw (above) with son, Zack Hawkins, pose after the race. Kim Cieslinski (left) accepts her award for her age group. Chris Strouse and son, Trace, (below) cross the finish line.

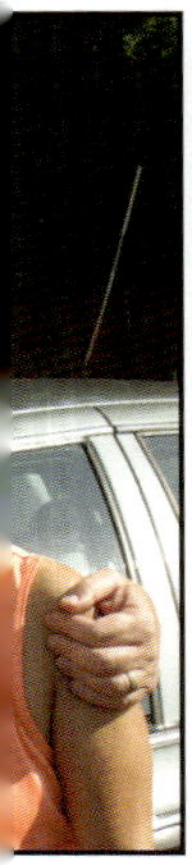

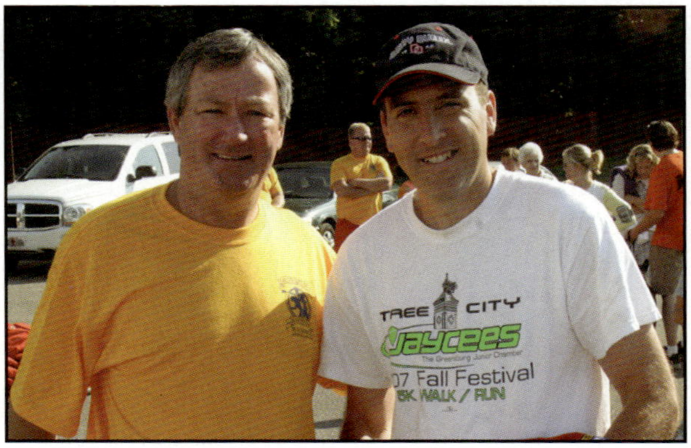

Madison Police Chief John Wallace and wife, Patti, (above left) pose after the race. Madison Mayor Tim Armstrong (above right) poses with men's overall winner, Jim Cole of Versailles, Ind.

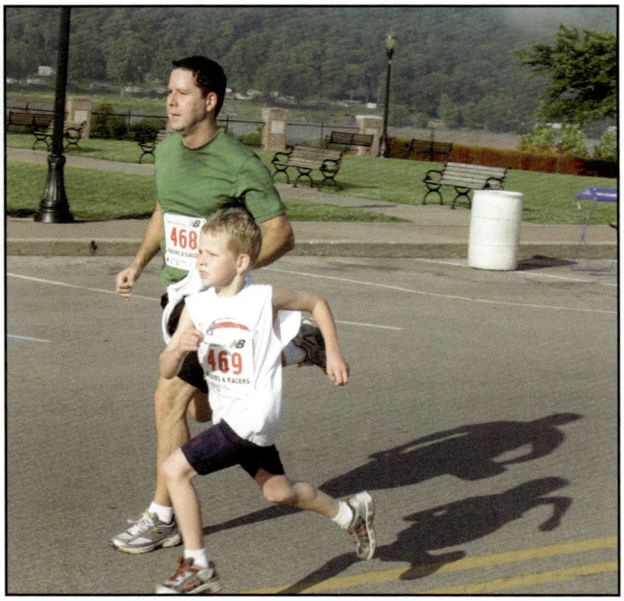

Bicentennial Mural VIP Party

Photos by Don Ward

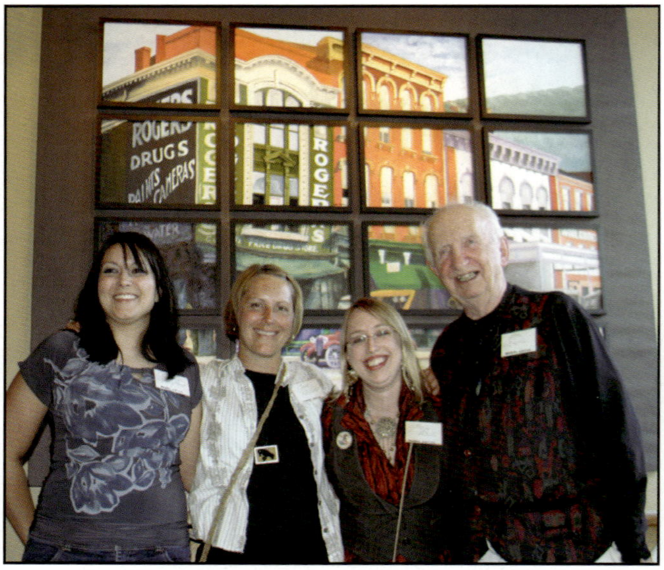

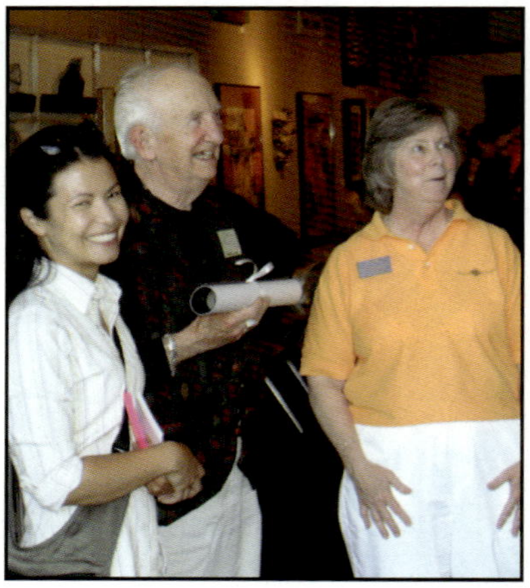

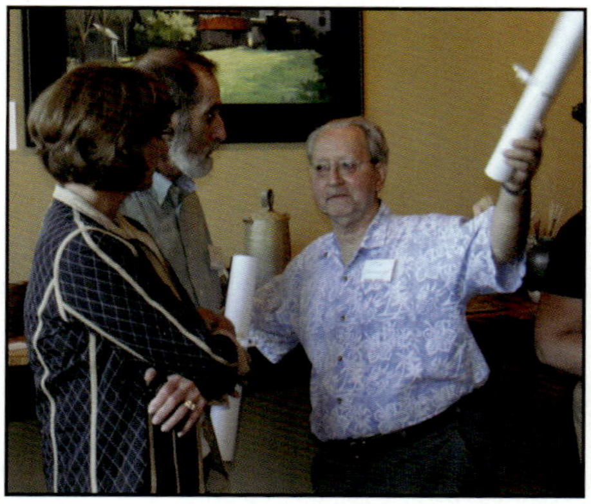

Posing above are four of the 16 artists who created separate panels of the Madison Chautauqua-sponsored mural. They are (from left) Jenny Straub Youngblood, Jane Devito, Patty Cooper Wells and Lou Knoble. Middle photo, Leticia Bajuyo admires the original paintings with Lou Knoble and Chautauqua coordinator Georgie Kelly. At right are Sally McWilliams with artists Bill Borden (center) and Bob Saueressig.

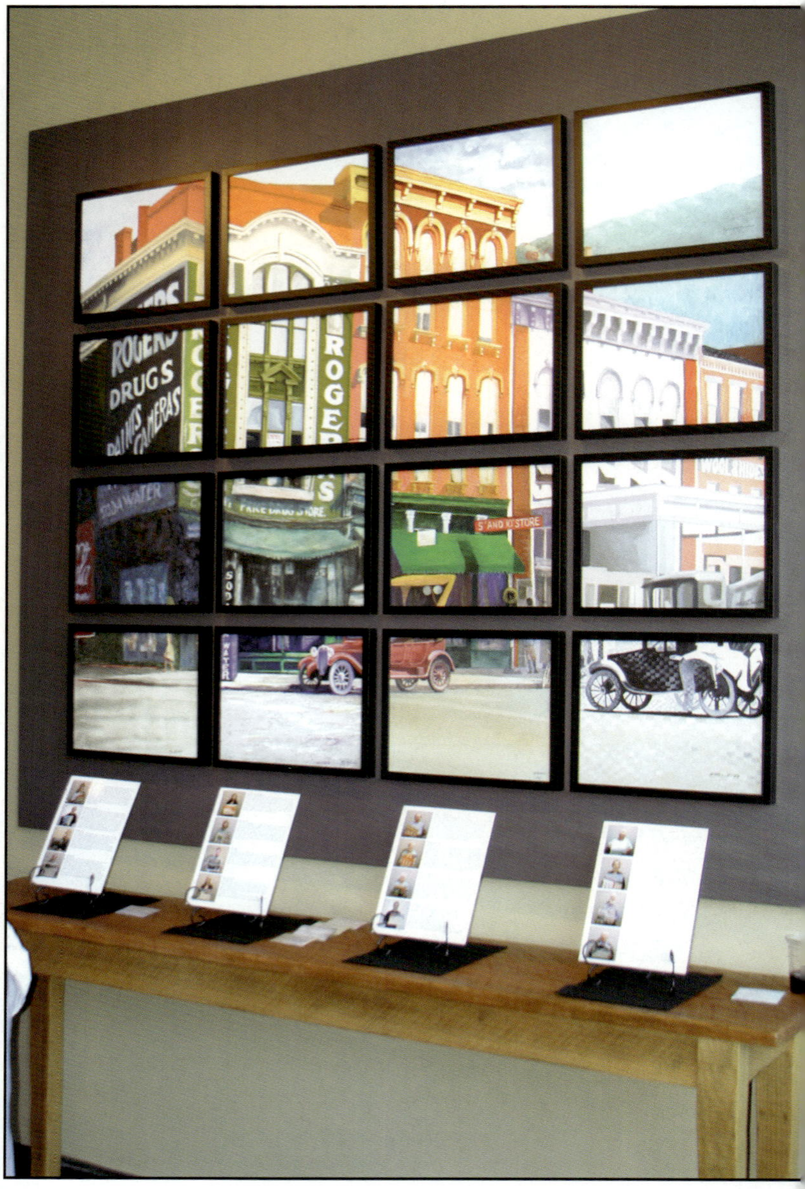

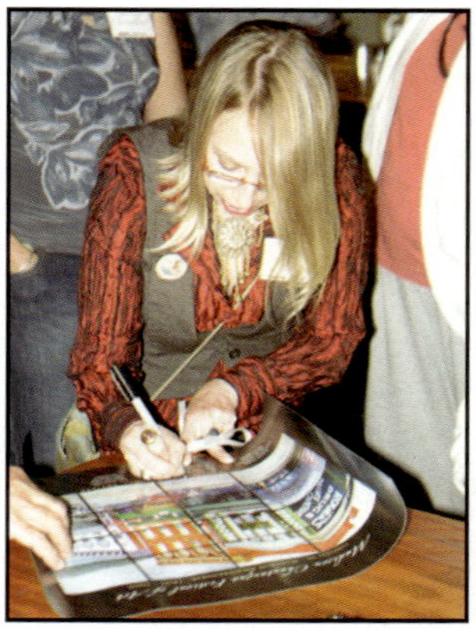

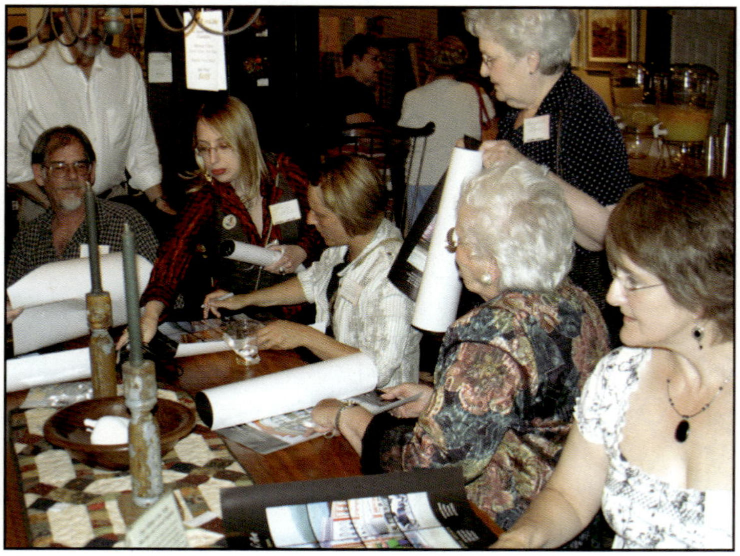

The original paintings (above of the mural were placed on the wall of the Madison Artisan Center by Timbers Custom Sign Co.

Left, several artists sign a poster of the mural, of which 12x16 sheet of vinyl was created and hung June 8 on the outside wall of Rogers Corne in Madison.

At far left, Patty Wells Coope signs what will become the Chautauqua poster for 2009.

Bicentennial Mural at Rogers Corner

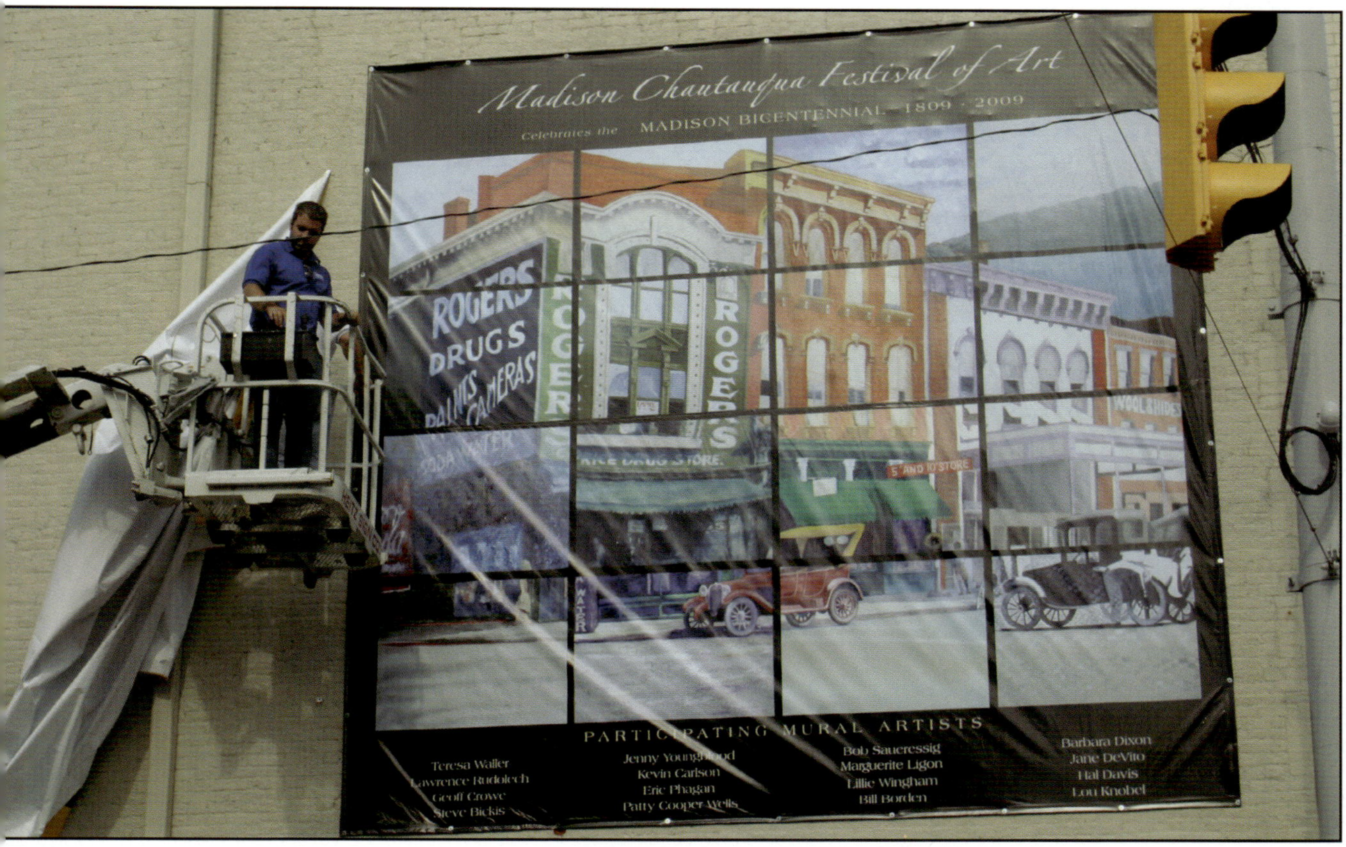

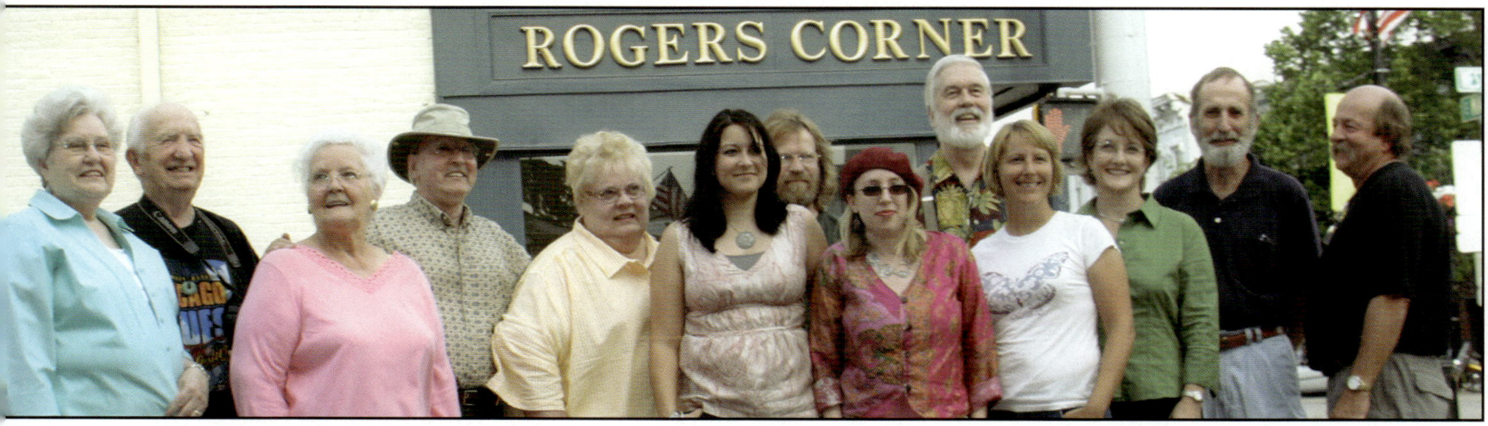

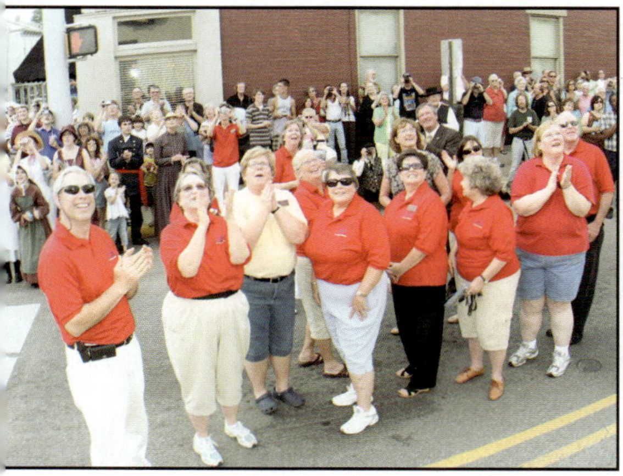

Above photo by Matt Griffith

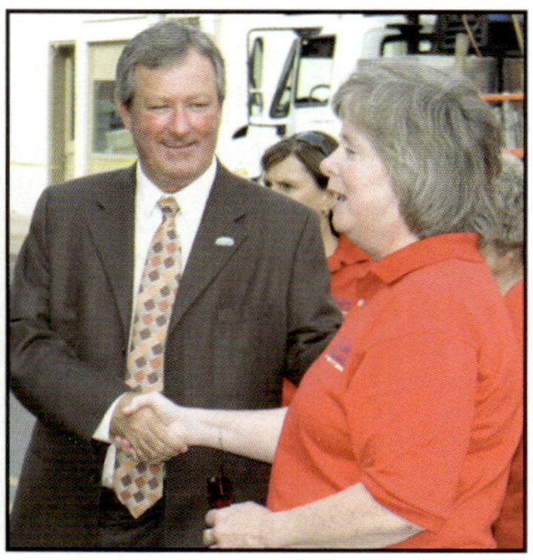

Chris Heitz of Heitz Sign Co. unveils the mural on the Rogers Corner building June 8. Artists attending include (from left) Marguerite Ligon, Lou Knoble, Lillie Wingham, Bob Saueressig, Barbara Walters-Dixon, Jenny Straub Youngblood, Kevin Carlson, Patty Cooper Wells, Hal Davis, Jane Devito, Teresa Waller, Bill Borden and Larry Rudolech. At far left, the Chautauqua committee applauds the unveiling as Madison Mayor Tim Armstrong thanks festival coordinator Georgie Kelly.

Photos by Don Ward

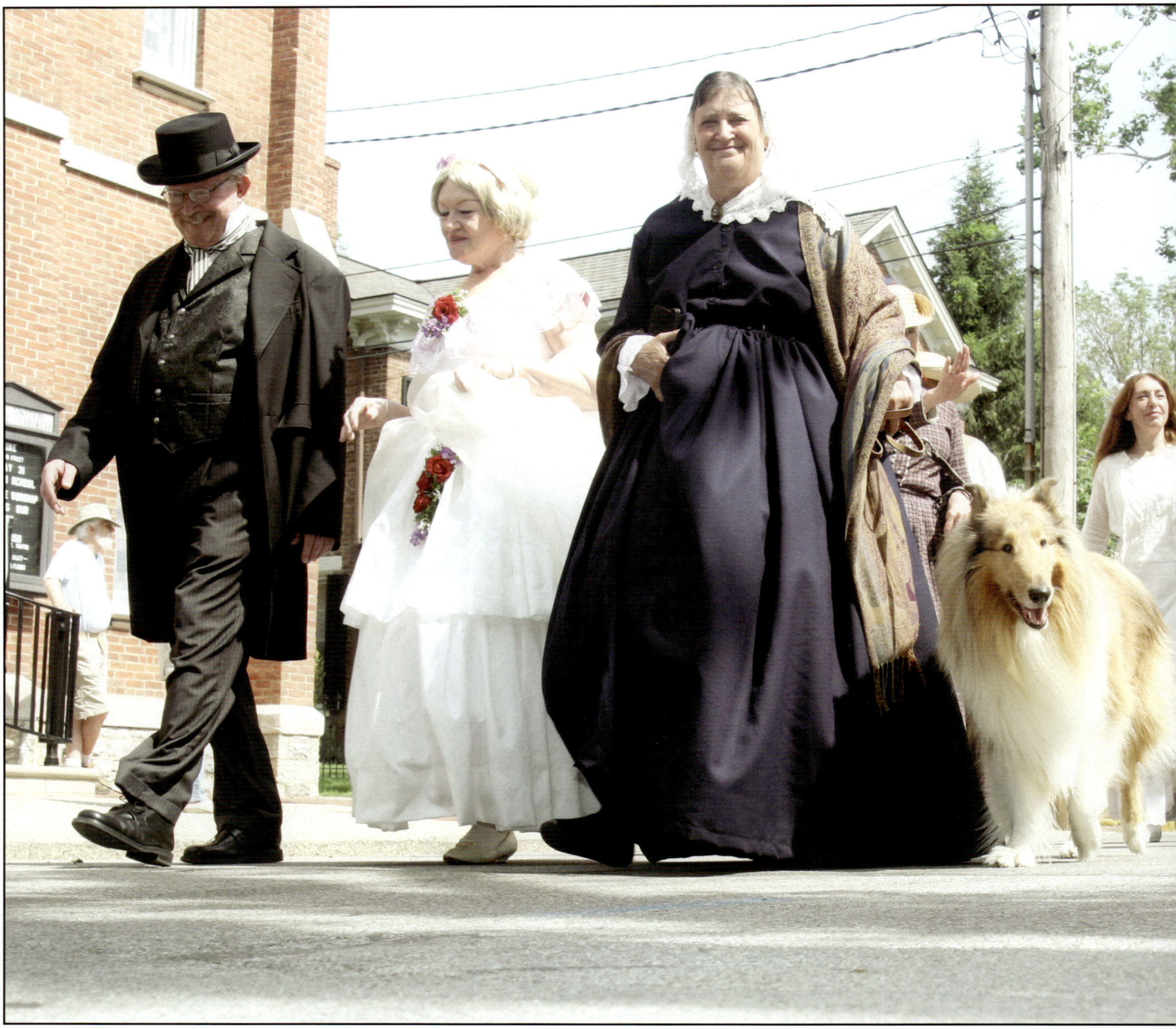

Photo by Matt Griffith

Bicentennial characters add color to the Founder's Parade on June 6 as it proceeded down Broadway to the riverfront stage for the Opening Ceremony. They are (from left) Wayne Engle, Camille Fife, Connie Partington and Bryce Worrell.

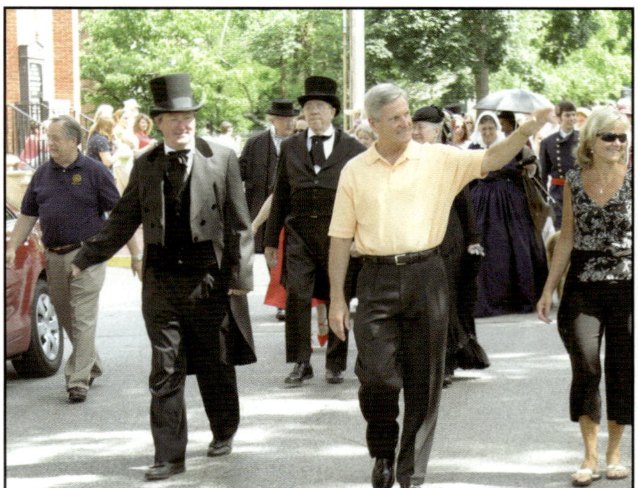

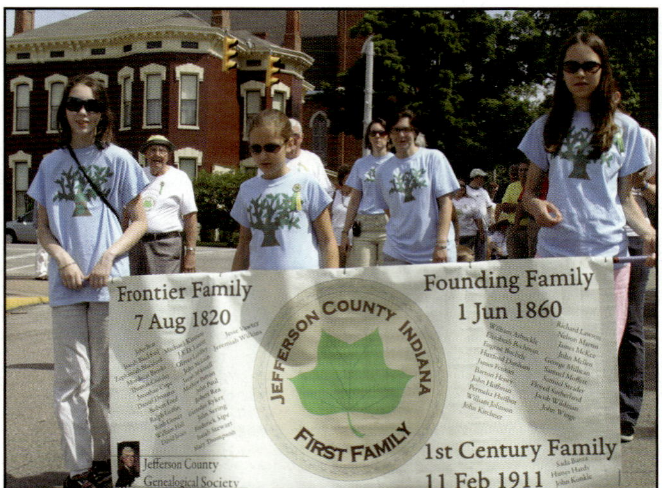

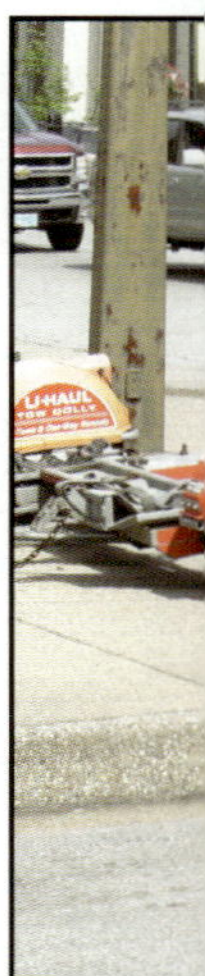

Founder's Parade

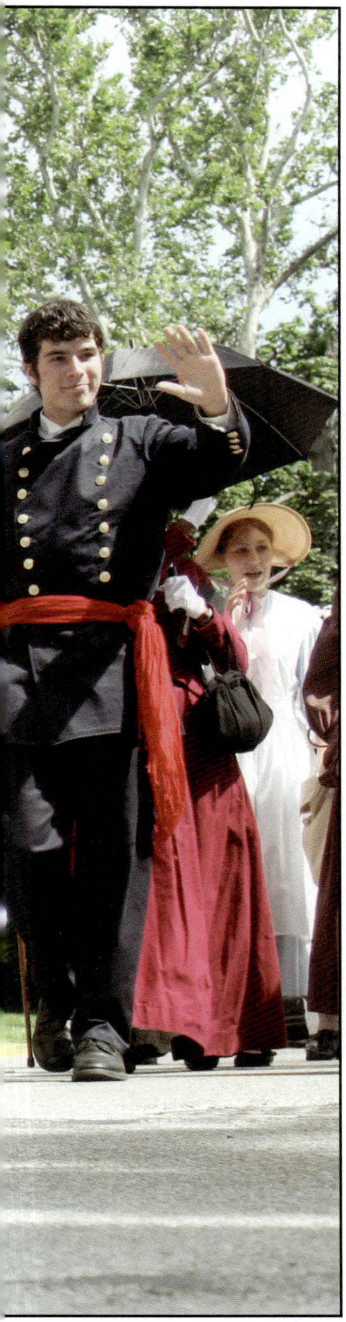

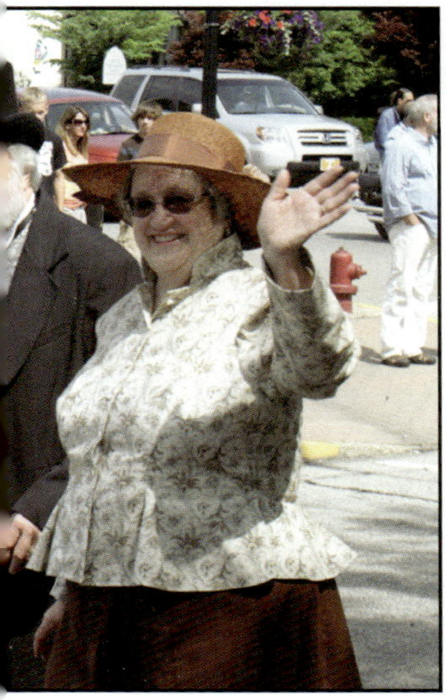

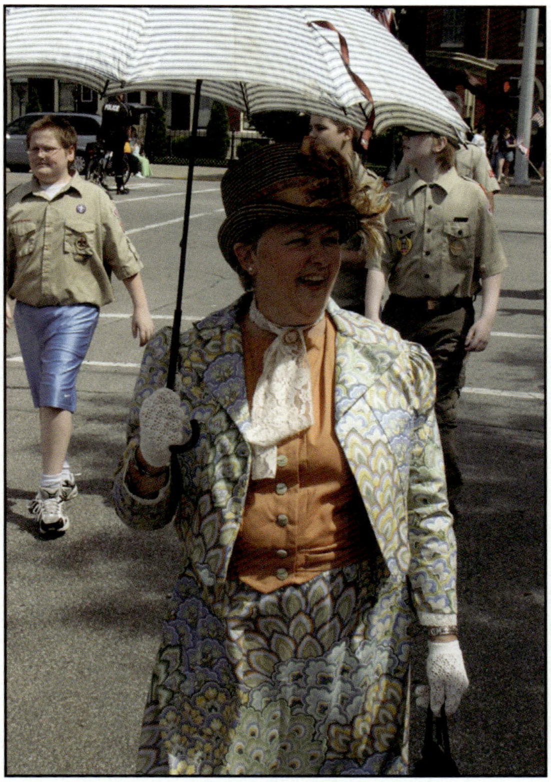

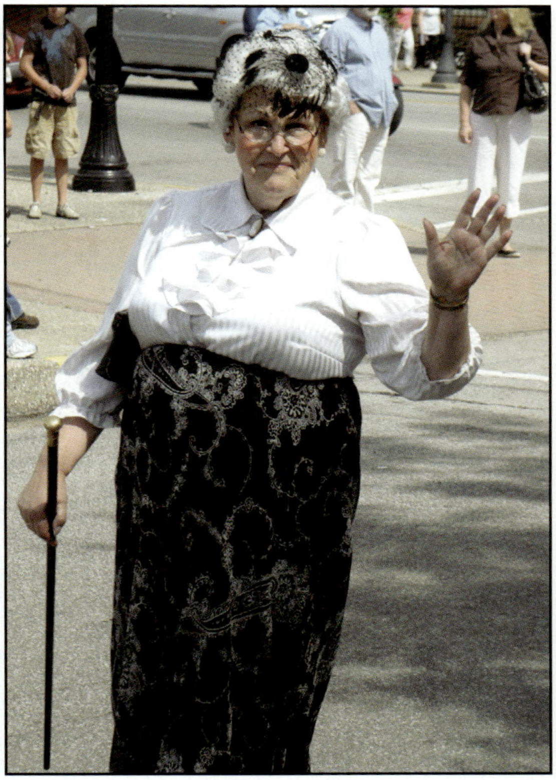

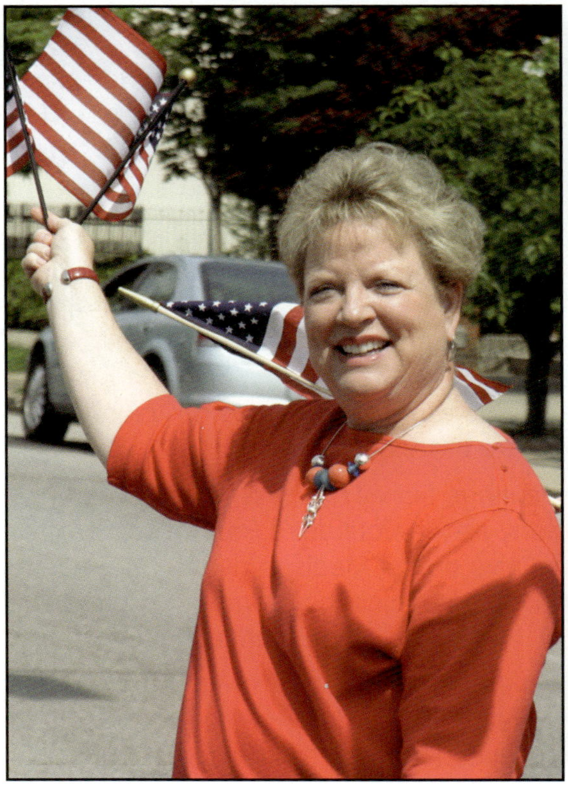

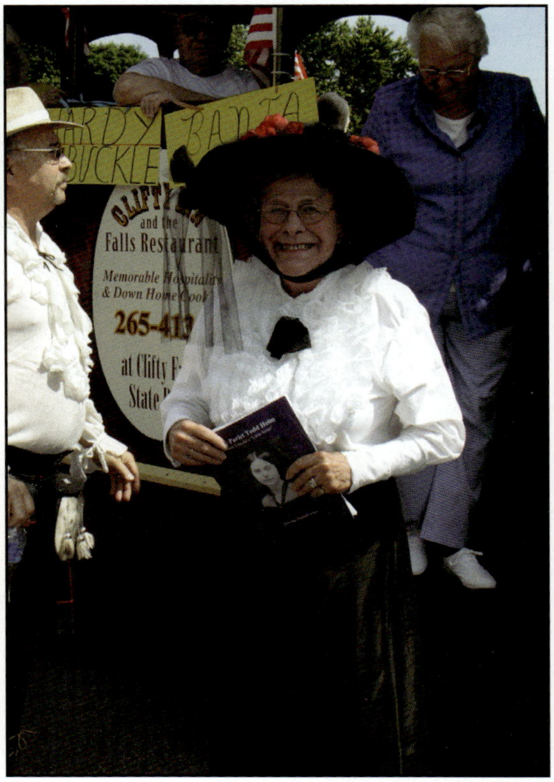

Photos by Don Ward

Above left is Victorian-dressed Joyce Wells; above right is Betsey Vonderheide portraying Drusilla Lanier Cravens; bottom left is Susan Ohlendorf; bottom right is Dorothy Jones portraying Emilie Todd Helm. At left is Bob and Merry Fourhman.

At far left, U.S. Rep. Baron Hill leads the Founder's Parade with his wife, Betty, Madison Mayor Tim Armstrong and former Mayor Al Huntington (at far left in photo).

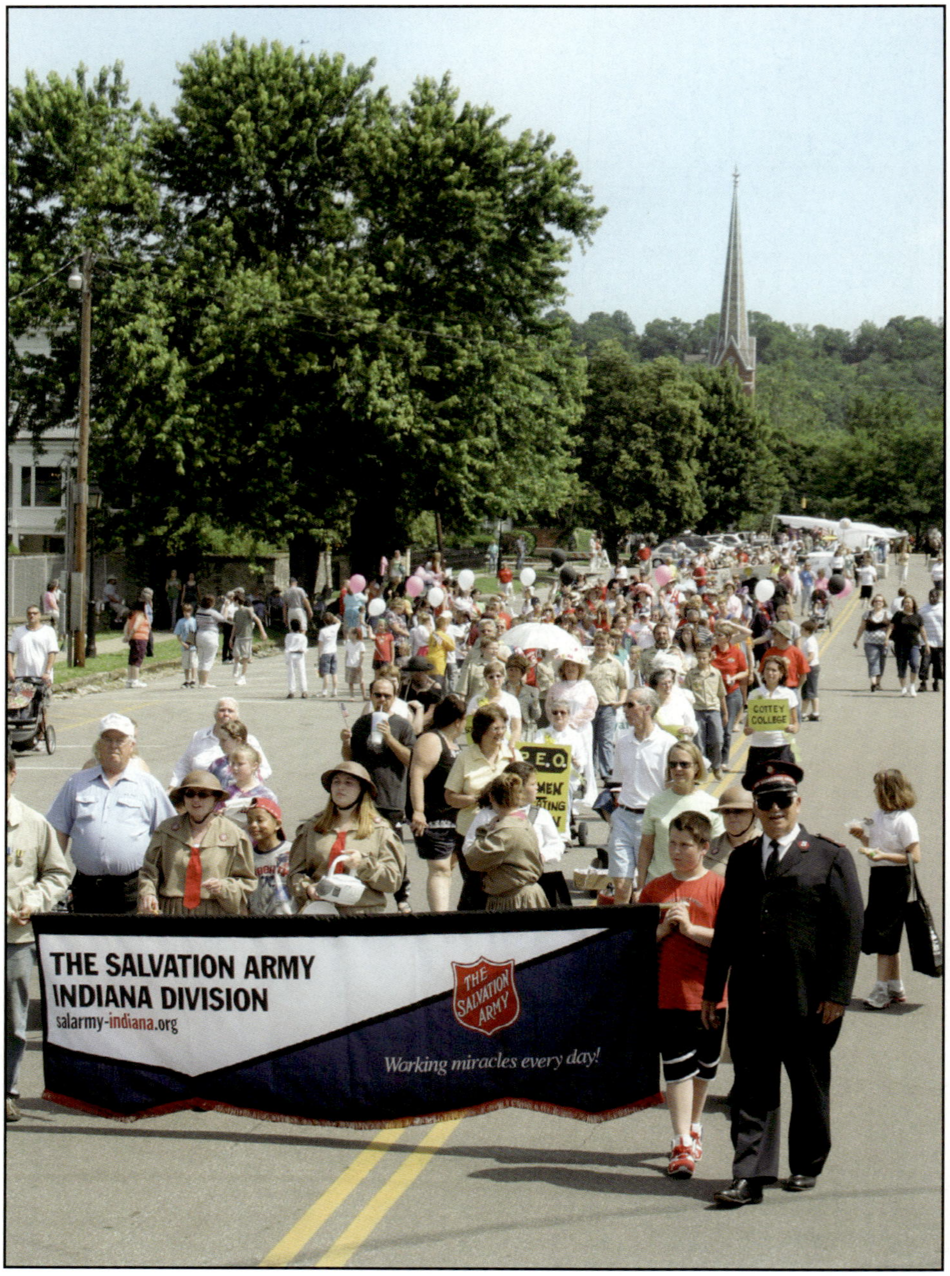

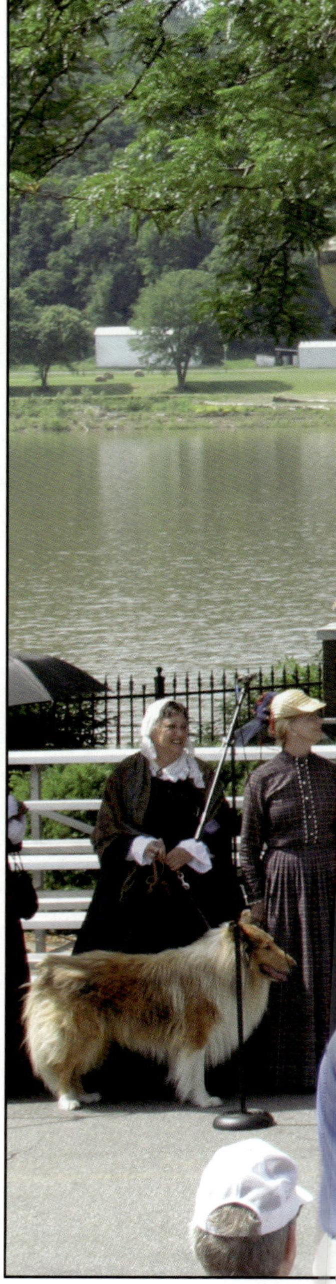

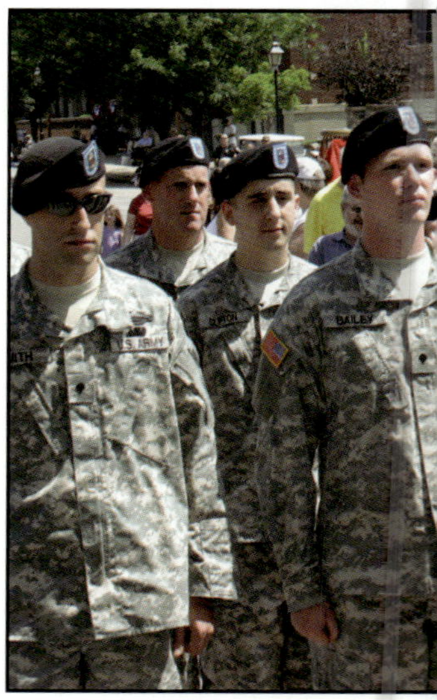

Above, a long parade of townspeople strings all the way up Broadway, from the riverfront to Main Street, as participants arrive at the stage on Vaughn Drive for the Bicentennial Opening Ceremony.

At top right, the stage slowly fills with participants for the ceremony as the Founder's Parade concludes at Vaughn Drive on the Madison riverfront. Emcee Al Huntington begins the program by introducing the Bicentennial Characters.

At right, members of the 152nd Alpha Unit-Indiana National Guard from Madison present the American Flag for the Pledge of Allegiance.

In the middle photo, enjoying the program are (from left) U.S. Rep. Baron Hill, his wife, Betty, State Rep. Dave Cheatham and former Madison Mayor and the program's emcee Al Huntington.

At far right is Janice Hardy Stanley of Chelsea. She is a descendant of one of Madison's founding families.

Photos by Don Ward

Opening Ceremony

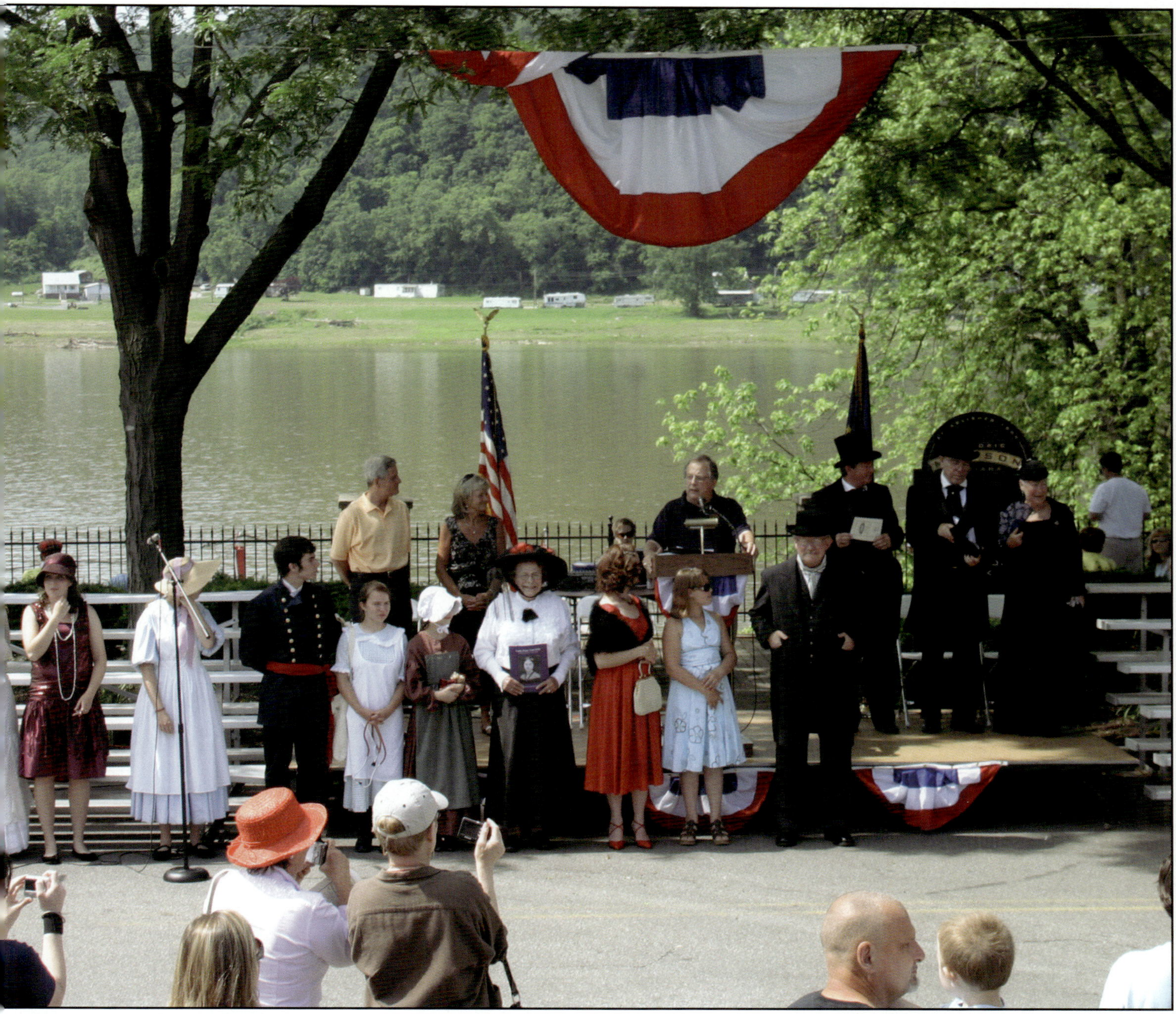

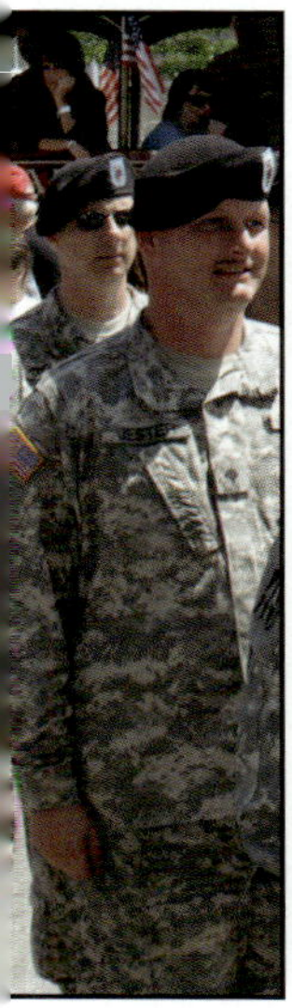

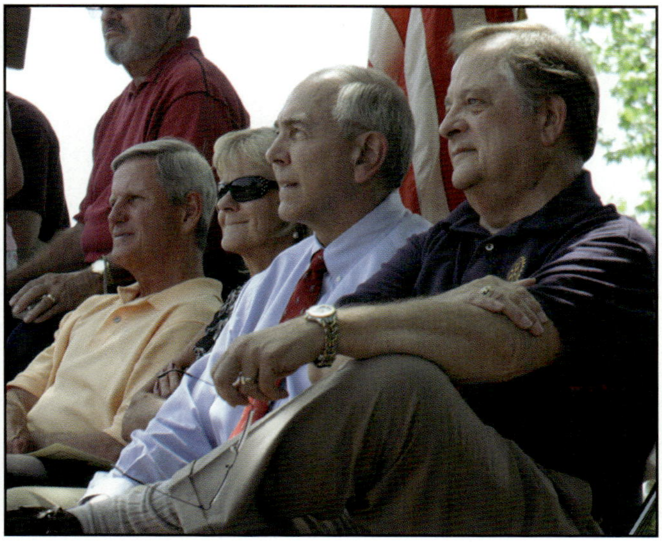

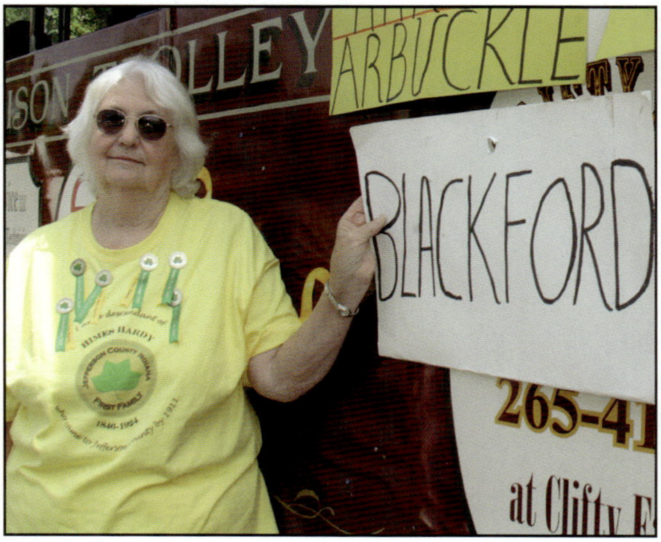

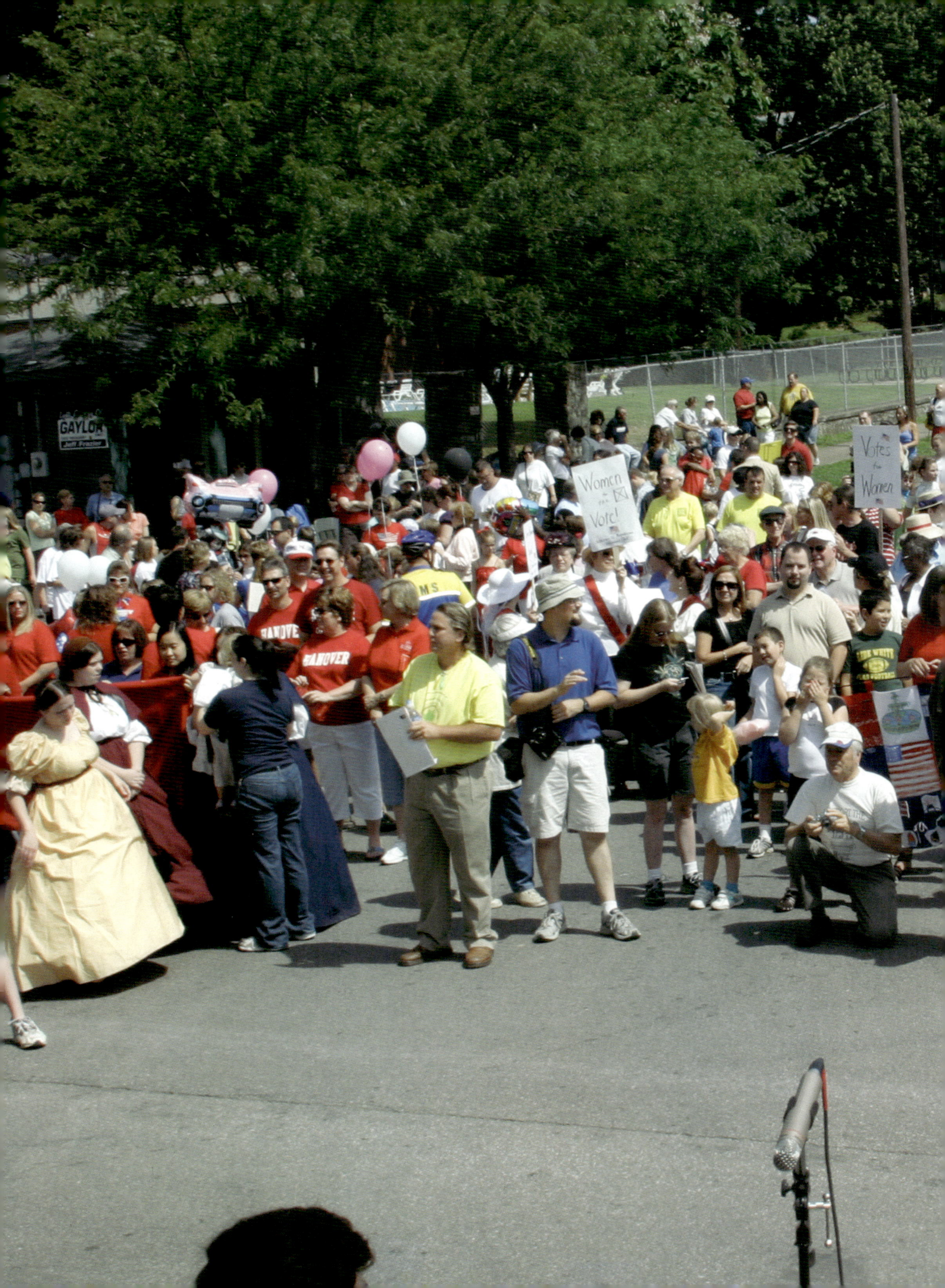
GAYLOR
Jeff Frazier
HANOVER
HANOVER
Votes for Women

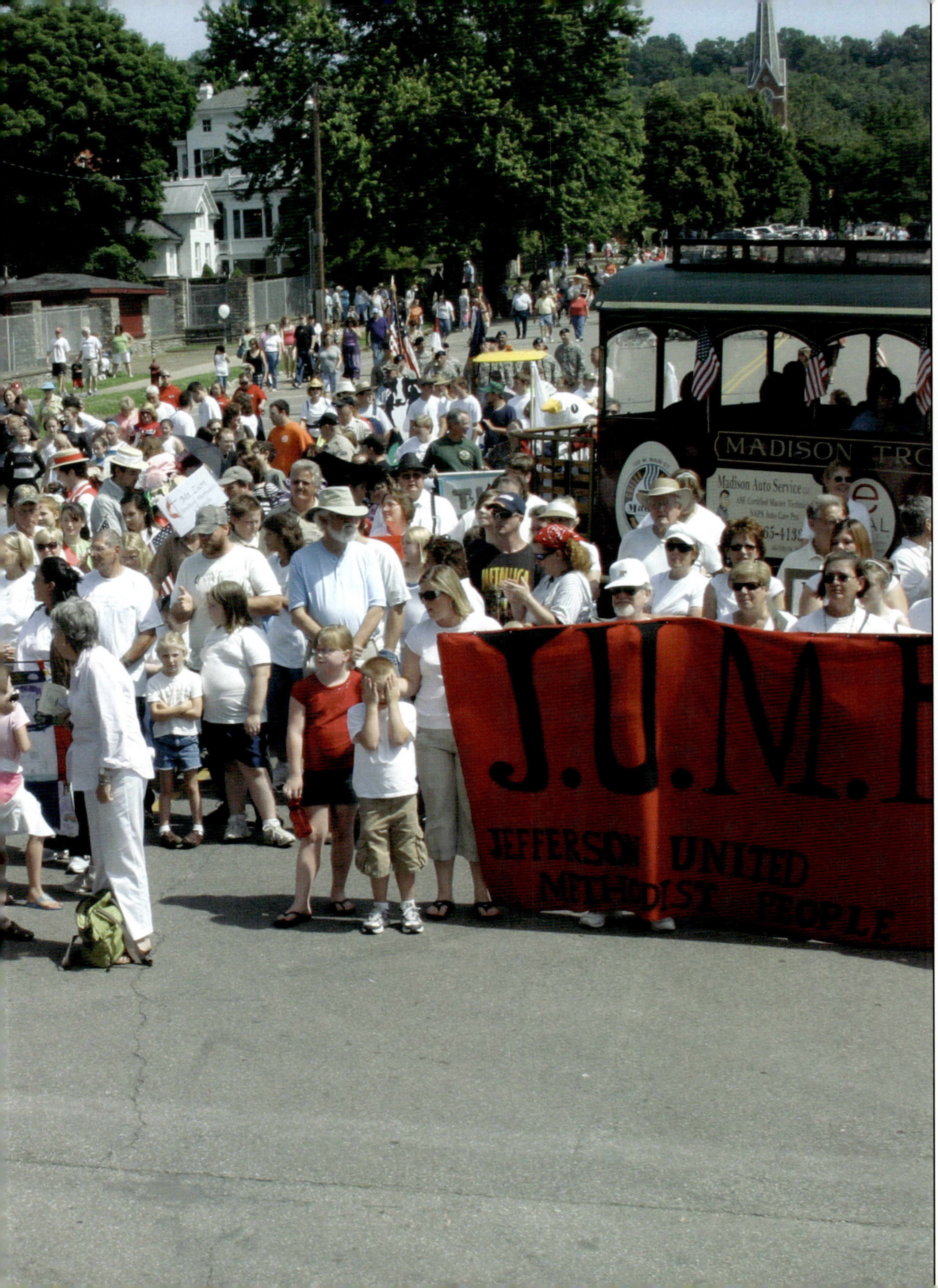
J.U.M.
JEFFERSON UNITED
METHODIST PEOPLE
MADISON
Madison Auto Service

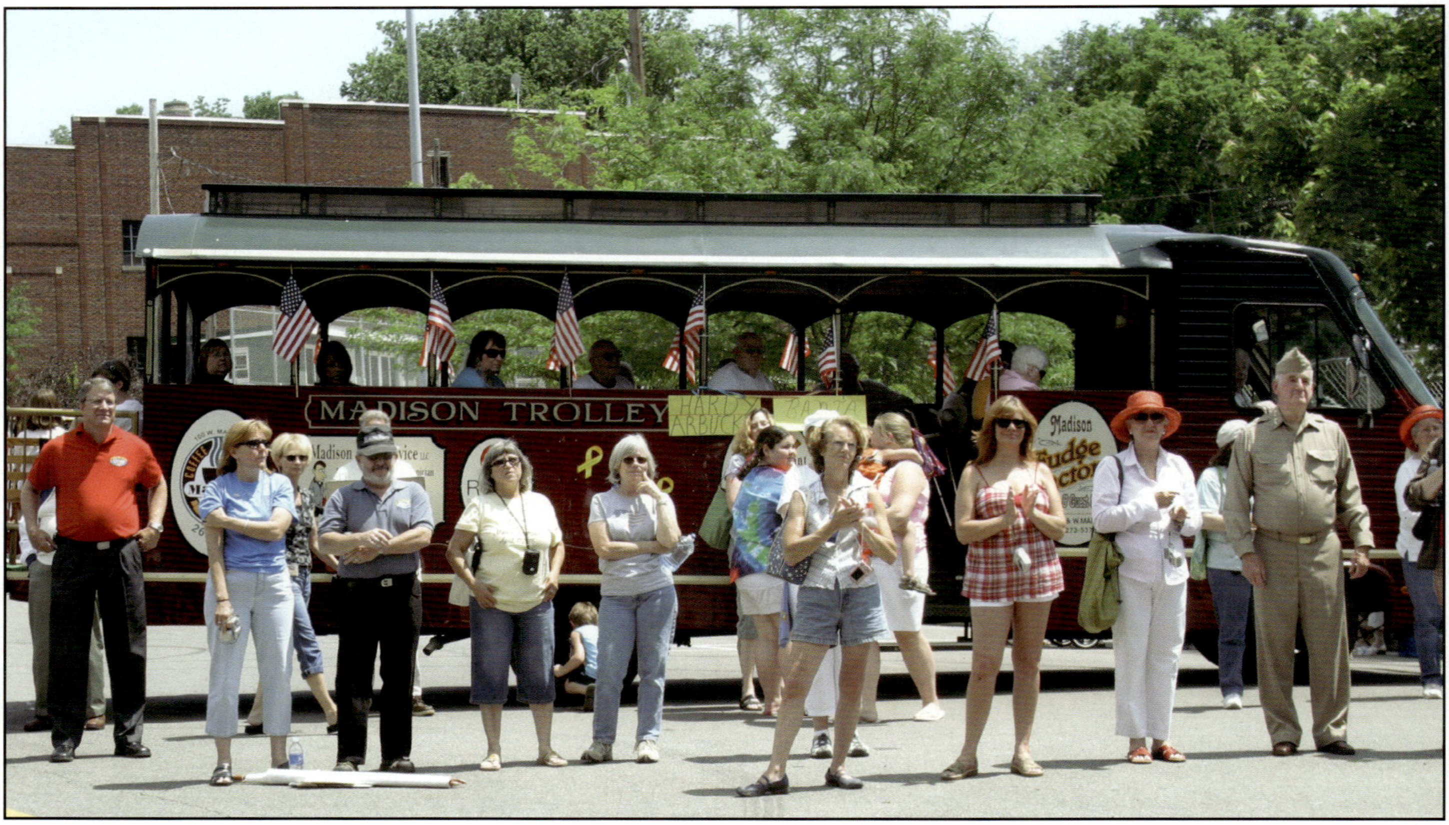

Descendants of the city's founding families arrived to the Opening Ceremony aboard the Madison Trolley.

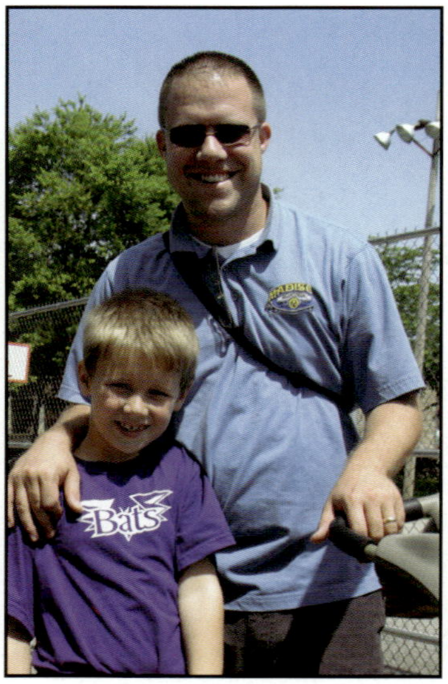

Corey Murphy
with his son, Evan, 6

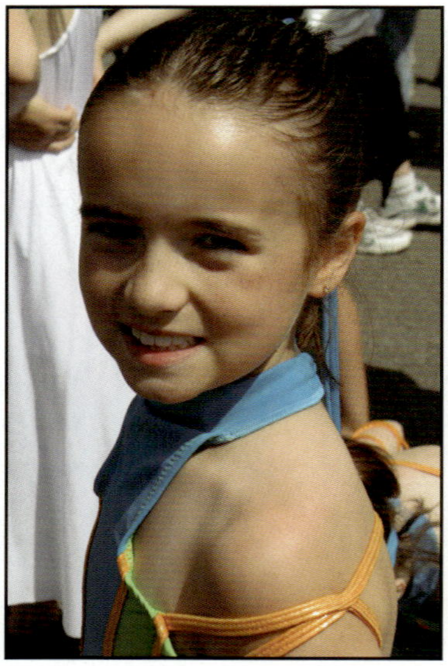

Musical Resource dancer
Erin Laufer, 9

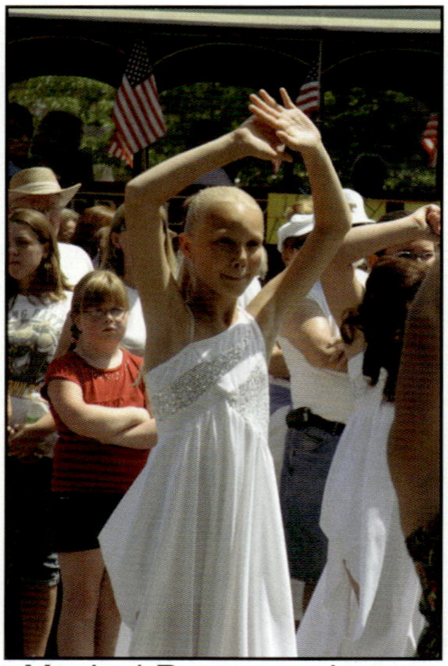

Musical Resource dancer
Lauren Cieslinski

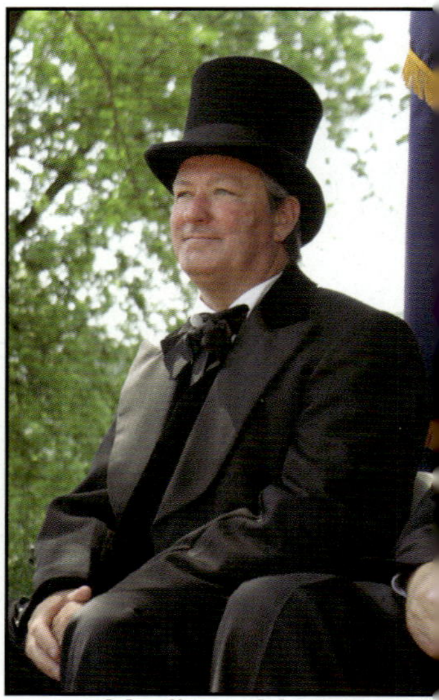

Madison Mayor
Tim Armstrong

At right, the current and four past mayors of Madison pose for the first ever such photo. They are (from left) Markt Lytle (1984-88), Tim Armstrong (2009-present), Morris Wooden (1988-Nov. 30, 1994 when he became a senator), Donald Vaughn (Oct. 1966-72, named by City Council after Markt A. Lytle Sr. died in office) and Al Huntington (1994-2007).

Photos by Don Ward

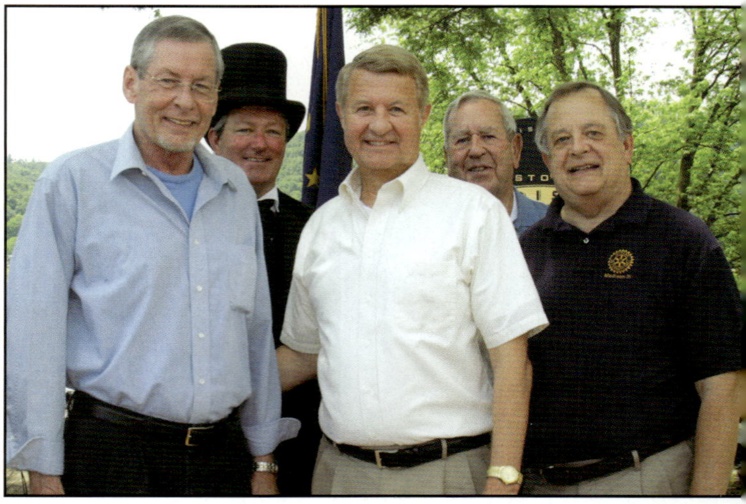

Previous page photo by Don Ward of the Opening Ceremony crowd on Broadway.

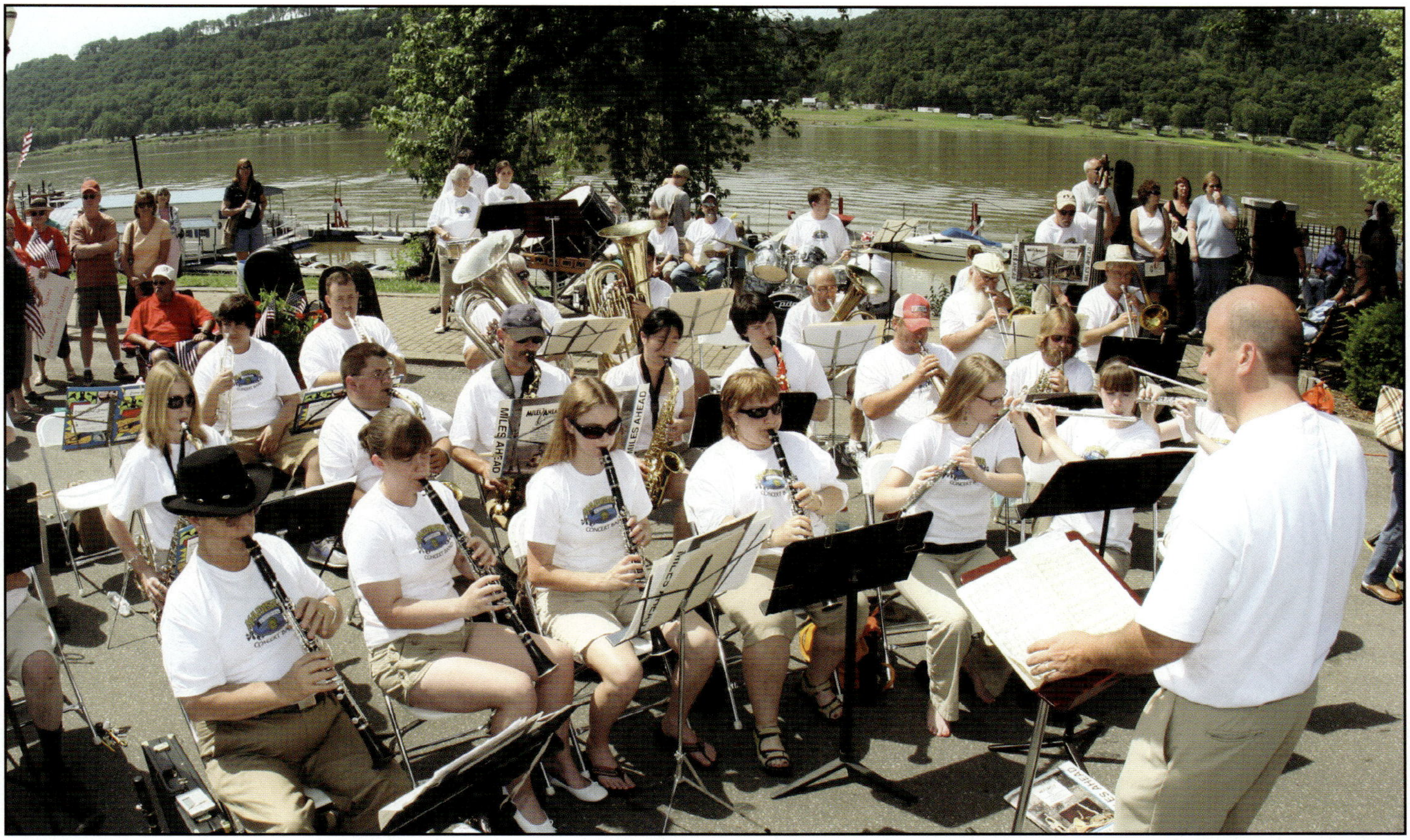

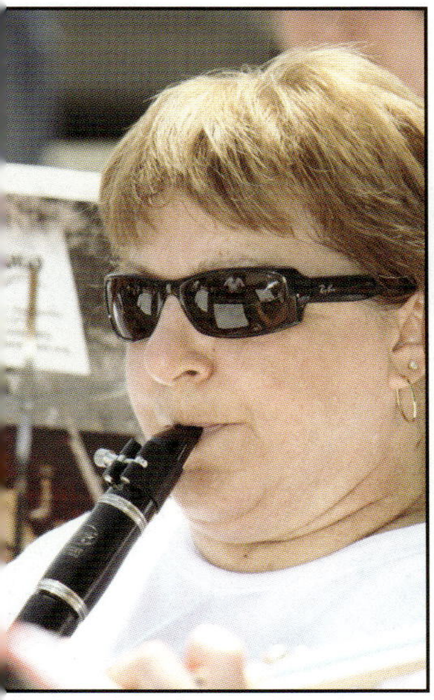

larinetist Karen Buchanan
of the Bicentennial Band.

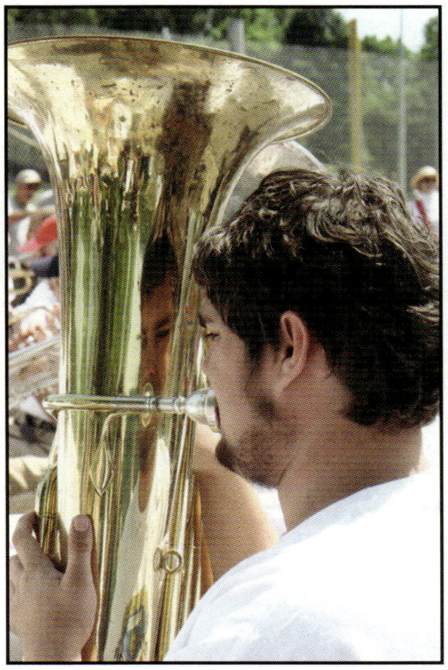

Kenton Mahoney, 19,
plays the tuba in the band.

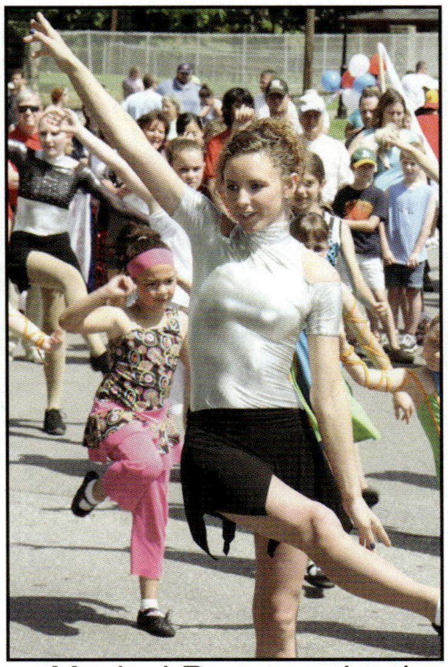

Musical Resource lead
dancer Addie Turner, 20.

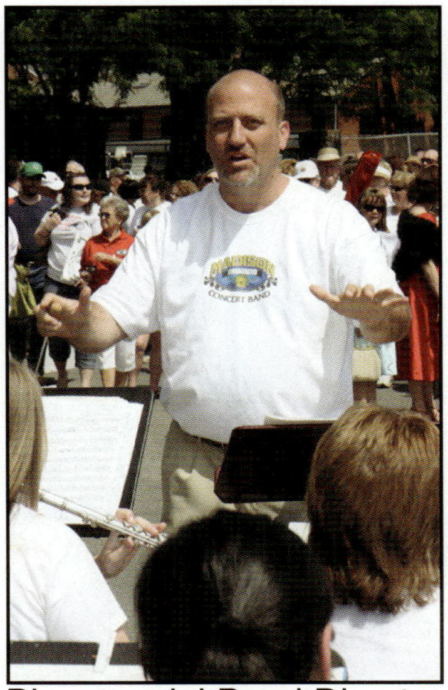

Bicentennial Band Director
Don Cochran.

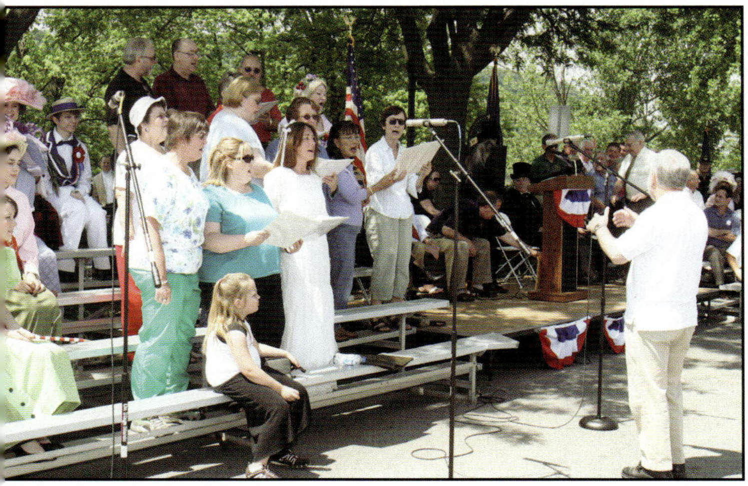

Top photo, the Bicentennial Band performs at the Opening Ceremony.

At left, Larry Wickersham directs the Madison Churches Choir as they sing for the crowd and dignitaries during the Bicentennial Opening Ceremony at the riverfront.

Photos by Matt Griffith

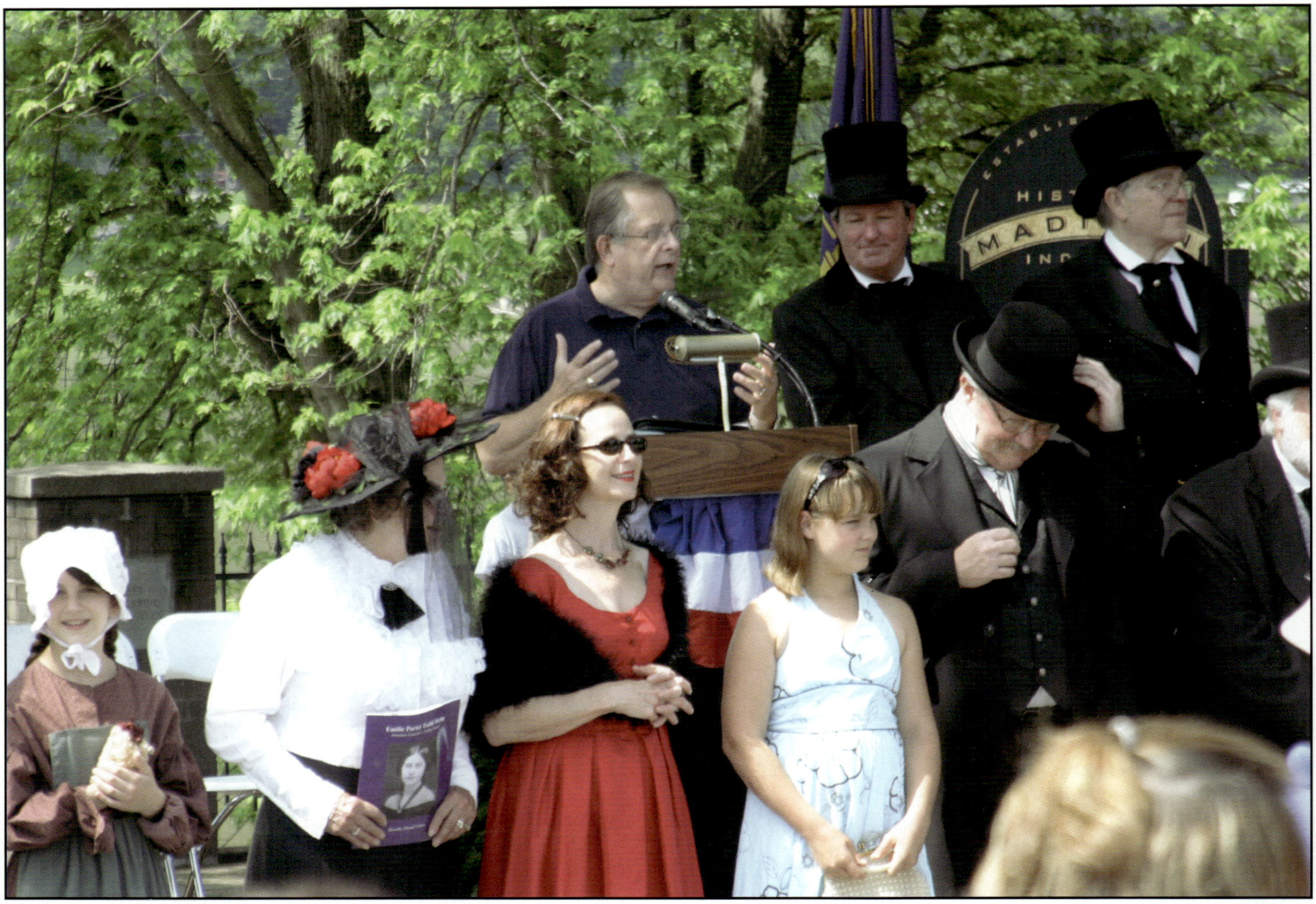

Emcee Al Huntington leads the Opening Ceremony program from the podium, located at the foot of Broadway.

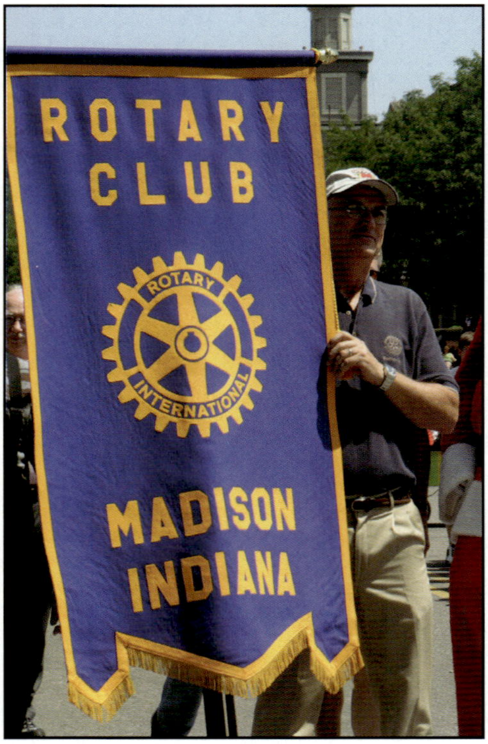

Ray Wilson displays the Madison Rotary Club banner to recognize one of the oldest chapters in Indiana.

Photos by Don Ward

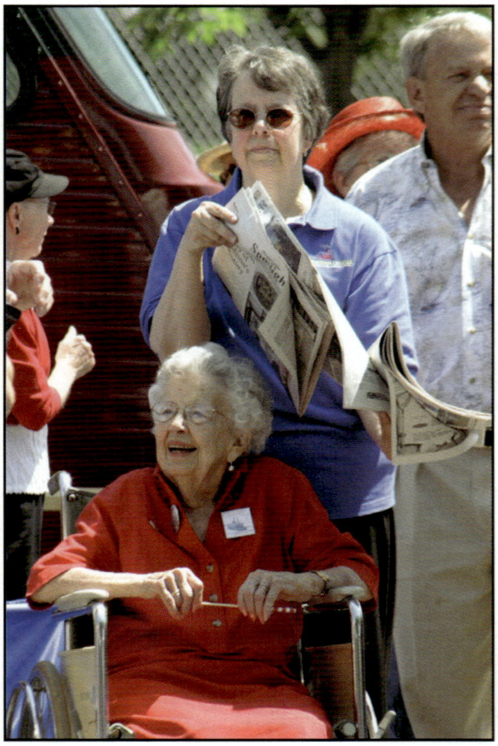

Madison Courier publisher Jane Jacobs uses one of her newspapers to shield her mother, Mary Goode Wallis, from the sun during the Opening Ceremony.

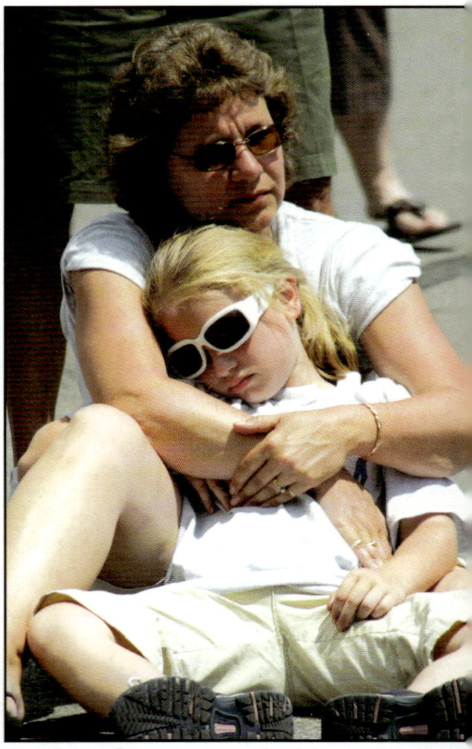

Debbie Snodgrass holds her sleep ing daughter, Kristen, as they both s on Broadway Street during th Opening Ceremony.

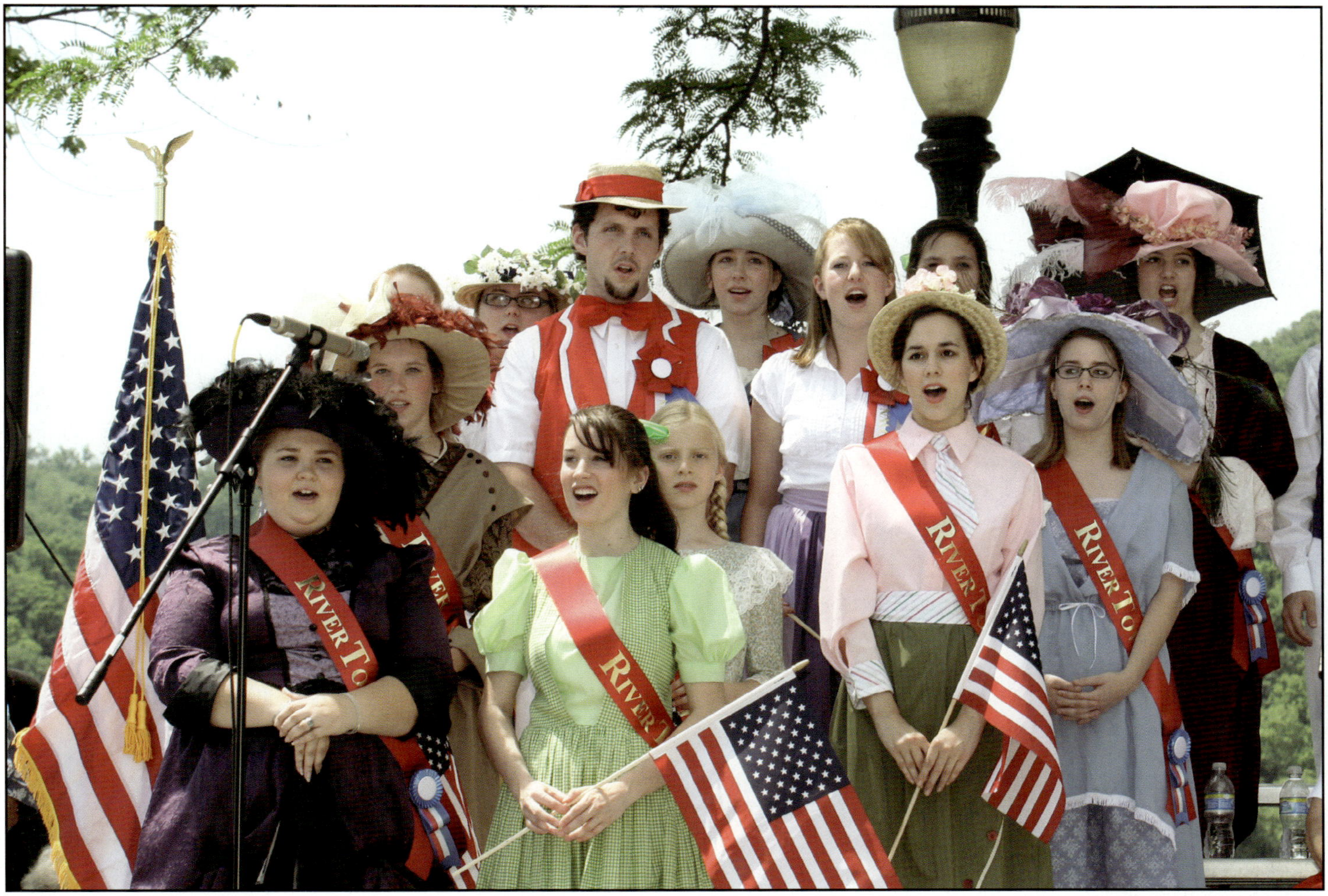

Photo by Matt Griffith

Members of the high school cast of “Rivertown, the Musical” perform at the Opening Ceremony.

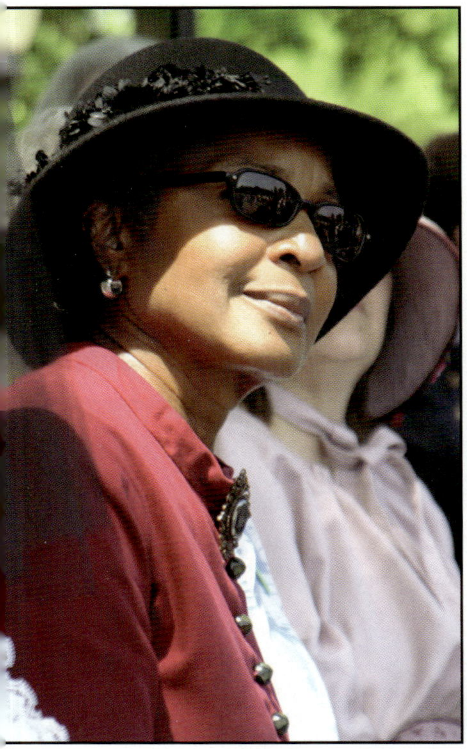

Photo by Don Ward

icentennial character re-enactor ue Livers watches the Opening eremony while portraying Patsy Ann arris, wife of Rev. Chapman Harris.

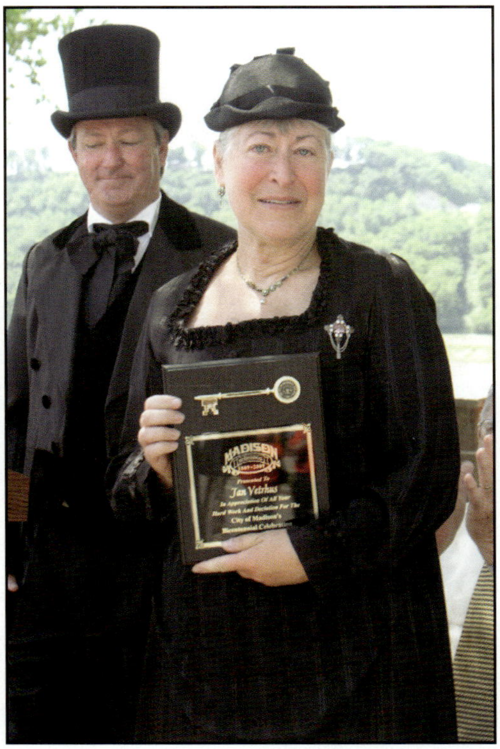

Photo by Don Ward

Madison Bicentennial Chairwoman Jan Vetrhus receives a plaque of appreciation for her work in organizing and leading the planning committee.

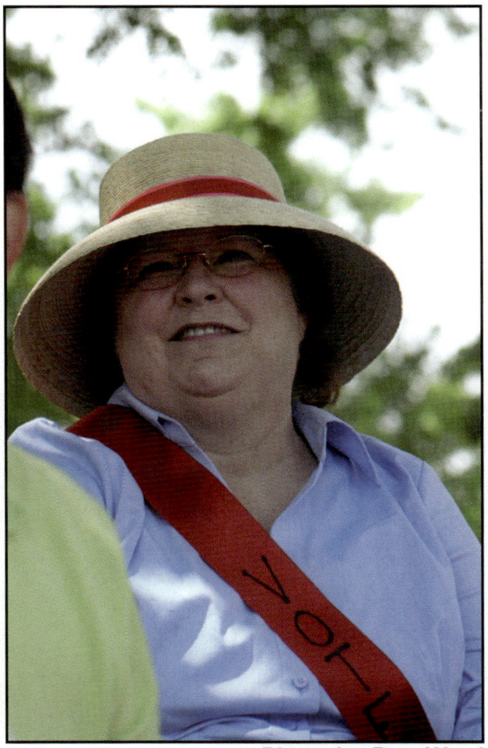

Photo by Don Ward

Madison Bicentennial Marketing Chairwoman and City Council member Laura Hodges enjoys the program from her seat near the podium.

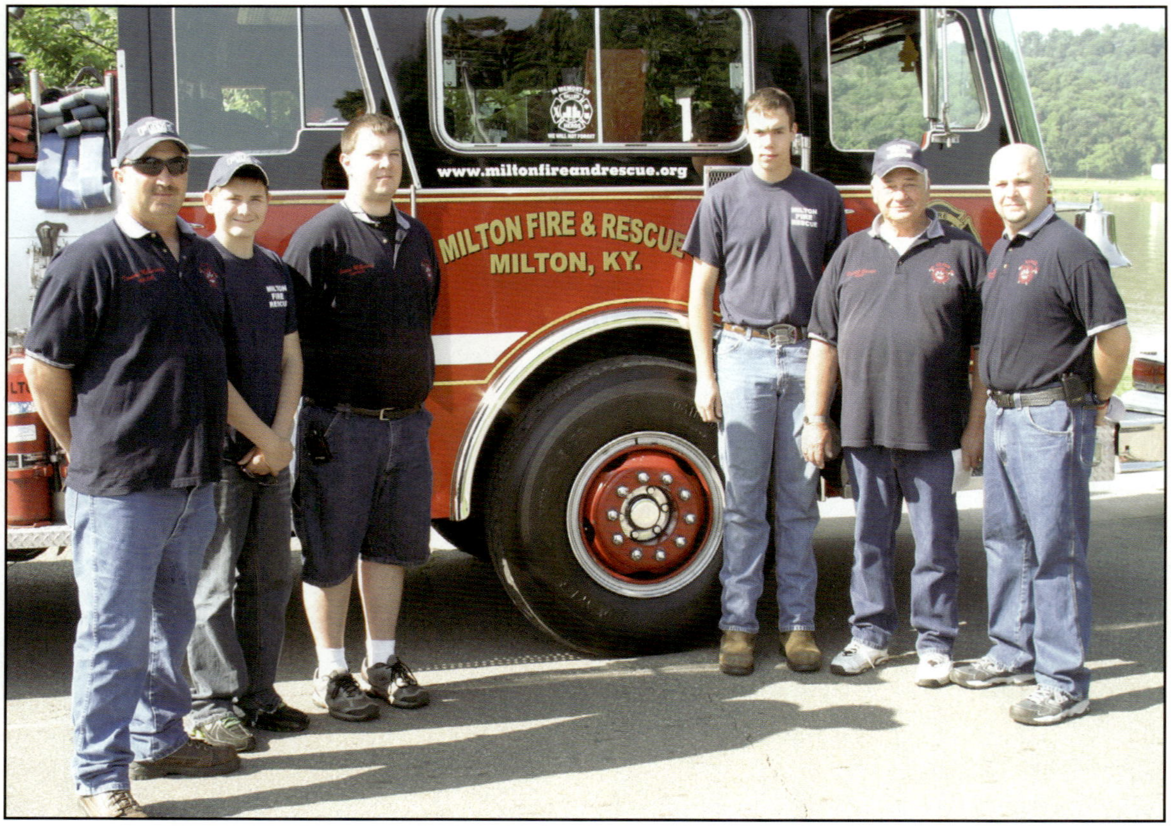

Photo by Don Ward

Members of the Milton (Ky.) Fire & Rescue team attending the Antique Fire Truck Muster on June 6 are (from left) Tommy McQueary, Taylor Starks, Justin McQueary, Adam Stewart, Chief Ronald Barnes and Mike Snell.

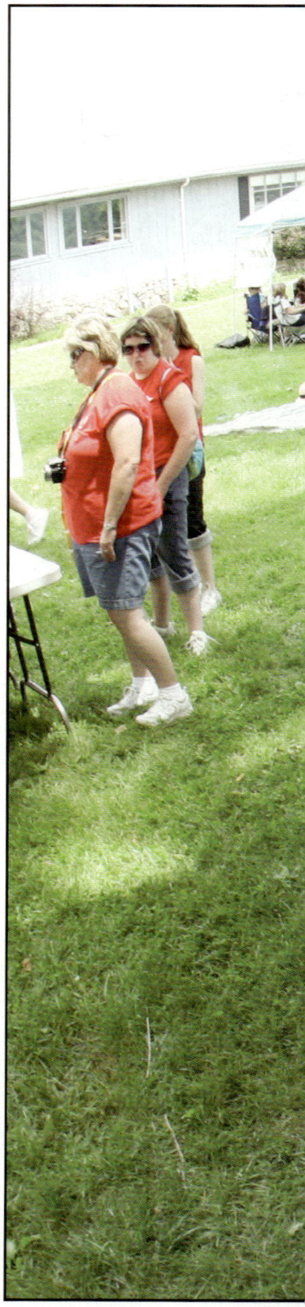

Antique Fire Truck Muster organizer Frank Taff poses beside this Ahrens Fox-City Service Ladder Truck that arrived at the Walnut Street Fire Co. No. 4 on May 20, 1929.

Photo by Tara Gentile

At right, Carl Morgan of Madison peers into the window of his 1950 GMC minipumper fire truck.

Second from left below, a family explores the fire trucks on display at Madison's Fireman's Park.

Third from left, Tim Monoghan of Jennings County, Ind., sells fire helmets.

Bottom right is an 1880s Seagrave hand-drawn Ladder Wagon on display.

Photos by Matt Griffith

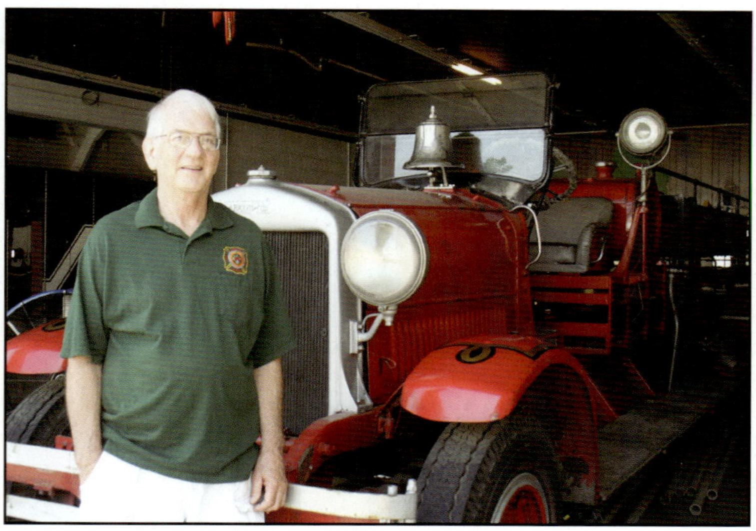

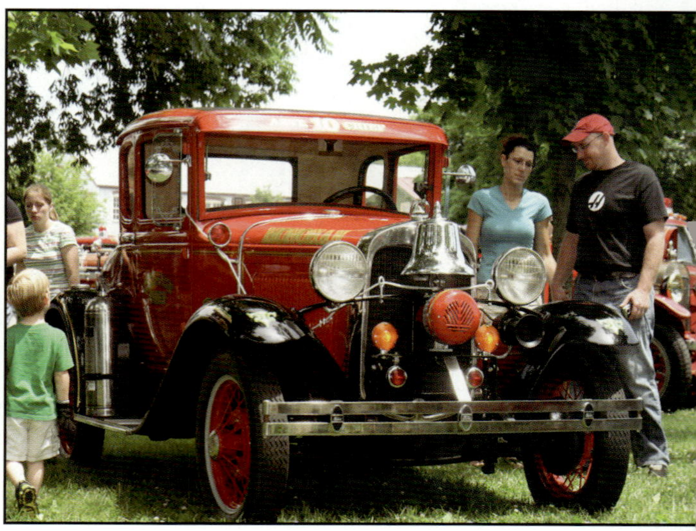

Antique Fire Truck Muster

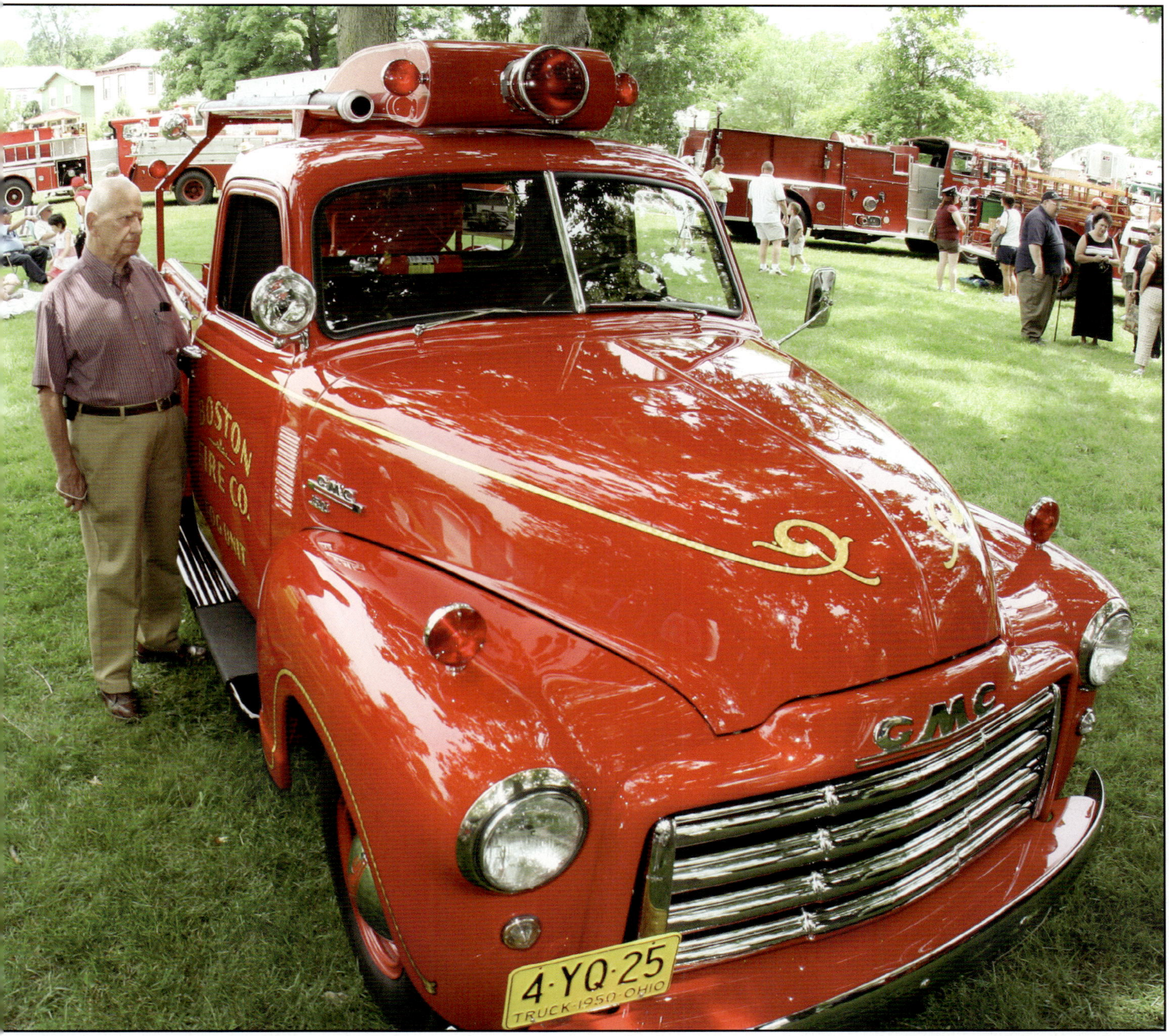

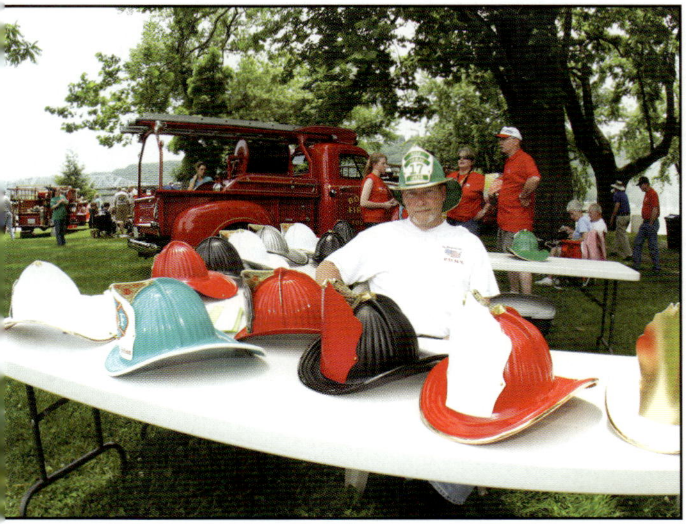

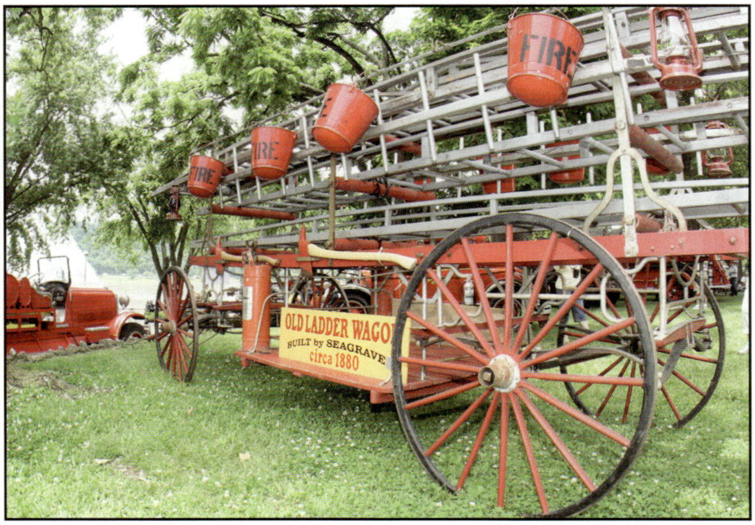

Lighted Boat Parade

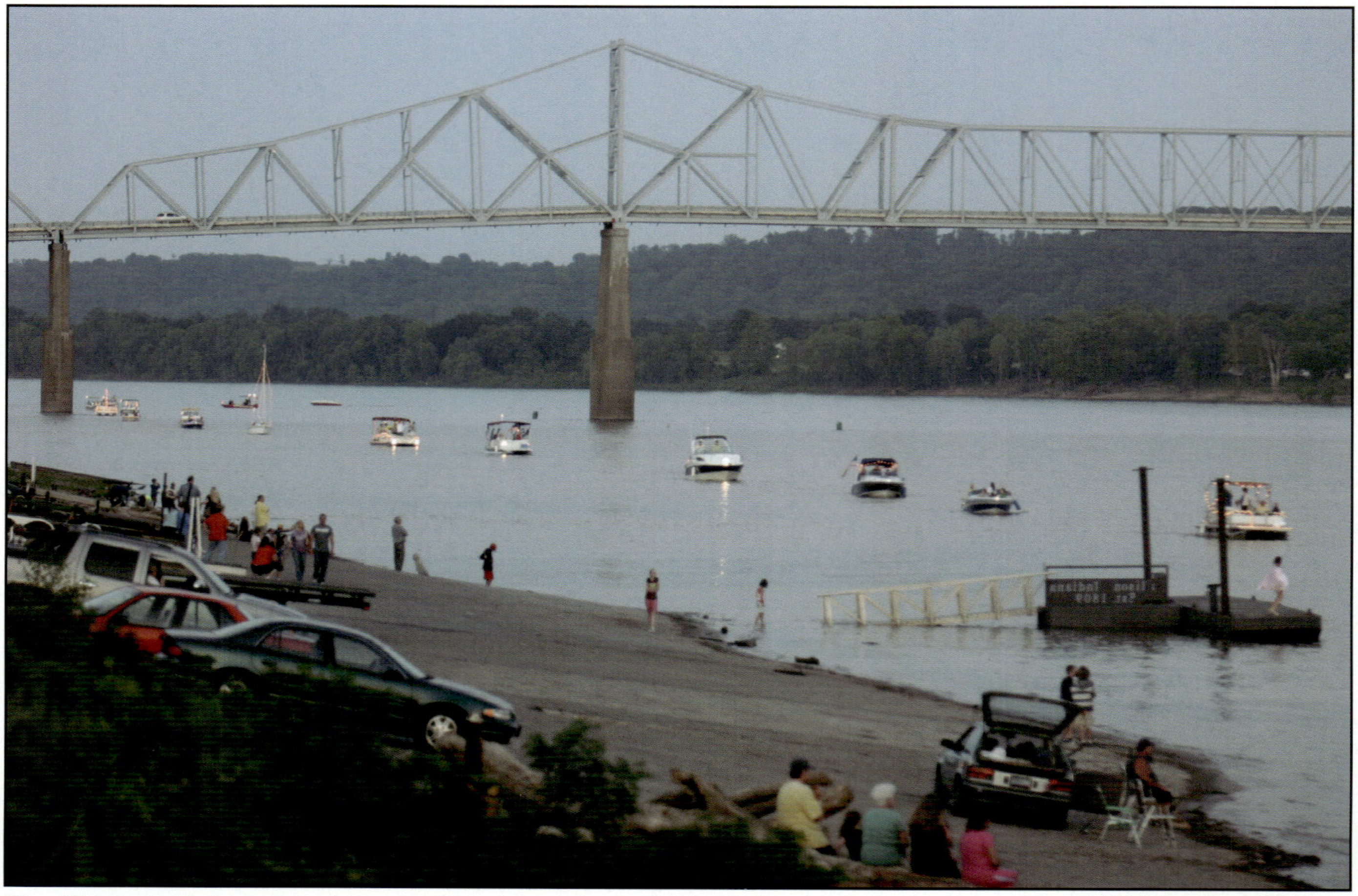

The Bicentennial crowd witnessed the first lighted boat parade in Madison on June 6 on the Ohio River. The event was so popular that a second boat parade was added to the 2009 Madison Regatta festivities.

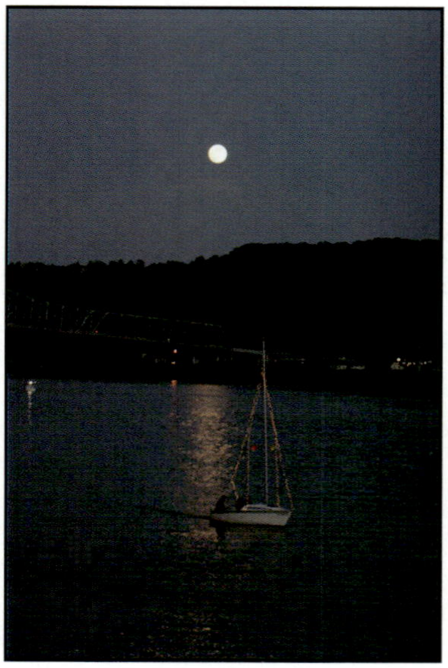

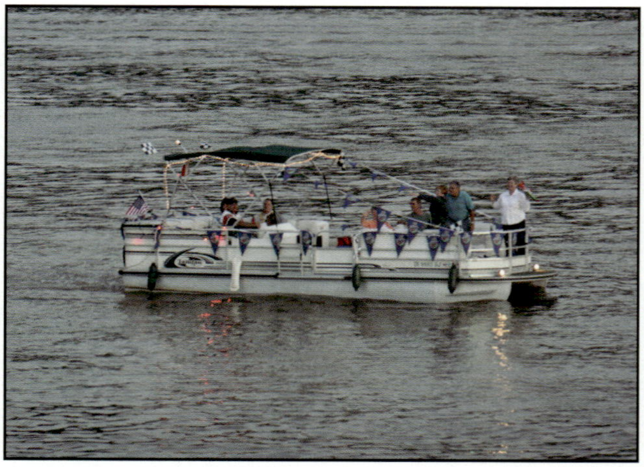

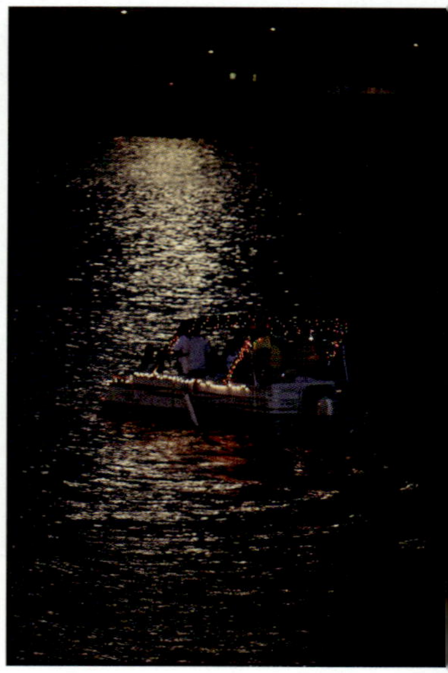

A full moon provided a beautiful backdrop to the Bicentennial Lighted Boat Parade. Boaters waved to the crowd watching from the riverbank.

Photos by Matt Griffith

Saturday Night Concert

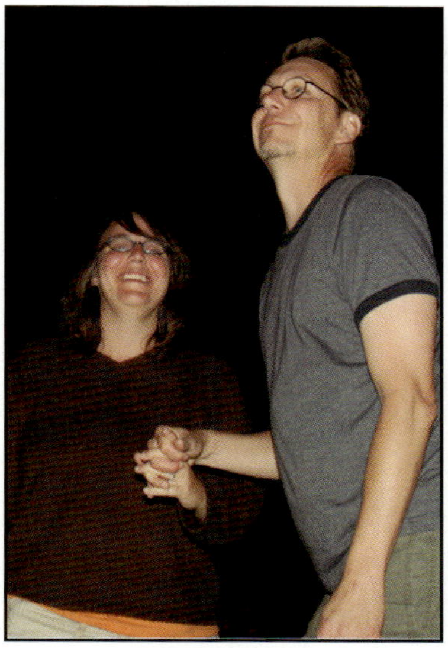

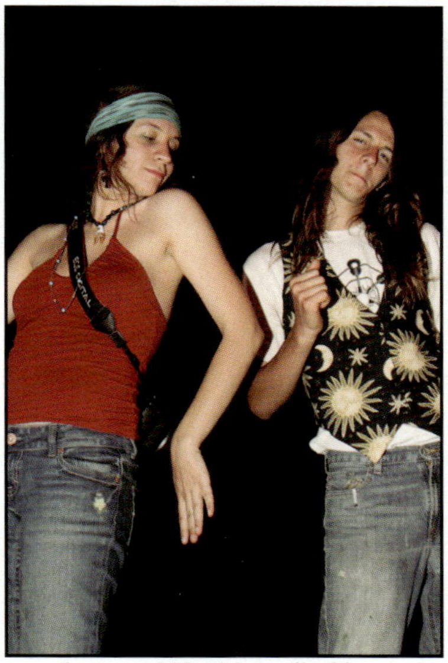

Jenna Watkins (left) and a friend tear up the dance floor along with another couple (top photo) who are enjoying the music.

Photos by Matt Griffith

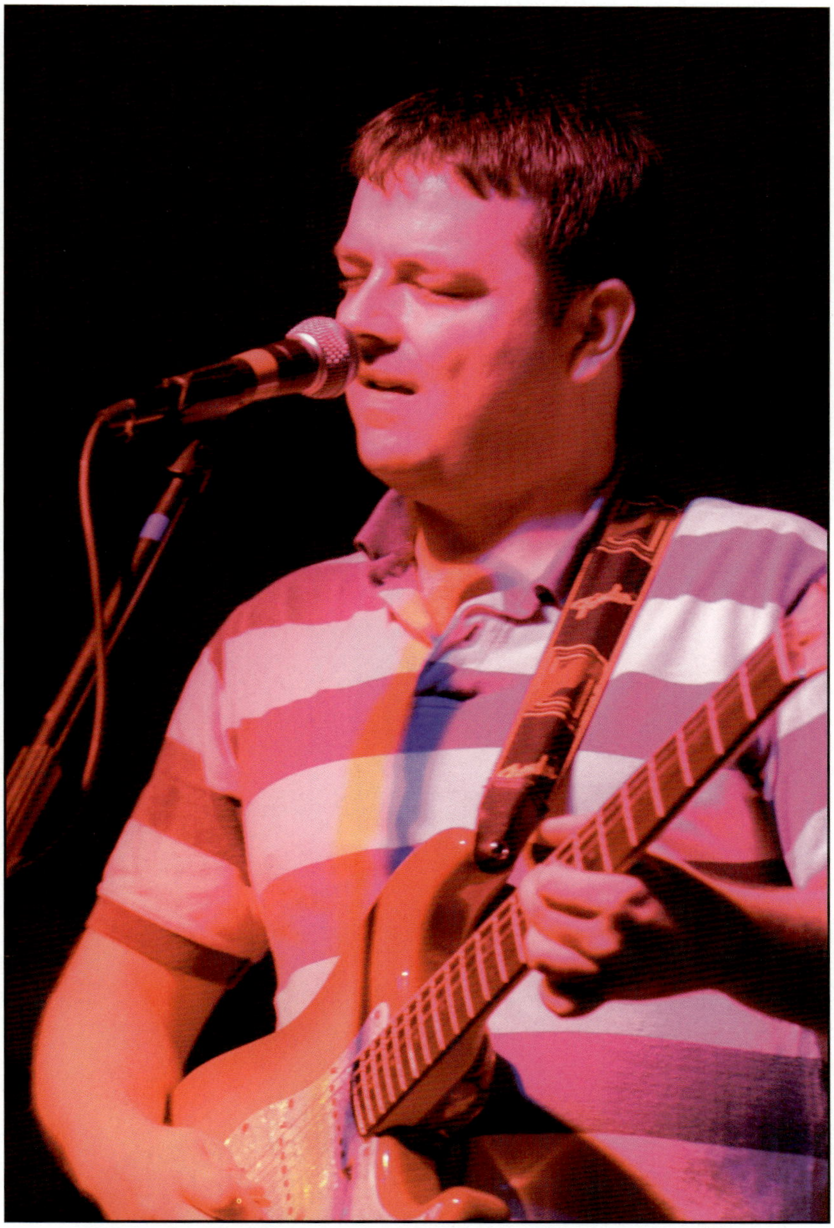

The Jimmy Davis Band entertained the crowd Saturday night, June 6. Davis (above) was accompanied by Brook Reindollar on trumpet and Rick Bennett on saxophone (below).

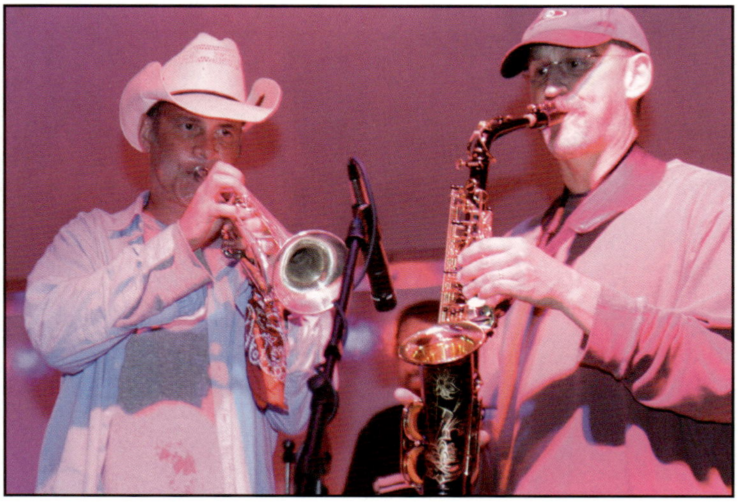

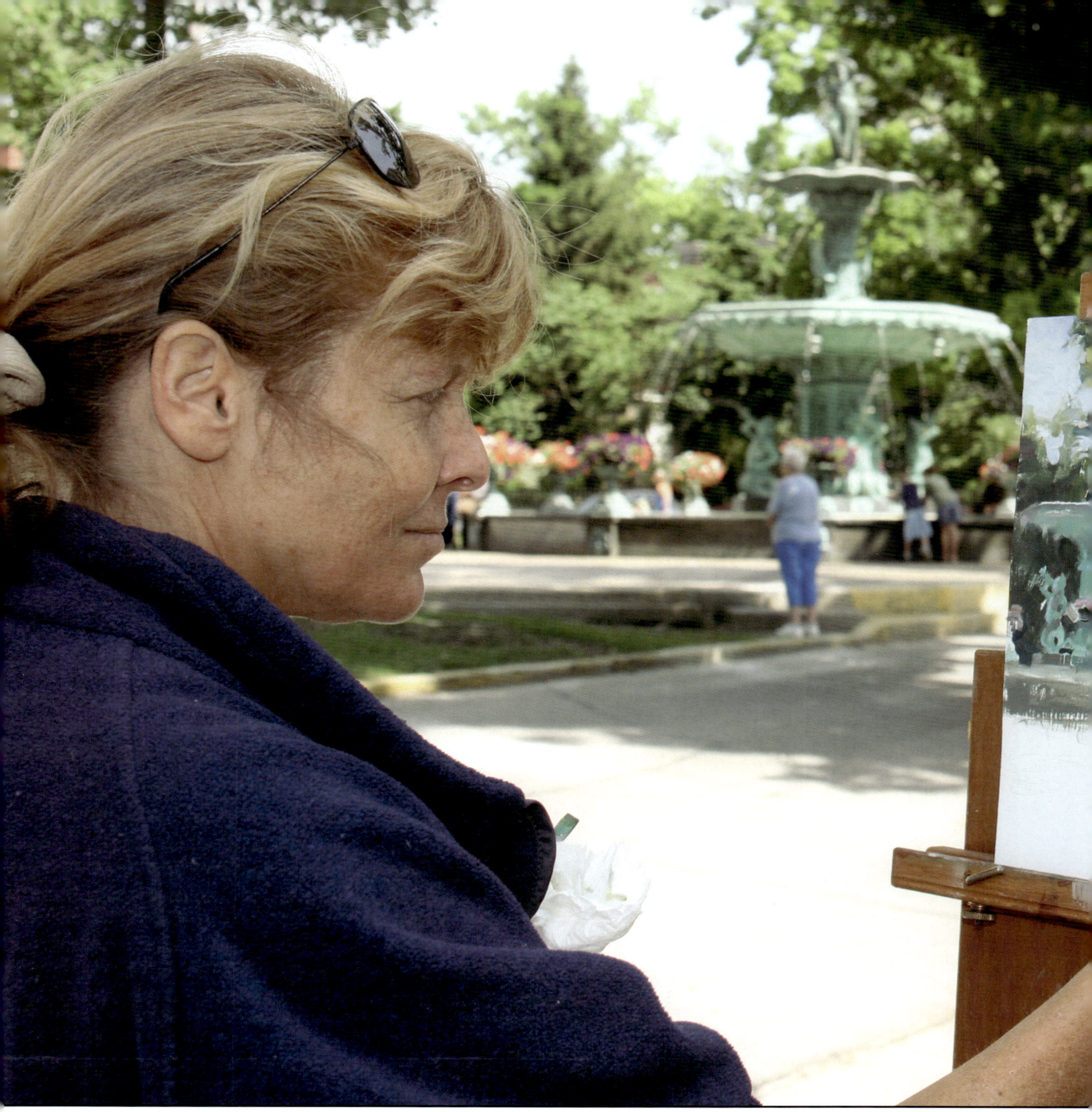

Above, artist Pamela Stockard, 43, of Louisville, Ky., paints a scene of Madison's Broadway Fountain during Sunday's Plein Air Painters Art Exhibit and Sale, held throughout the downtown.

Right, artist Matthew Williams, 6, admires his two paintings, on the lower right.

In the second photo, Pam Quick of Versailles, Ind., feeds an apple to her horse, Amy.

Photos by Matt Griffith

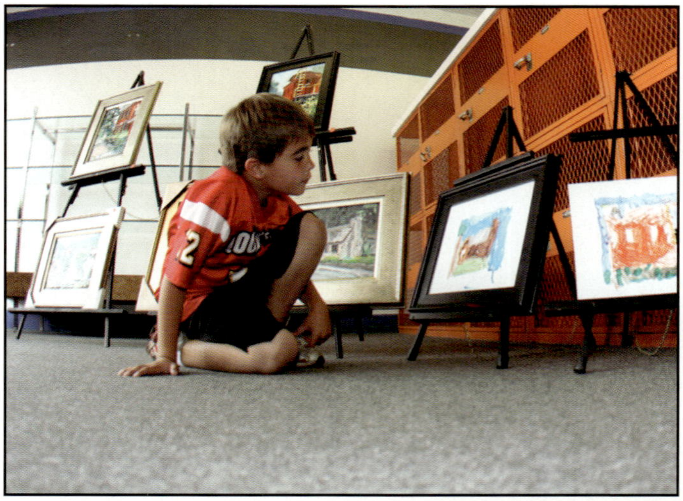

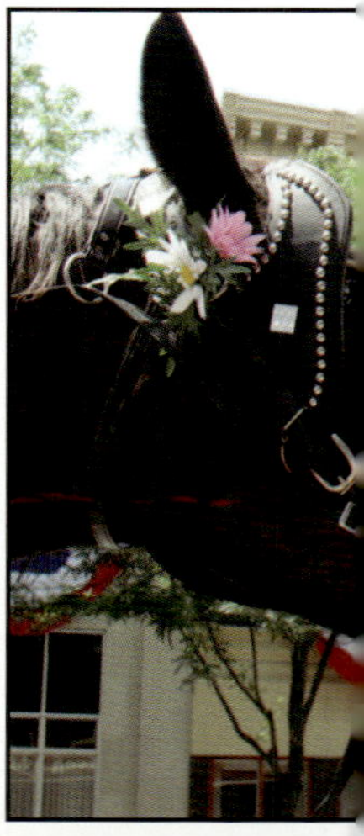

Sunday Afternoon on Main Street

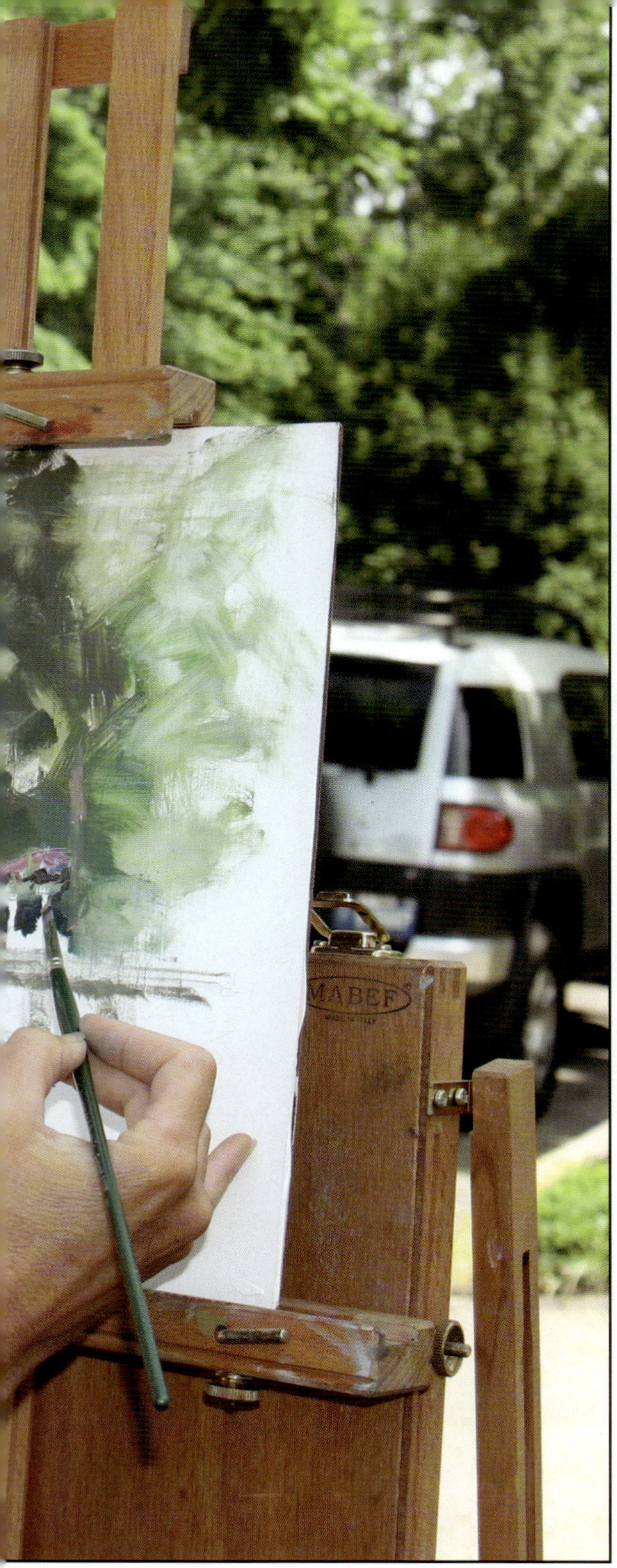

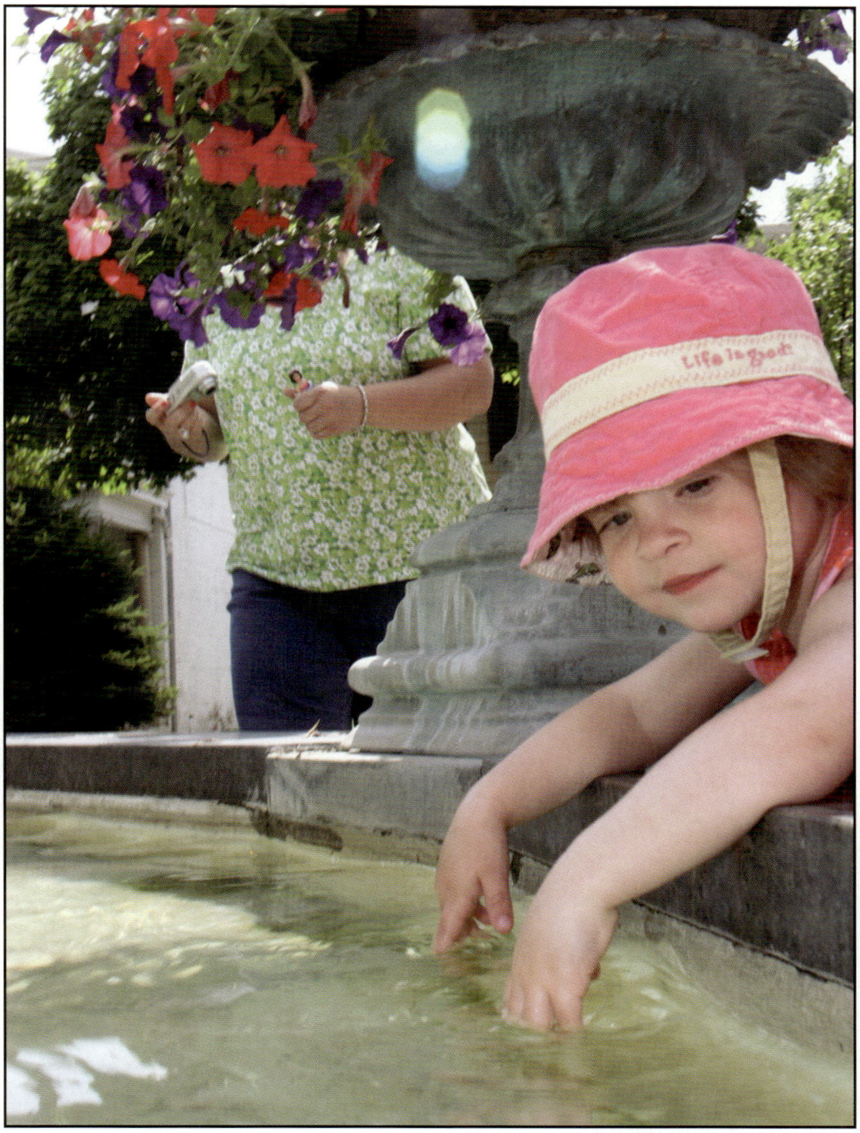

Photos by Matt Griffith

Above, Sarah Adams, 2, of Madison plays in the cool water of the Broadway Fountain in downtown Madison.

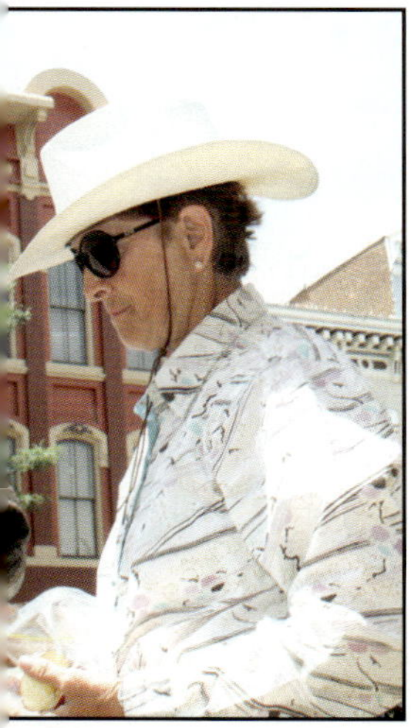

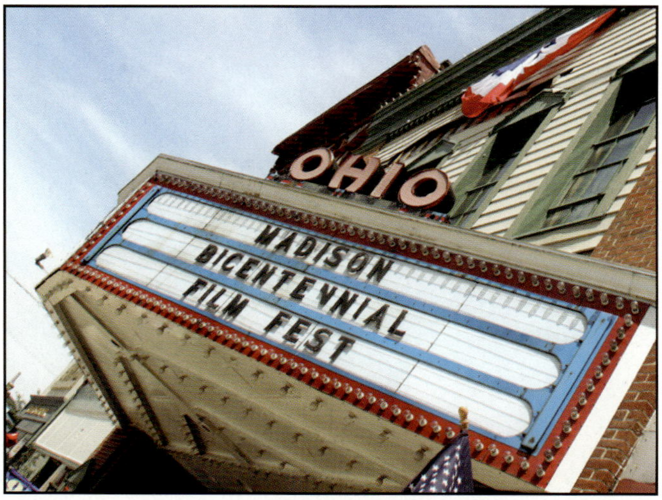

All through the nine-day Bicentennial week, the Ohio Theatre offered free movies for the public. All the movies were either filmed in Madison or had some Madison connection in their making. Perhaps the most popular film was the movie, "Madison," about the 1971 Unlimited Hydroplane Gold Cup race, won by the hometown boat.

Photo by Randy Porter

At right, the Cincinnati Symphony Regional Pops Orchestra conductor Vince Lee coordinates the music with solo vocalist Lauren Ringel.

Second photo from left, a musician plays.

Photos by Randy Porter

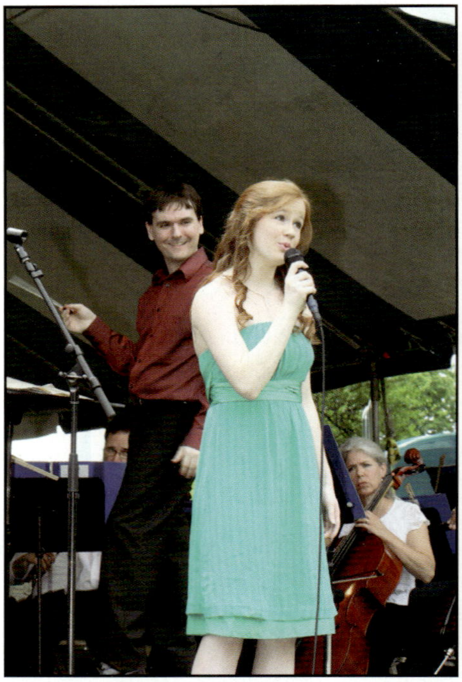

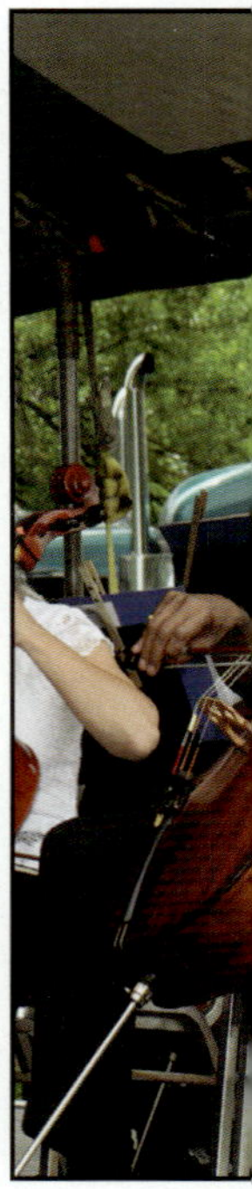

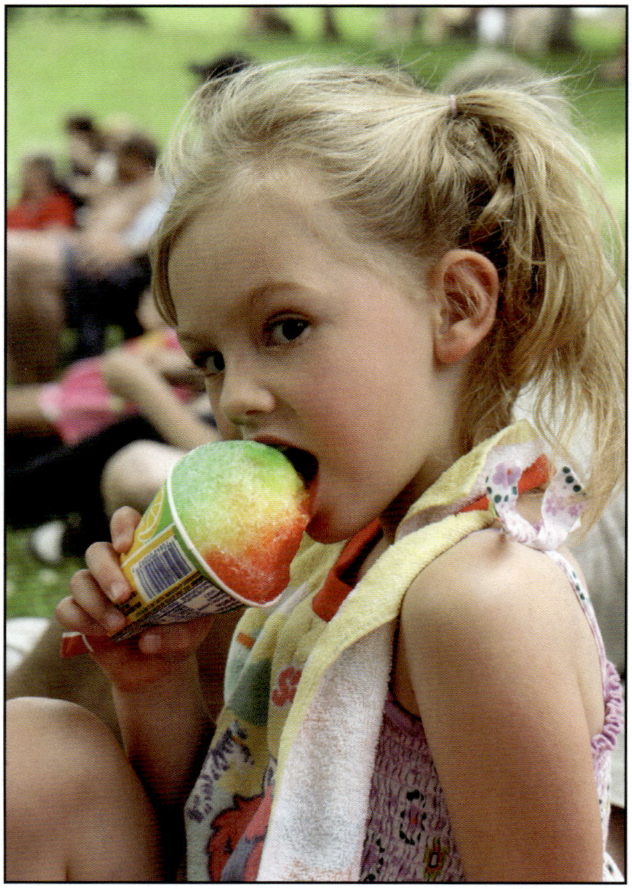

Above, 4-year-old Ava Rowland eats a sno-cone during the concert at Lanier Mansion State Historic Site. The family oriented event featured many popular songs and free ice cream treats for the first hour

At Right, the orchestra plays to a large crowd on the Lanier Mansion's South Lawn.

Photos by Matt Griffith

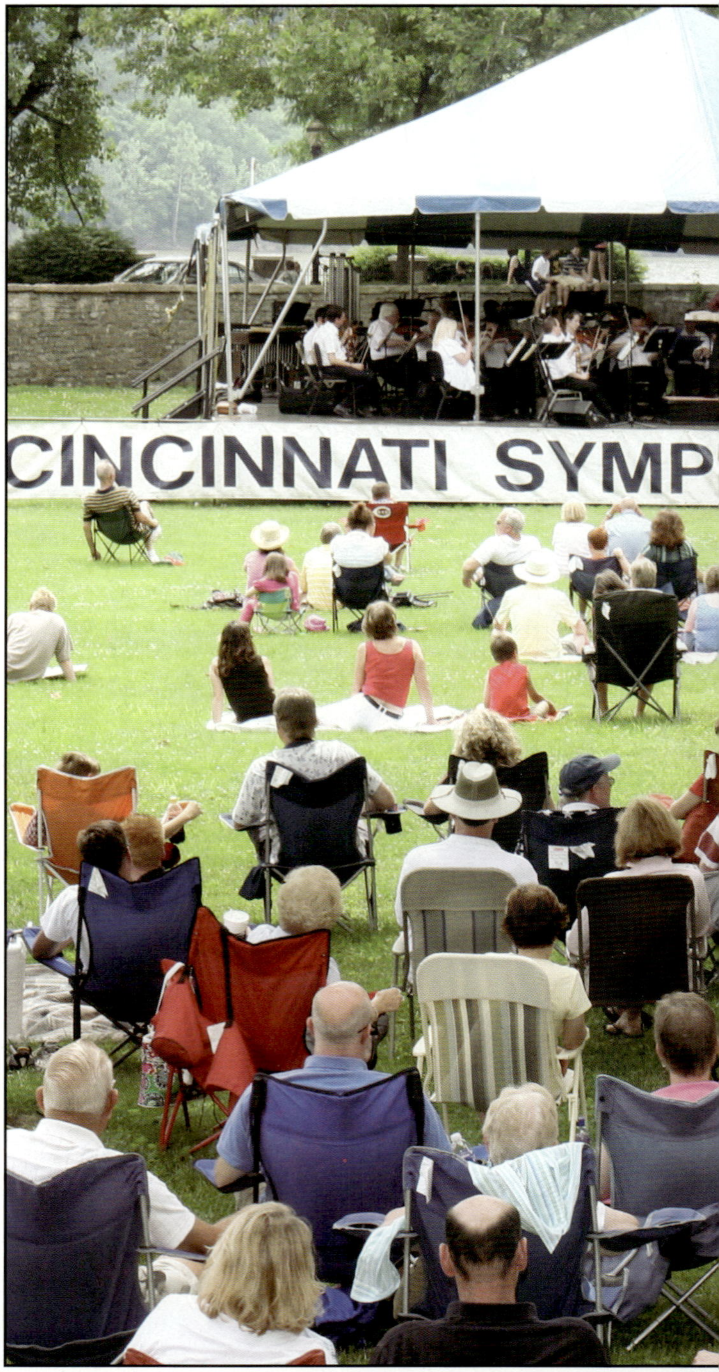

Cincinnati Symphony Orchestra

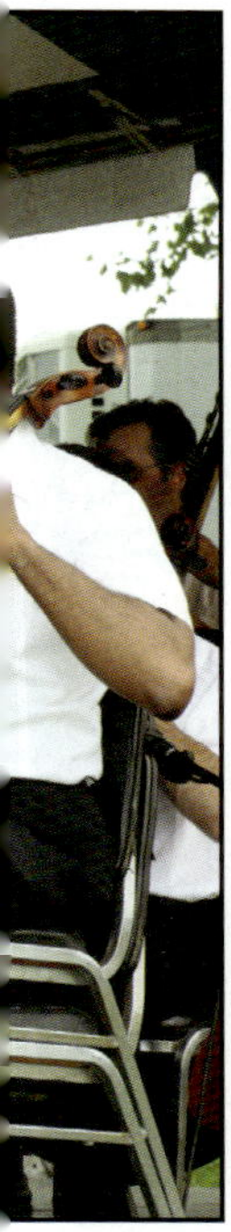

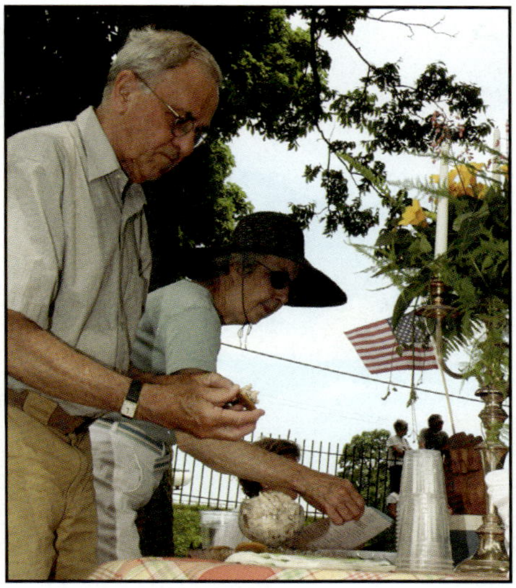

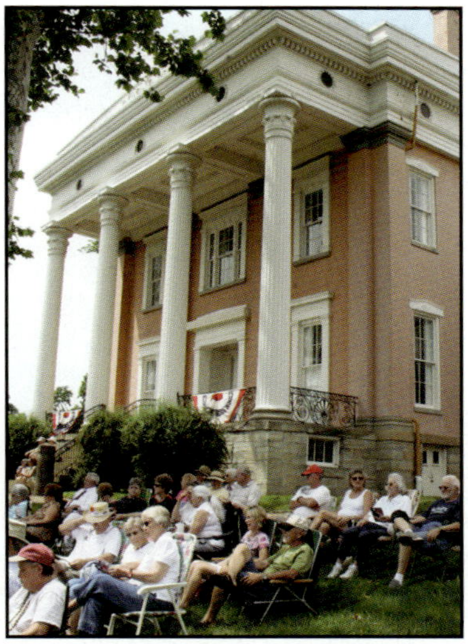

At left, the crowd enjoys the concert on the south lawn of the Lanier Mansion State Historic Site in downtown Madison.

Second from right, Frank and Carolyn Gunter of Madison sample the free ice cream that was available at the concert.

Photos by Randy Porter

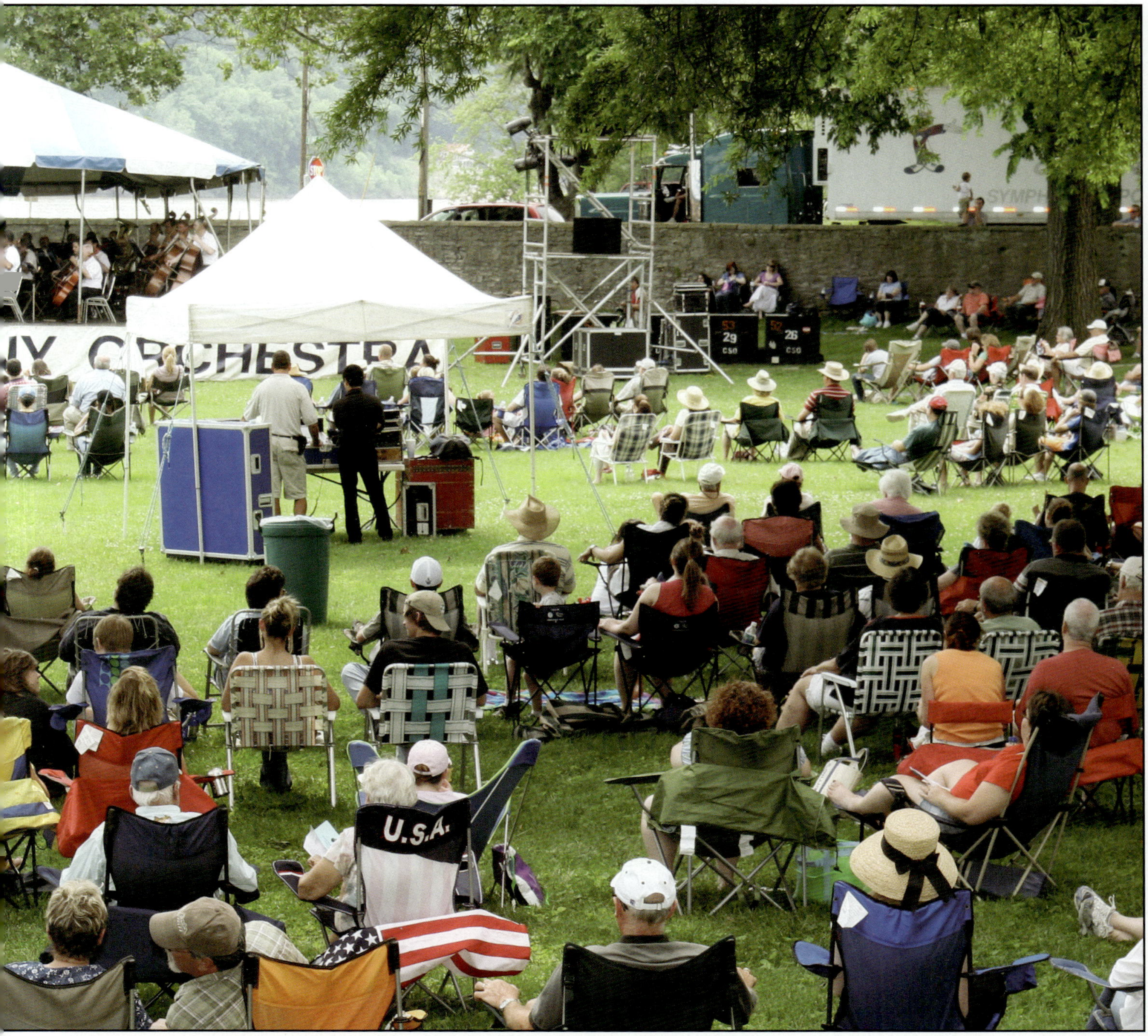

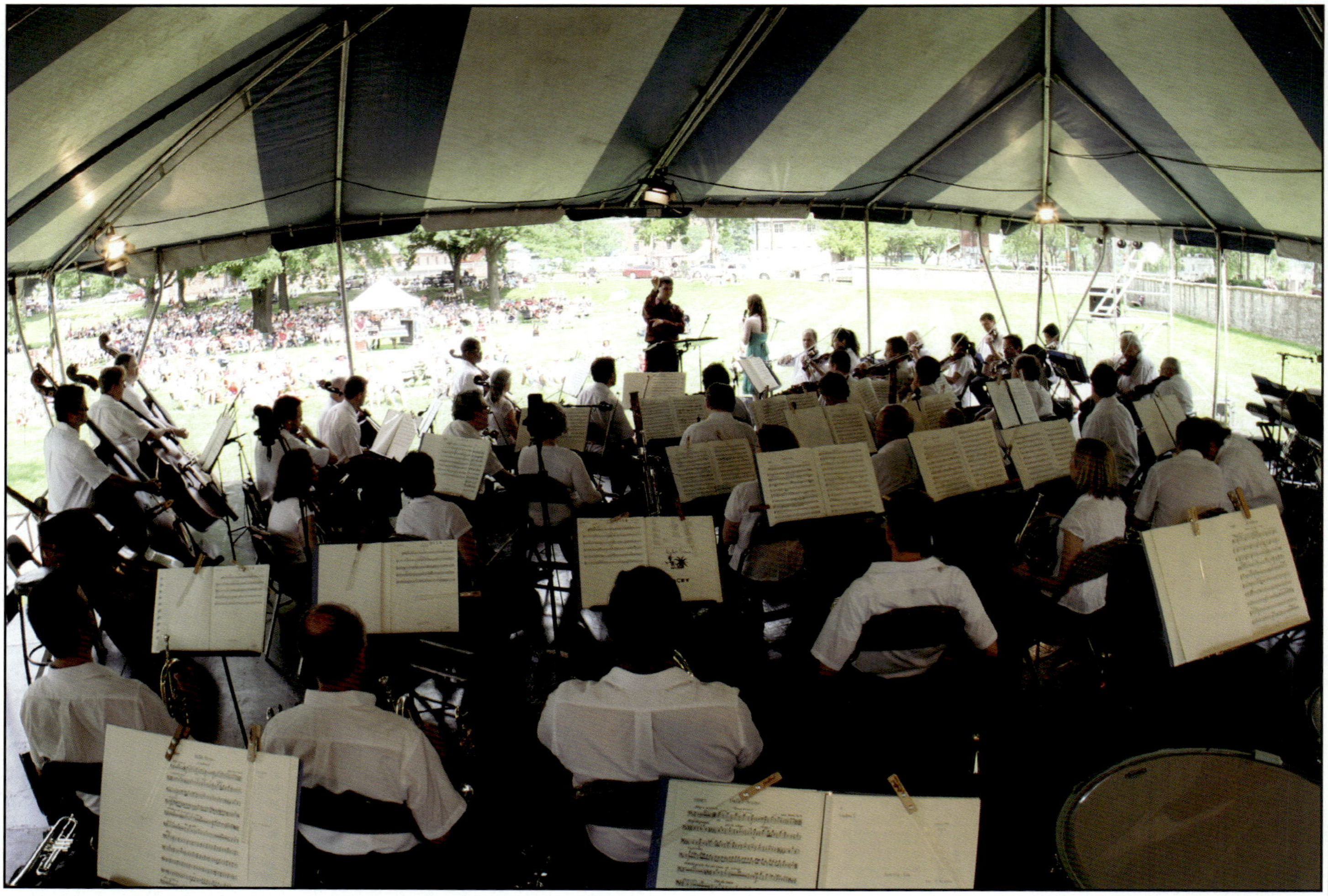

The Cincinnati Symphony Regional Pops Orchestra plays songs from popular American composers.

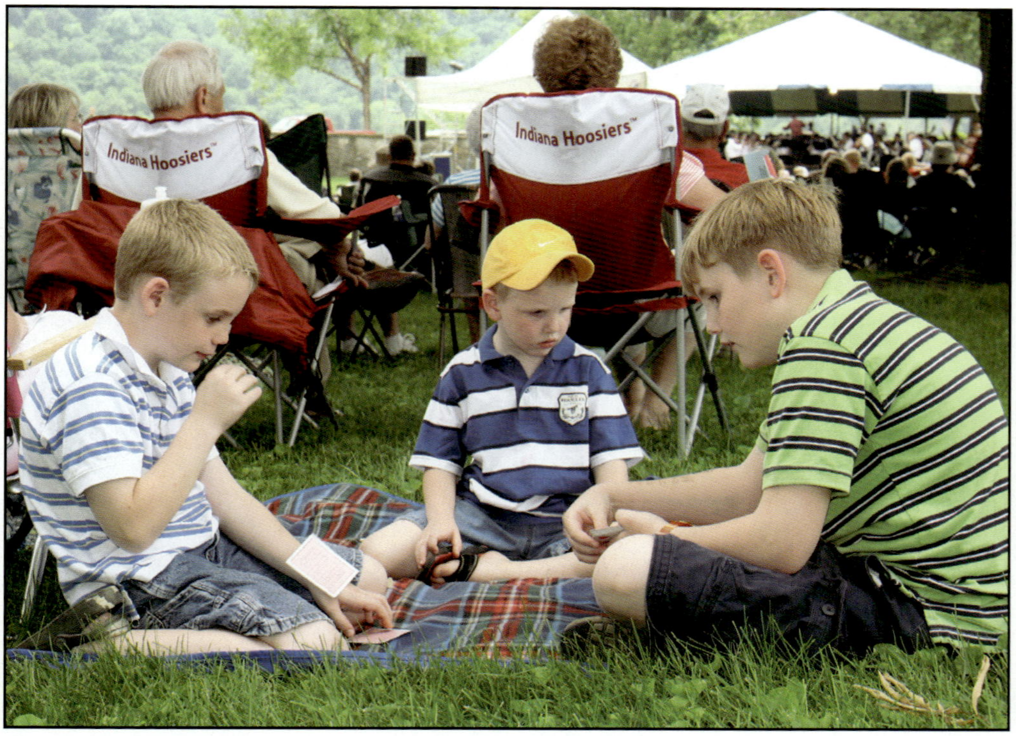

From left, Erin McMahon, 8, Gavin McMahon 4, and Gabriel McMahon, 11, of Madison play cards on the lawn during the Cincinnati Symphony Orchestra concert on Sunday, June 7.

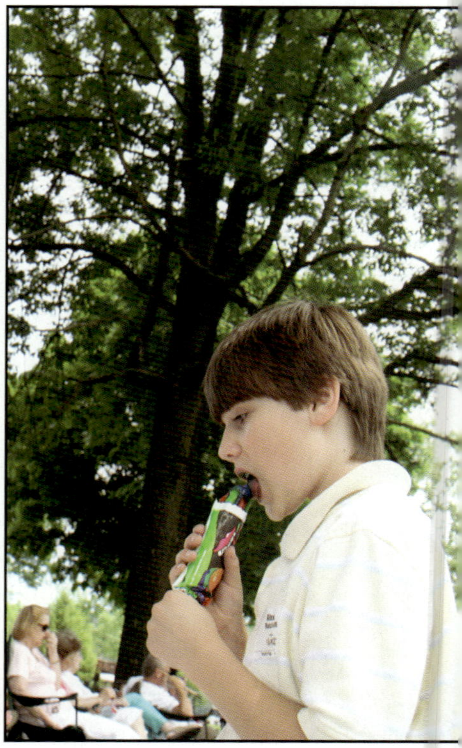

Alex Ratcliff, 8, of Madison enjoys popsicle at the concert.

Photos by Matt Griffith

Sunday Street Scenes

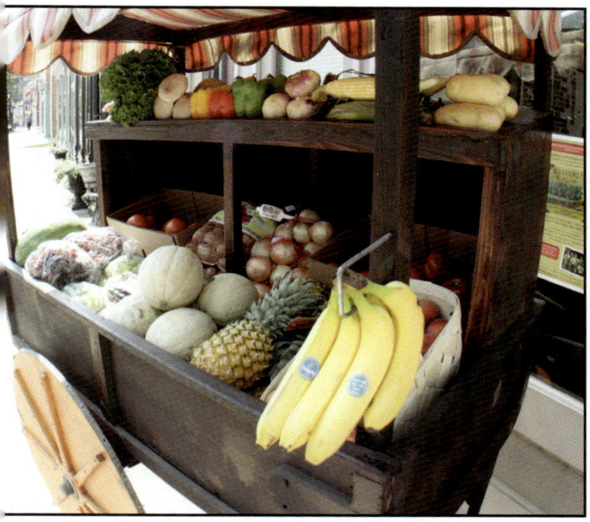

At left, the A. Dattilo's Fruit Co. cart sits outside the store on Main Street. Bottom photo, Crystal Beach City Swimming Pool offered a free swim day.
Photos by Matt Griffith

Right, Bryce Worrell walks past the Ohio Theatre dressed as Civil War soldier, Lt. Col. Alois Bachman.
Photo by Laura Hodges

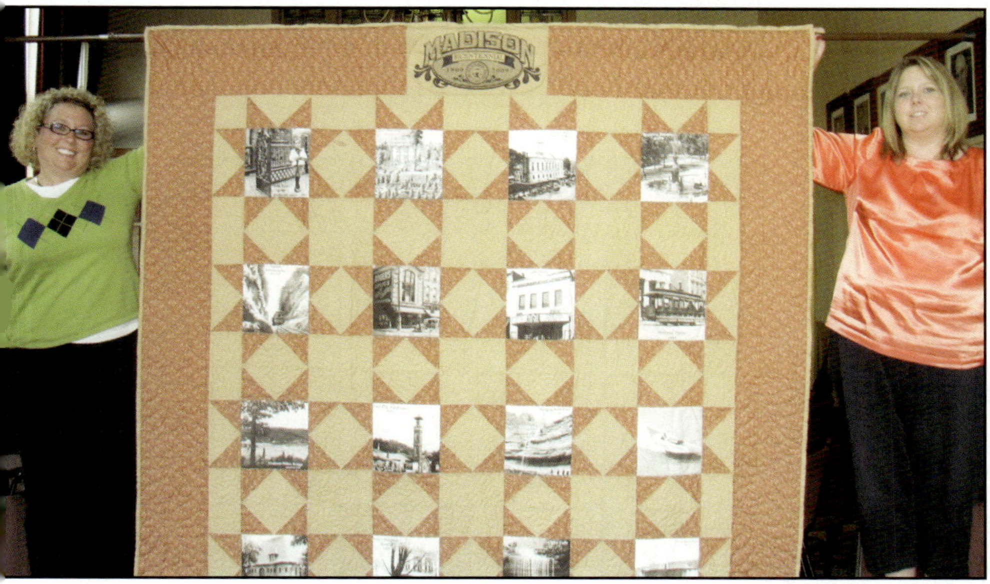

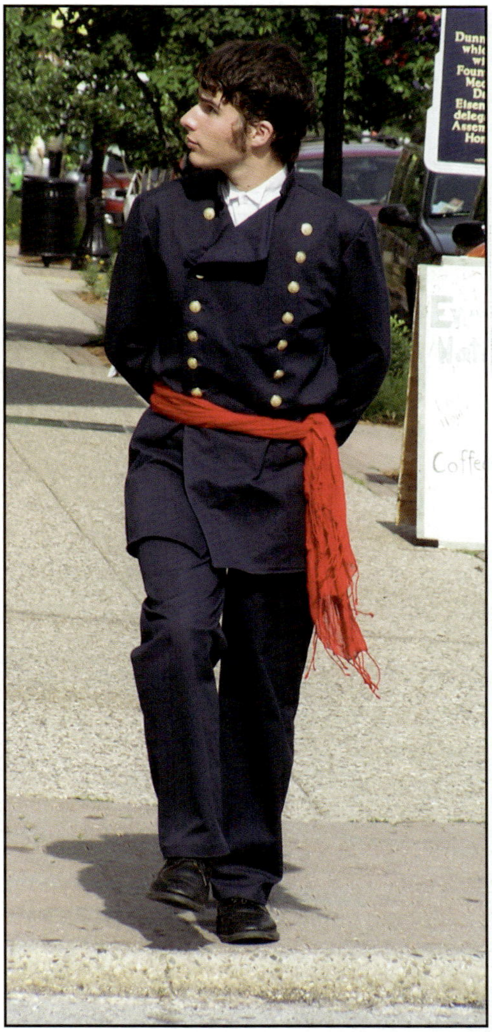

Photo by Cristina Evans

is quilt was made by a group of local quilters for the Madison Bicentennial. hung in the window of Madison City Hall for several weeks in May and June 09. It will hang in various locations throughout the year. Holding the quilt are adison City Hall employees Gina Center (left) and Tammy Boldery.

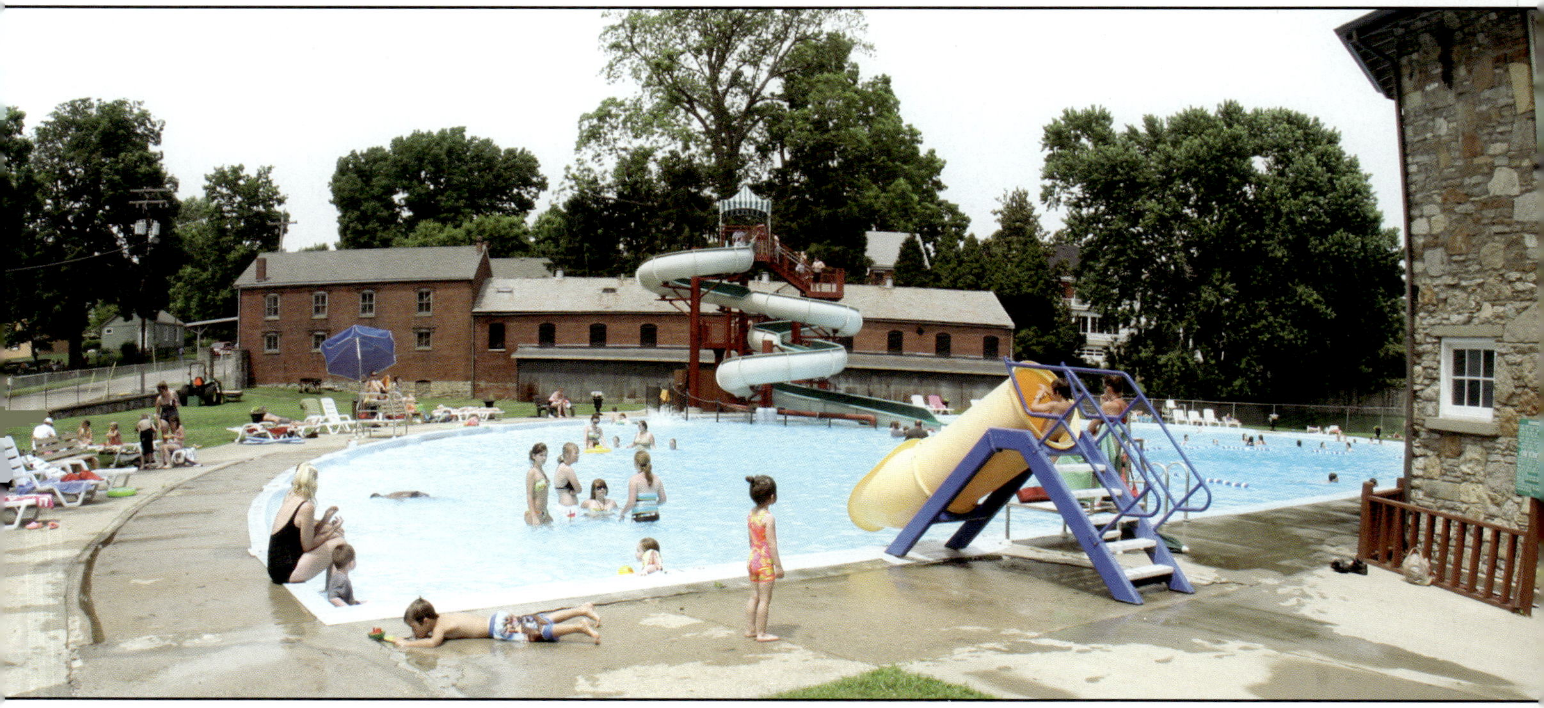

At right, Kathie Petkovic (in red) kicks up her heels to a jazzy song with "Rivertown" musical cast members (from left) Kate McKay, Nichole Waldon and Sadie Courtney.

Below, the 1920s and 1930s era band, Different Hats Dance Orchestra of Dayton, Ohio, gets the crowd going with a selection of lively dance songs. The band featured vocalist Elizabeth Hayes.

Photos by Matt Griffith

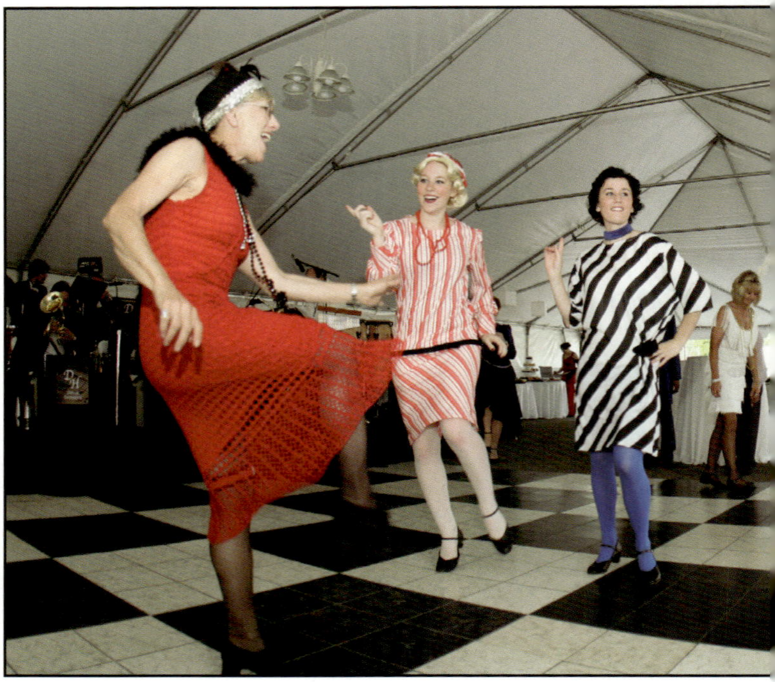

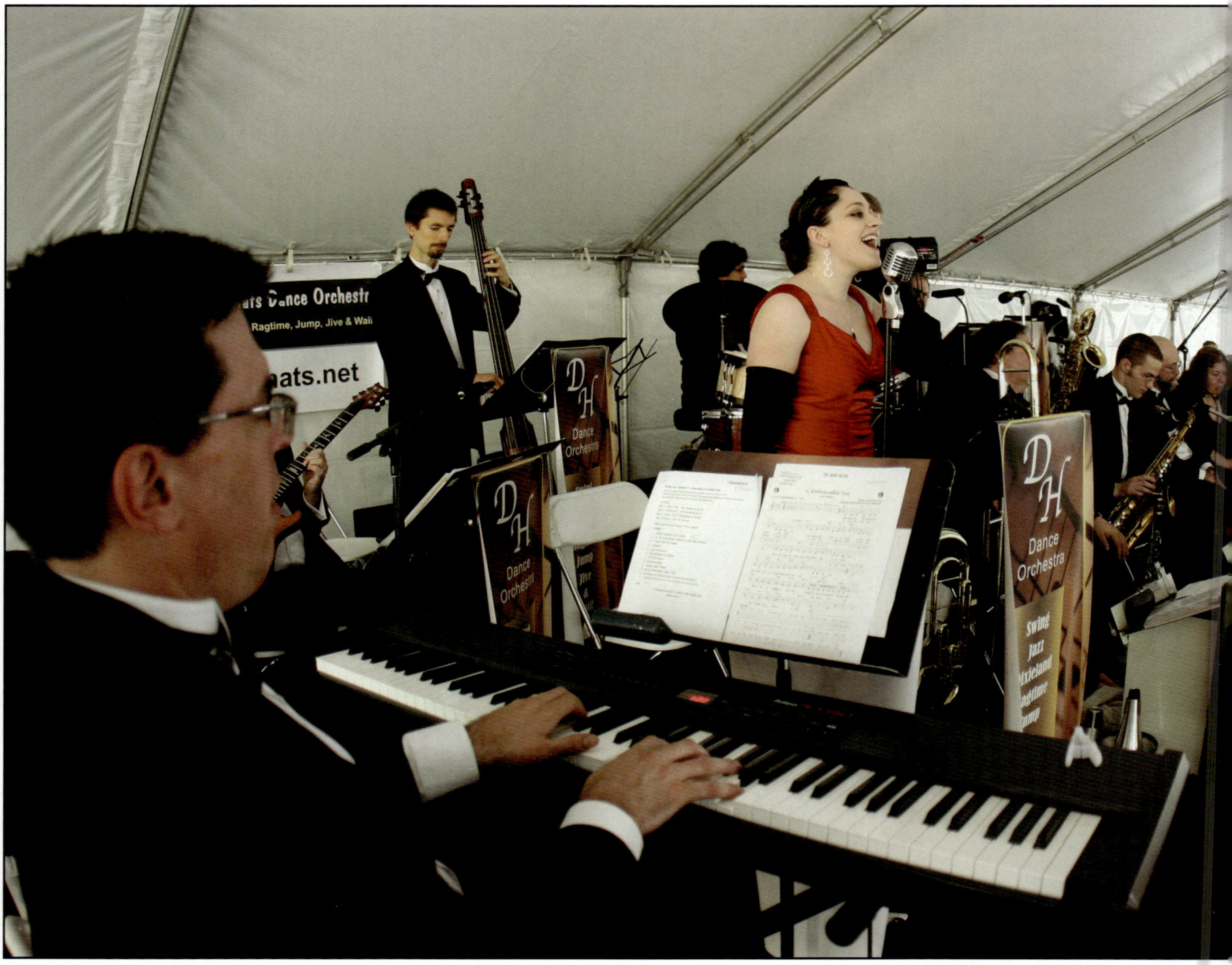

1920s Gala Cocktail Party

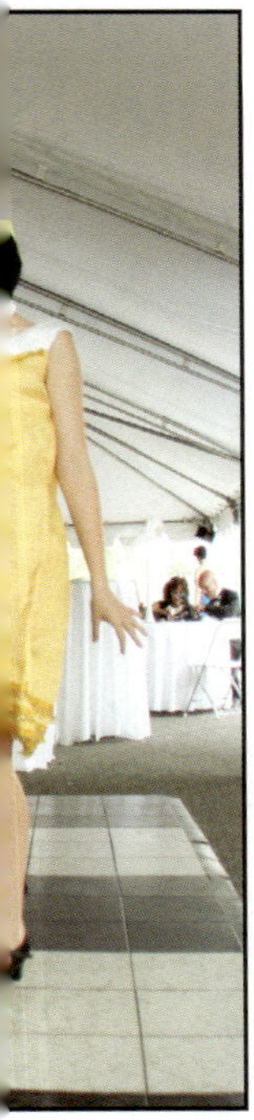

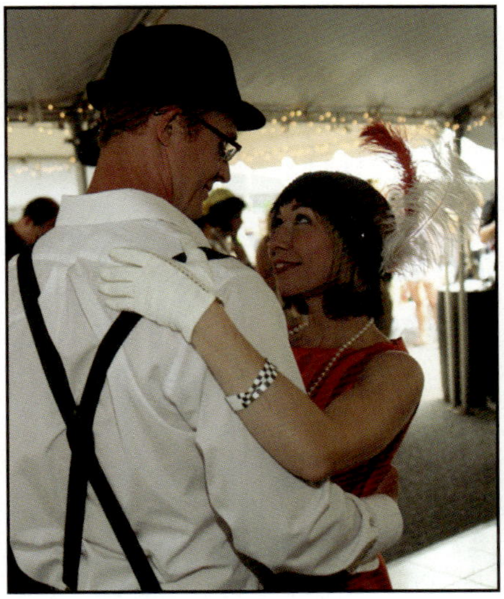

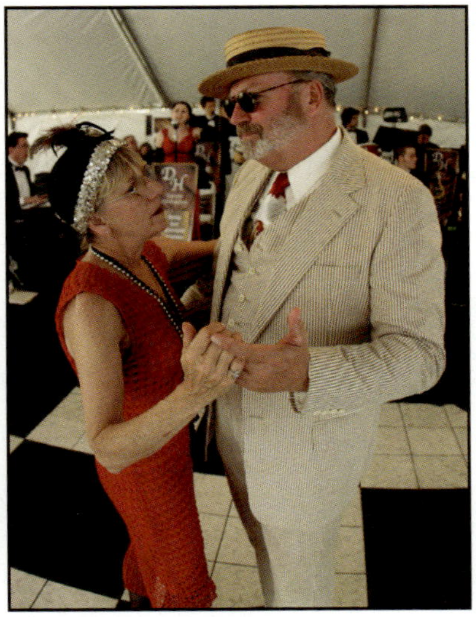

At left, Kathie Petkovic and Jim Grant dance to the music of Different Hats Dance Orchestra.

Second photo from right, Eric and Kelly Rector on the dance floor.

Photos by Matt Griffith

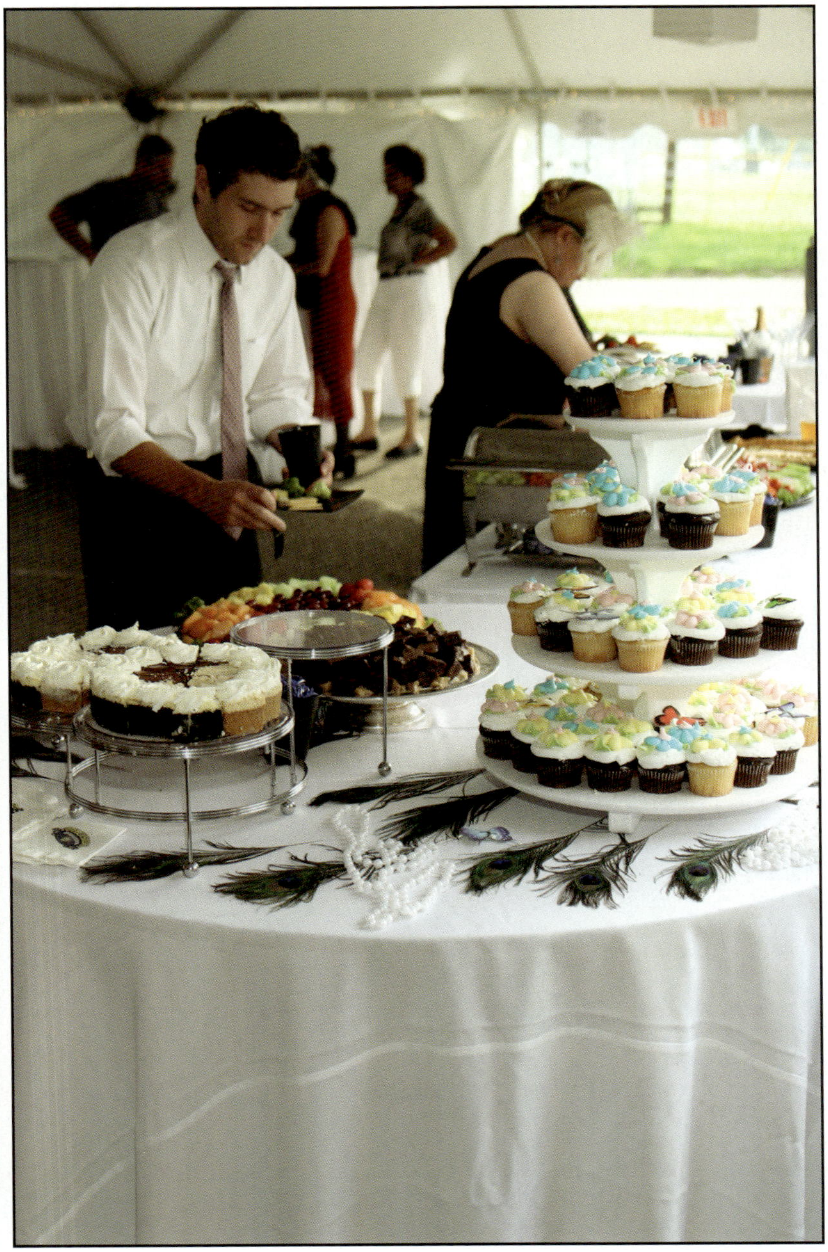

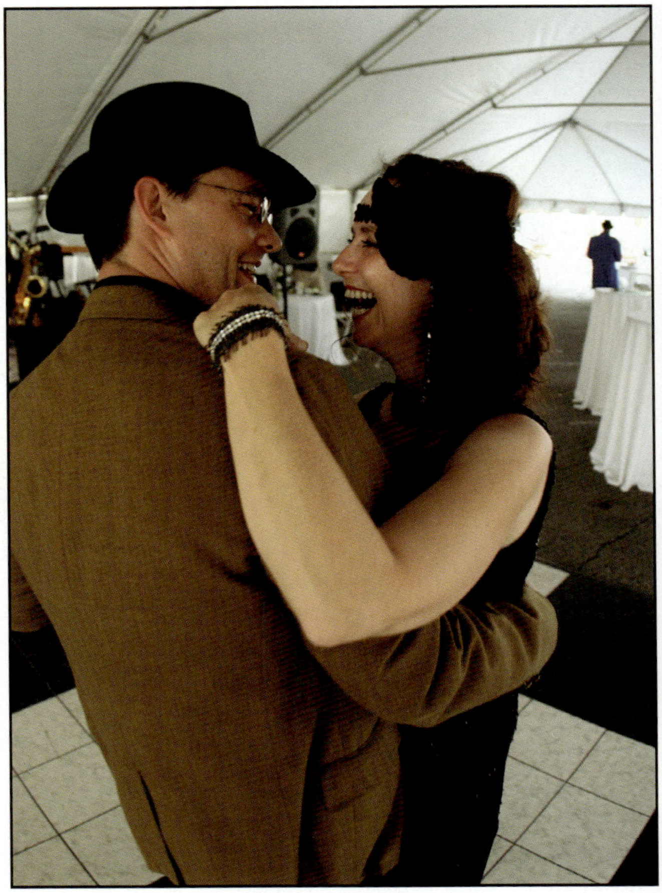

Above, Kevin and Margo Watkins dance to a slow song during The Gala.

At left, guests were treated to a wide selection of appetizers and sweets, all donated by local restaurants. An open bar, featuring a special "Bicentini" cocktail drink, was available. The event served as a Bicentennial fundraiser.

Photos by Matt Griffith

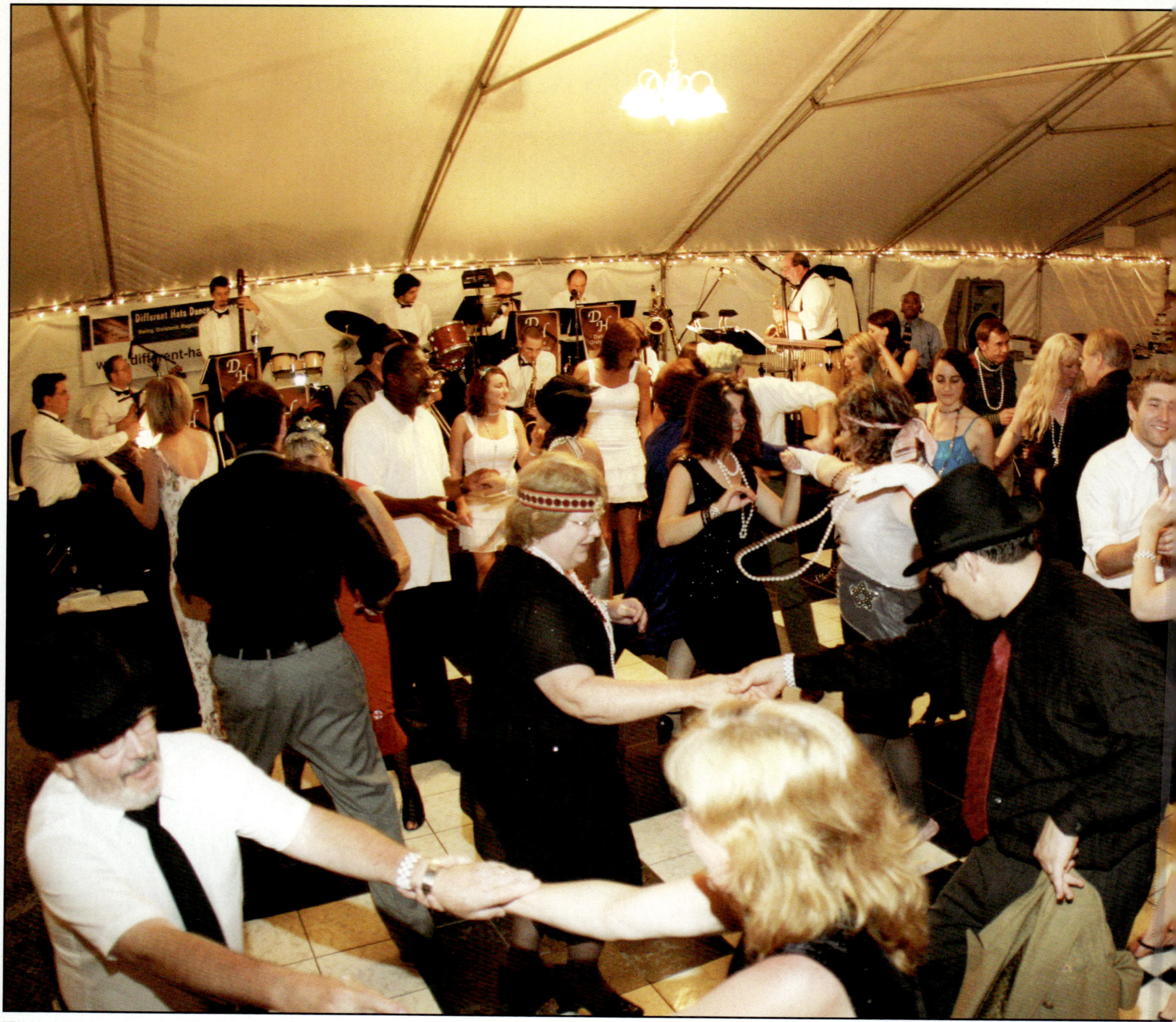

The 1920s-1920s Gala Cocktail Party was a hit with dancers who were first taught the "Charleston" and then turned loose to try out their new skills.

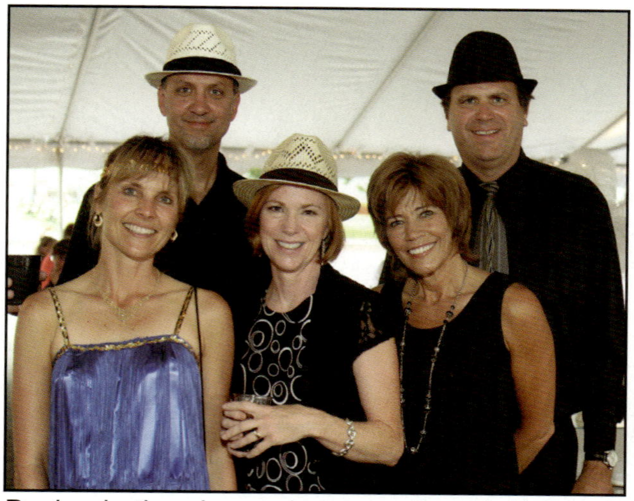

Posing in the above photo are (from left) Candi Miller, Charlie Rohlfing Kathy Rohlfing, Mary and Tom Davee.

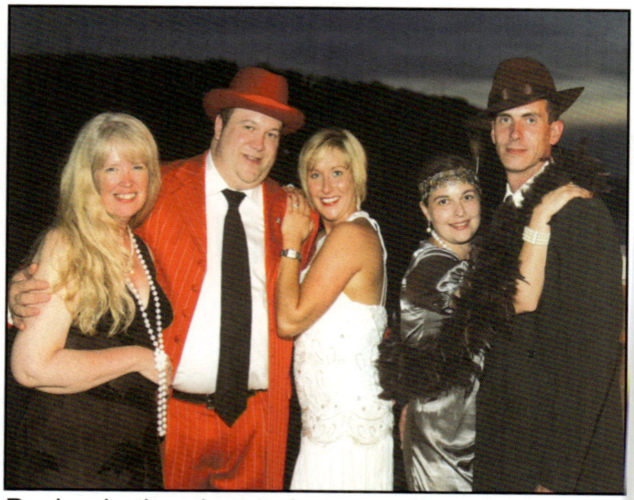

Posing in the above photo are (from left) Nancy Gruner, Erik and Jennifer Grove, Whitney and Bill Settles.

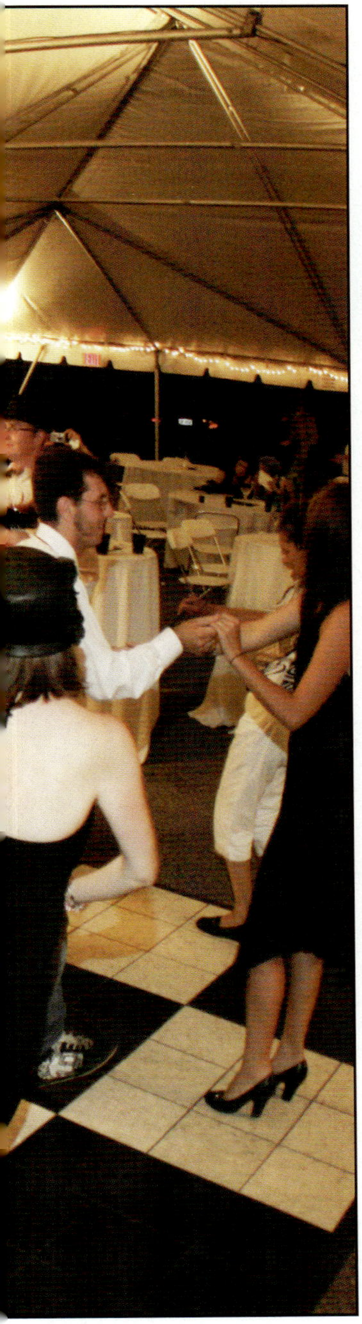

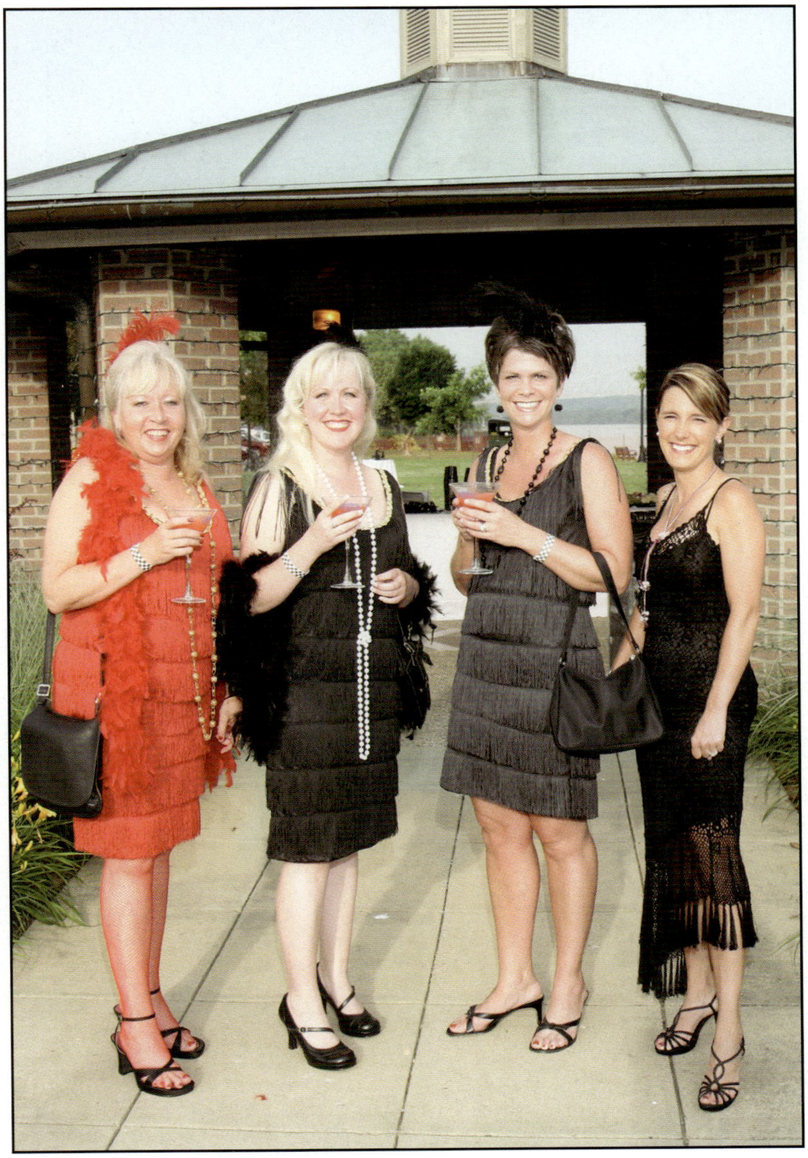

This group of ladies dressed the part for the 1920s-1930s Gala Cocktail Party on June 7 at the Madison riverfront. They are (from left) Sandra Straub of Cincinnati, her niece, Dr. Sarah Marshall of Madison, Jill Turner and Dr. Holly Robinson, both of Madison.

Photos by Matt Griffith

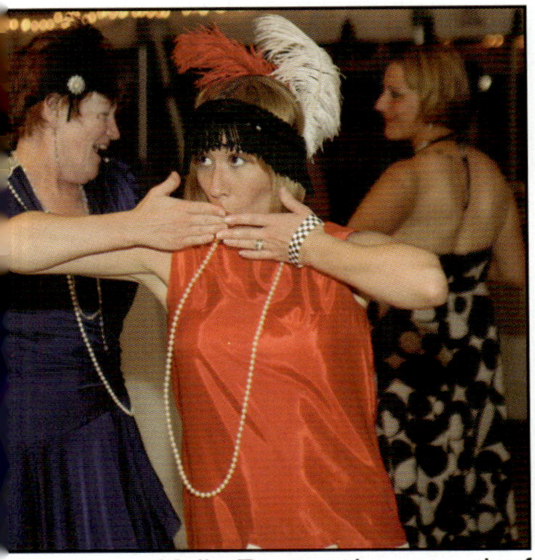

Kelly Rector shows a playful move while dancing at the Gala. Behind her are Camille Fife and Jane Devito

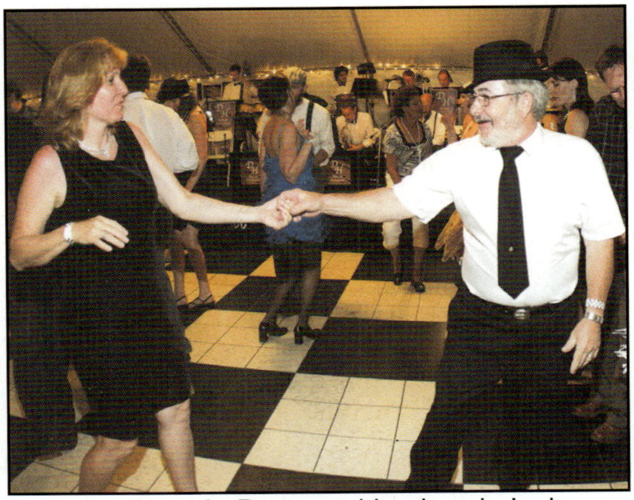

Dancers Rhonda Deeg and husband, Jack Patchin, turn it on after learning some new "Charleston" moves at the Gala Cocktail Party.

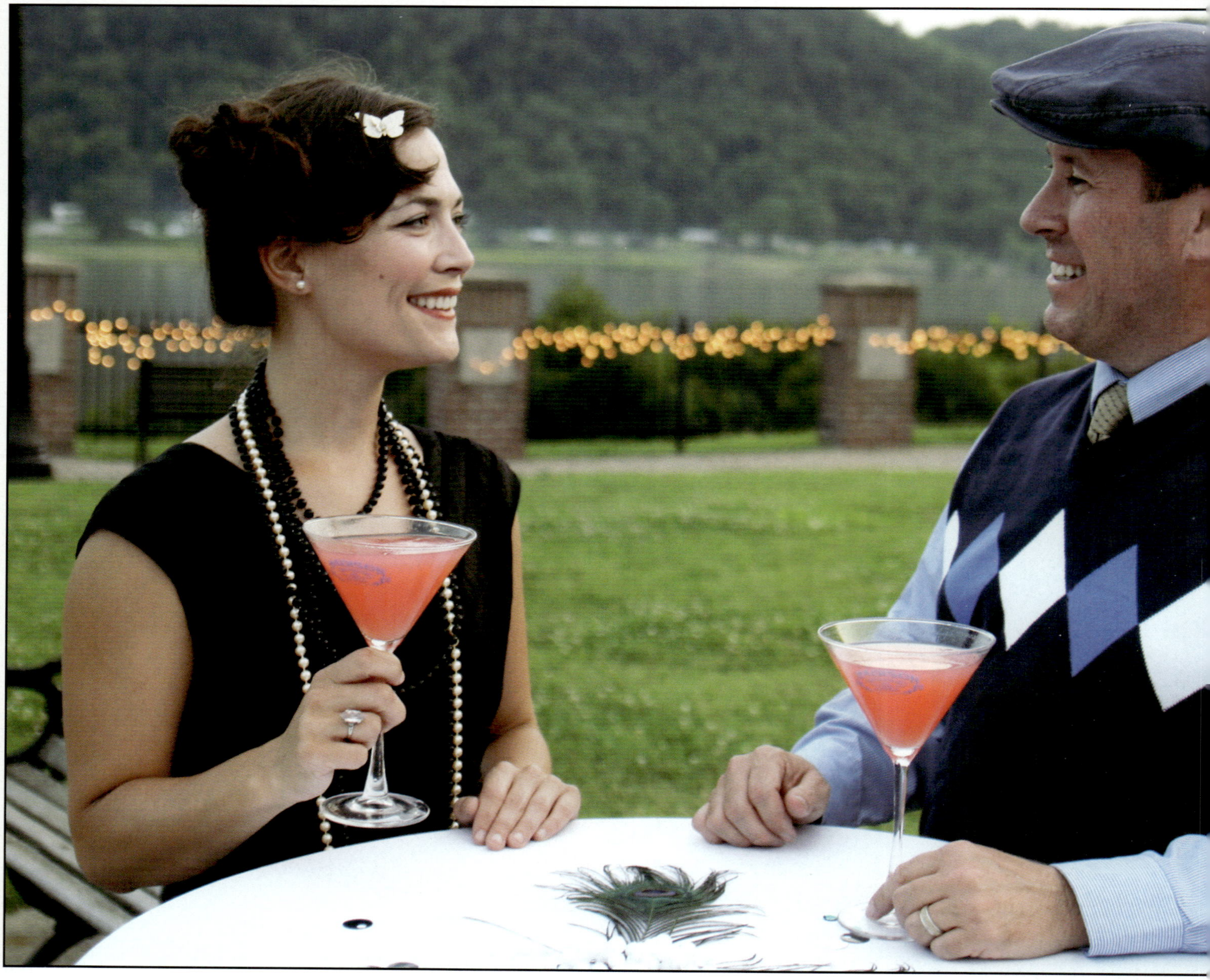

Photo by Matt Griffith

Posing for this vintage 1920s photo are Amy Vaughn and Sean Cleary. Cleary, wearing a 1920s-style golf outfit, won an award at the Gala Cocktail Party for "Best Themed Costume." The two are holding a special "Bicentini" cocktail drink. The drinks, which included the glass, were sold at the June 7 event.

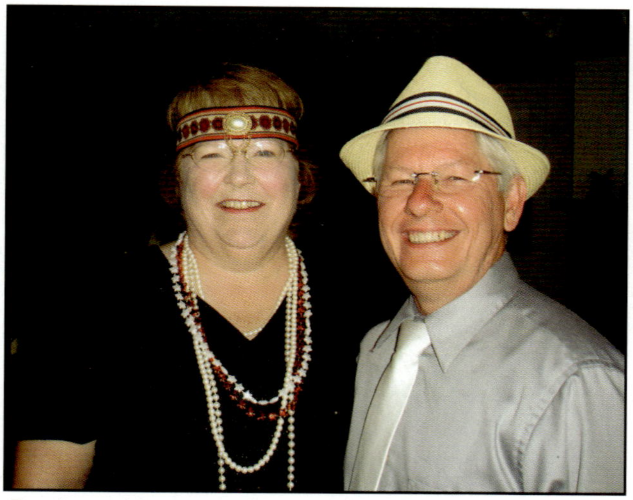

Posing above are Laura and Dan Hodges at the Gala Cocktail Party.

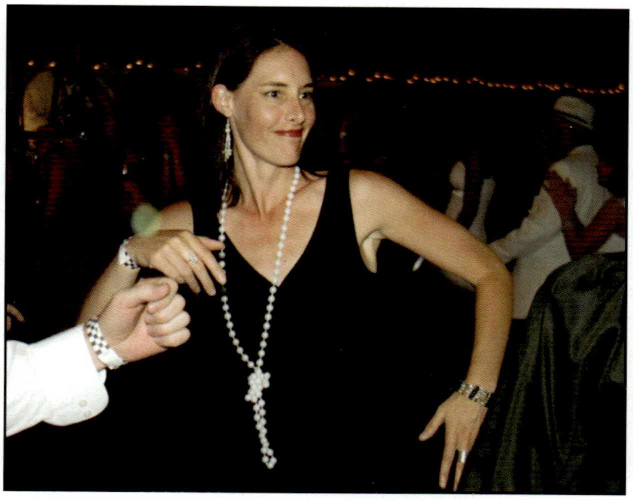

Photo by Don Ward

Jennifer Wright of Madison shows her moves on the dance floor at the Gala.

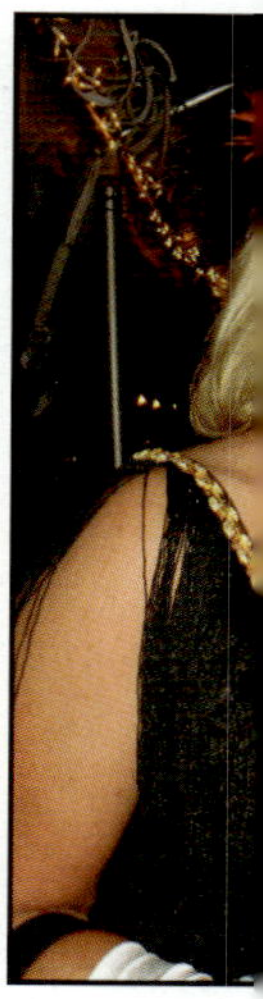

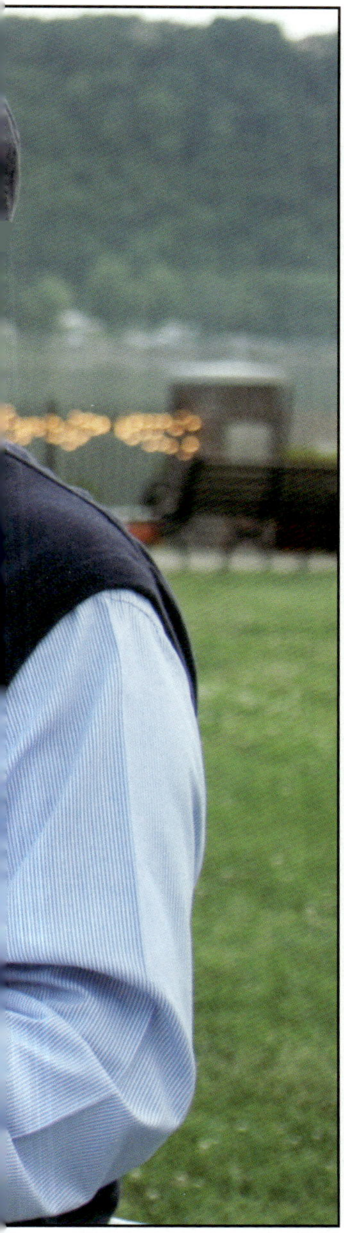

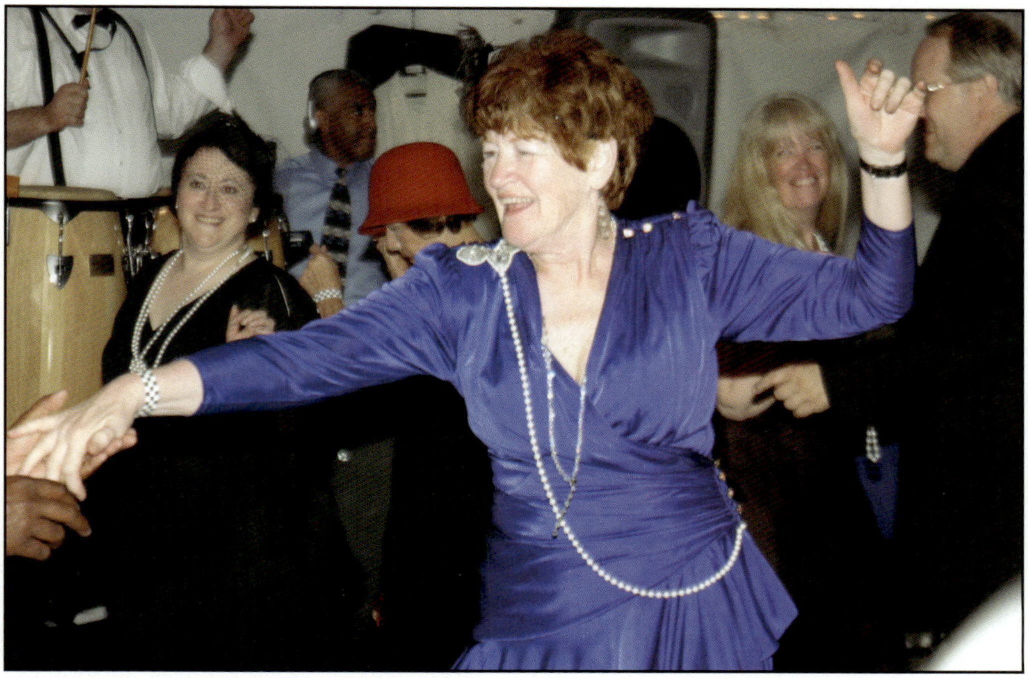

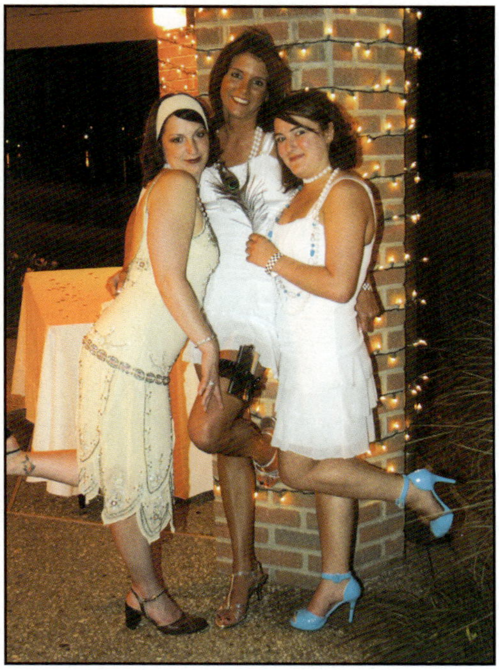

Above, Camille Fife takes a spin across the dance floor at the Gala Cocktail Party.

Photo by Don Ward

At left, these gals hammed it up for the camera in their 1920s outfits. They are (from left) Elizabeth Sorba, Miranda Jackson and Tristen Walters.

Photo by Randy Porter

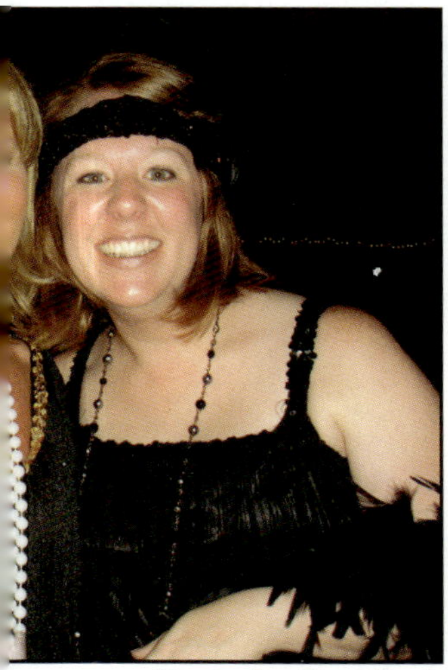

Photo by Dan Hodges

Posing above are Debbie Armstrong (left) and Jenny Eggenspiller.

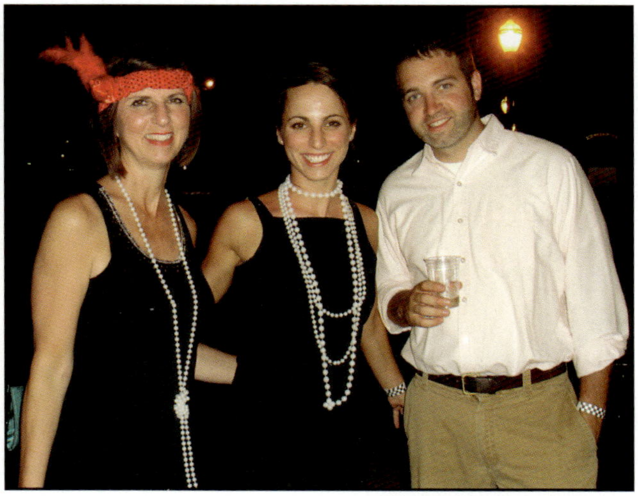

Photo by Dan Hodges

Posing in the above photo are (from left) Catherine LaSaux, daughter Meredith Terrell and Chris Heitz.

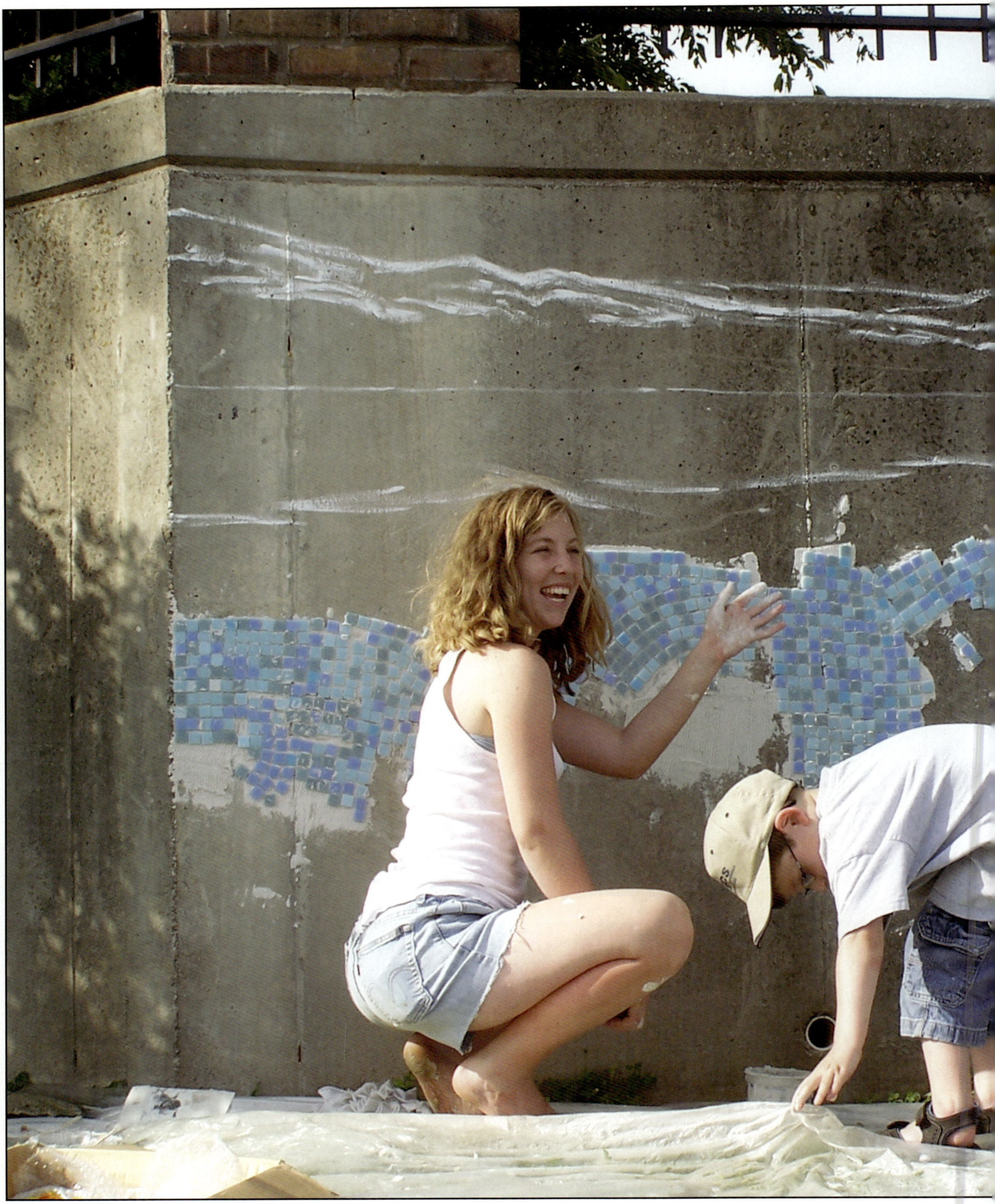

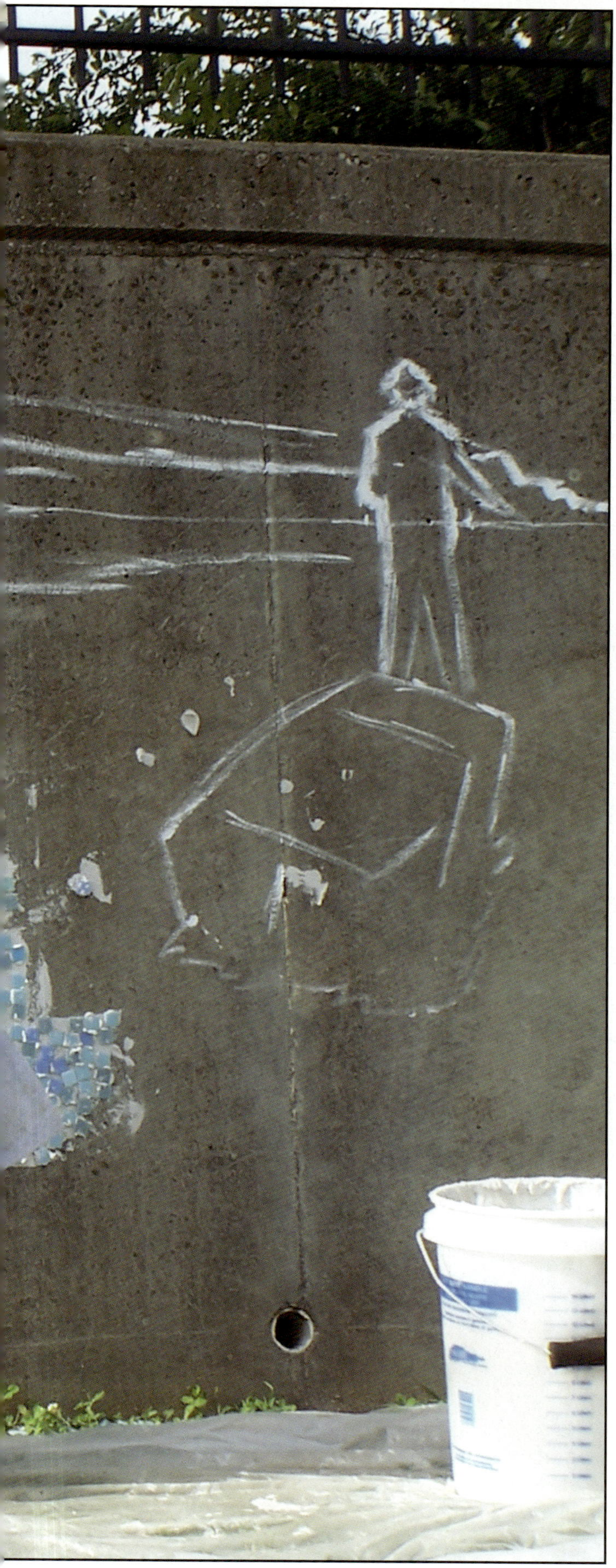

Arts Day

Arts Day on June 8 at the Madison Bicentennial featured a variety of activities for adults and children, including paintings, sculpture, video game contests, art exhibitions, dance, poetry workshops and the creation of this public mosaic on a wall at the Madison Riverfront Walk.
At left, artist Tiffany Black gets help from a young assistant in pasting on the mosaic pieces of a what will become a river scene.

Photo by Laura Hodges

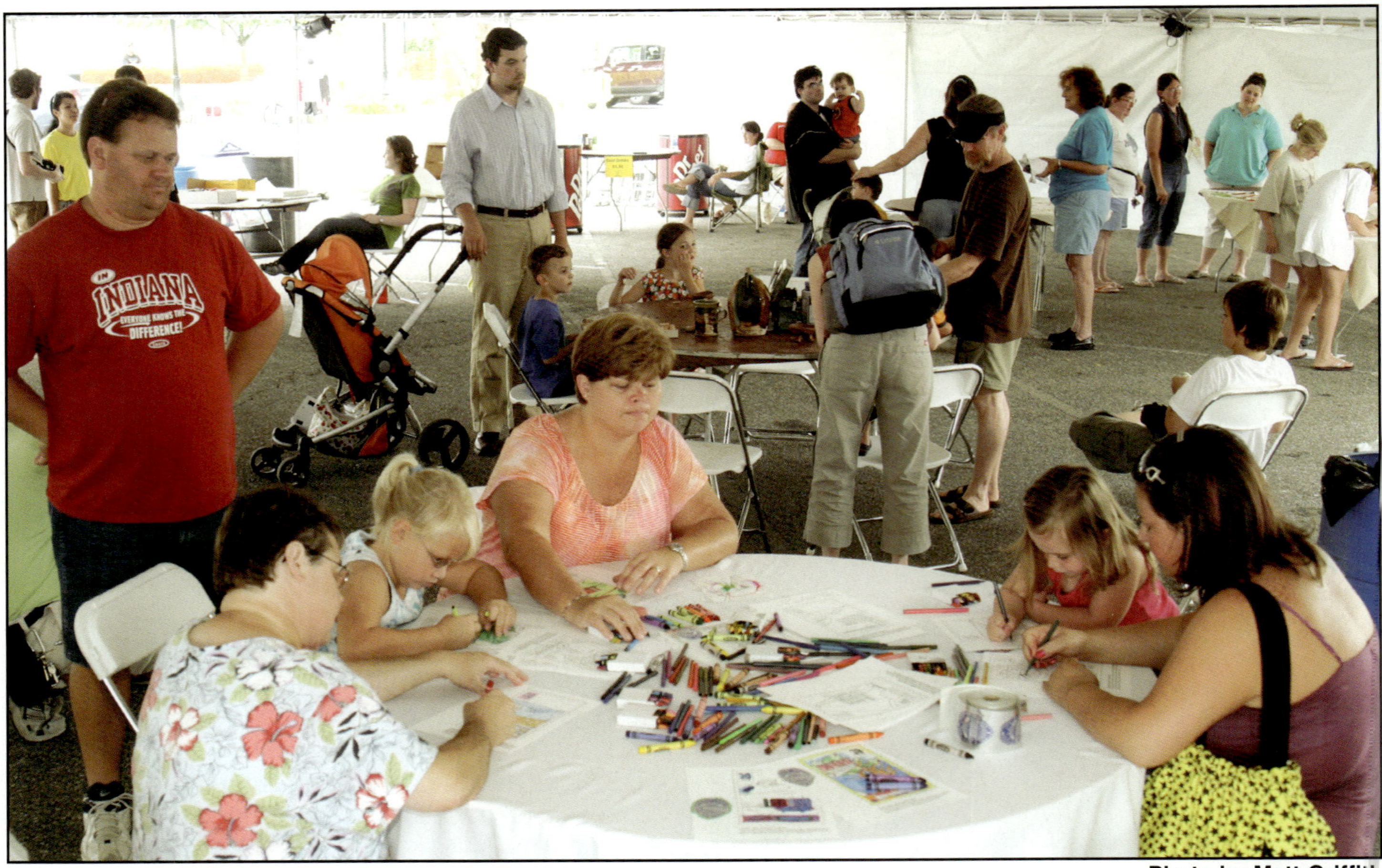

Photo by Matt Griffith

Arts Day offered all types of activities for families, especially children.

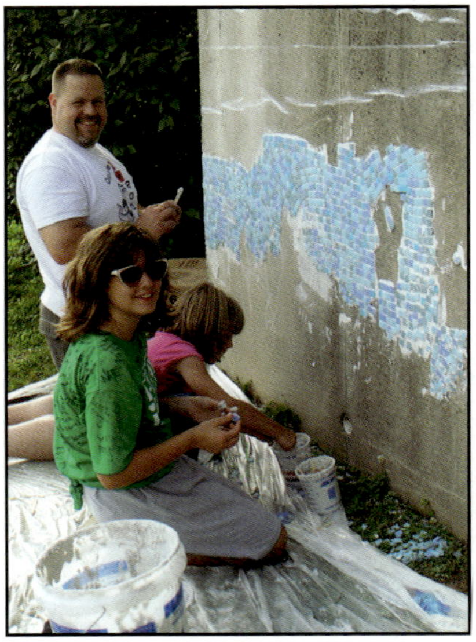

Photo by Laura Hodges

Working on the riverfront mosaic are Kevin Snyder with his daughters, Emma, 8, and Kayla, 11.

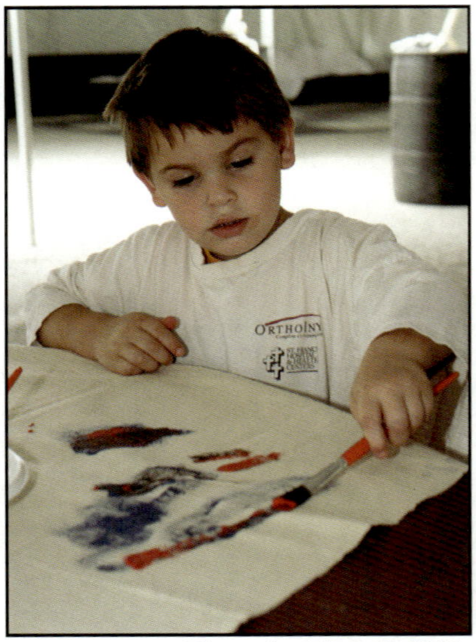

Photo by Matt Griffith

Trey Ashby, 4, of Columbus, Ind., paints on canvas.

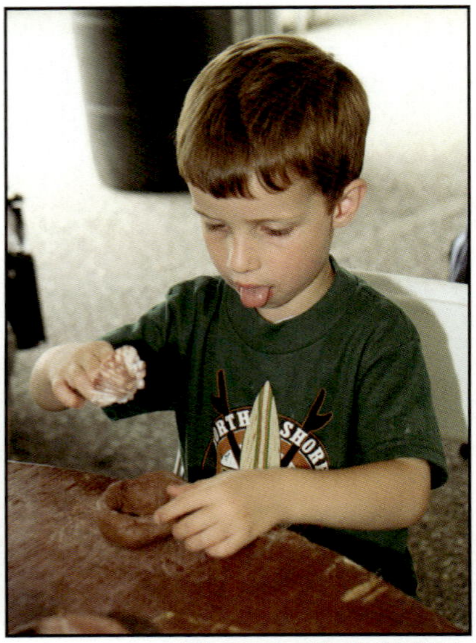

Photo by Matt Griffith

Owen Altermatt, 4, of Hanover, Ind., works on a pottery project.

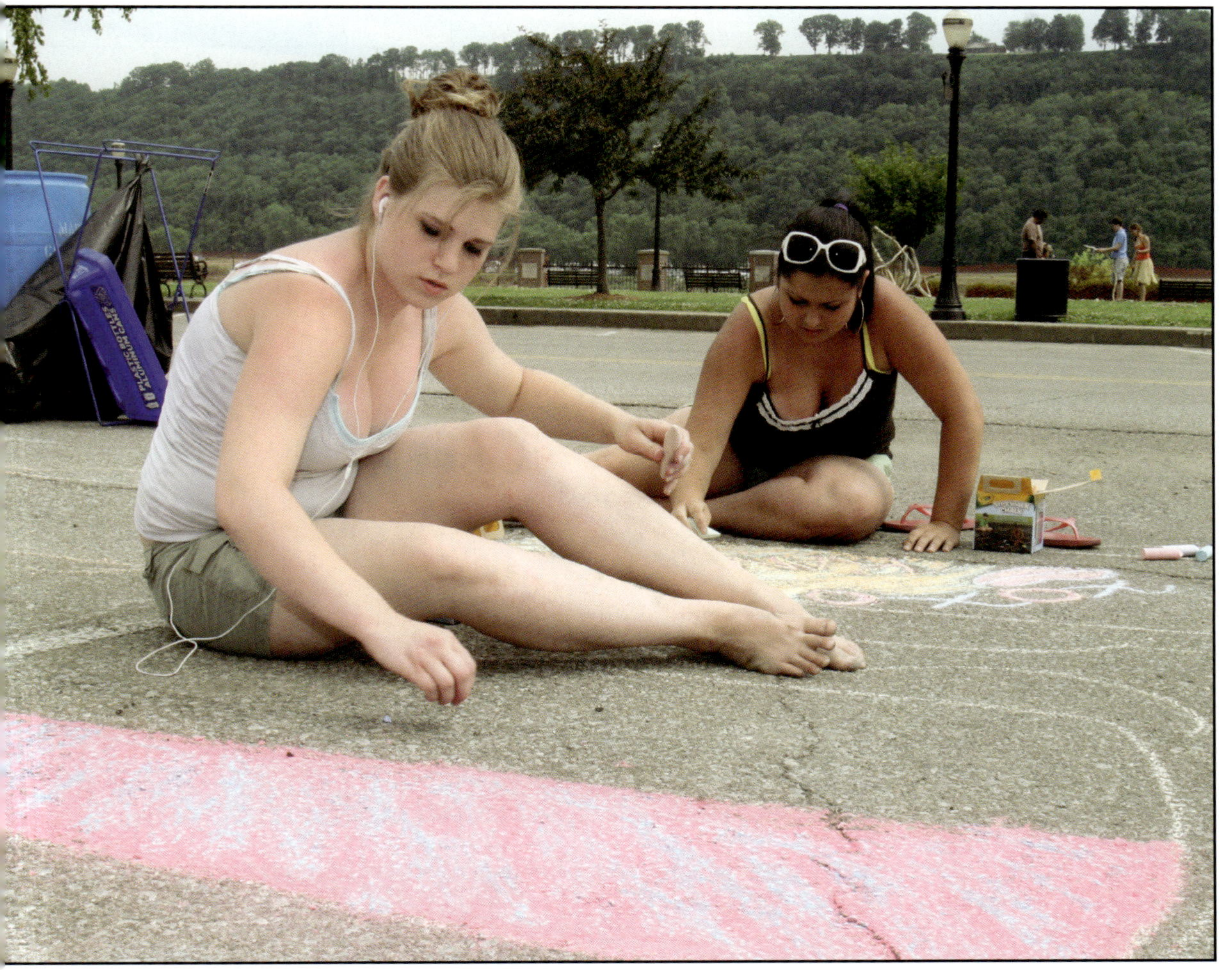

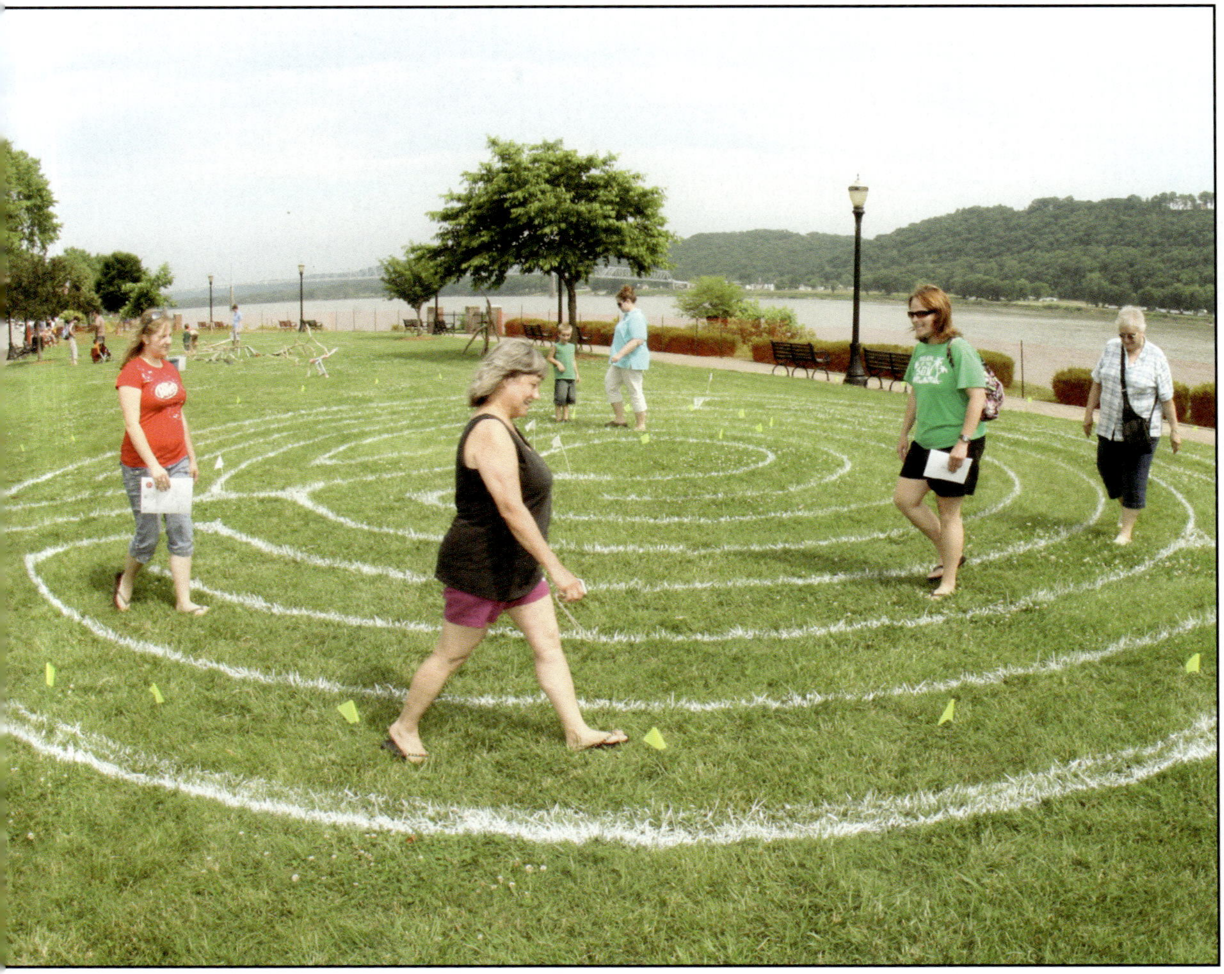

TOP: Trimble County, Ky., residents (from left) Randie Carson, 16, and Tasha Carson, 19, work on a sidewalk chalk art project.

BOTTOM: Annalisa Strickland (center) and others try to solve the labyrinth maze painted on the grass for Arts Day at the Madison riverfront.

Photos by Matt Griffith

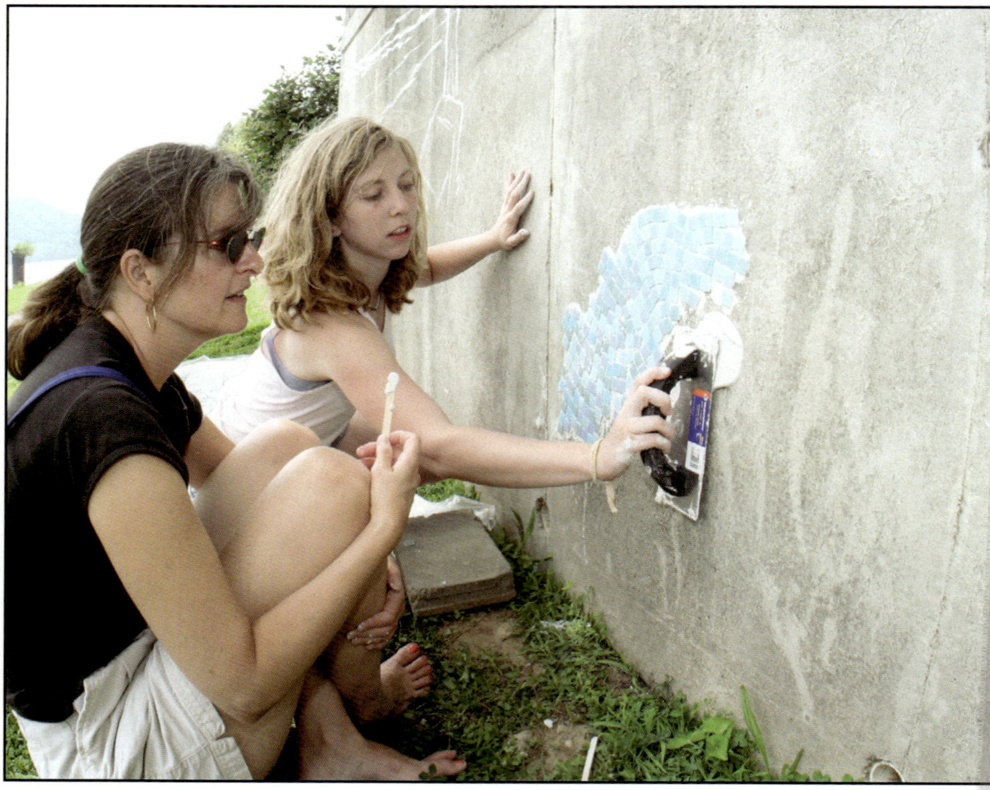

RIGHT: Artist Tiffany Black (right) gets help from Kay Stokes in creating the Madison Riverfront public mosaic during Arts Day.

BOTTOM: Tiffany Black carefully glues the pieces into place to create the river scene.

Photo by Matt Griffith

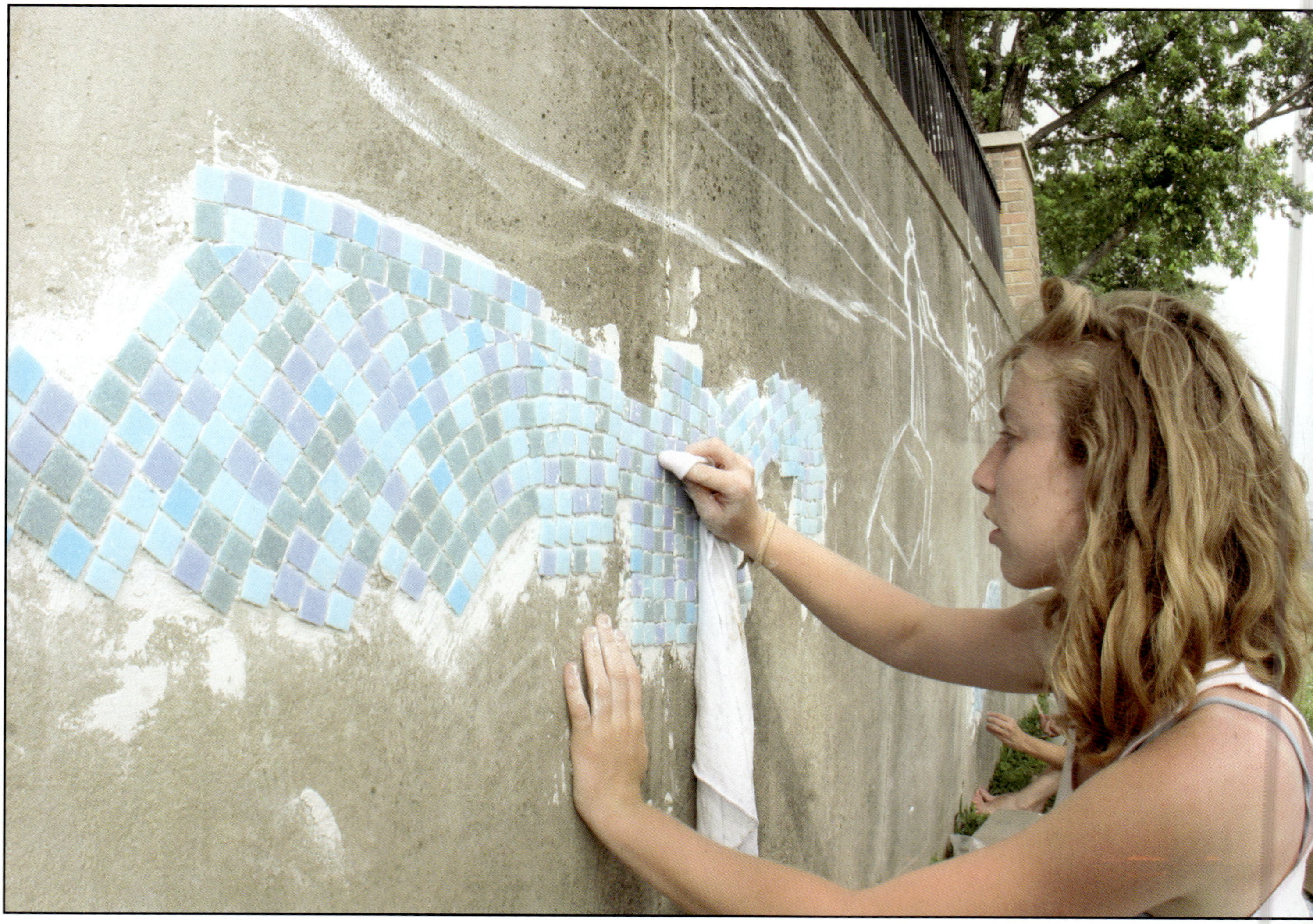

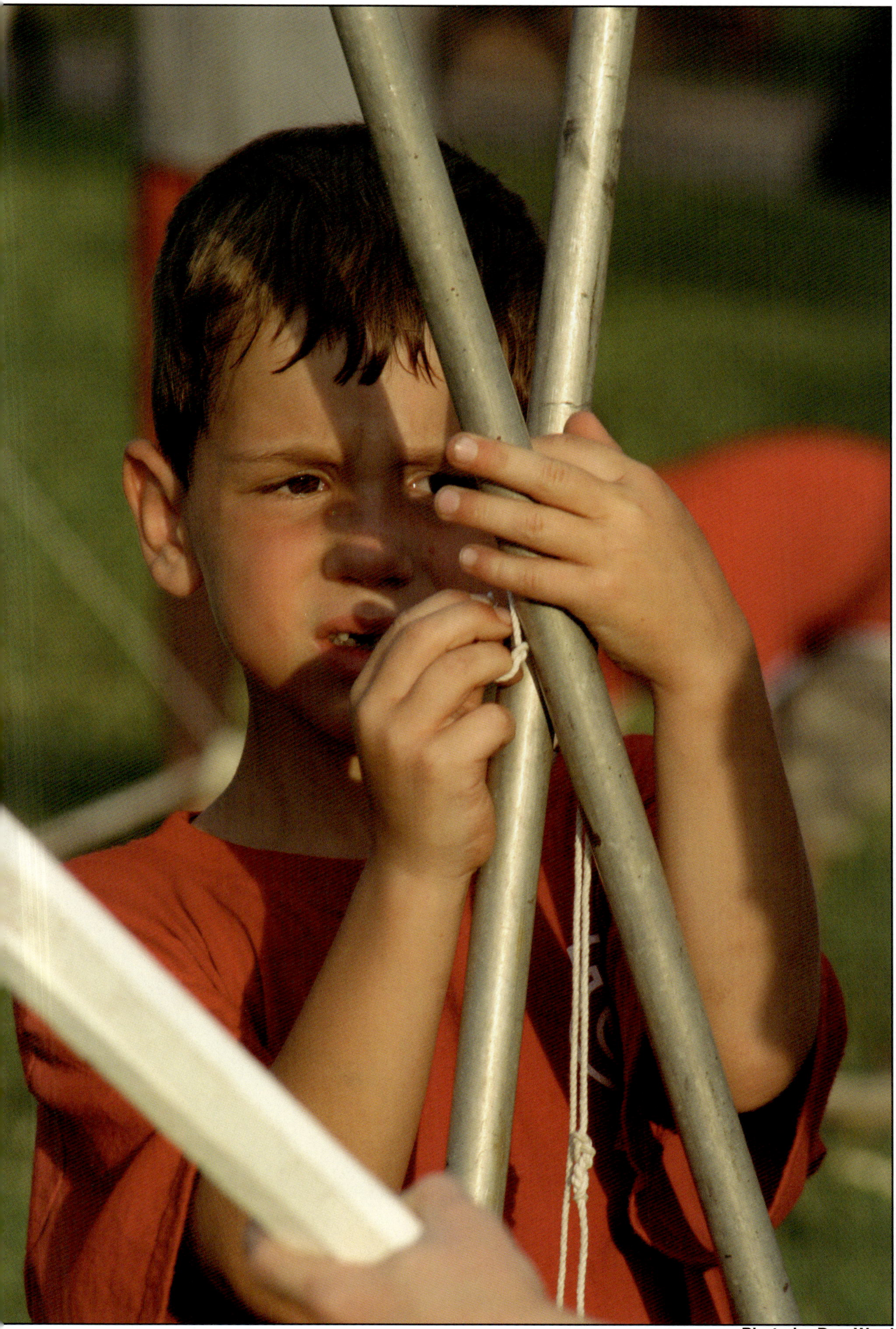

Photo by Don Ward

ırson Denton, 7, of Madison works on a sculpture from sticks during Arts Day at the riverfront.

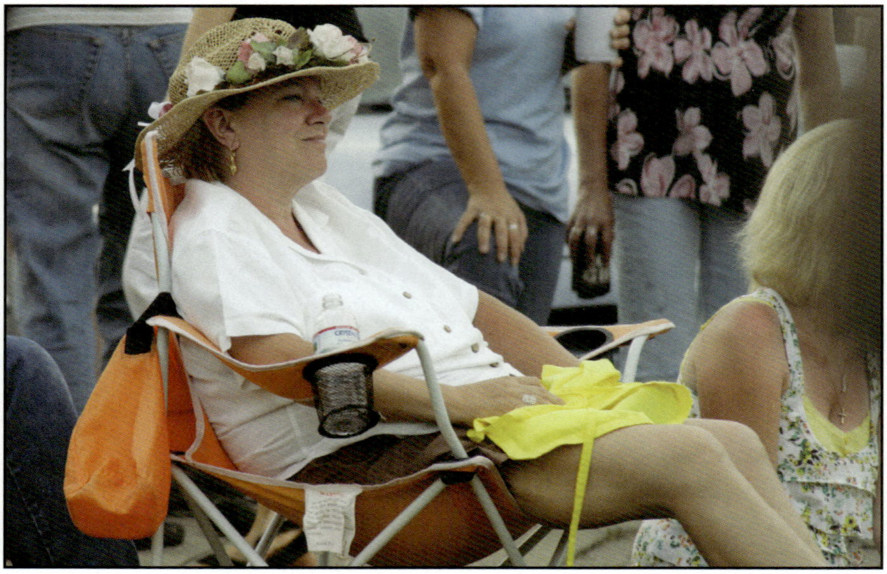

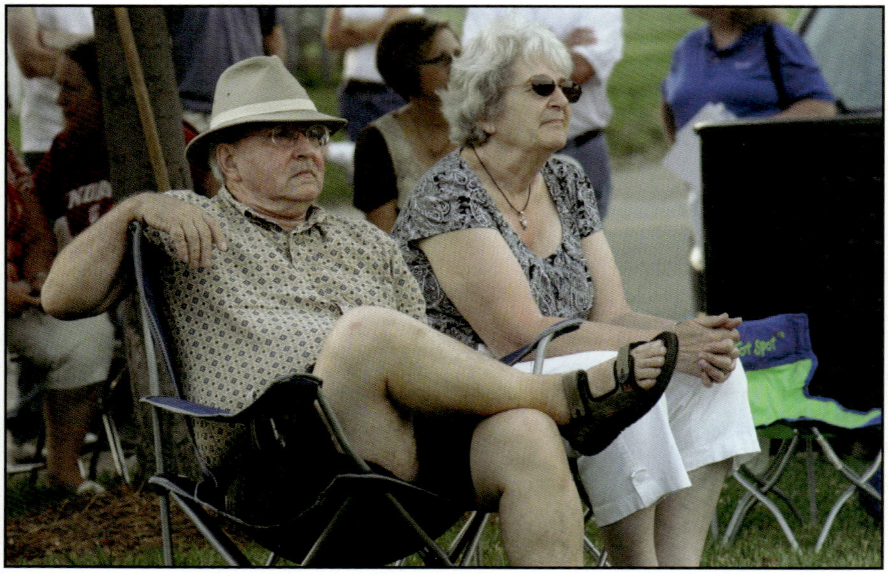

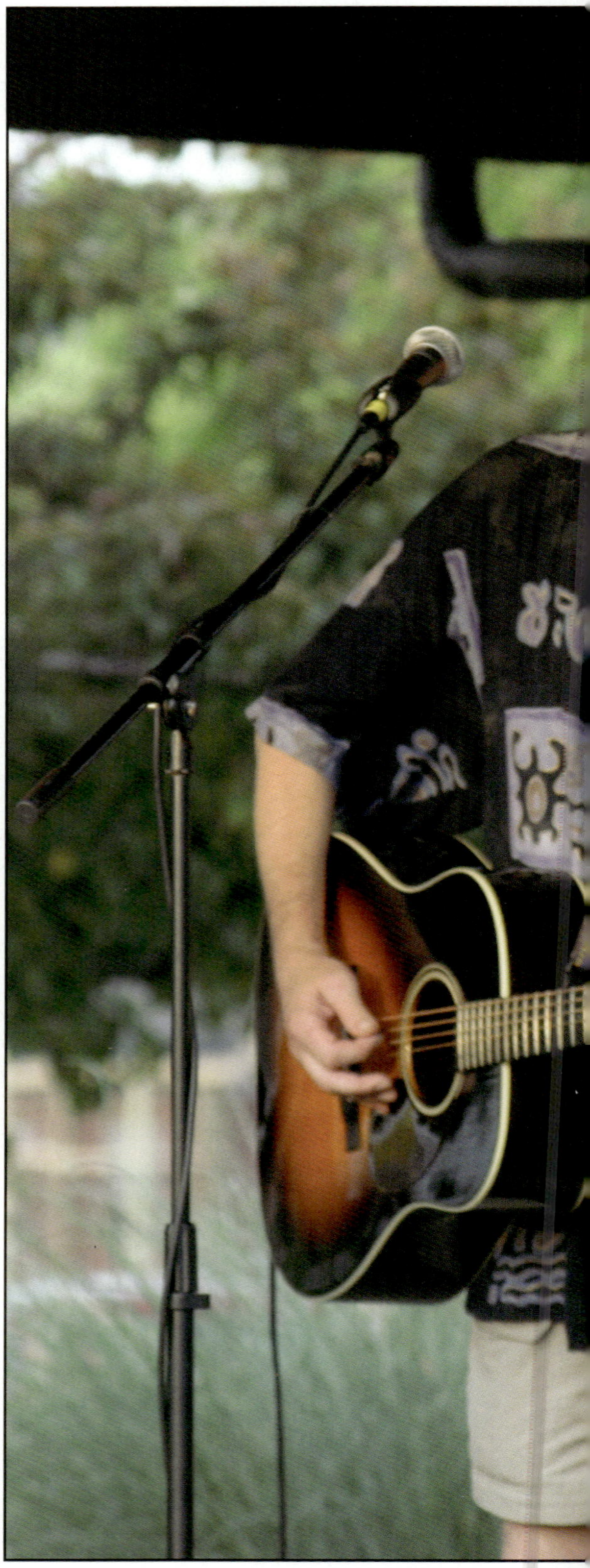

RIGHT: Greg Ziesemer and Kriss Luckett perform at the Madison Riverfront Gazebo on June 8.

TOP: Susan Brewer.

ABOVE: Bob and Heidi Saueressig.

Photos by Don Ward

Music on the Riverfront

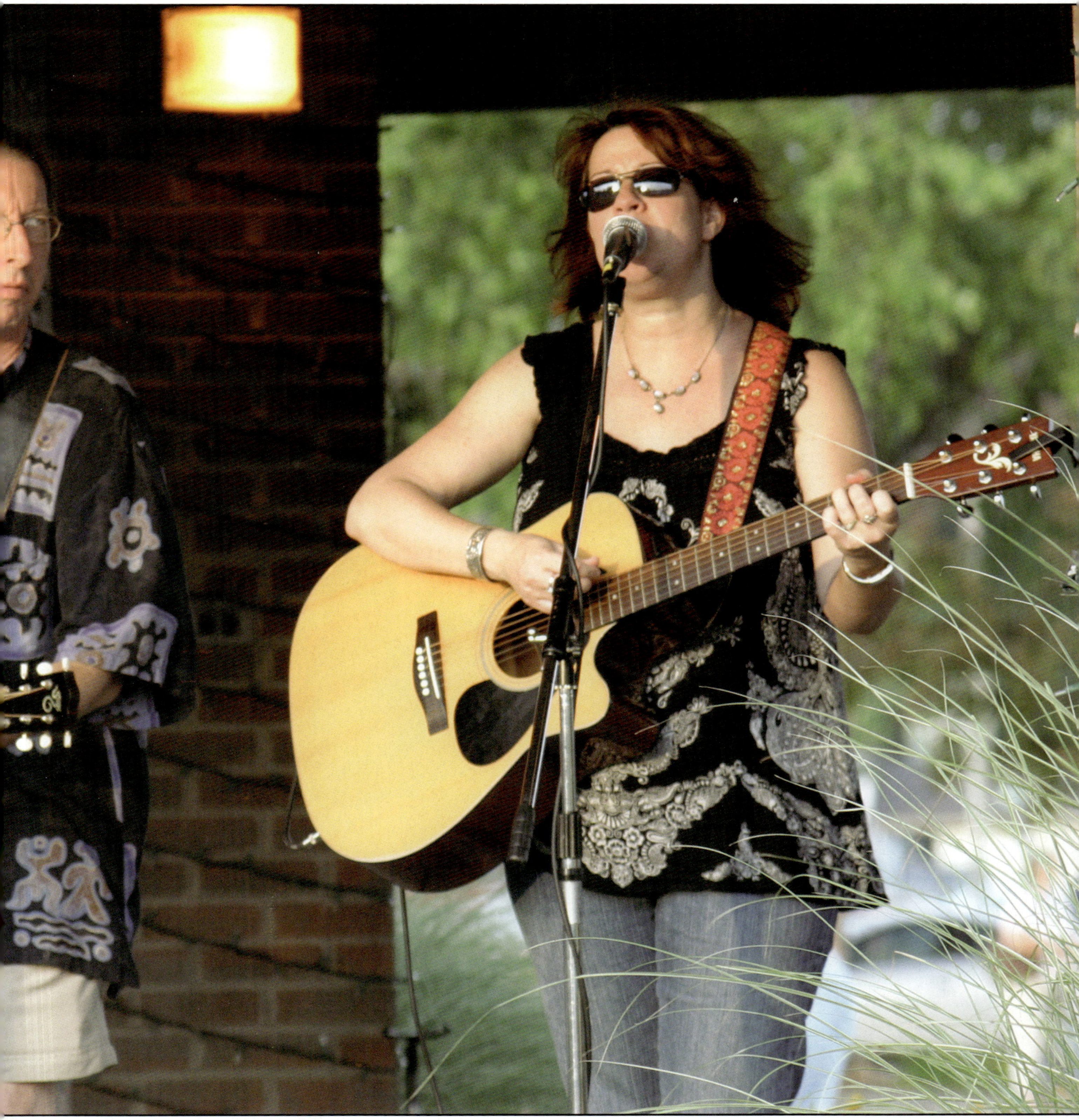

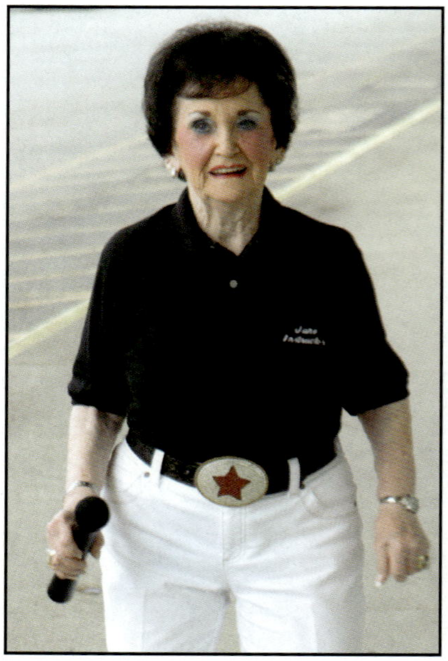

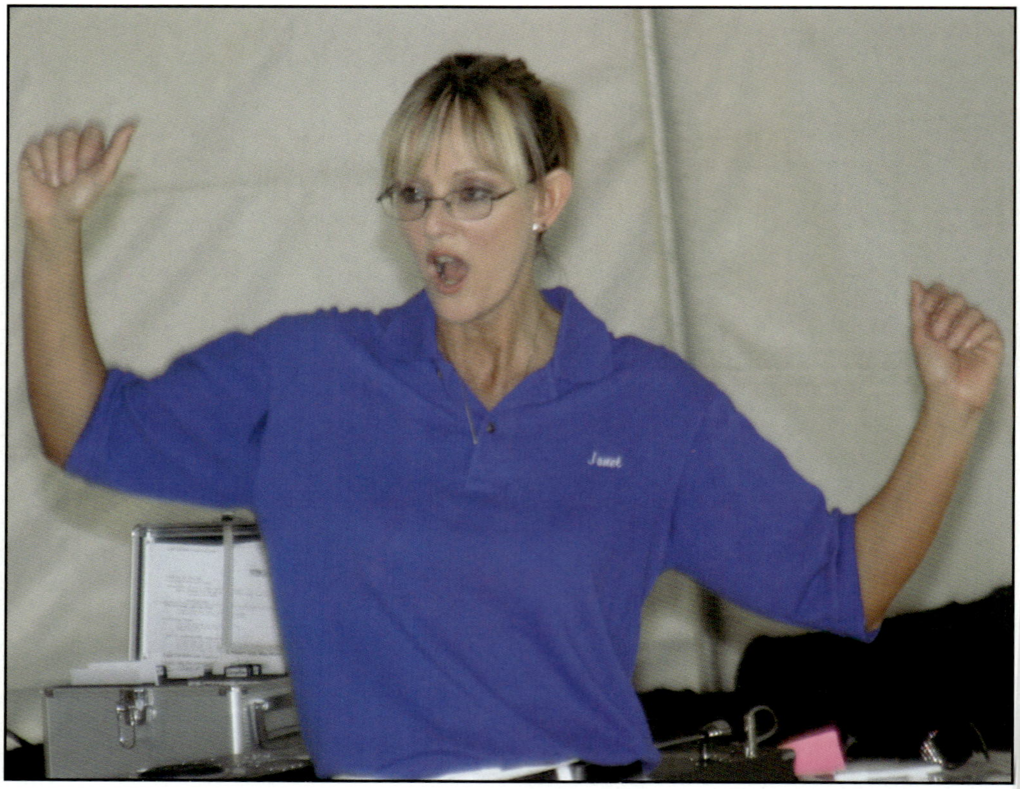

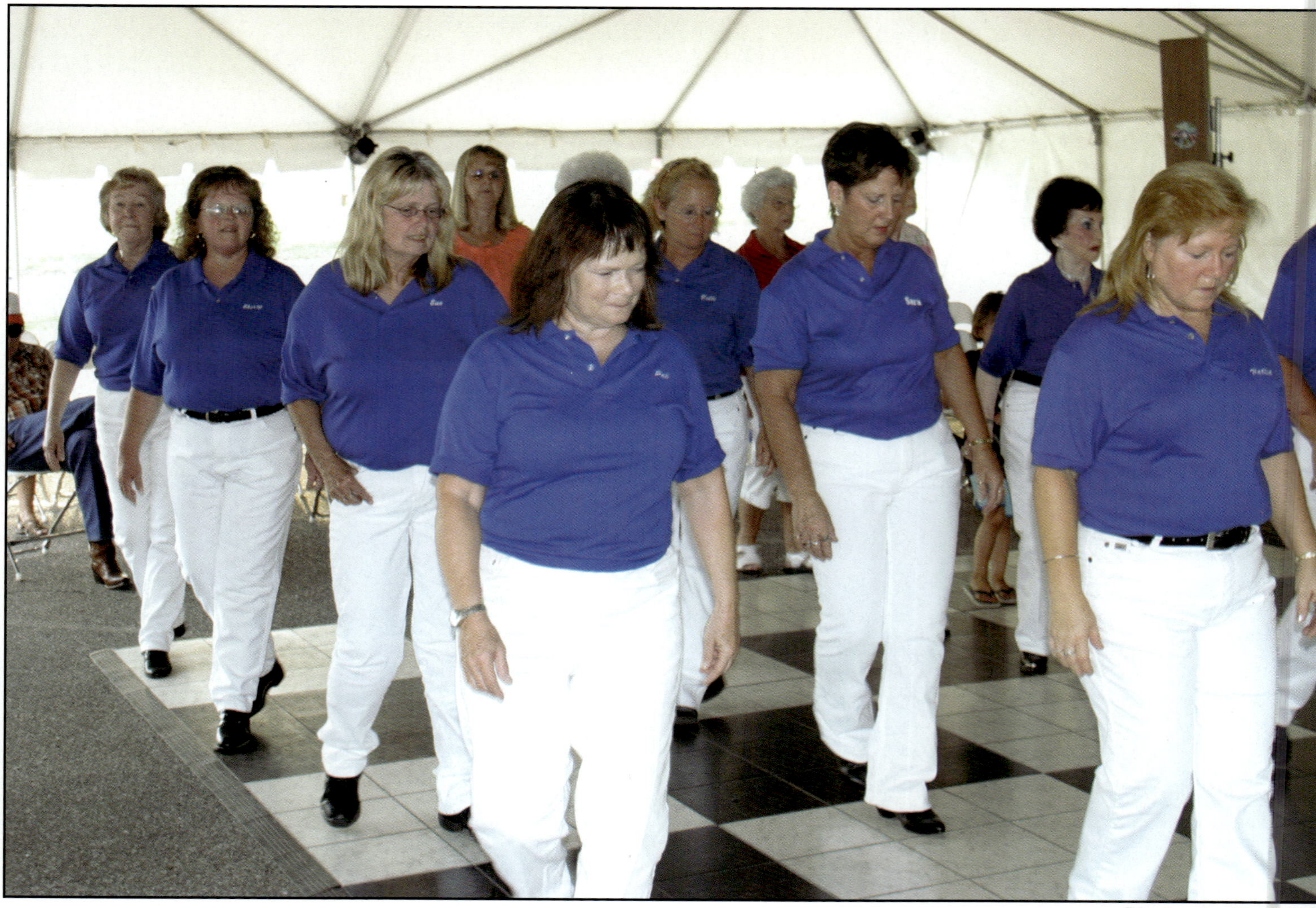

Photos by Don War

At top right, **Boots and Jeans** dancer Janet Furnish spins around on the floor during one of the group's routines. Above, the Boots and Jeans dancers perform at the riverfront on June 8. At top left, group leader June Ritchie calls out the steps during a performance June 11 at the Big Lots parking lot on the Madison hilltop.

Pie-Baking Contest

LEFT: Pie-baking contest coordinator Juanita DeWeese reviews the entries for the contest.
MIDDLE: Janet Faubush checks in her pie.
RIGHT: Roselle Schmabel checks in her pie.
Photos by Kathy Chandler

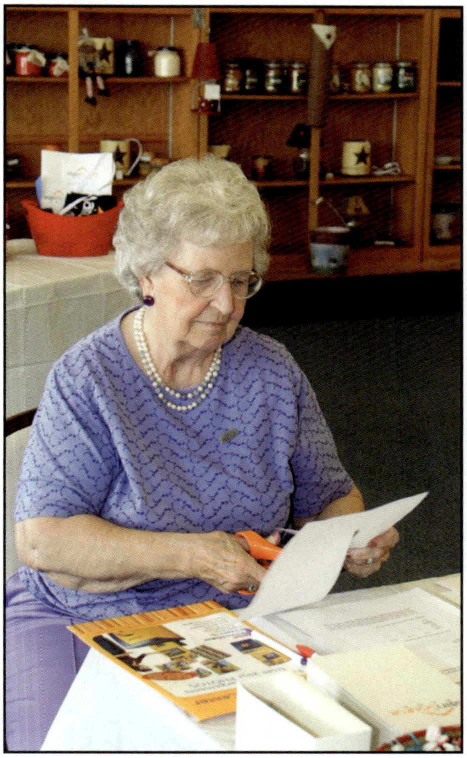

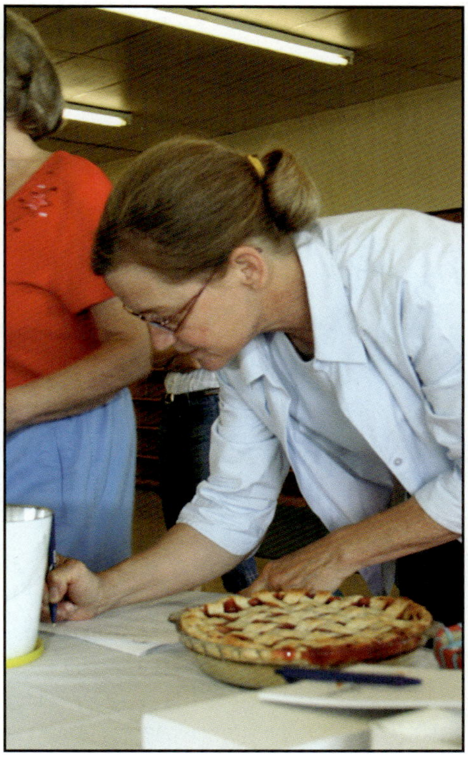

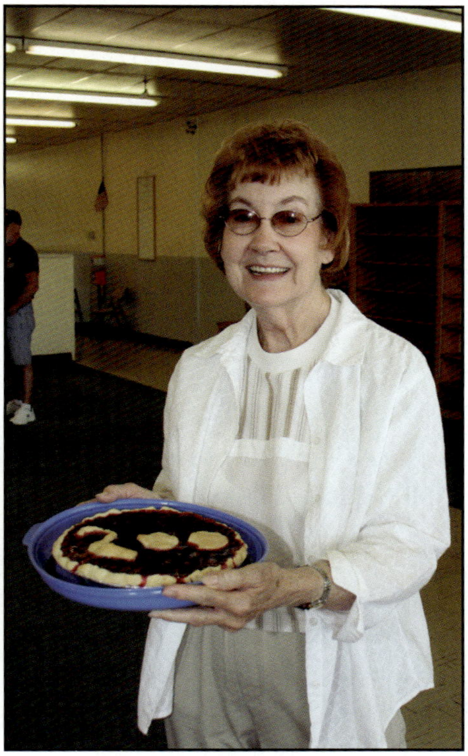

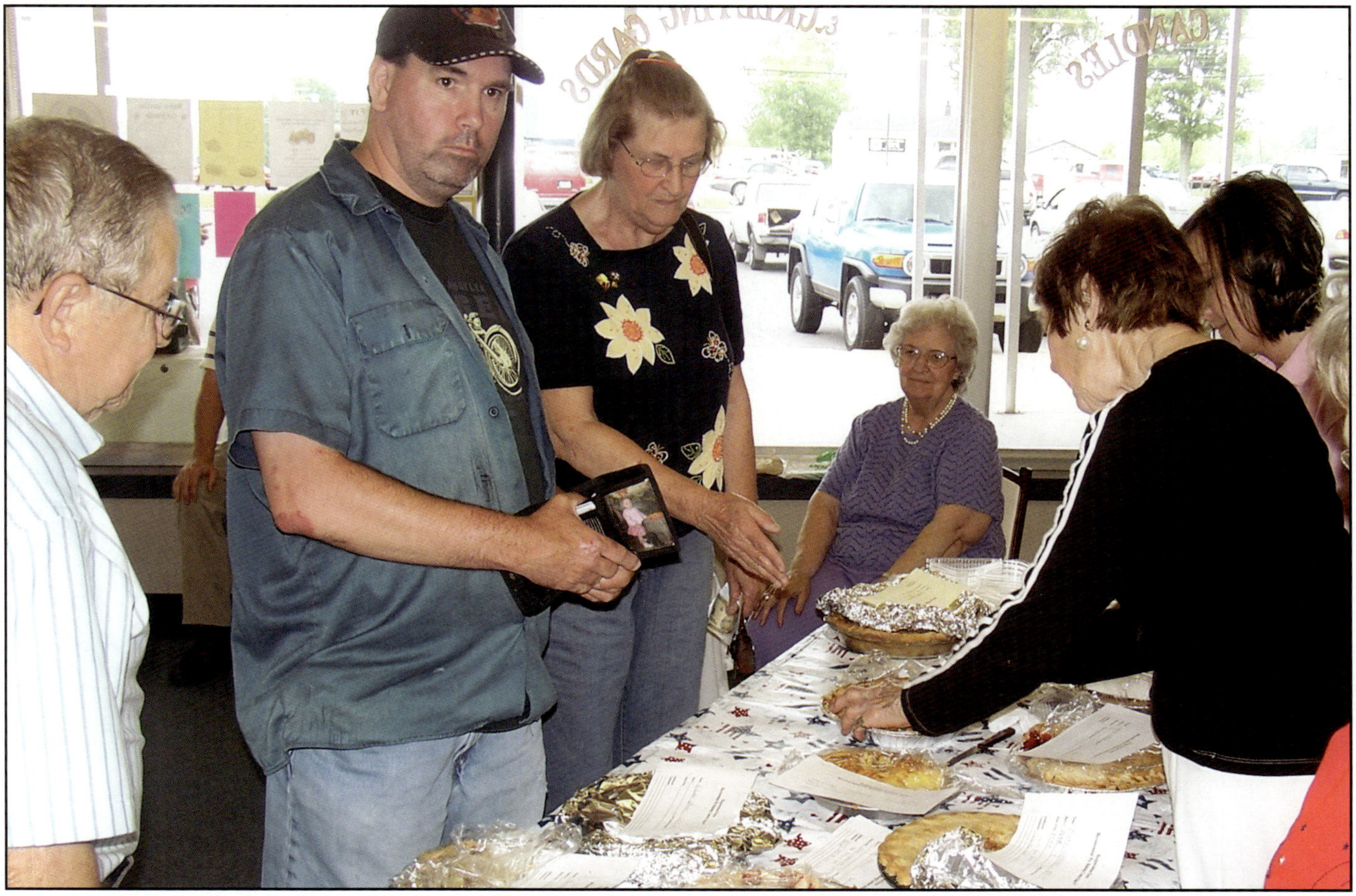

Sara Minor (center) makes a donation for a pie at the pie-baking contest, held June 9 at Mike's Grill. Sitting in back is contest director Juanita DeWeese.

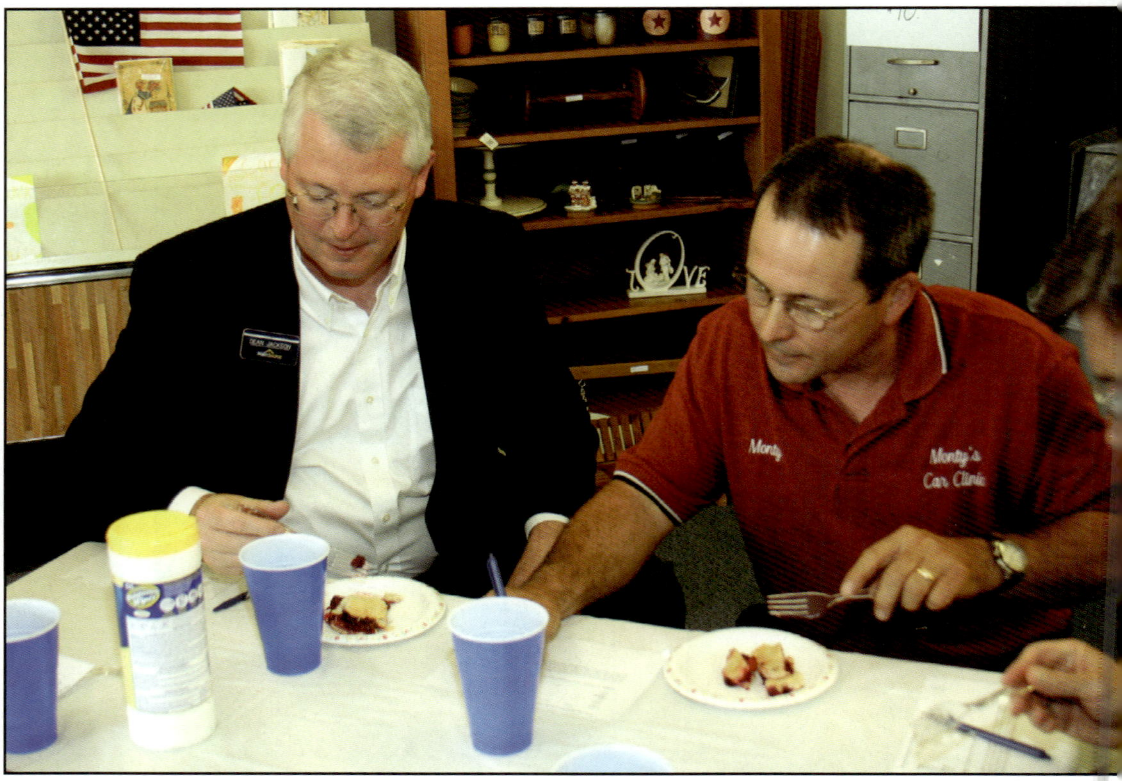

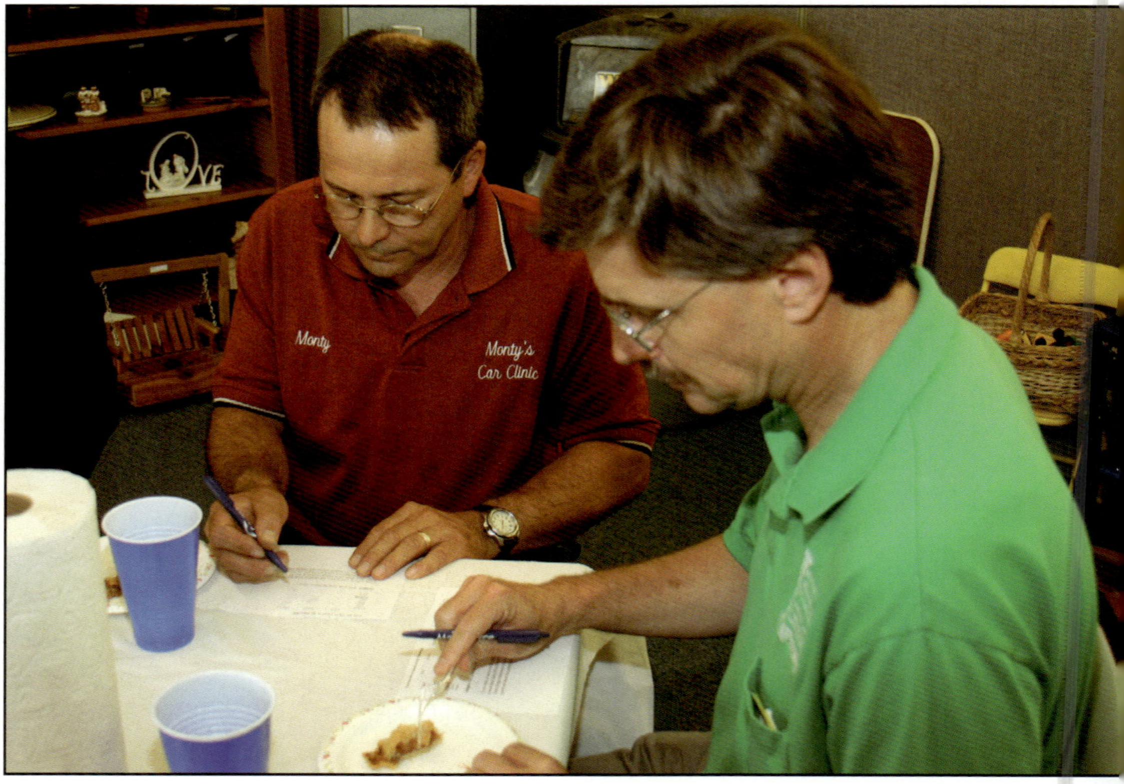

TOP: Pie-baking contest judges (from left) Dean Jackson of MainSource Bank and Monty Geisler of Monty's Car Clinic make their selections. MainSource Bank was a sponsor of this event.

BOTTOM: Monty Geisler and John Staicer of Historic Madison Inc. taste and judge the pies. Dave Stucker also helped judge the contest. In all, 22 pies were submitted. Lisa Forner won with her strawberry pie. The event raised $120 in donations for the Bicentennial.

Photos by Kathy Chandler

Parks Day - Community Picnic

BELOW LEFT: Trumpeters (from left) Dave Butler and Brook Reindollar perform as part of the band, Soundz Like Dixieland, at the Community Picnic, held June 9 at Clifty Falls State Park's Shelter House.

BELOW RIGHT: Members of Soundz Like Dixieland Band are (from left) drummer Jim Polley, clarinetist Jack Martindale and sax player and band leader Charlie Schnabel. **Photos by Laura Hodges**

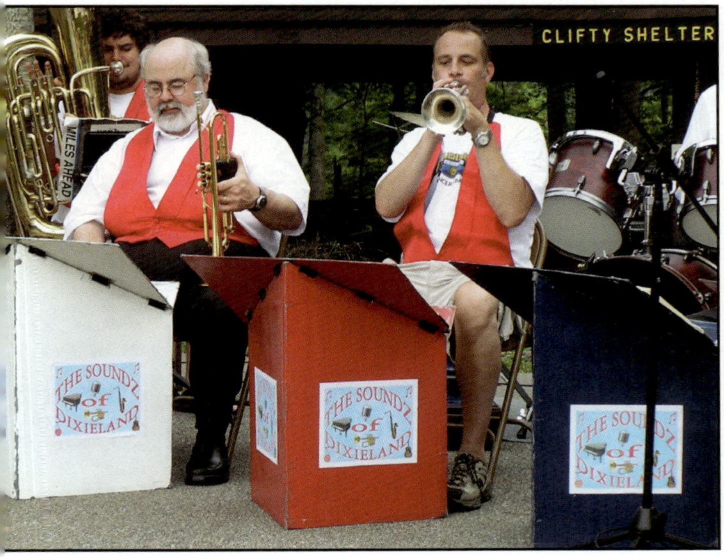

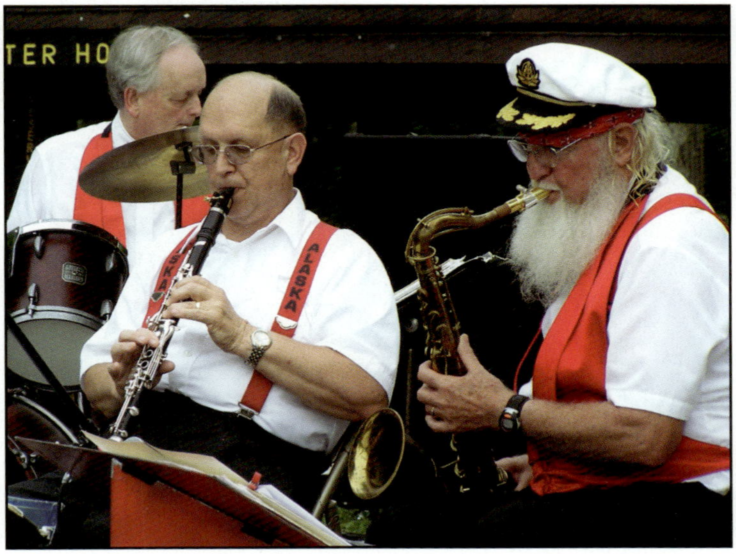

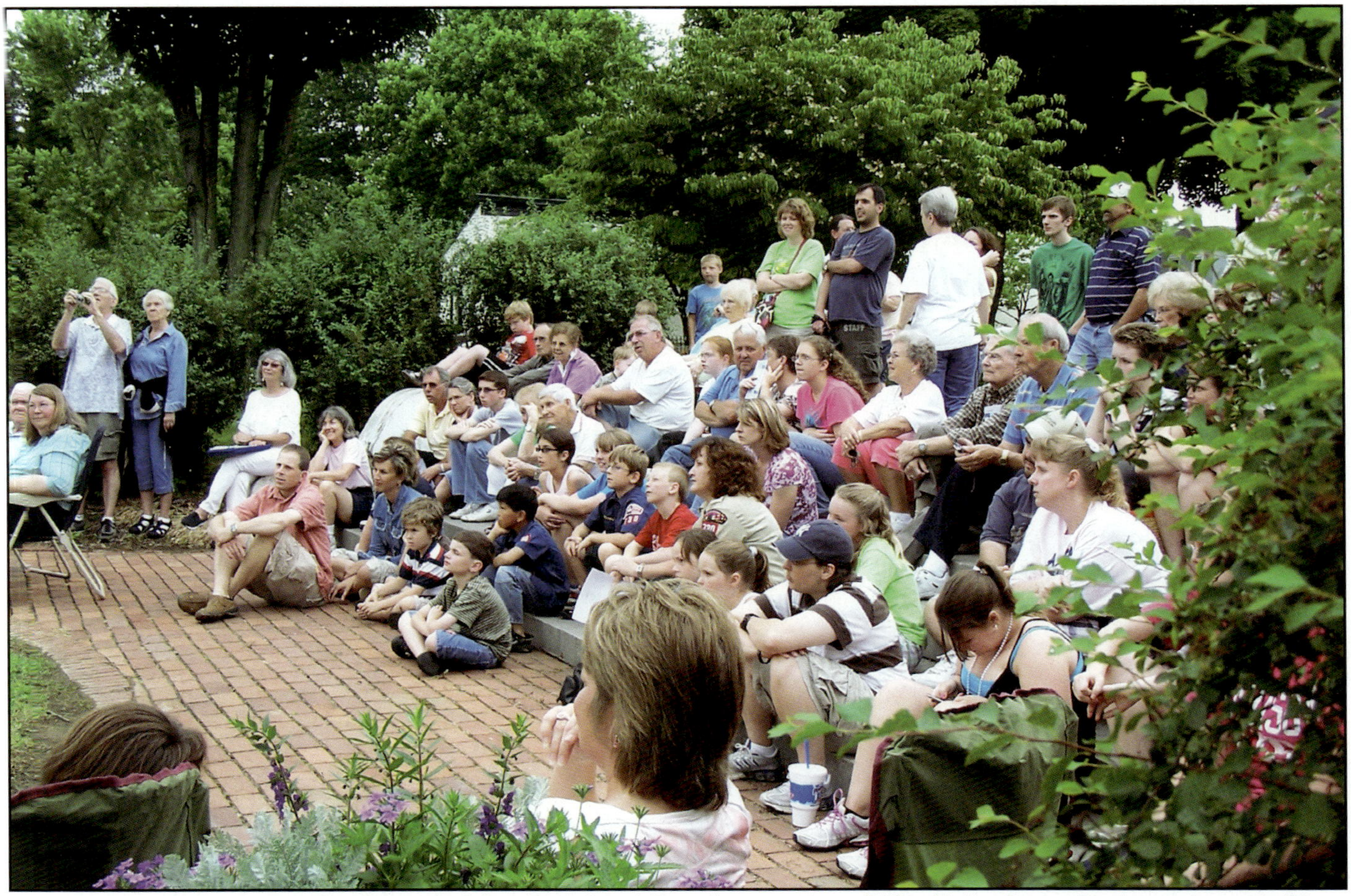

A large crowd listens to the Soundz Like Dixieland Band concert at Clifty Falls State Park on June 9. The Bicentennial Band also performed that evening.

Old-Fashioned Ice Cream Social

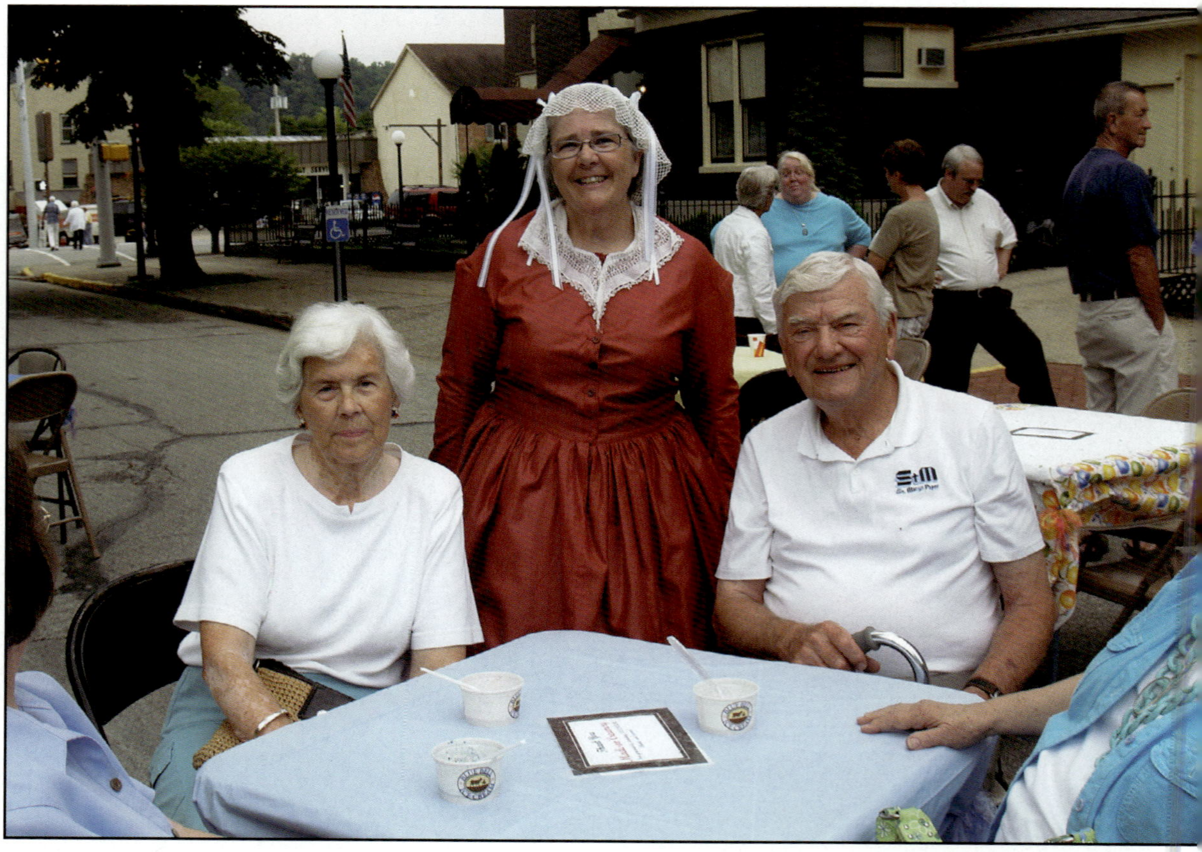

RIGHT: Madison Bicentennial re-enactor Stephanie Hellmann portrays Underground Railroad character Delia Webster as she visits with Fred and Mary Lou Hill during the Trinity United Methodist Church Old-Fashioned Ice Cream Social on June 10.

In the two photos below, visitors enjoy delicious homemade ice cream around the Broadway Fountain.

Photos below by Stephanie Hellmann

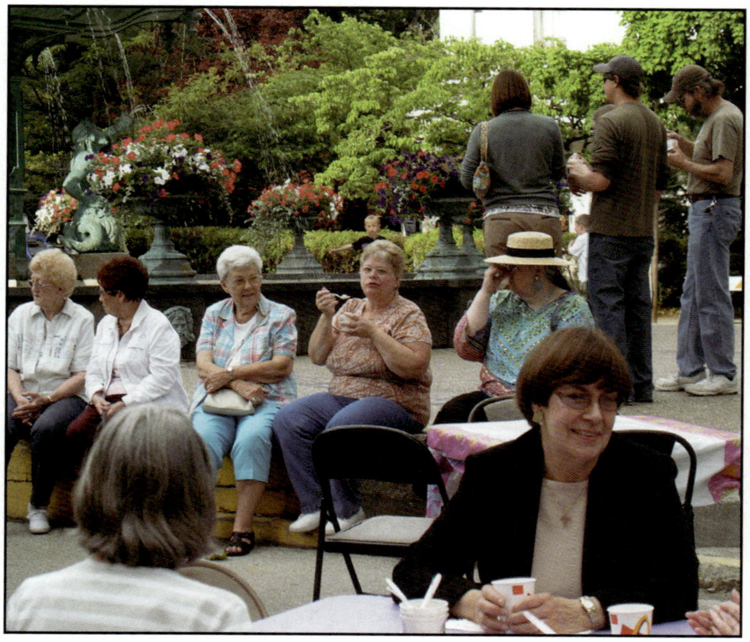

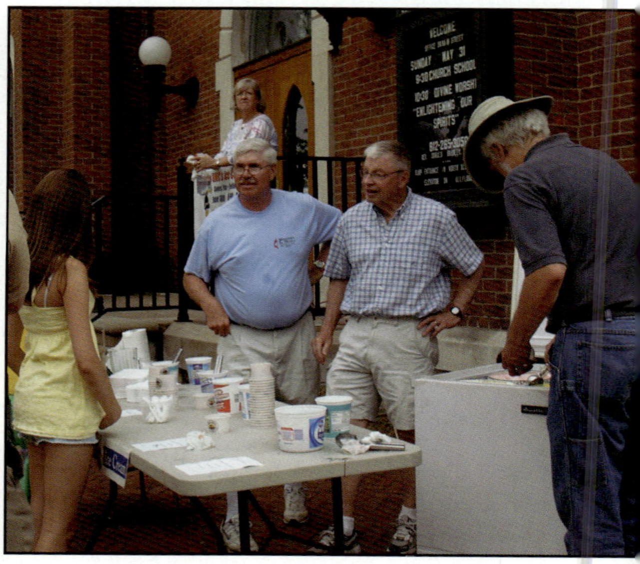

The Lincolns at Lanier

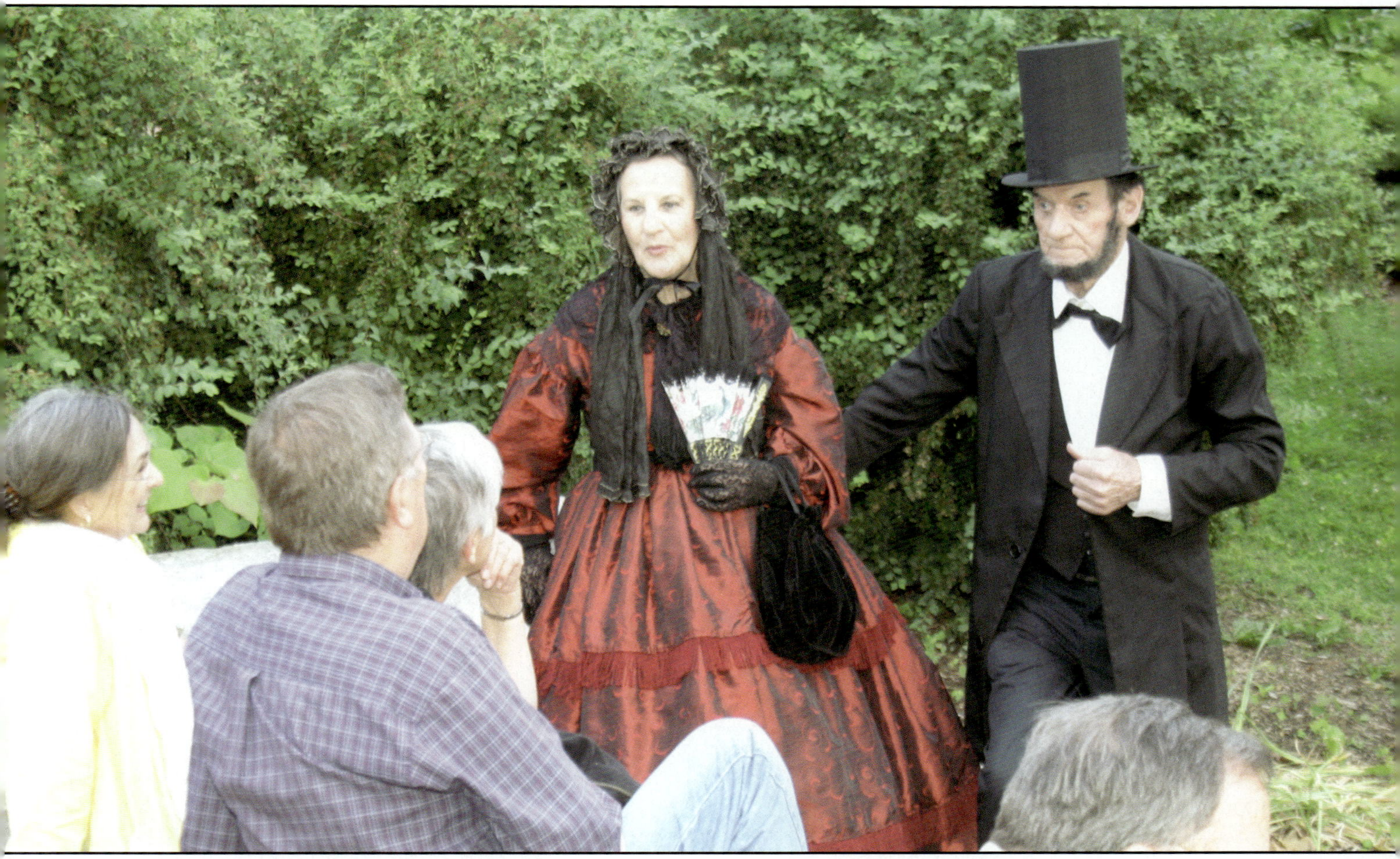

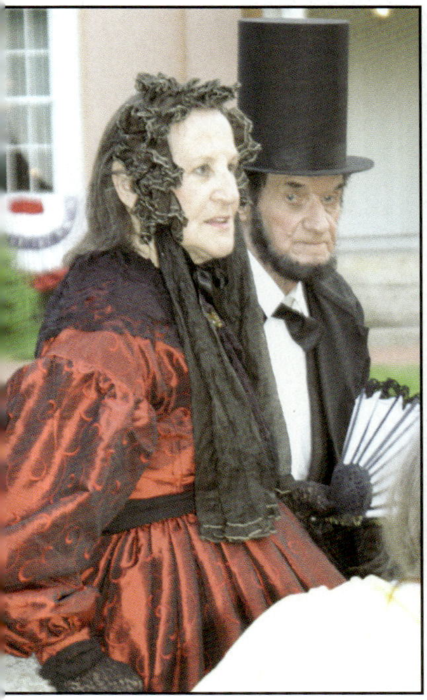

Top and above photos by Don Ward

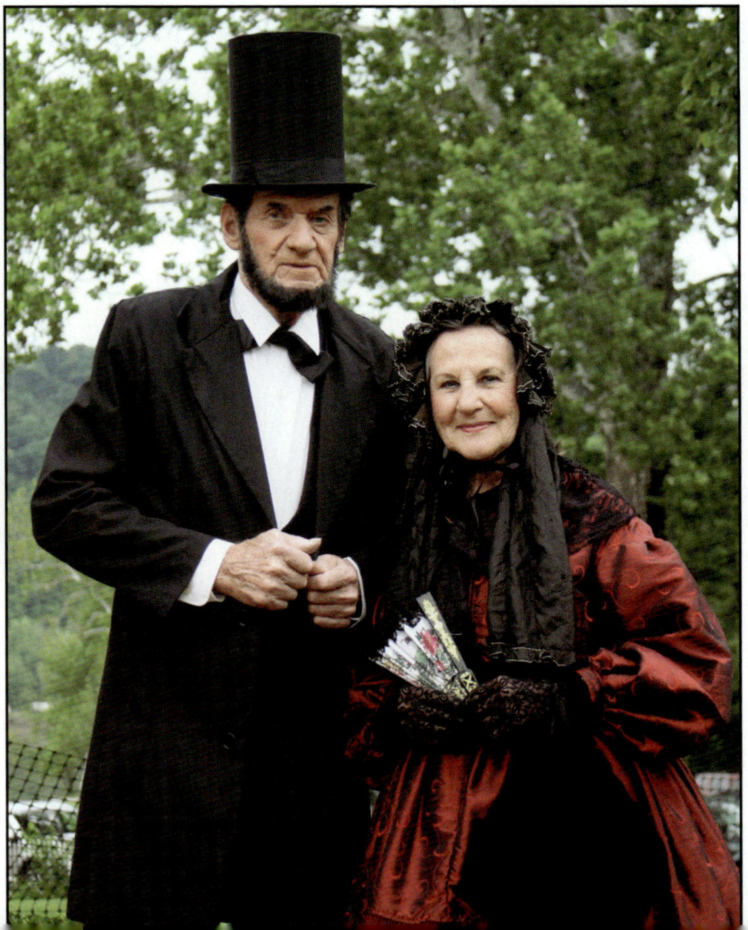

Bill and Stasia Wiseman of Vevay, Ind., play President Abraham and Mary Todd Lincoln during Historic Sites Day, June 10, at the Lanier Mansion State Historic Site. They held a program on the Lincolns for an audience on the lawn. The couple has played the Lincolns at events and Lincoln-related historic sites throughout the country.

Left photo by Kathy Chandler

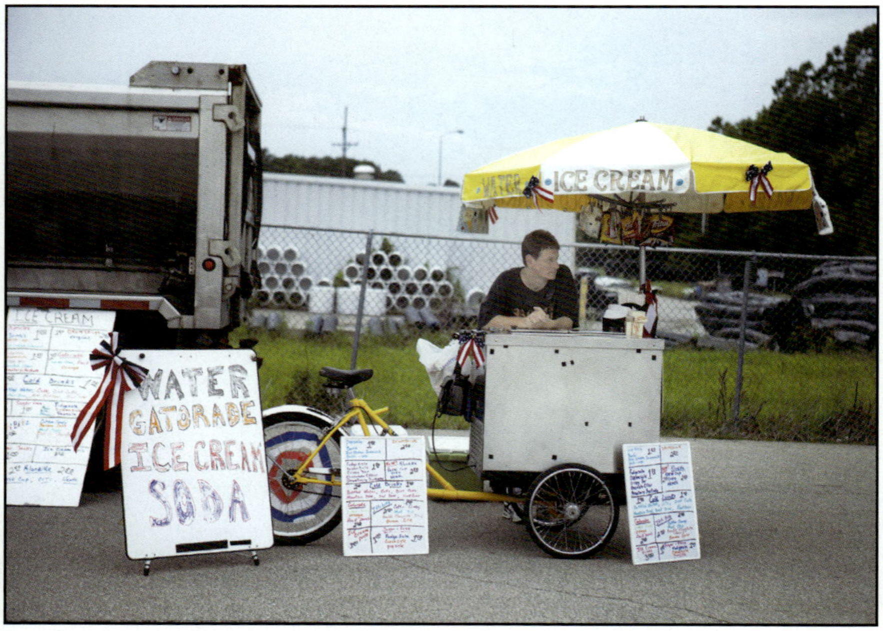

ABOVE: Steve Taylor sells hot dogs, drinks and ice cream treats June 11 during the "Music on the Hilltop" event.

RIGHT: Chip Binzer and son, Aiden, watch the concert, which took place in the parking lot in front of Traderbaker's.

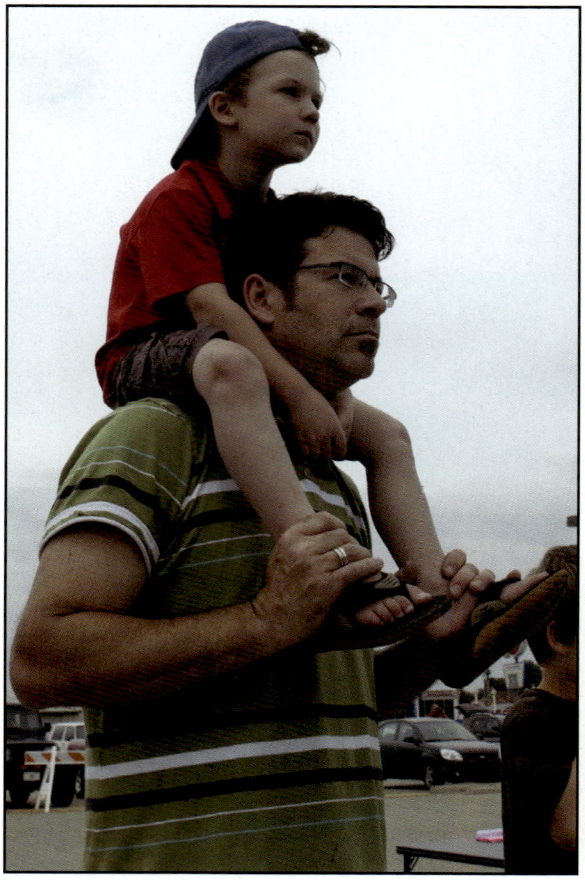

Photos by John Palmer Gregg

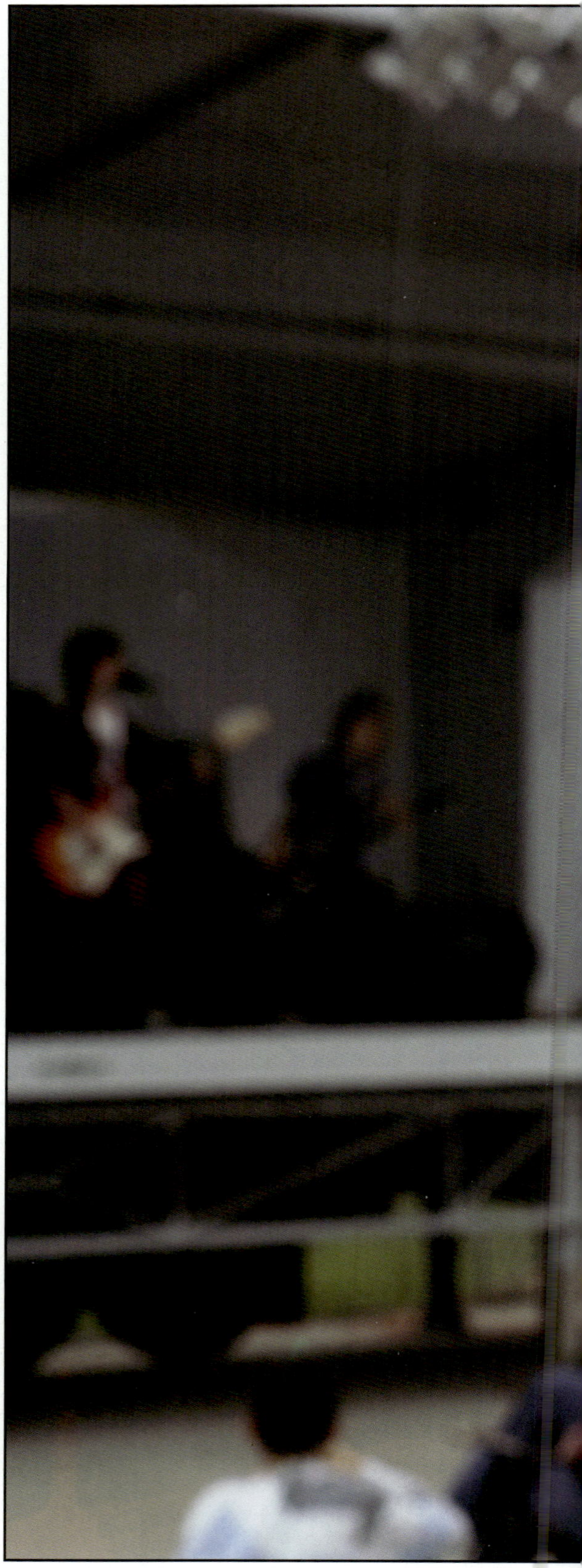

Teen Band Music on the Hilltop

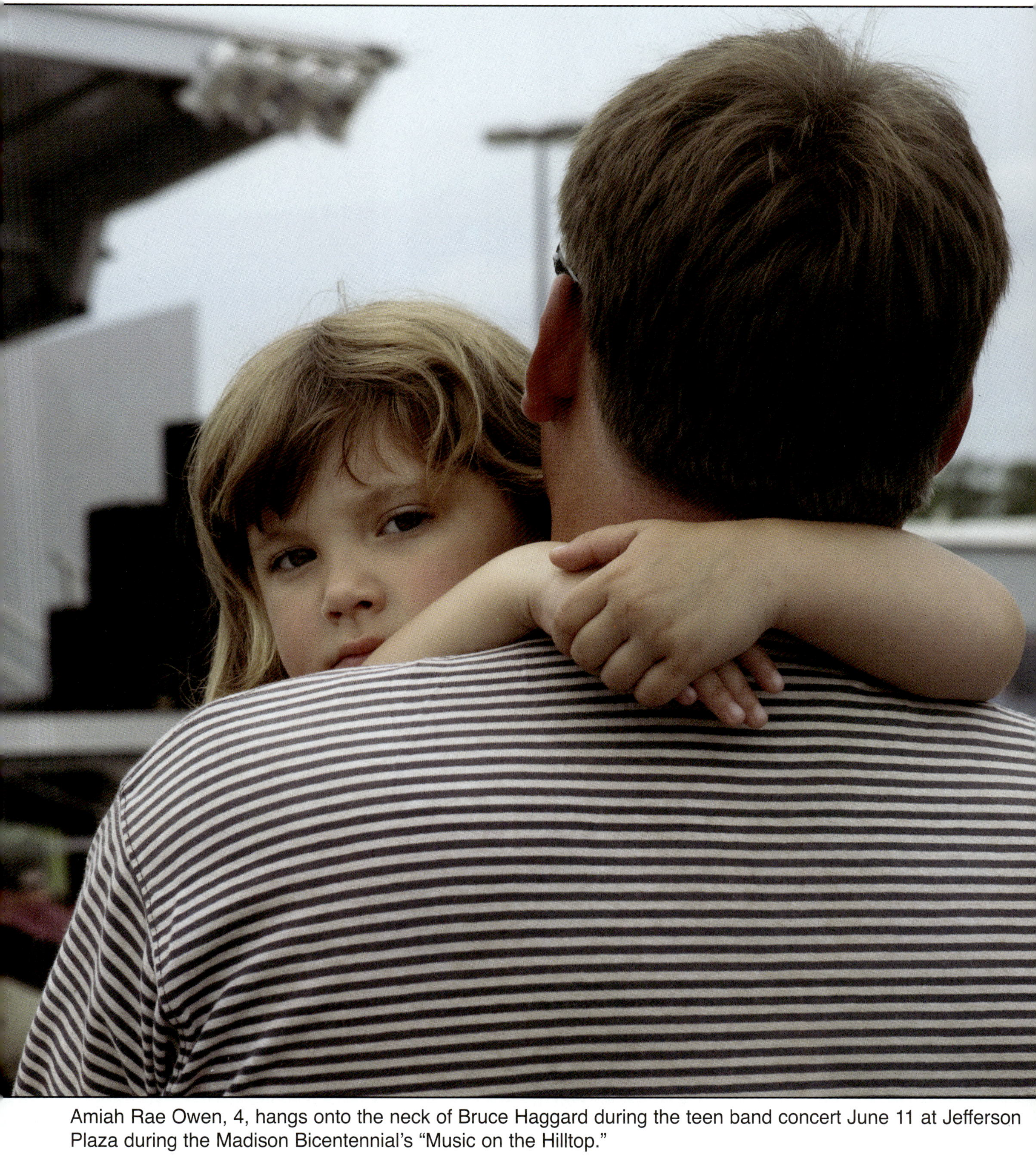

Amiah Rae Owen, 4, hangs onto the neck of Bruce Haggard during the teen band concert June 11 at Jefferson Plaza during the Madison Bicentennial's "Music on the Hilltop."

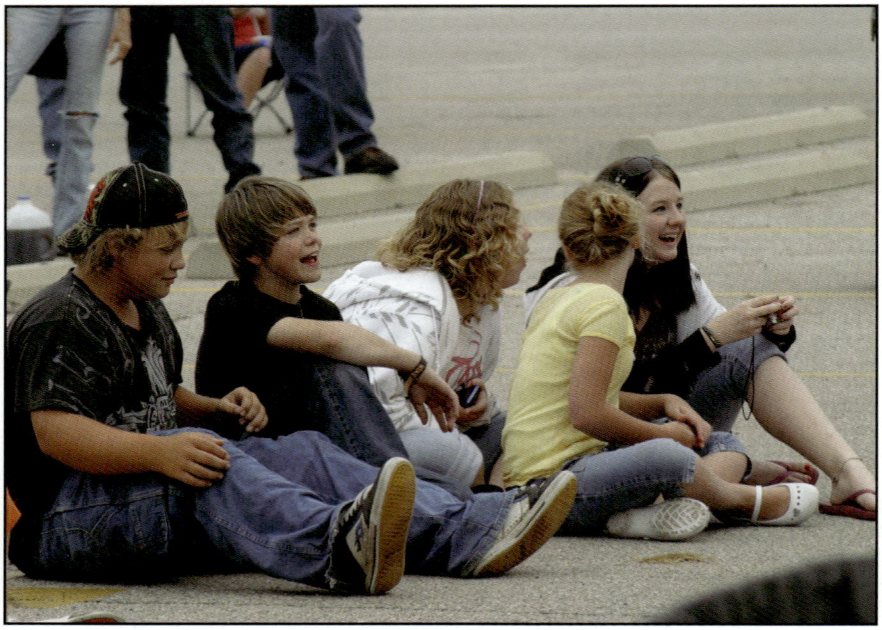

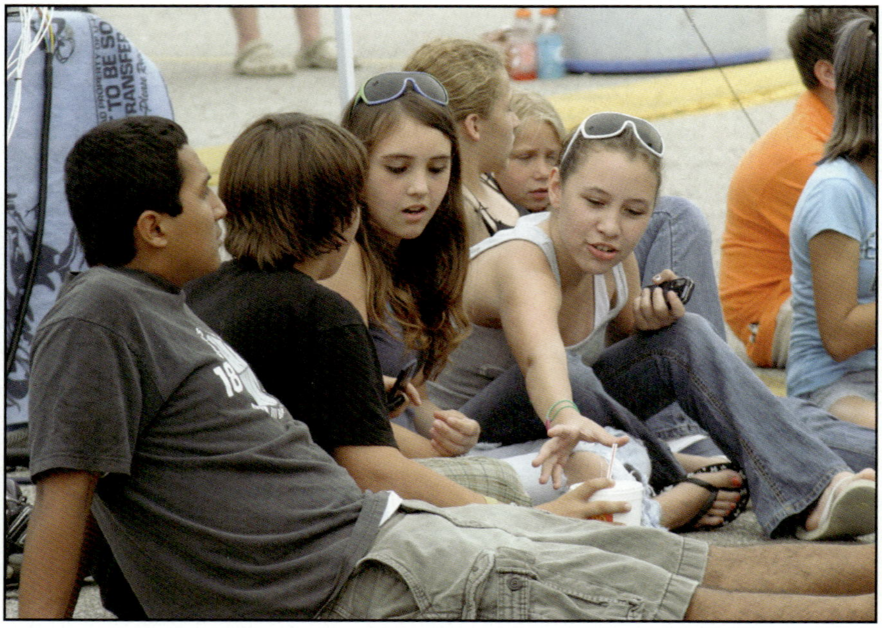

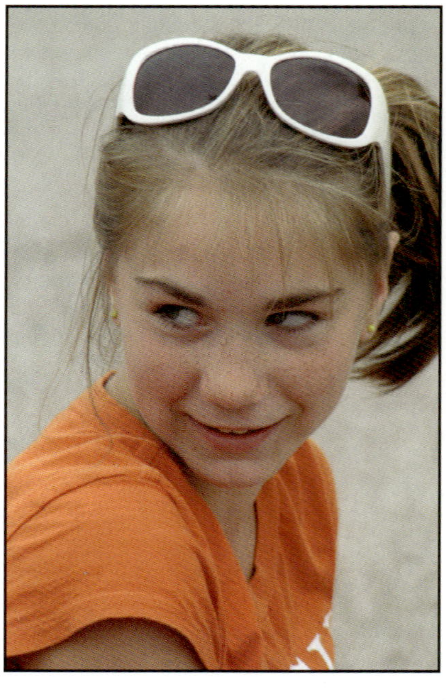

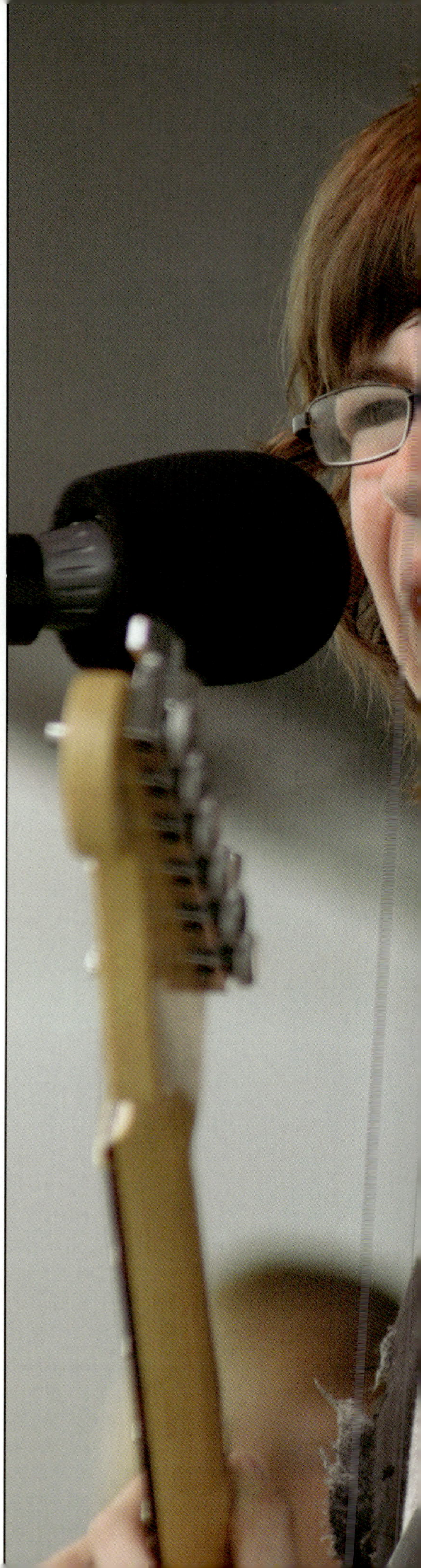

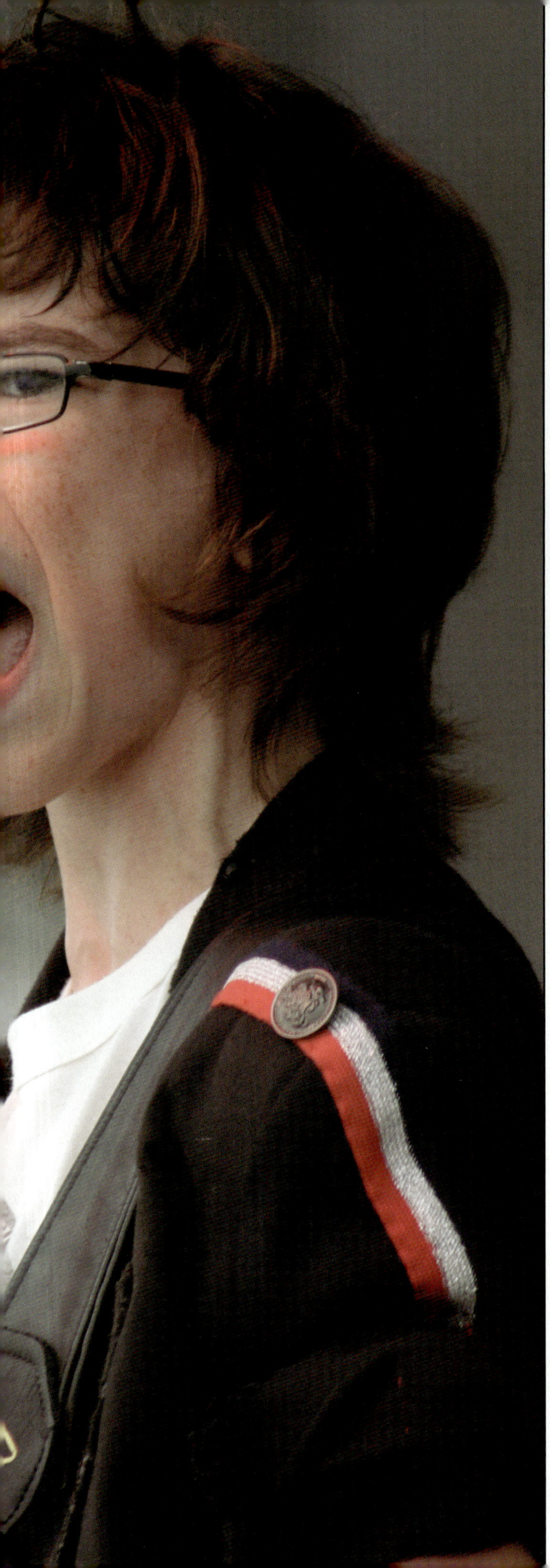

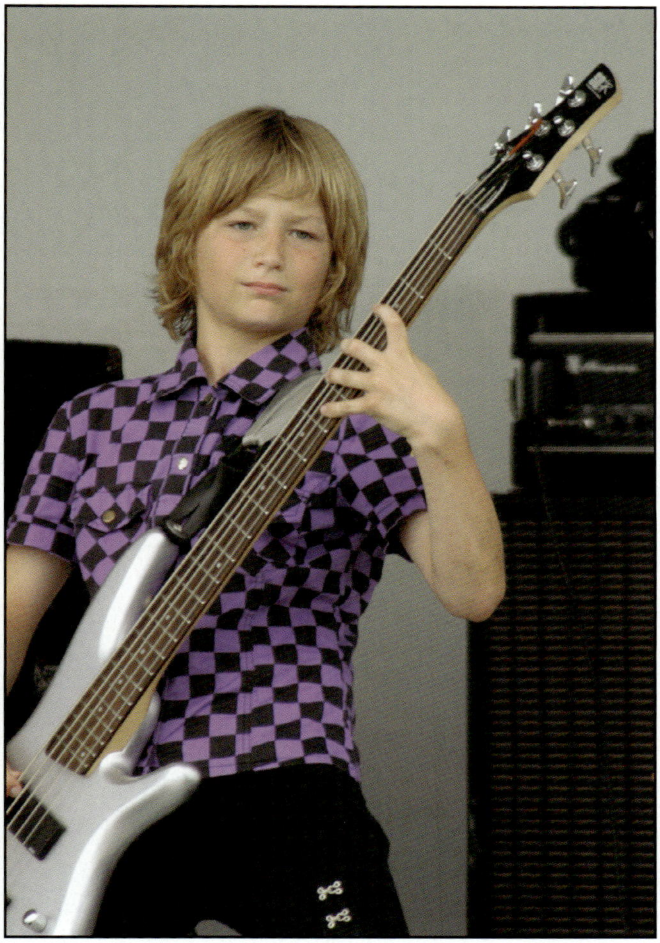

ABOVE: Eleven-year-old singer-guitarist Matt Marsh of Madison performs with the band, The Trouble With Boys, during the "Music on the Hilltop" concert June 11 at Jefferson Plaza.

LEFT: The Trouble With Boys' lead singer Conner Brough of Sellersburg, Ind., performs oldies rock-n-roll songs for the audience of adults and teens.

TOP AND MIDDLE LEFT: Teenagers listen to the music played by the teen bands.

BOTTOM LEFT: Skyla Judkins joins her friends in listening to the music at the teen concert.

Photos by Don Ward

River Valley Financial Bank Customer Appreciation Cookout

RIGHT: River Valley Financial Bank employees prepare free meals for customers during their Customer Appreciation Cookout, held Friday, June 12, at the main branch on the Madison Hilltop.

BELOW: Andrew Forrester (left), son of bank President and CEO Matt Forrester, and bank Board Chairman Fred Koehler man the hamburger grills.

Photos by Laura Hodges

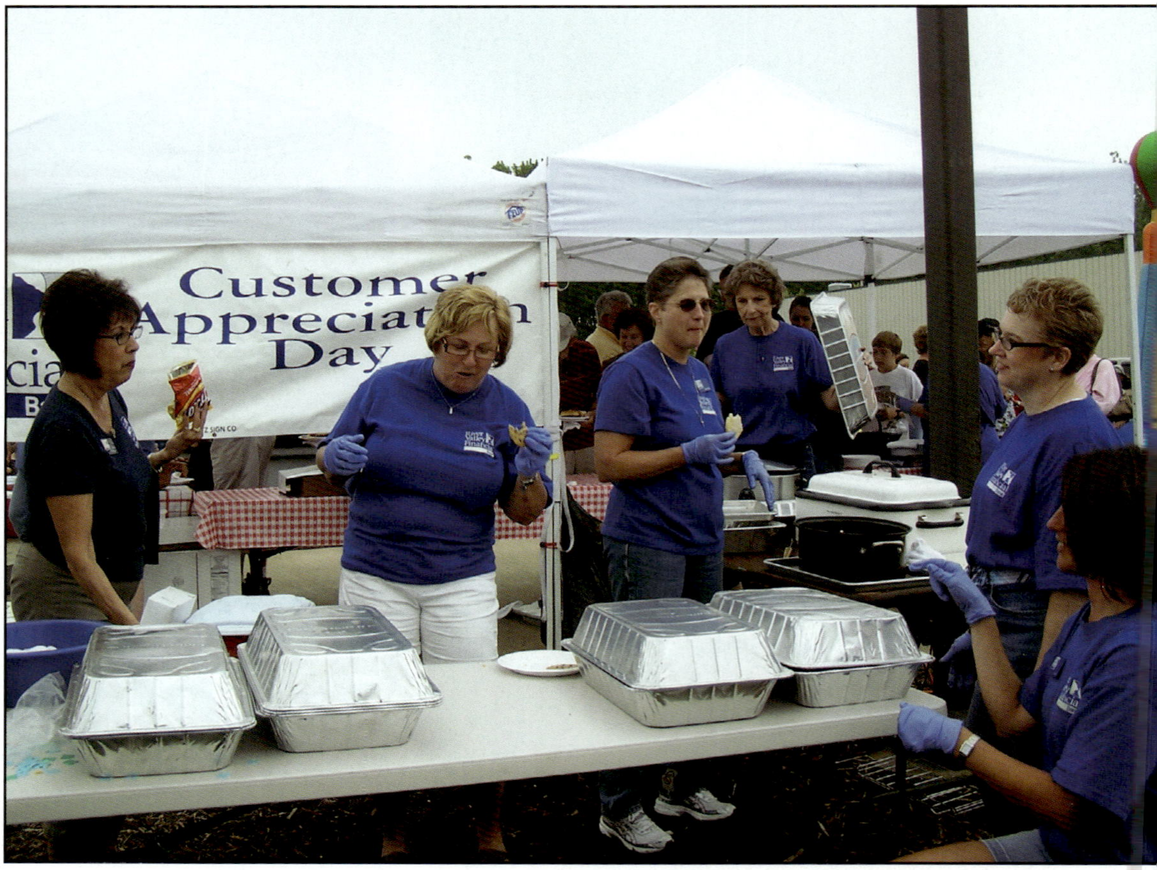

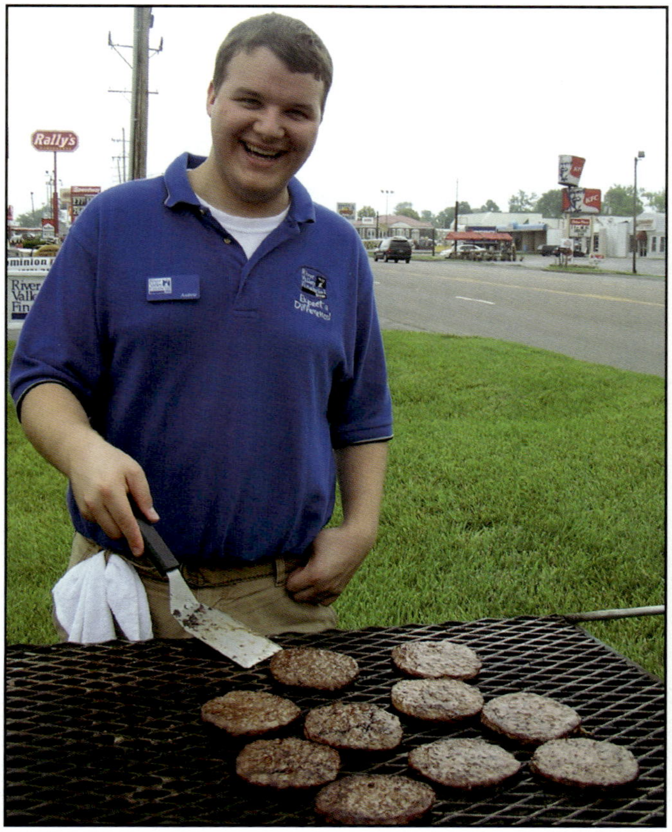

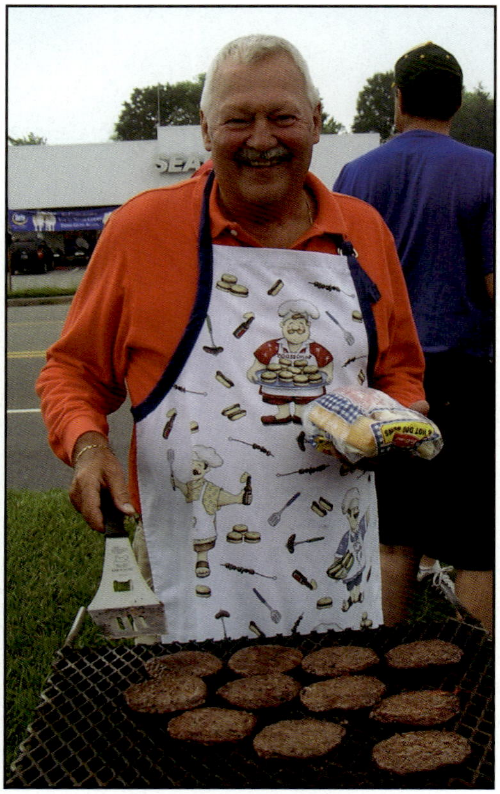

1920s-1930s Car Show at Clifty Falls State Park

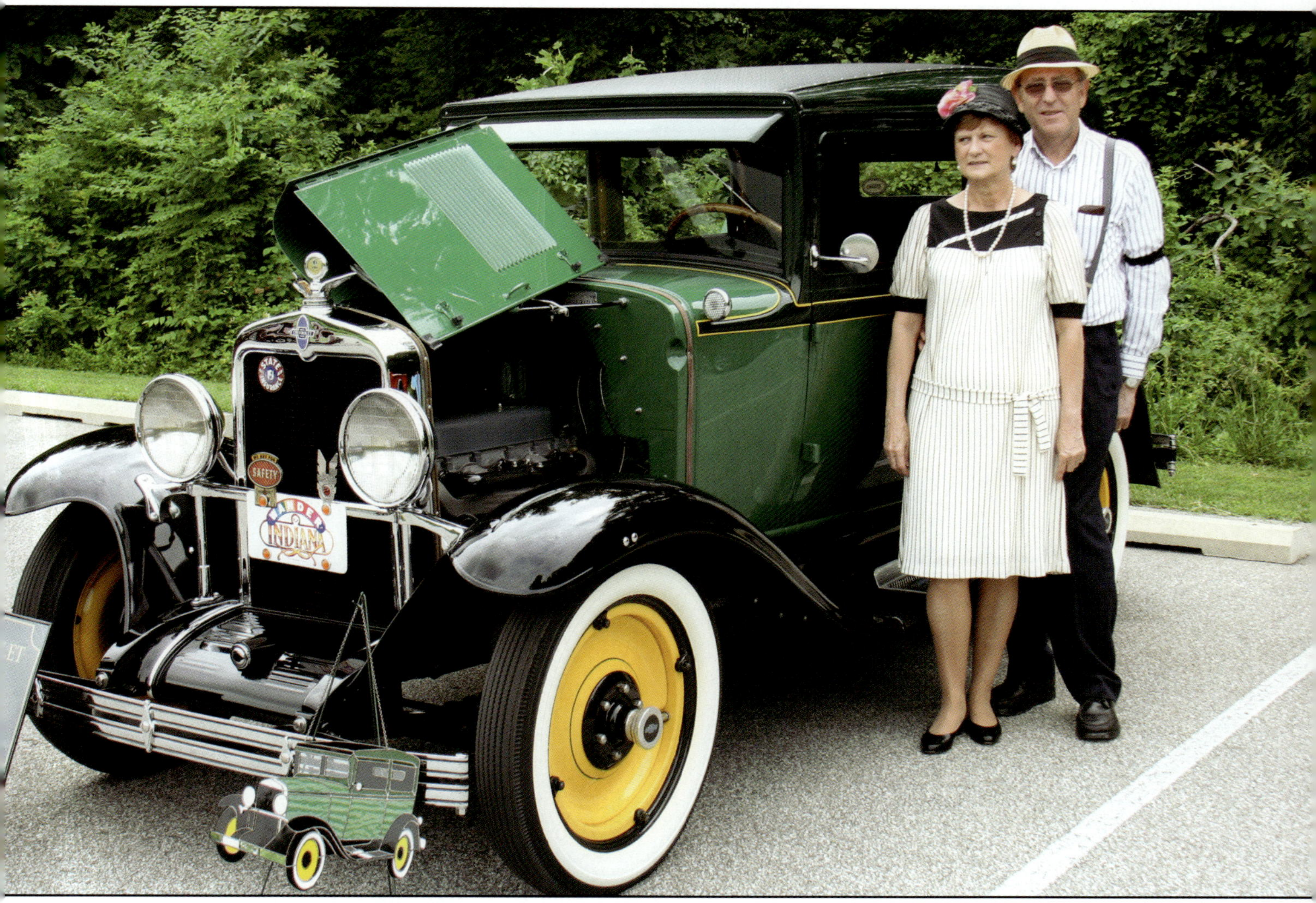

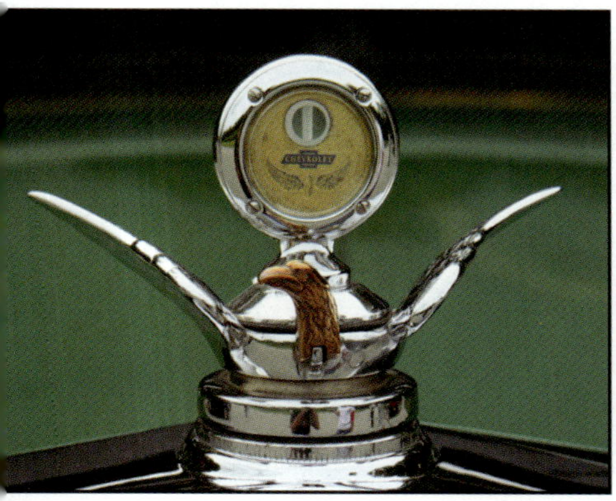

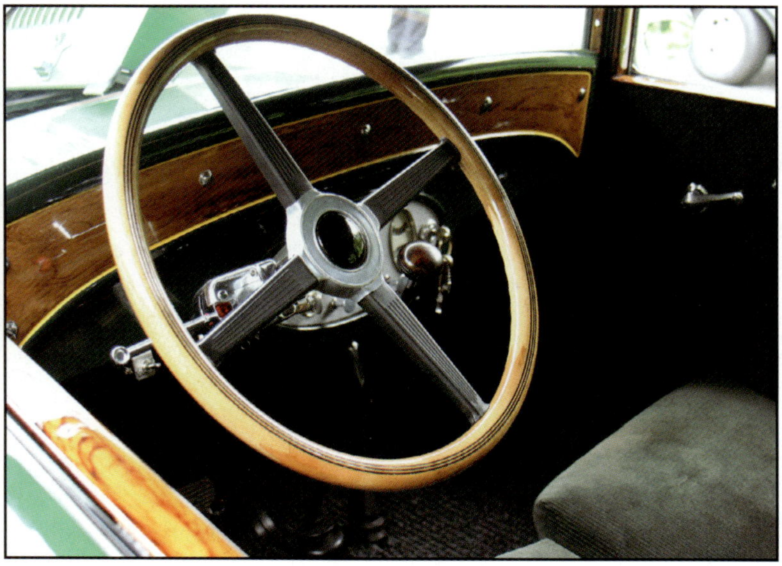

Betty and Lewis Stoner of Charlestown, Ind., dress the part as they display their 1929 Chevrolet.
Photos by Kathy Chandler

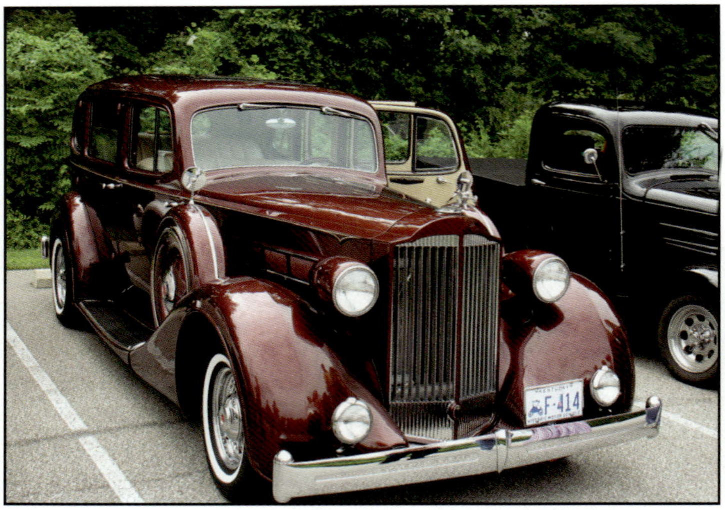

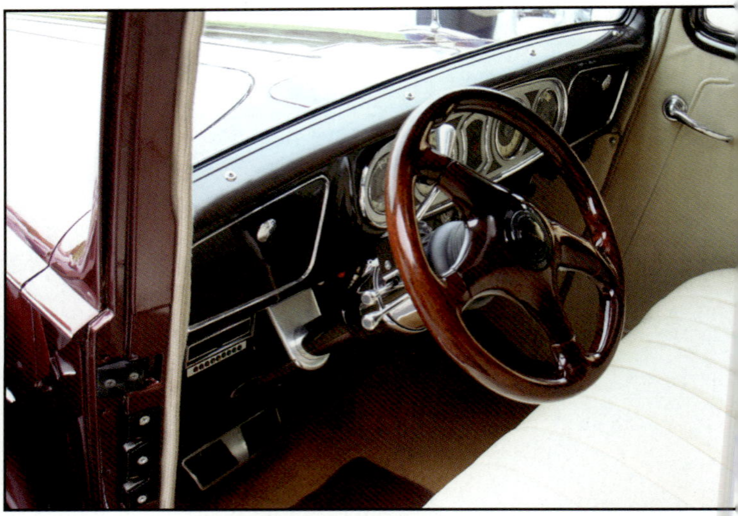

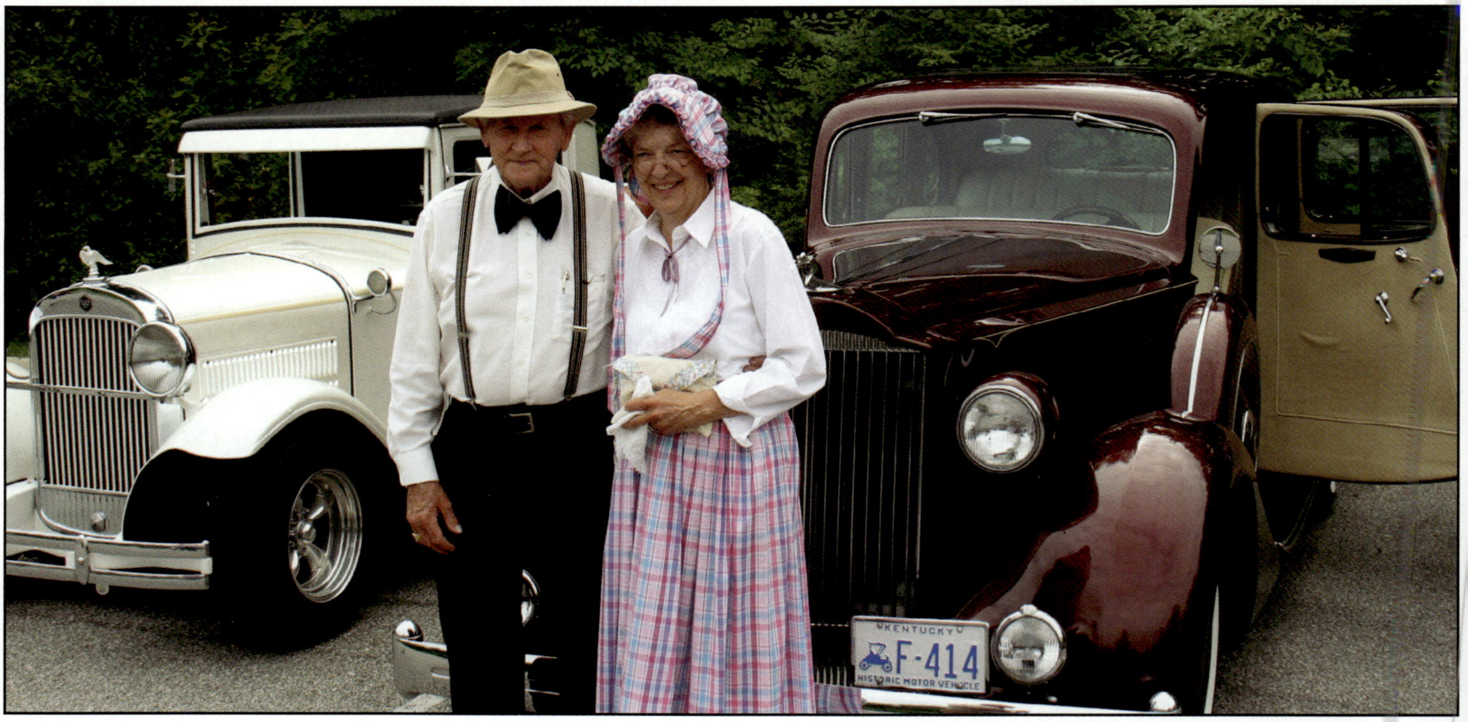

Howard and Elaine Long of Milton, Ky., display their classic cars, a 1935 Packard (top left) and a 1929 Essex Coupe.

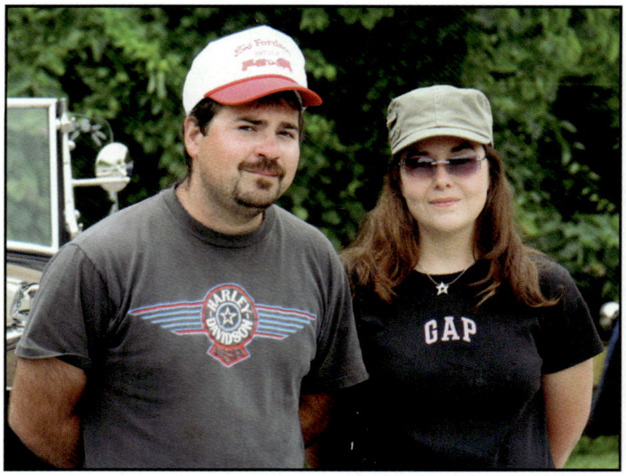

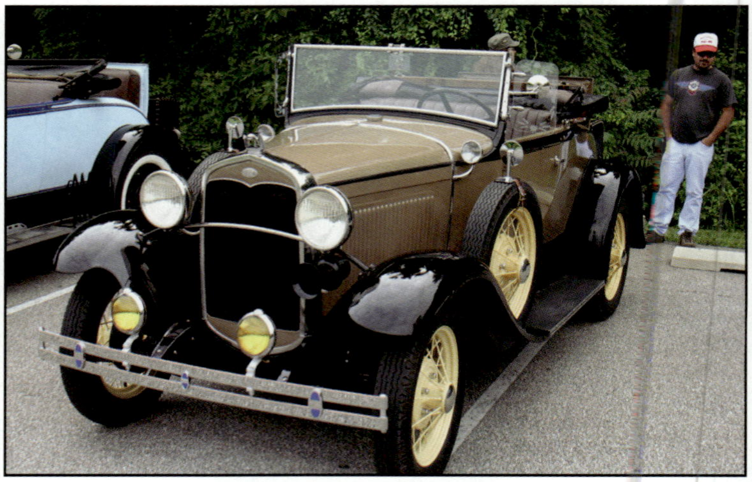

Chris and Janice Rider (left) of Uniontown, Ind., display their 1931 Model A Ford Roadster (above) at the car show.

Photos by Kathy Chandler

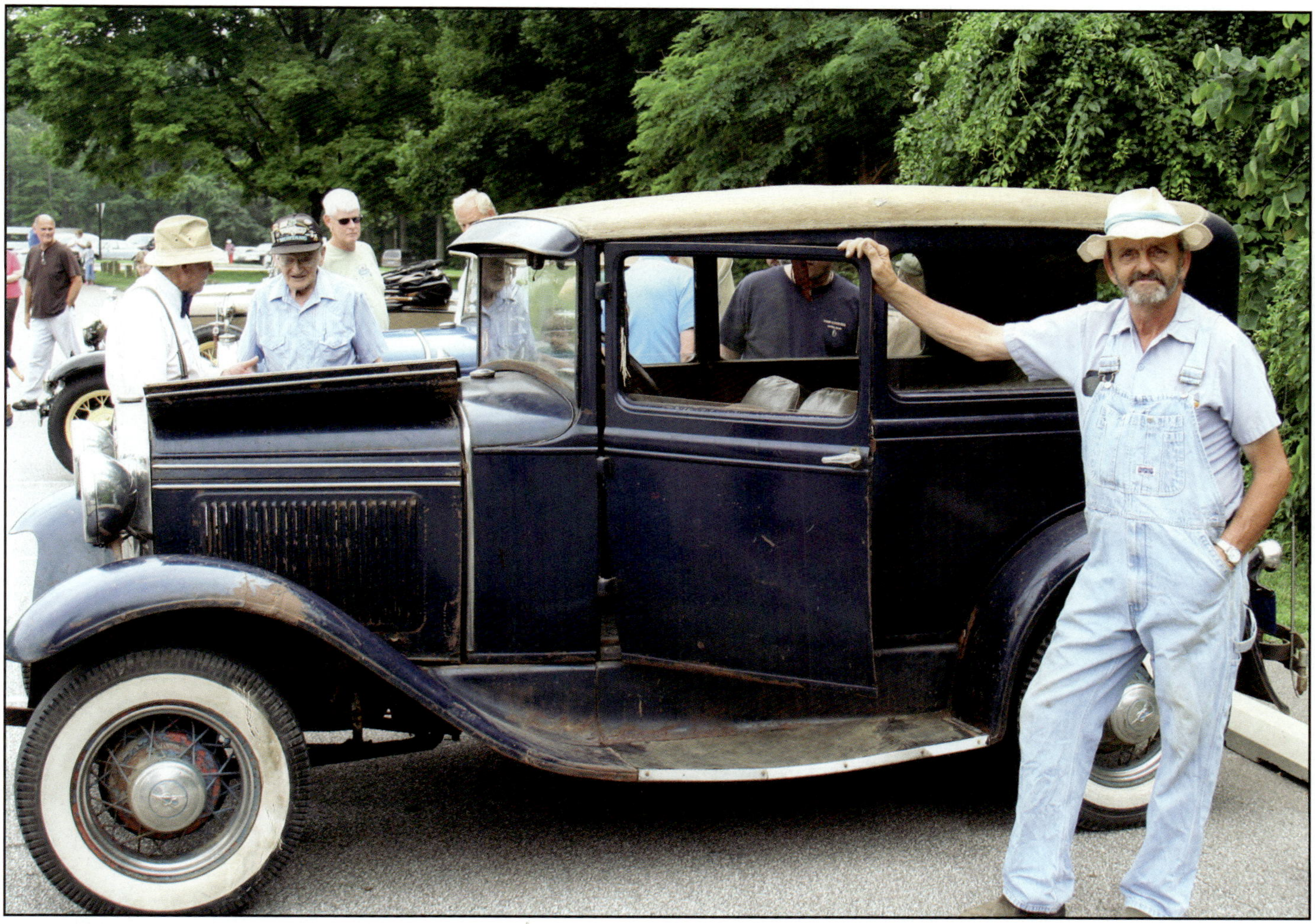

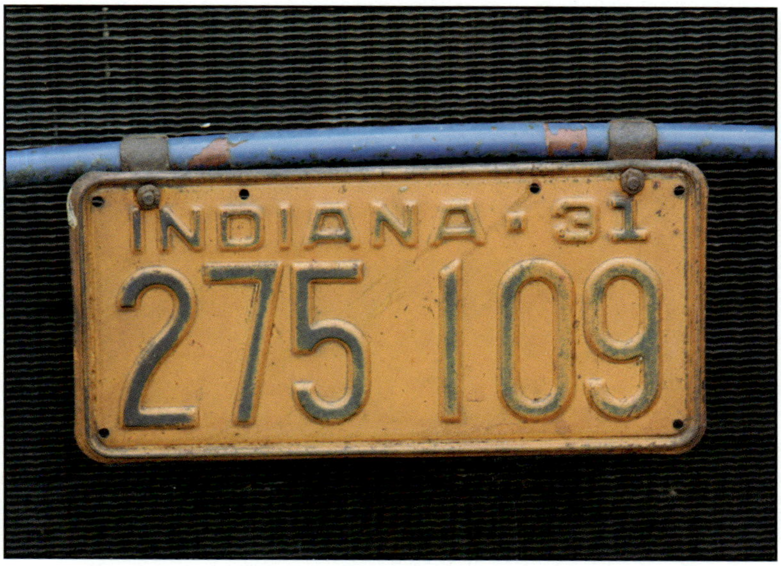

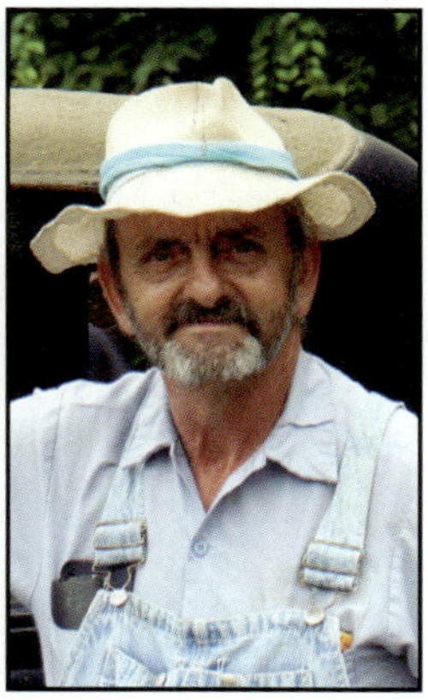

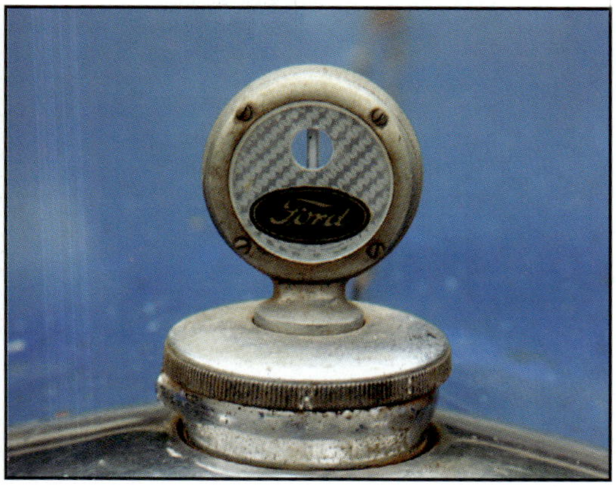

Bob Schafer of Madison displays his 1930 Model A Ford at the 1920s-1930s Car Show at Clifty Falls State Park on June 12.

Photos by Kathy Chandler

The 1920s-1930s Car Show offered spectato
an array of color as they browsed among th
vintage vehicles of yesteryea

Photos by Kathy Chandl

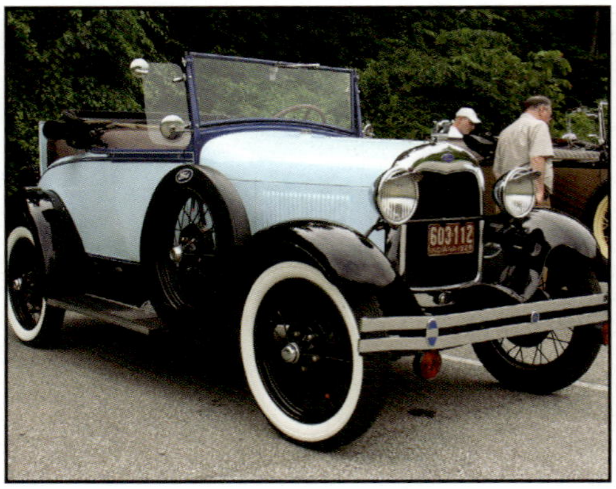

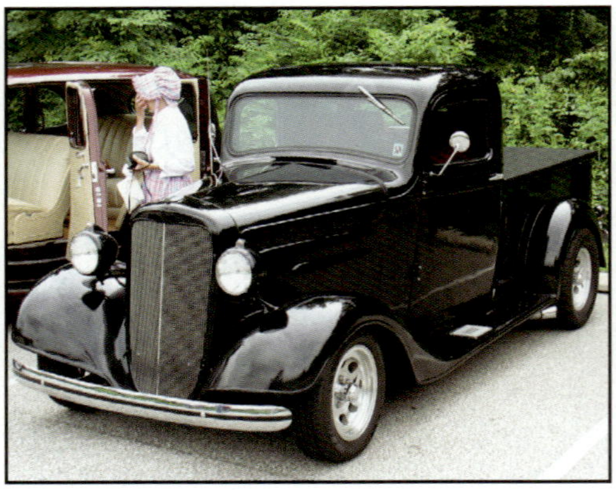

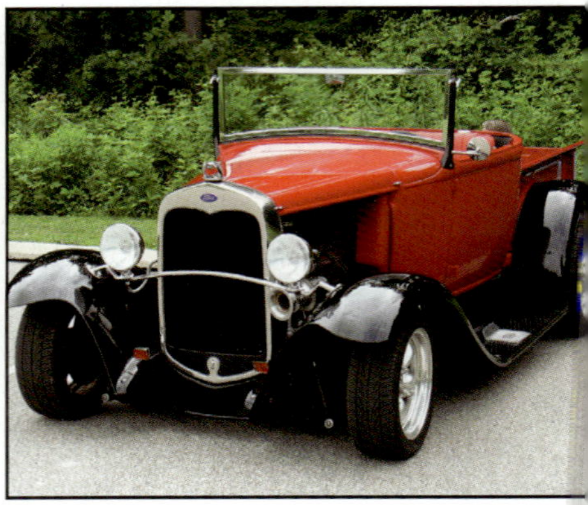

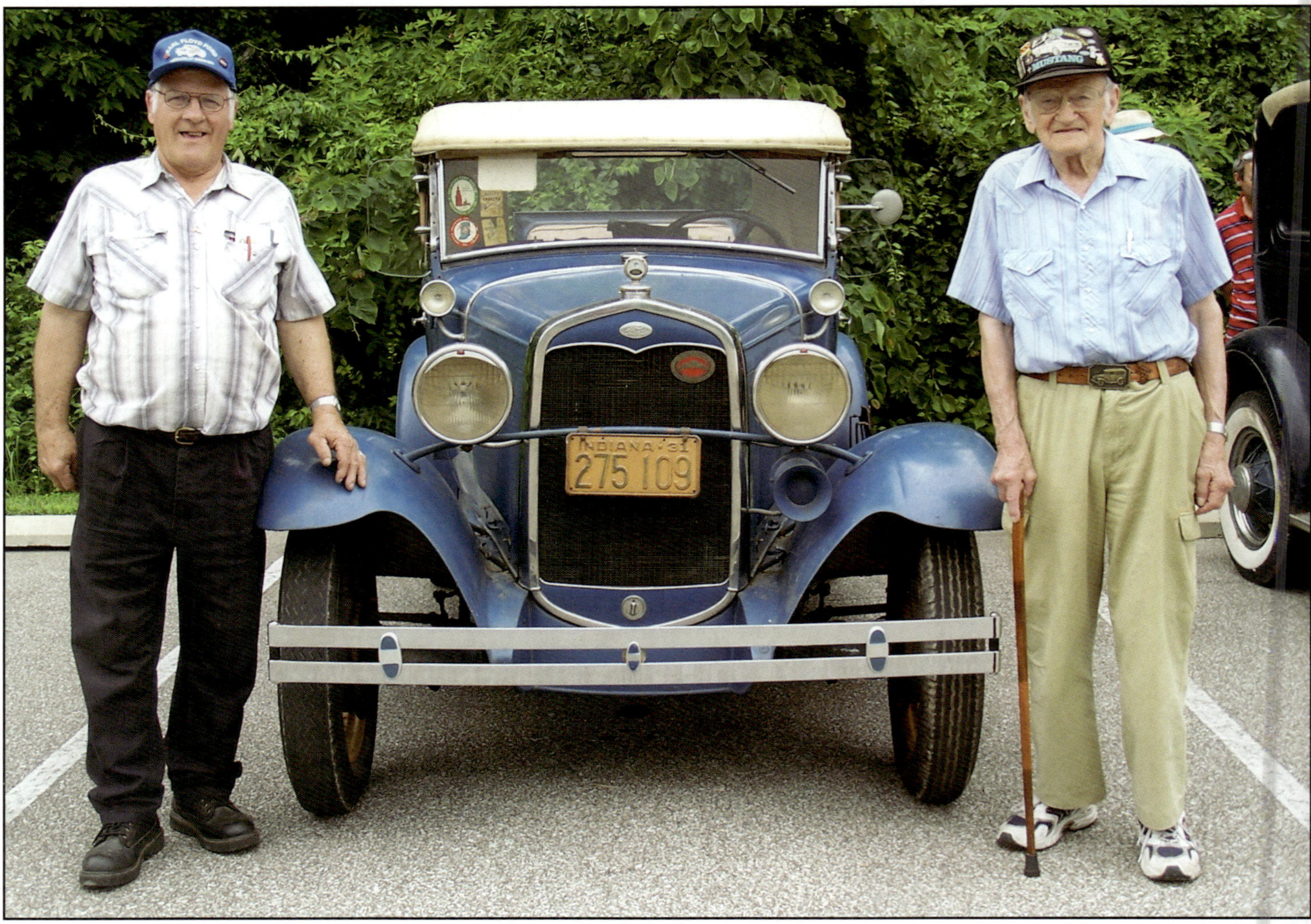

Photo by Laura Hodges

Ron Young (left) of Madison bought this Model A Ford from Louis Munier (right).

Good to the Bone

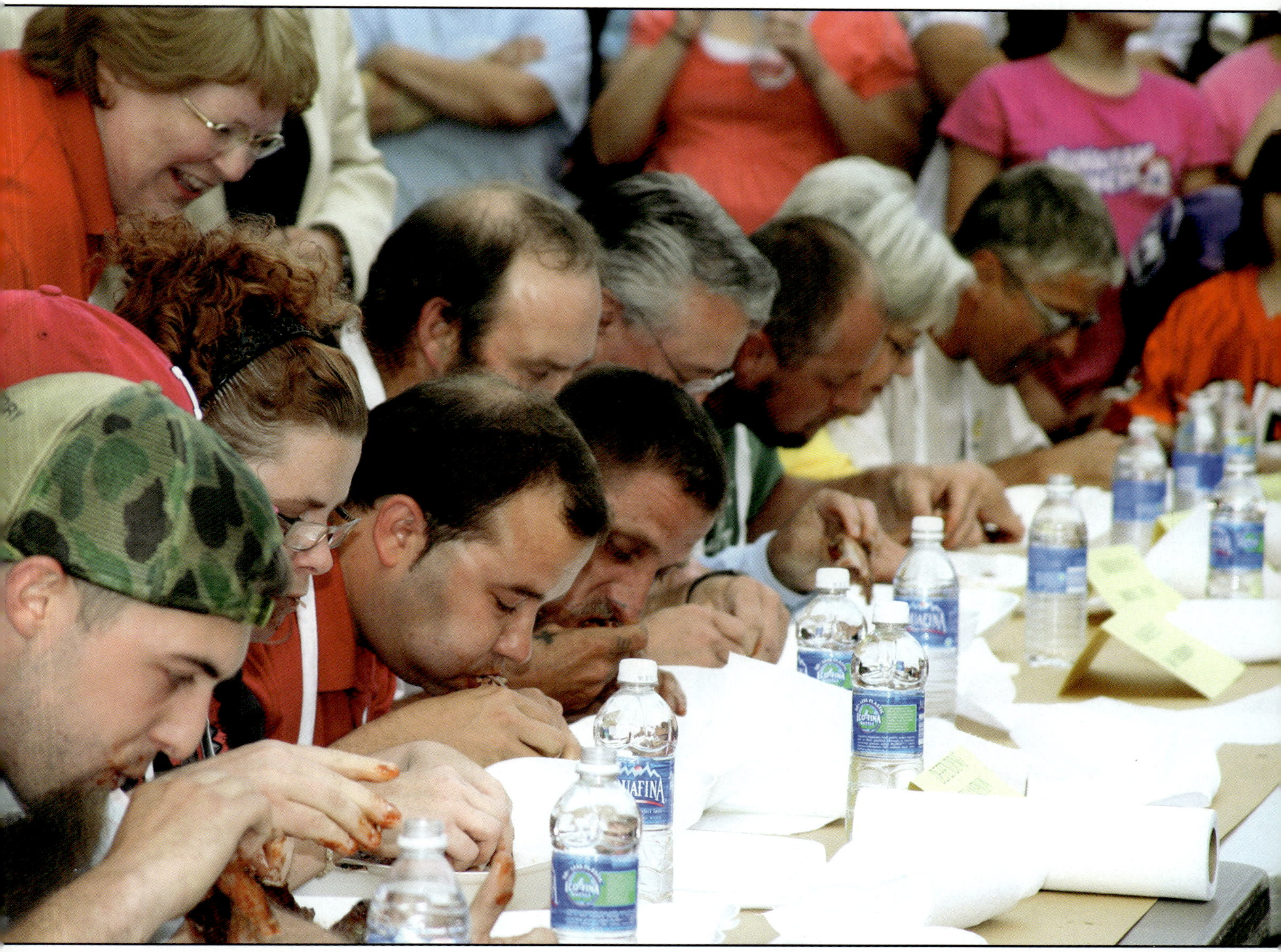

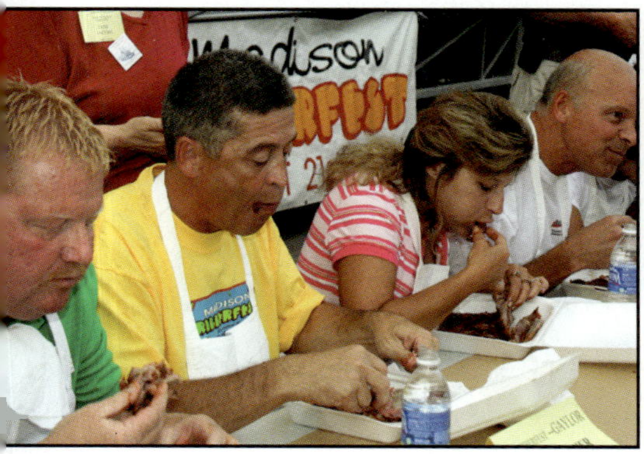

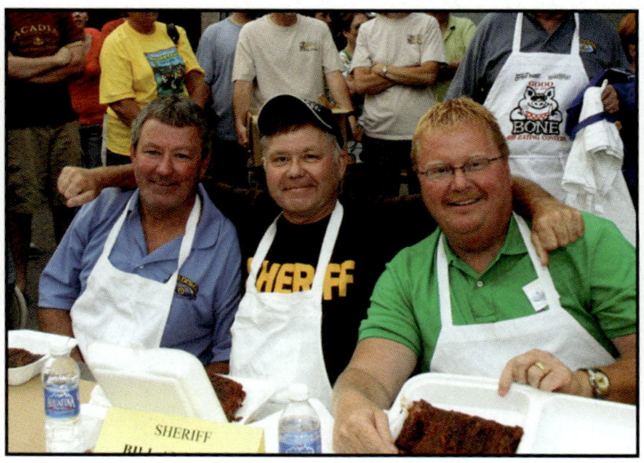

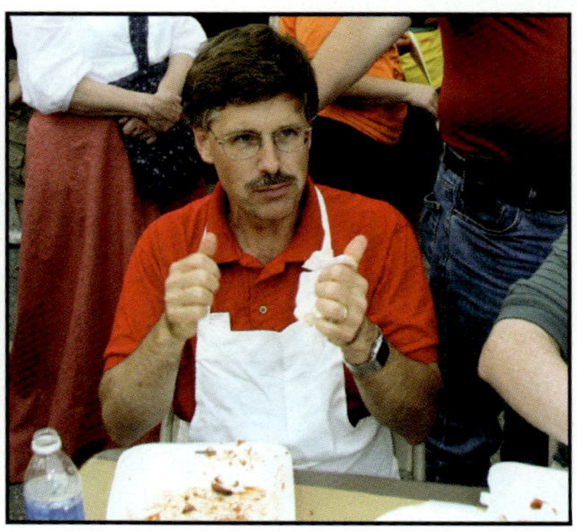

he Madison Ribberfest Committee sponsored the "Good to the Bone")-eating contest (top photo) June 12 at the Bicentennial Block Party, ɘld on Madison's Main Street. In all, 24 people competed. Dan Cole of adison won, with John Staicer (far right) finishing second. bove, Madison Police Chief John Wallace, Jeff Frazier of Gaylor, the ibberfest's title sponsor, an audience volunteer (pink shirt) and oundAbout Madison publisher Don Ward stuff their mouths with meat. the middle photo, (from left) Mayor Tim Armstrong, Jefferson County heriff Bill Andrews and City Police Chief John Wallace prepare to eat.

Photos by Kathy Chandler

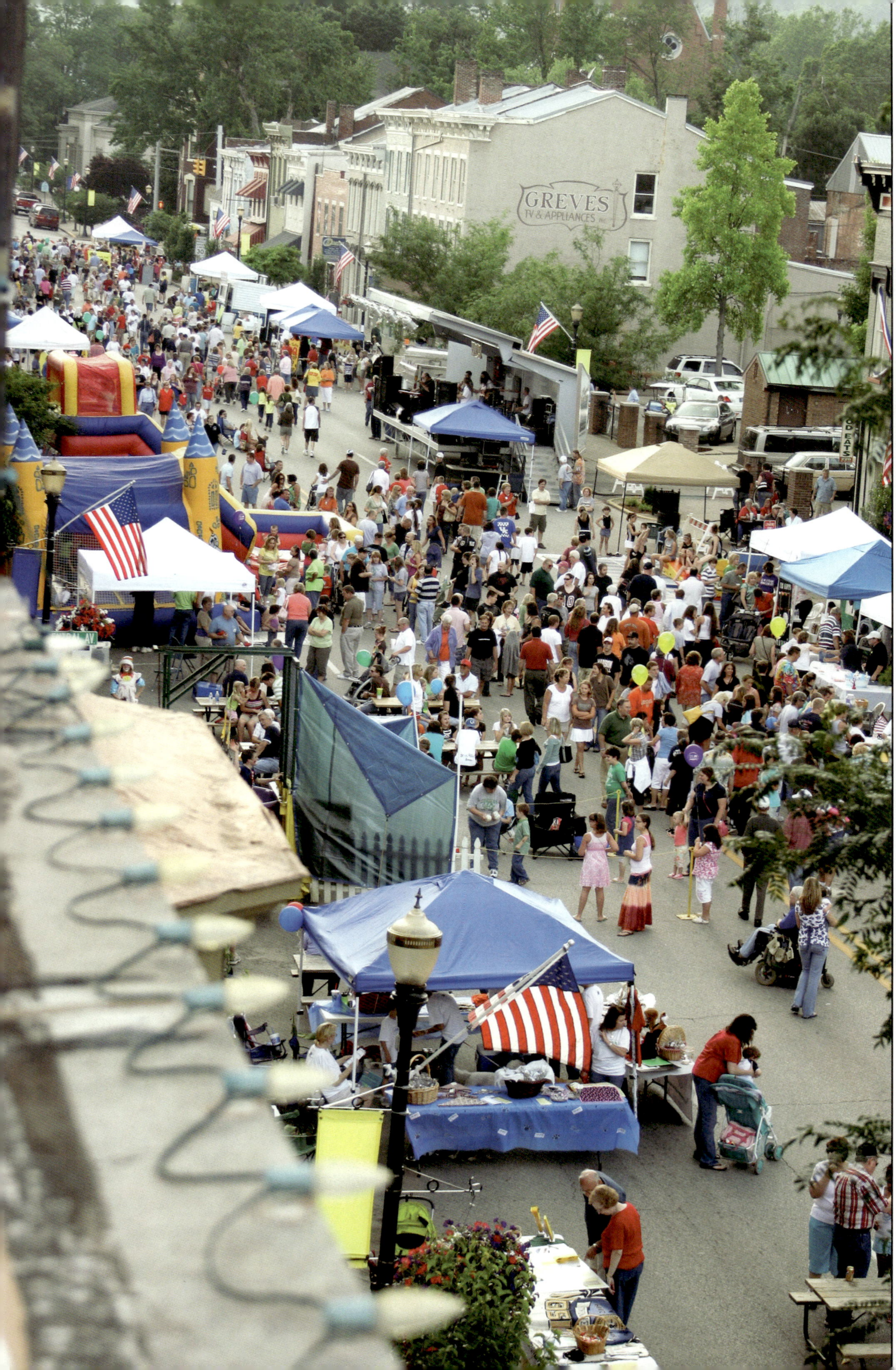
GREVES
TV & APPLIANCES INC

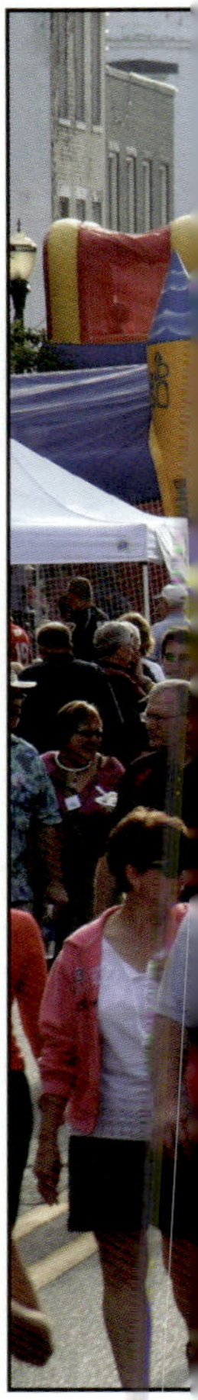

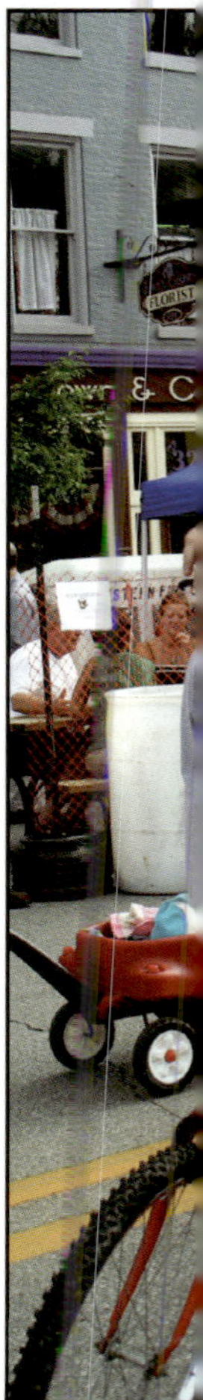

Block Party on Main Street

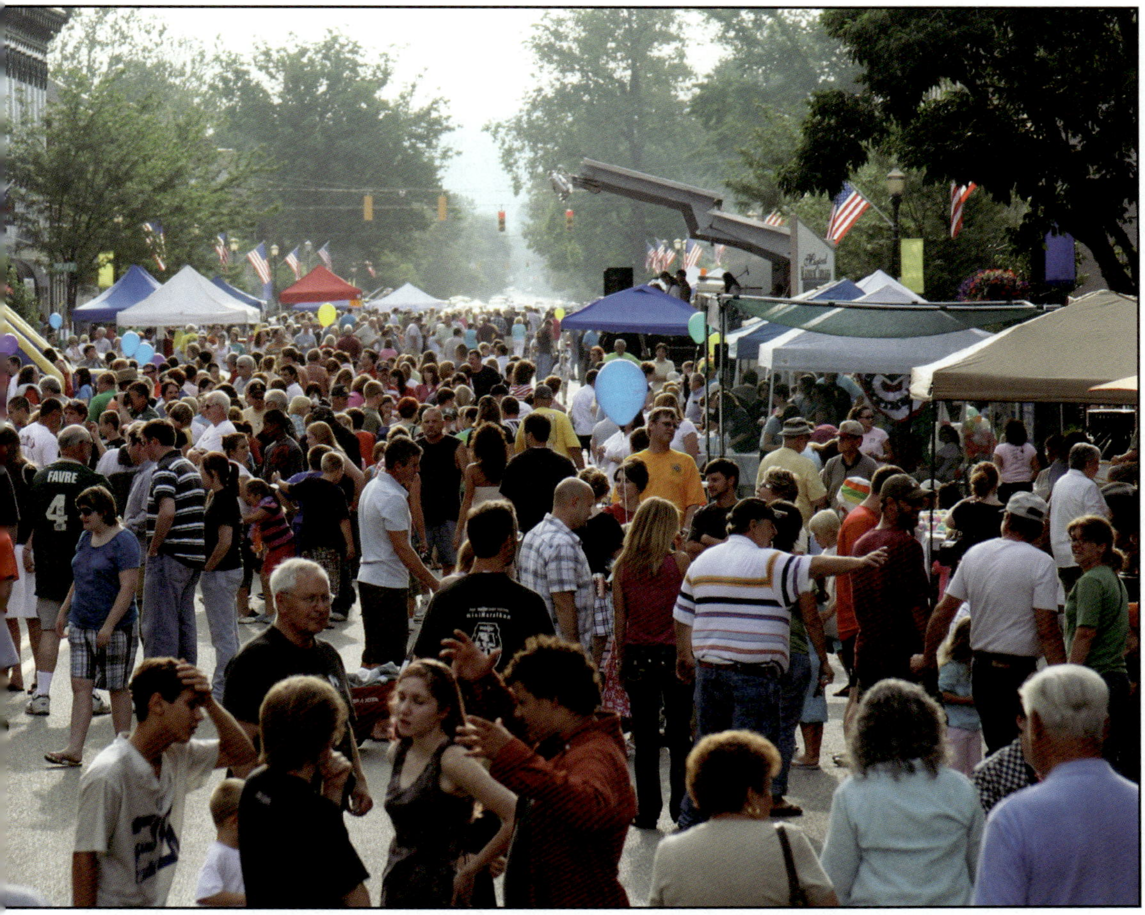

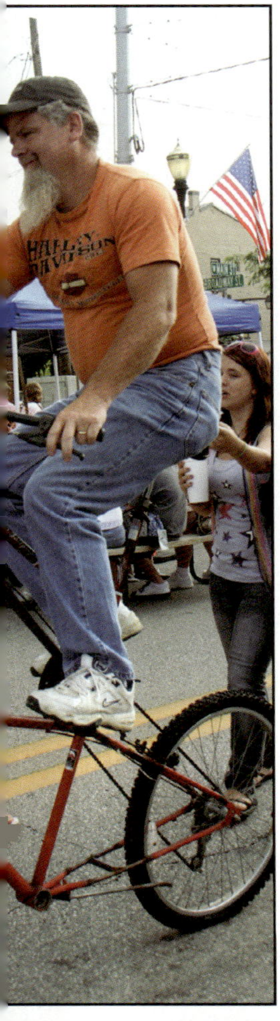

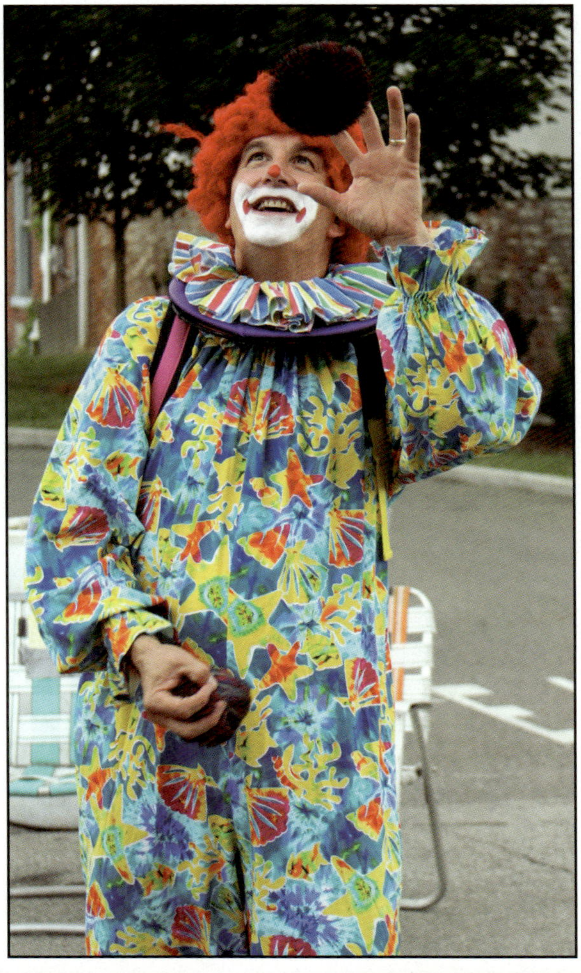

FAR LEFT: The Bicentennial Block Party on June 12 attracted the largest crowd of any event during the nine-day celebration. This photo was taken from the roof of Madison City Hall, looking west up Main Street.

ABOVE: The Block Party featured live music, dozens of community booths, food and a beer garden.

LEFT: A man rides a funny bicycle through the crowd.

SECOND FROM LEFT: "Conner the Clown," a.k.a. Paul Kelly, juggles his way through the throng of people on Main Street.

Photos by Kathy Chandler

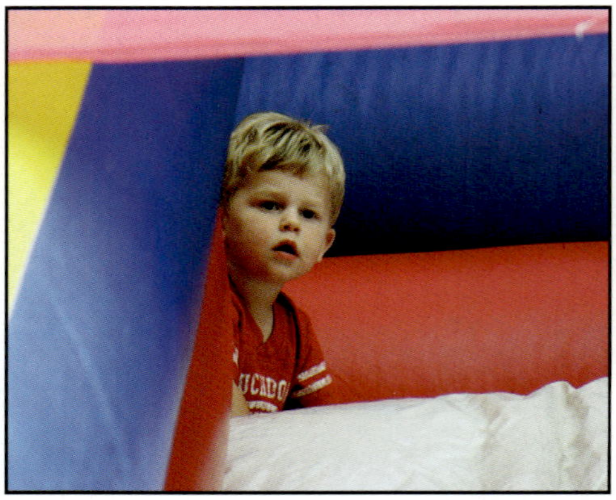

Photo by Kathy Chandler

A toddler peeks out from an inflatable slide after climbing up to the top.

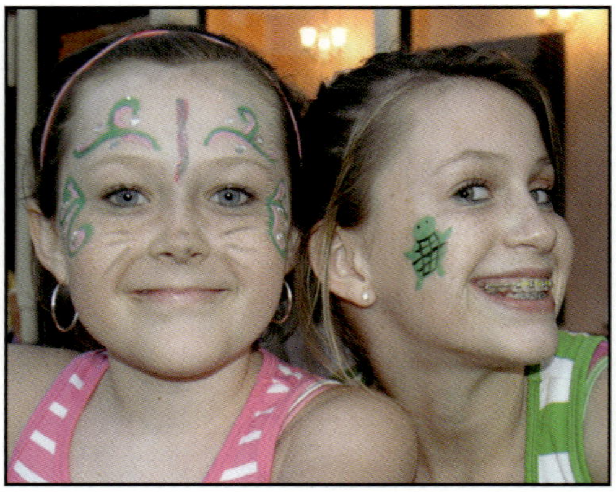

Photo by Don Ward

Brooke and Hailey Bayless show off their face paintings.

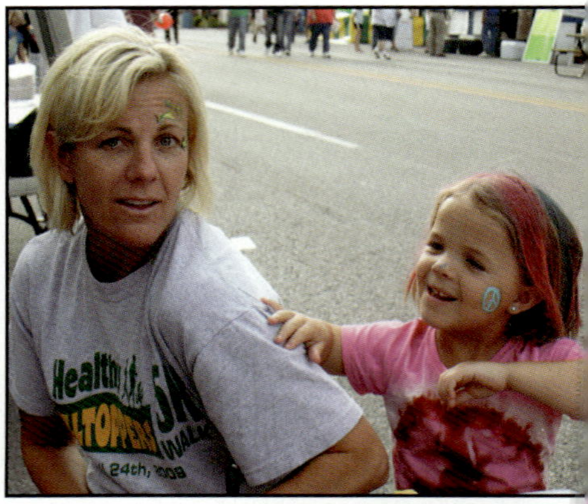

Photo by Kathy Chand

Patti Grote and her daughter, Caroline, explore the Block Party fu

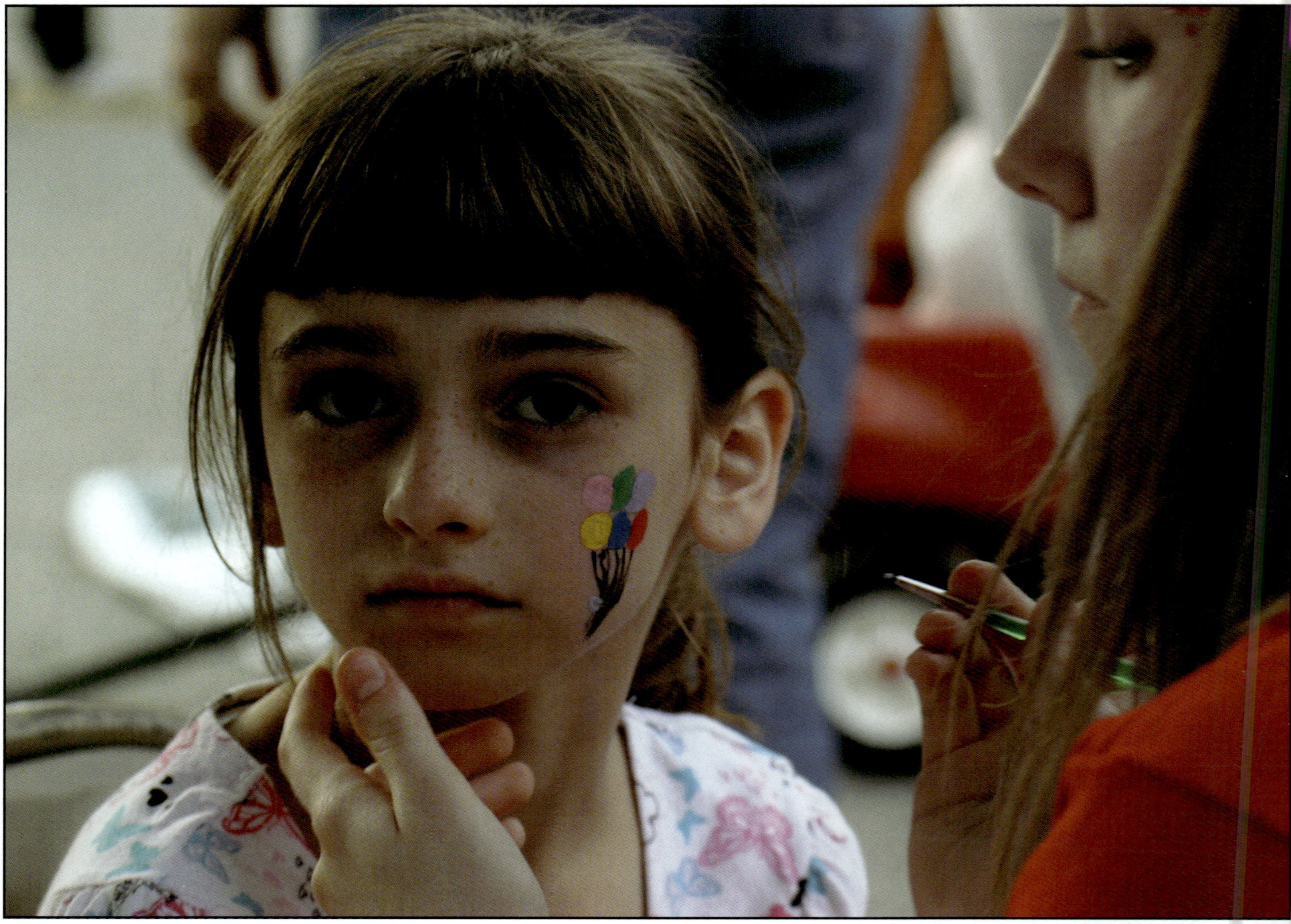

Photo by Don Ward

A young girl gets her face painted at the Madison Bicentennial Block Party.

Bernard Kelley (far left) repeatedly dunks Madison Mayor Tim Armstrong in the Dunk Tank during the Block Party on Main Street.

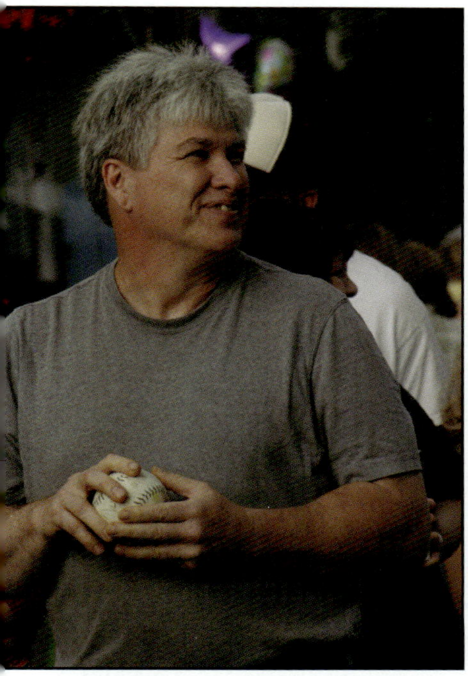

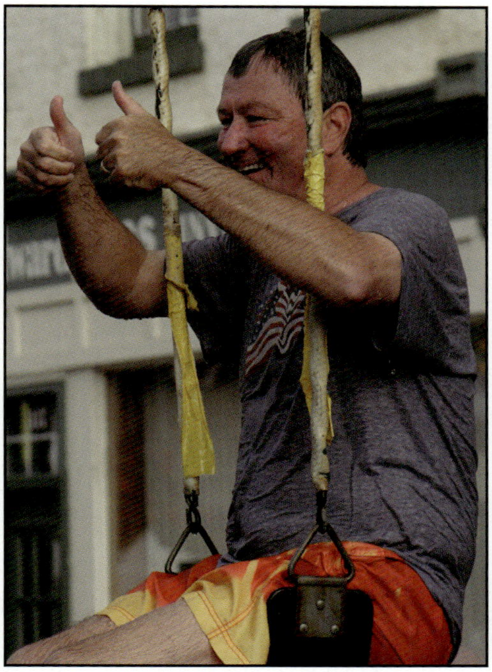

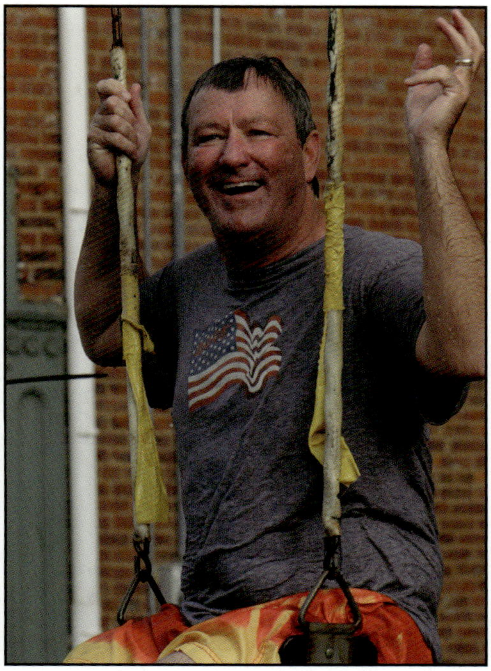

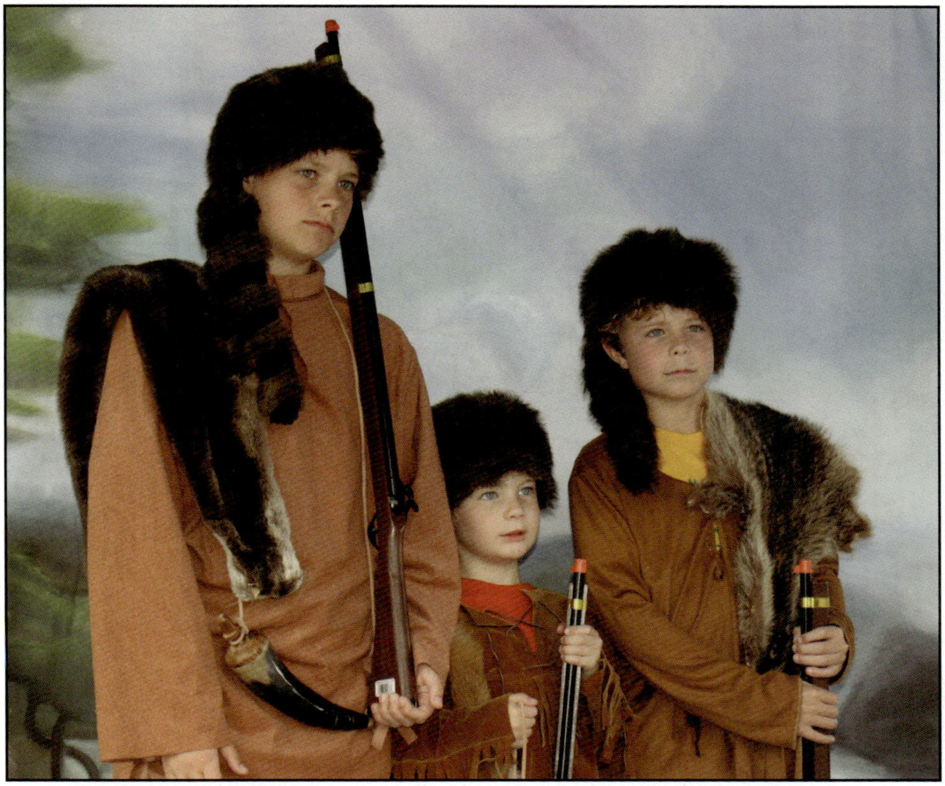

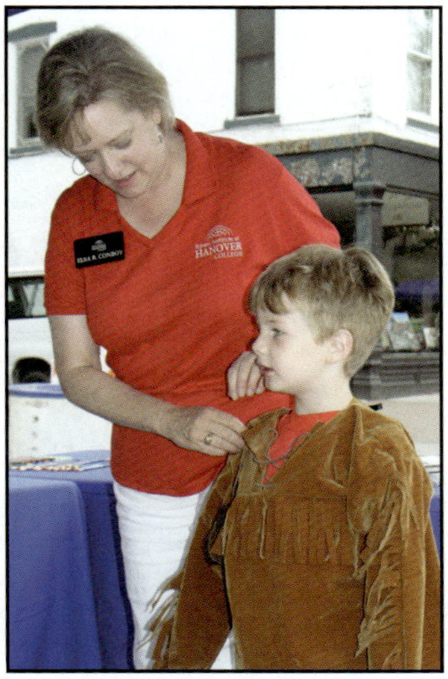

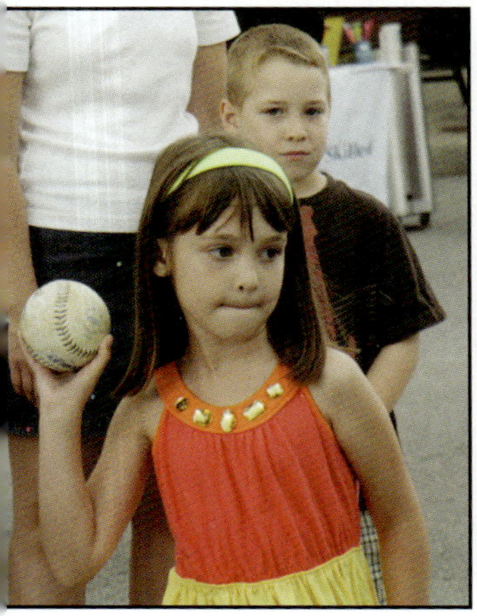

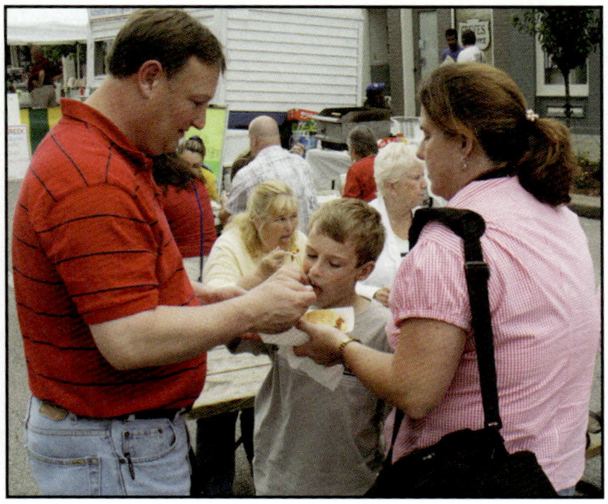

ABOVE LEFT: Whit, Jack and Christopher Grote don pioneer clothing and props to pose for a photo at a booth sponsored and staffed by members of the Rivers Institute at Hanover College.

ABOVE: Elsa Conboy of Rivers Institute helps Jack Grote with his pioneer costume.

FAR LEFT: Maria Stoner, 7, tries to dunk the mayor at the dunk tank.

LEFT: Rick, Holly and son, Kyle, Barton of Bloomington, Ind., try out the barbecue.

Photos by Don Ward

FAR RIGHT: Samesoul band members Chris Jesse (right) and Joe Devito perform for the Block Party crowd.

MIDDLE: Samesoul keyboardist John Adkins.

RIGHT: Harlan Kelly, dressed as a clown, rides through the crowd on a tricycle.

BELOW RIGHT: A young girl watches all the action.

BELOW: Leticia Bajuyo collects money for food and beverage tickets.

BELOW MIDDLE: David Jenkins grills burgers and hot dogs at the Western Volunteer Fire Co. No. 3 food booth.

Photos by Don Ward

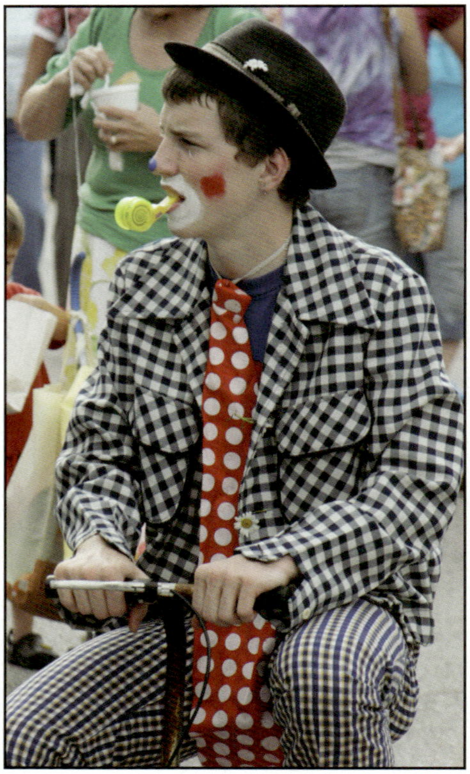

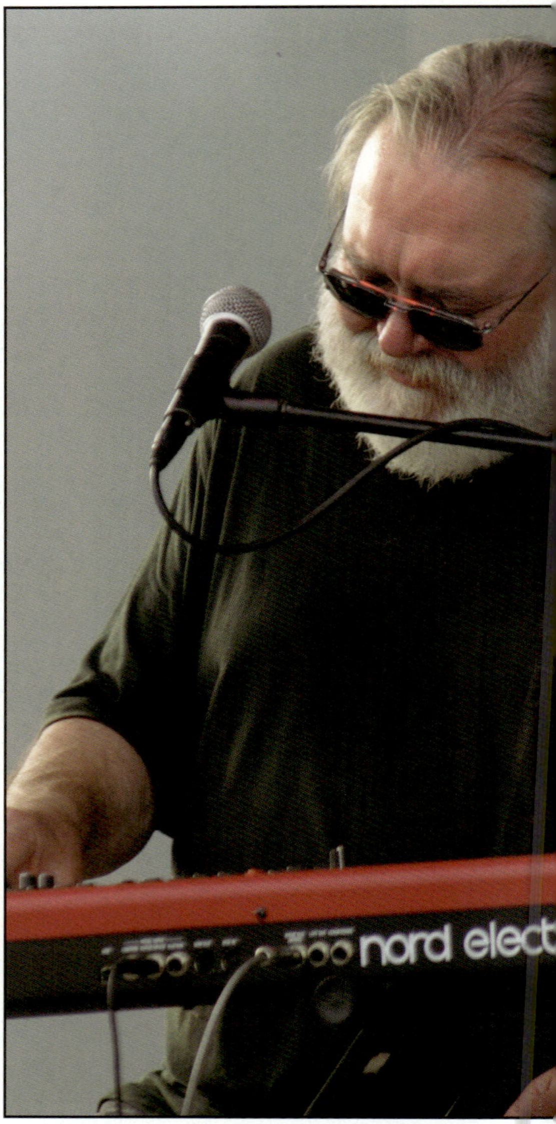

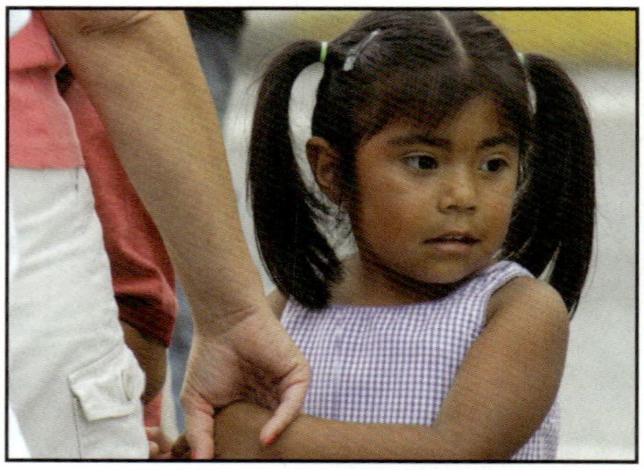

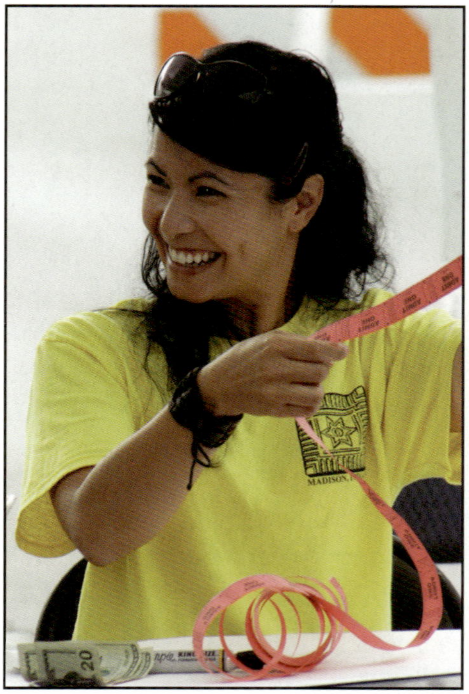

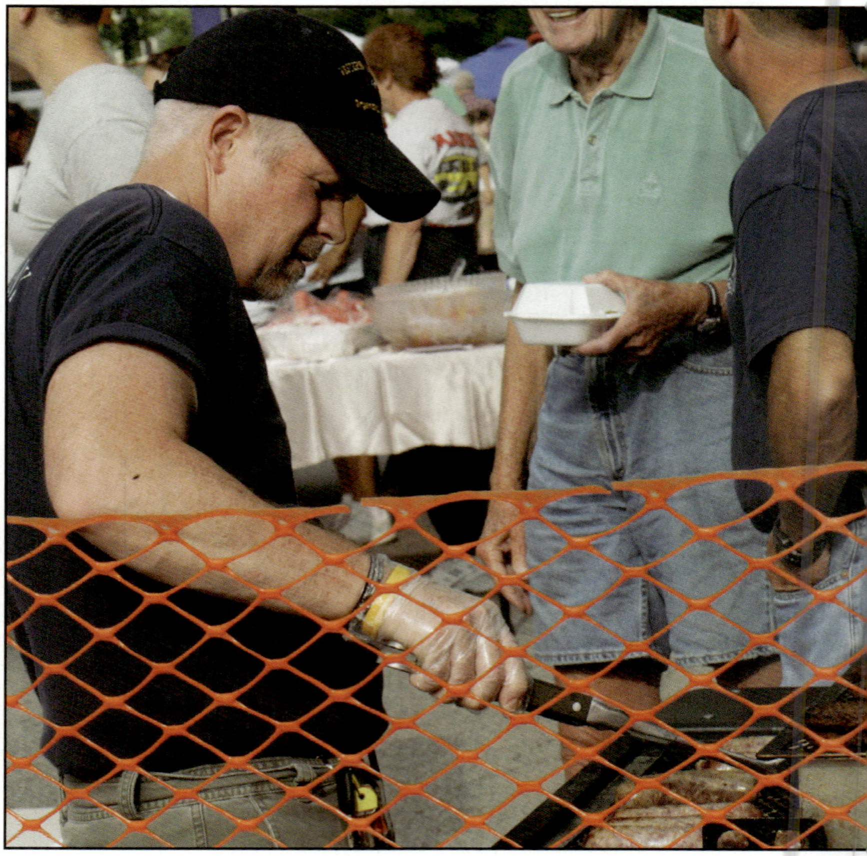

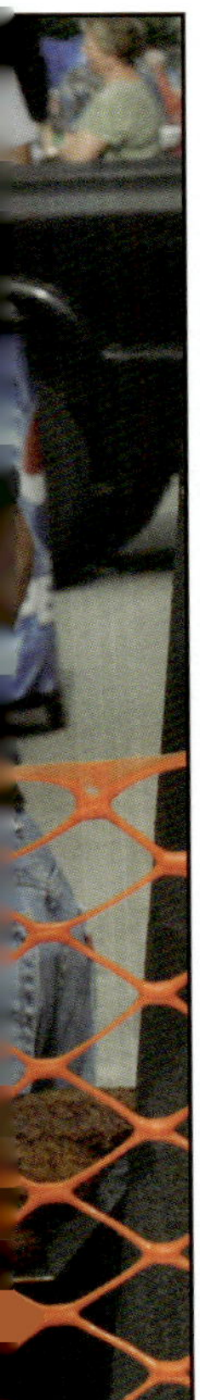

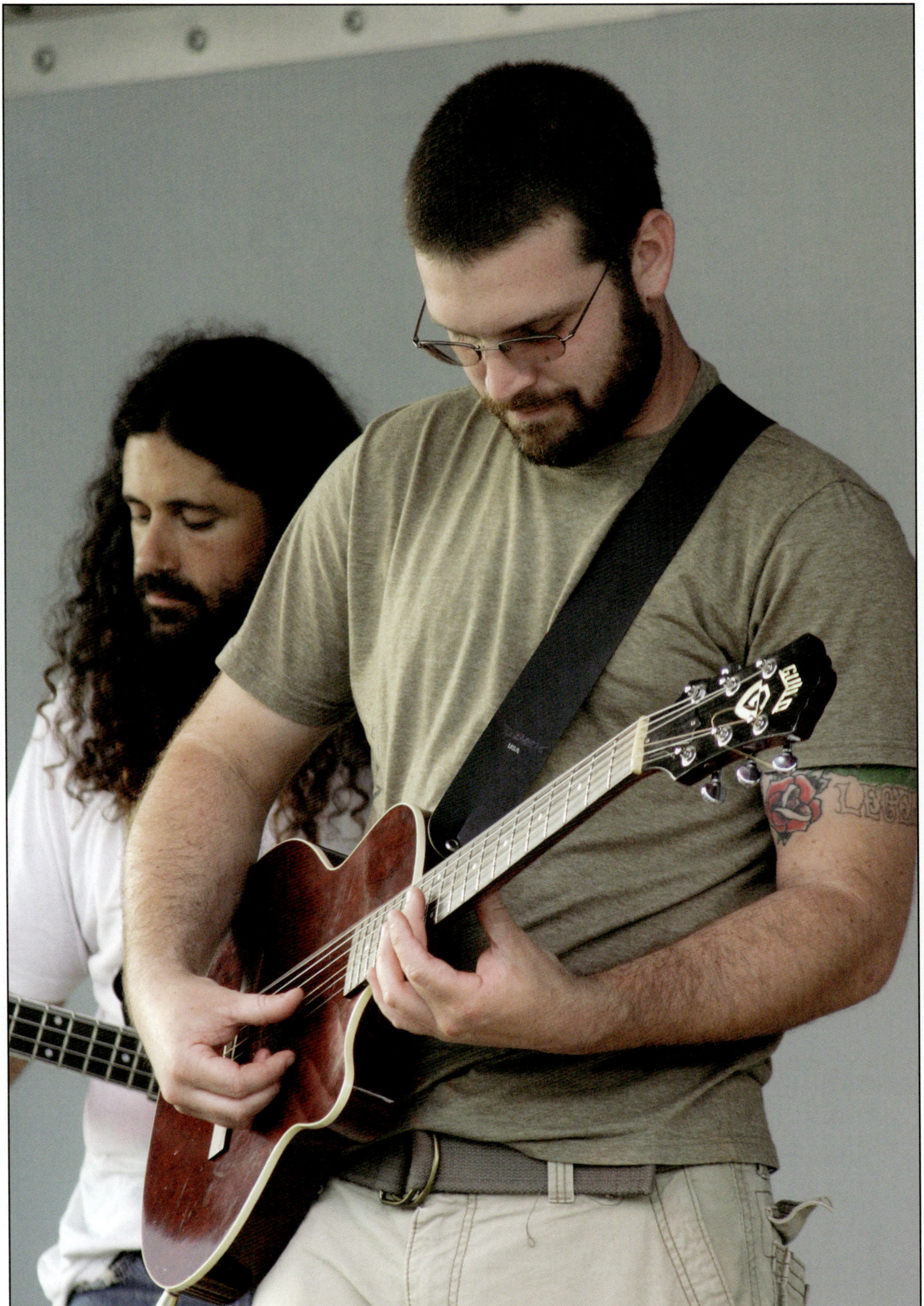

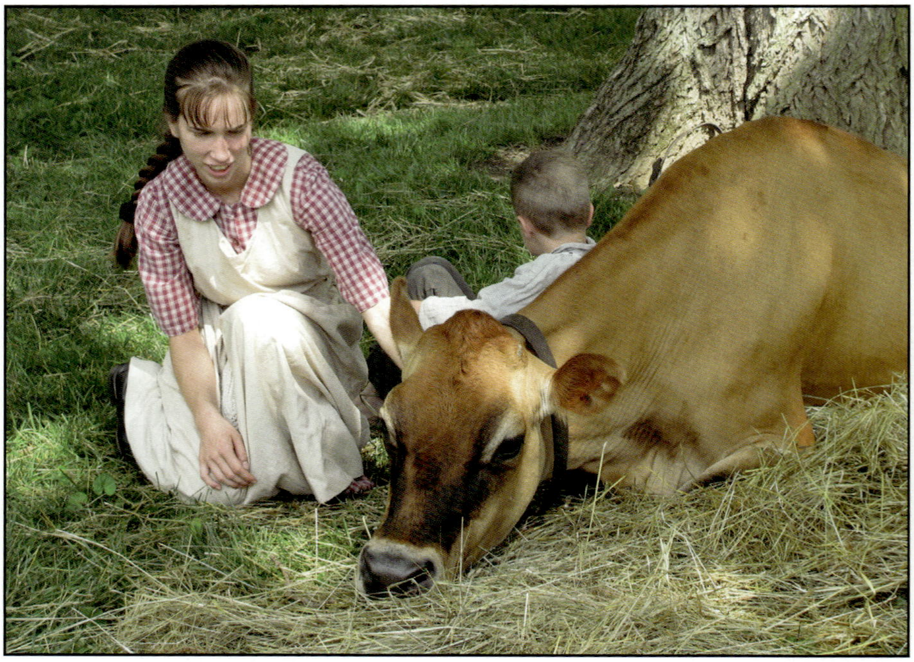

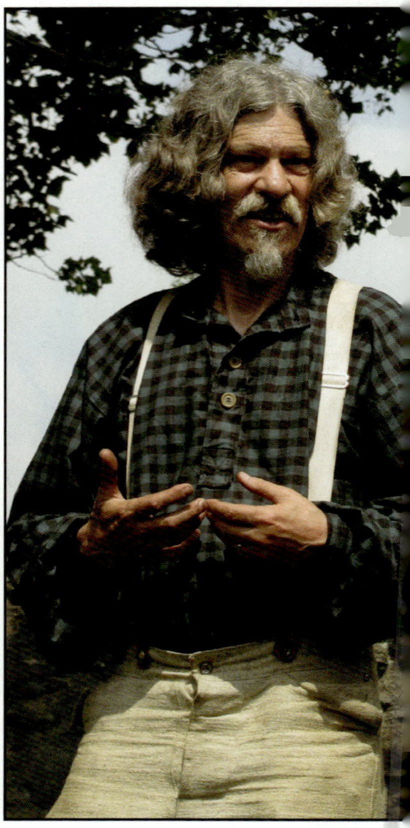

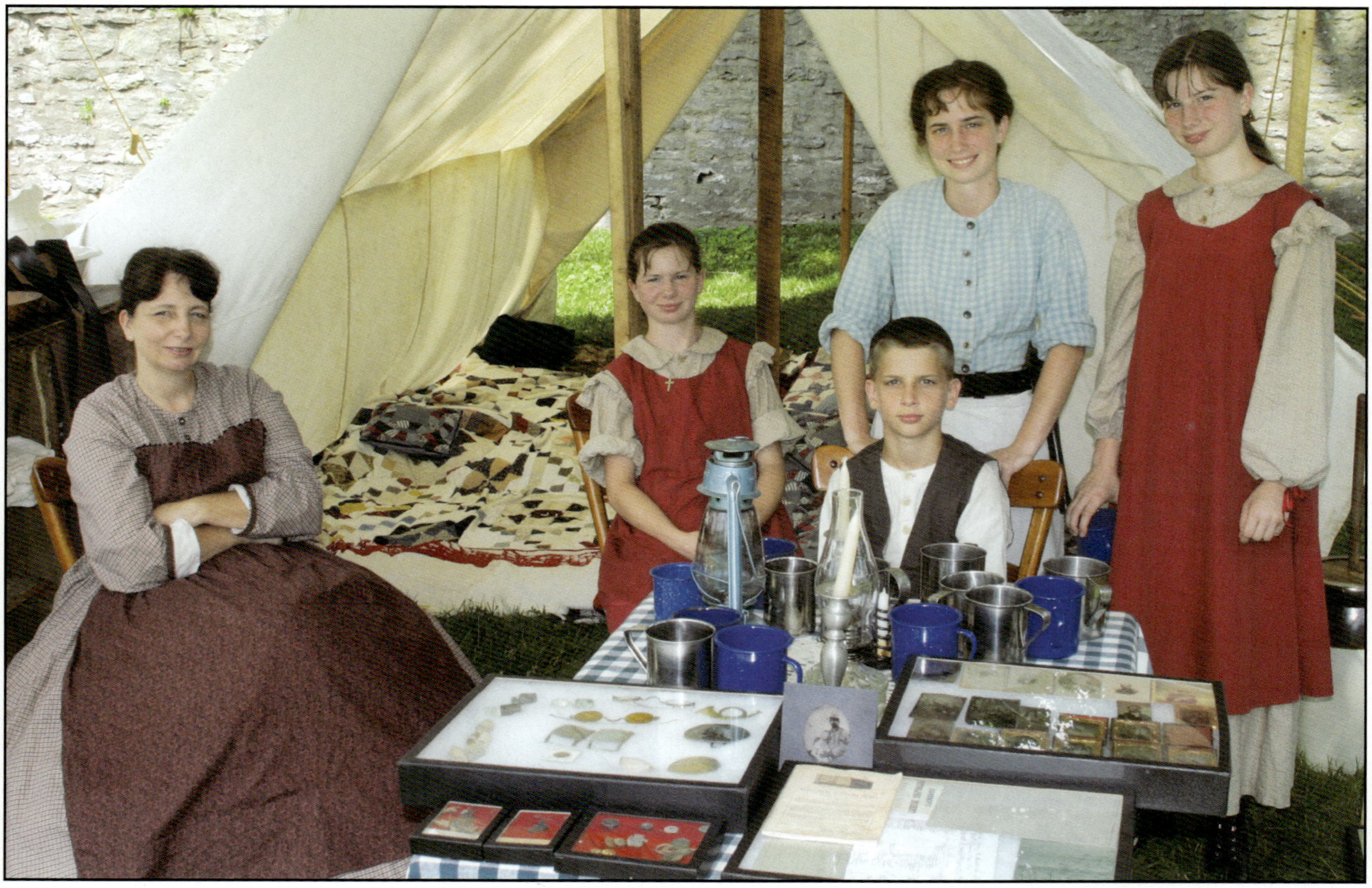

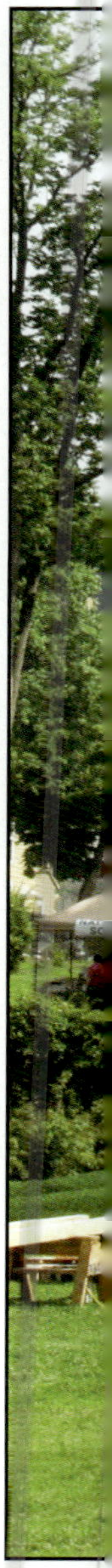

ABOVE: The re-enacting Recknor family poses for a photo at their Lanier Days tent on the lawn of the Lanier Mansion. They are (from left) mother, Kathy (sitting), with Bethany (twin), 14, Brystol, 20, Kimberly (twin) 14, and Emery, 11.

RIGHT: The Lanier Mansion State Historic Site was the location of the two-day re-enactment and trades show event.

Photos by Don Ward

Lanier Days & Historic Trades Fair

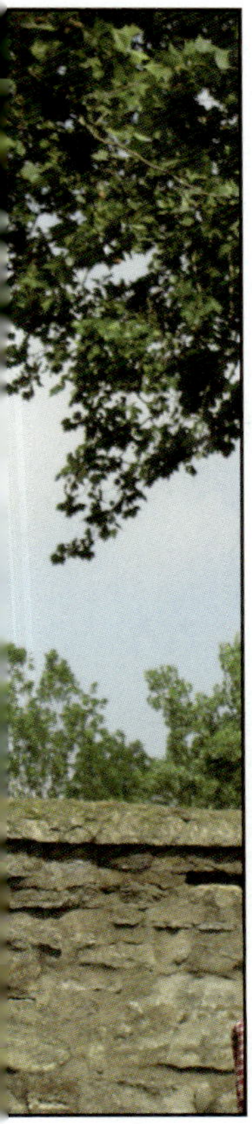

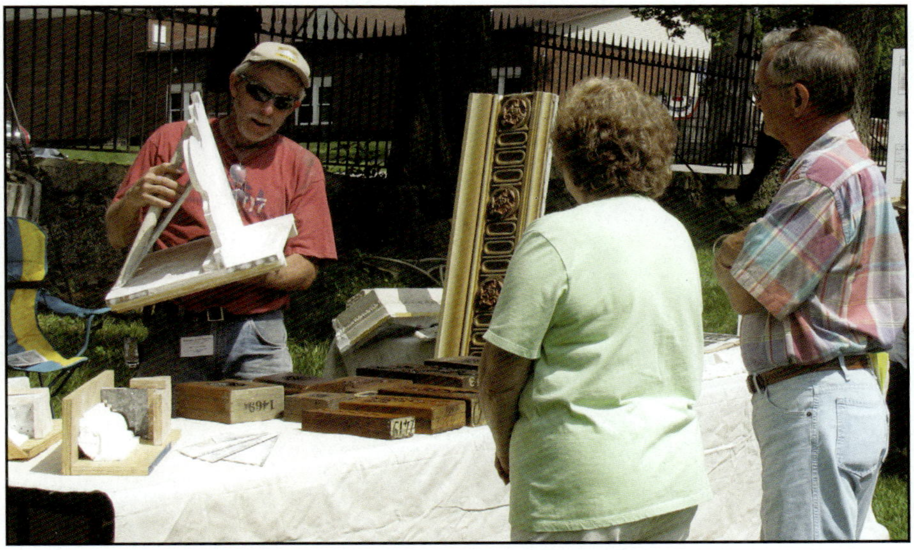

FAR LEFT: Lindsae Recknor, 20, of Sebree, Ky., cares for her cow "Rosie" on June 13 at Lanier Days.

SECOND FROM LEFT: Re-enactor Michael Totten of Madison explains weaponry of the Civil War.

LEFT: Plaster restoration expert Terry Wullenweber discusses his craft with visitors.

Photos by Emily Ward

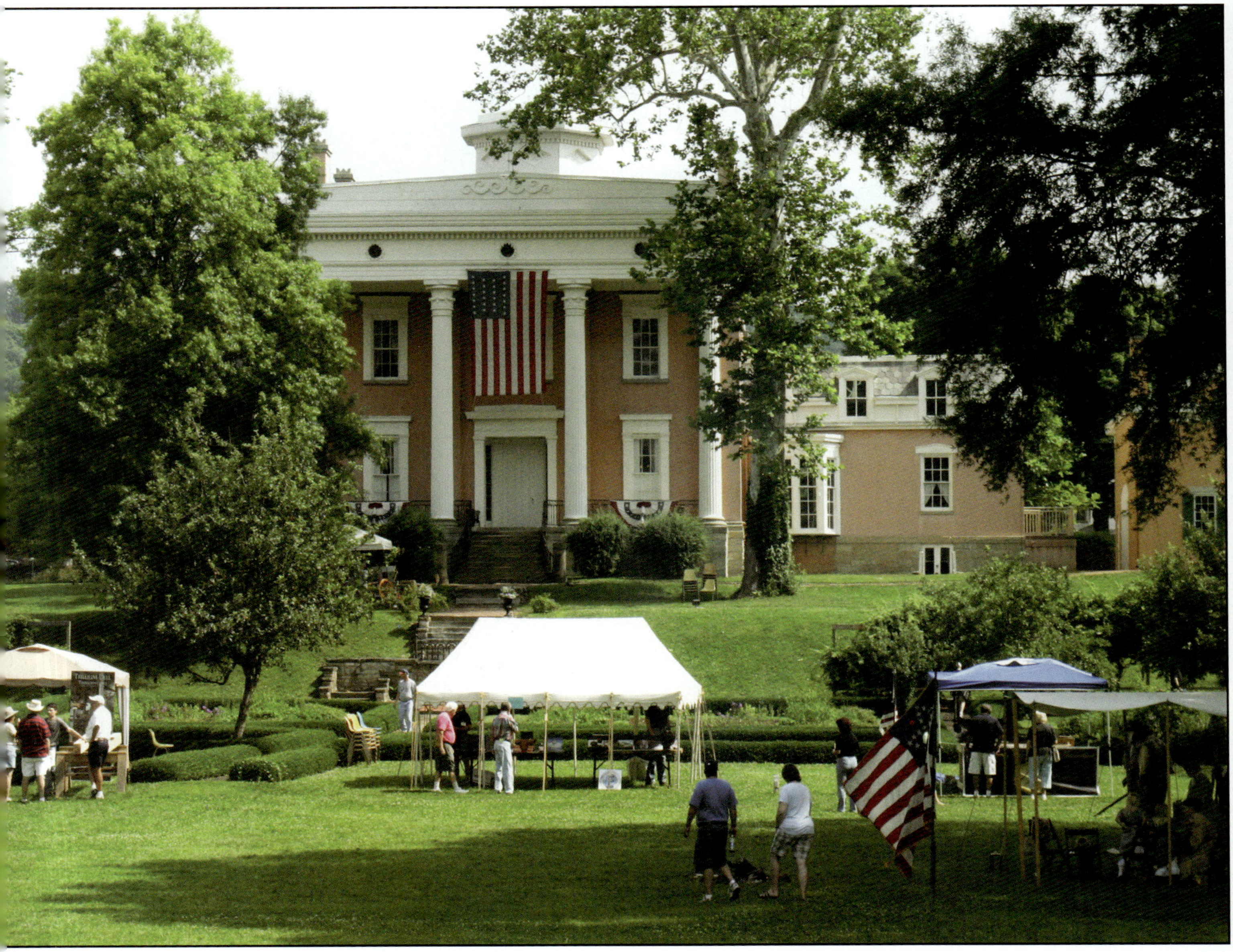

BELOW LEFT: Macy Reno of Gaston, Ind., plays a Union soldie

MIDDLE: Jim Coon of Indianapolis explain
the Confederate weaponry to visitor

BELOW RIGHT: Jim King of Auburn, Ind., takes a brea

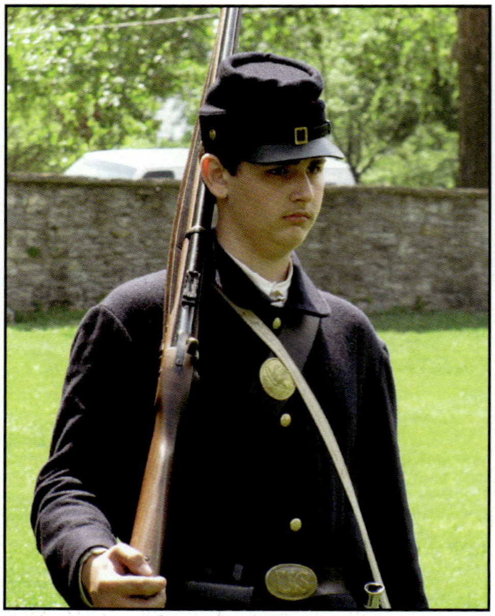

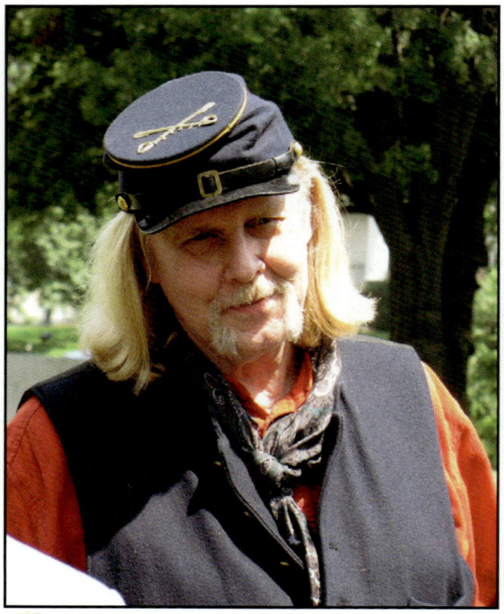

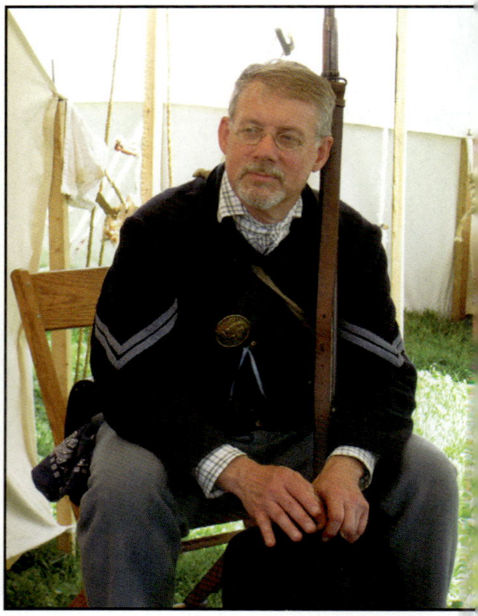

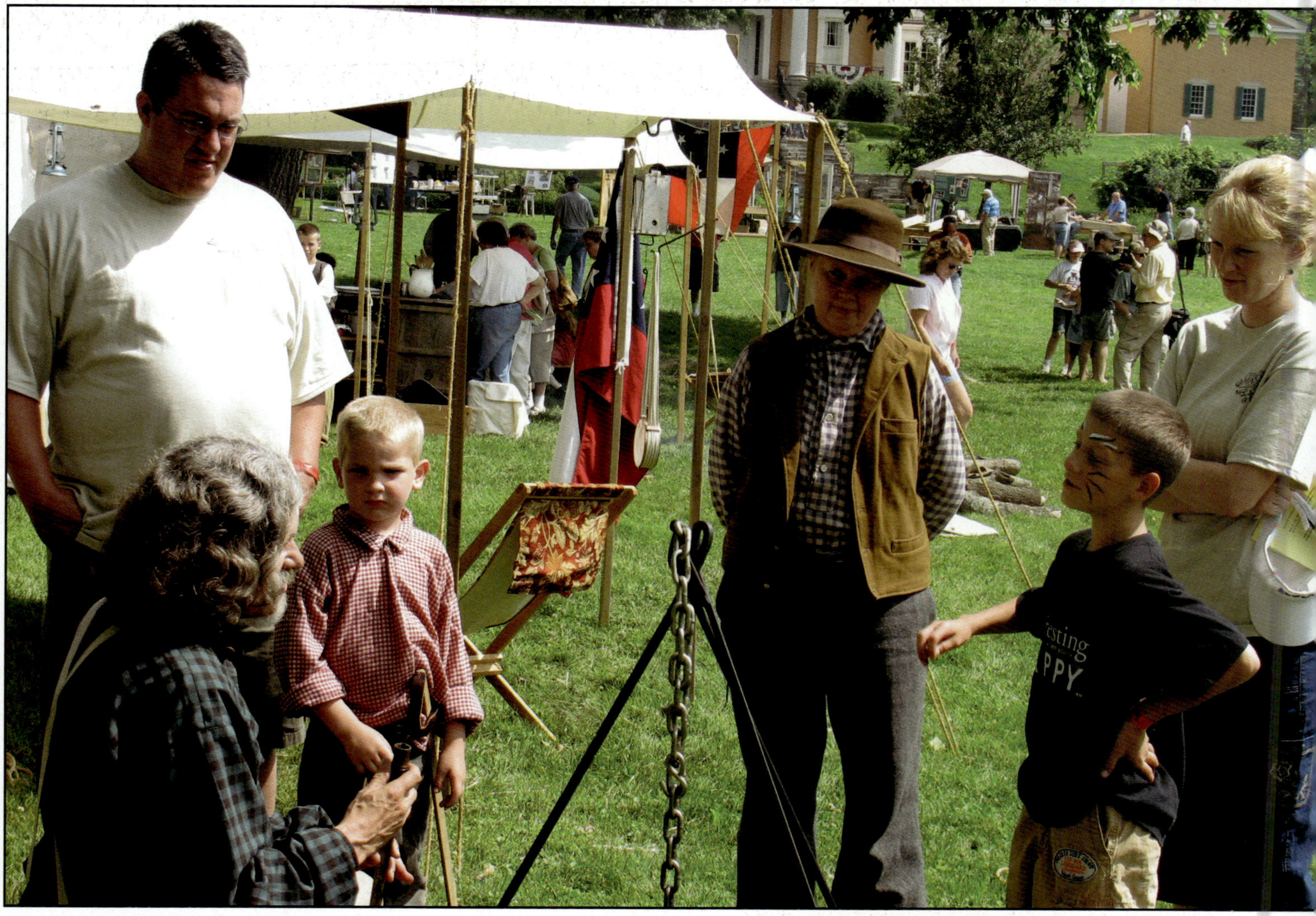

The Dryden family of Madison gets a lesson on Civil War-era tools and weapons from re-enactor Michael Totten (kneeling at far left). Standing at far left is John Dryden. His wife, Sara, and son, Jack, are at far right. Totten's wife, Brigitte, is third from right and re-enacts. Clayton Recknor, third from left, listens.

Photos by Emily Ward

Stephen Bowman (below left) teaches Sonya Hoffman of Hartford City, Ind., how to work with lace. Child re-enactor Clayton Recknor, 7, (middle photo) watches a demonstration. **Photos by Emily Ward**

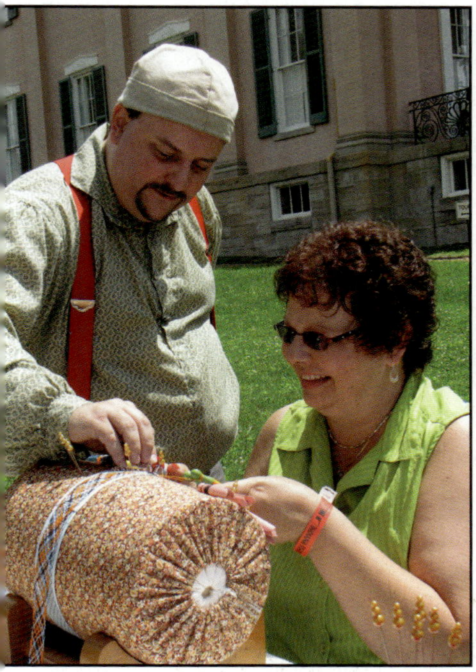

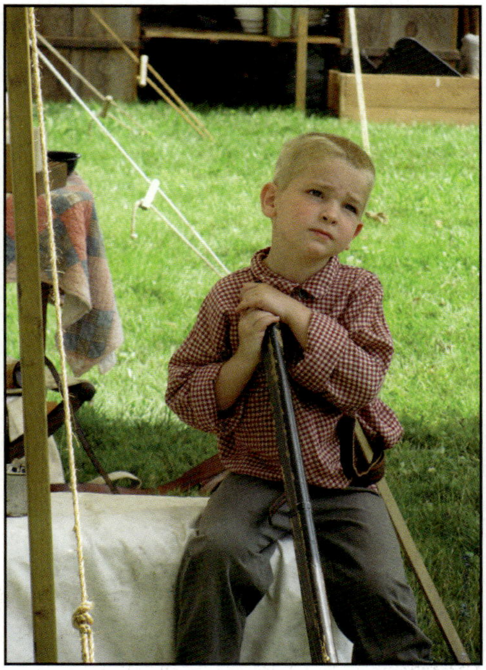

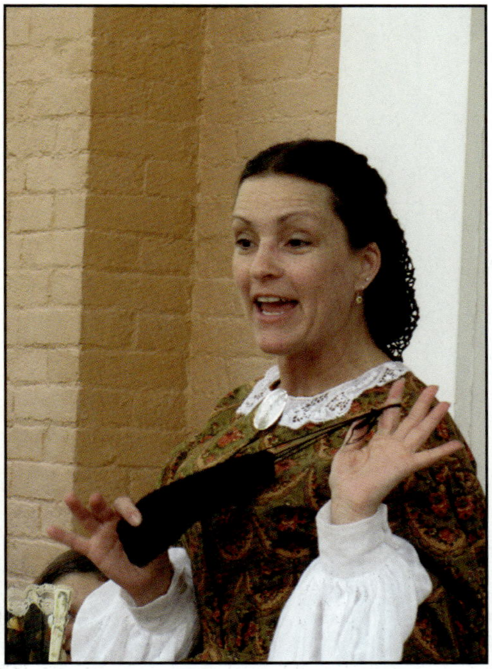

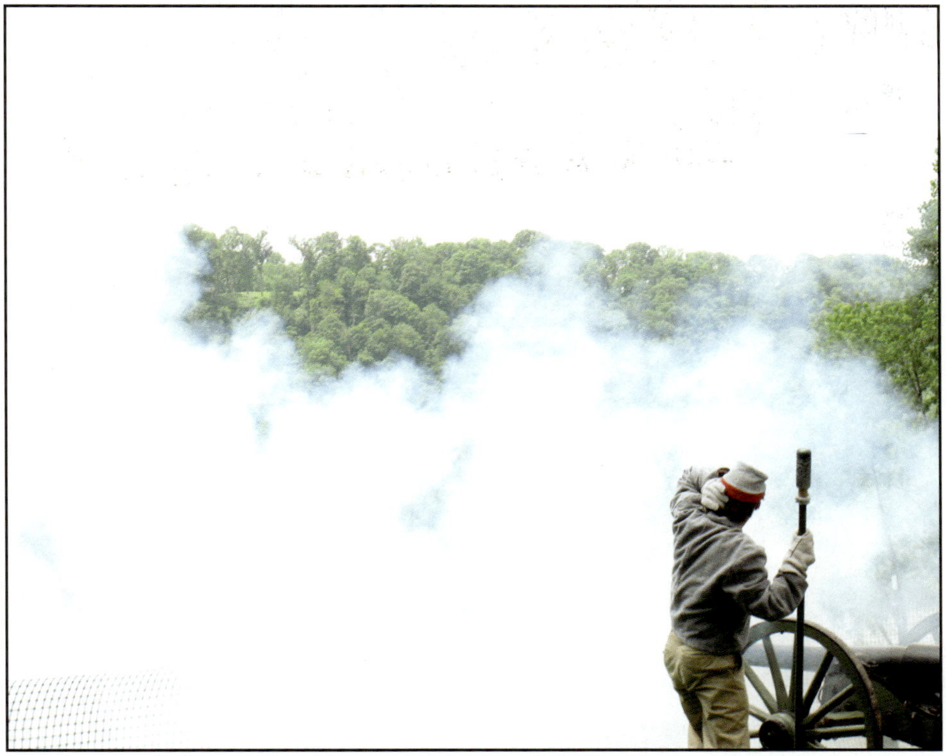

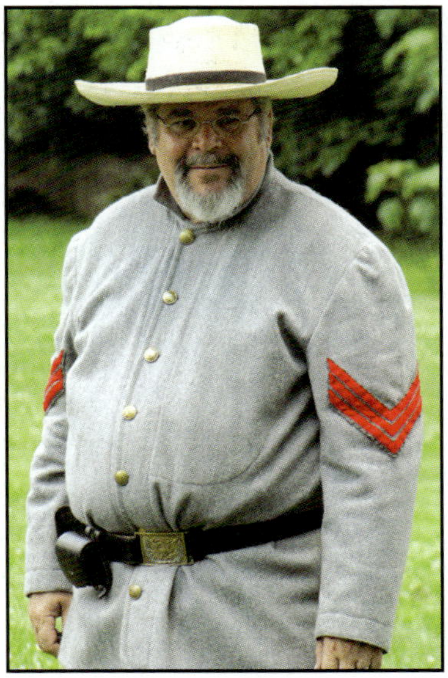

Dennis Jorgensen (above) of Madison prepares to fire a cannon as part of Lanier Days. **Photo by Don Ward**

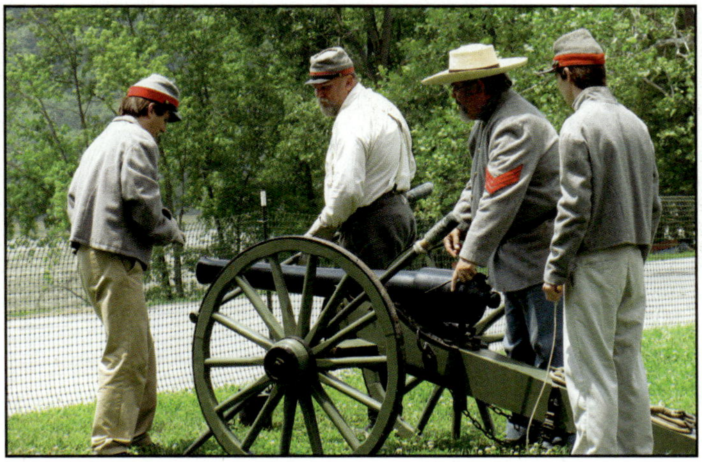

TOP RIGHT: Re-enactor Susan Walters of North Vernon, Ind., discusses what a typical home life was like during the Civil War era.

ABOVE LEFT: John Krantz of Hanover, Ind., holds his ears as the cannon fires.

LEFT: Confederate soldiers representing the Nelson County, Va., Artillery Co. prepare to fire the cannon. They are (from left) John Krantz of Hanover, Dennis Vermillion of Corydon, Ind., Dennis Jorgensen of Madison, and Daniel Krantz.

Photos by Emily Ward

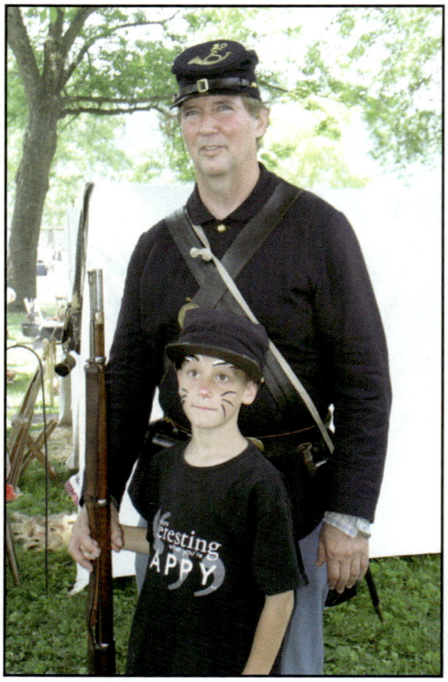

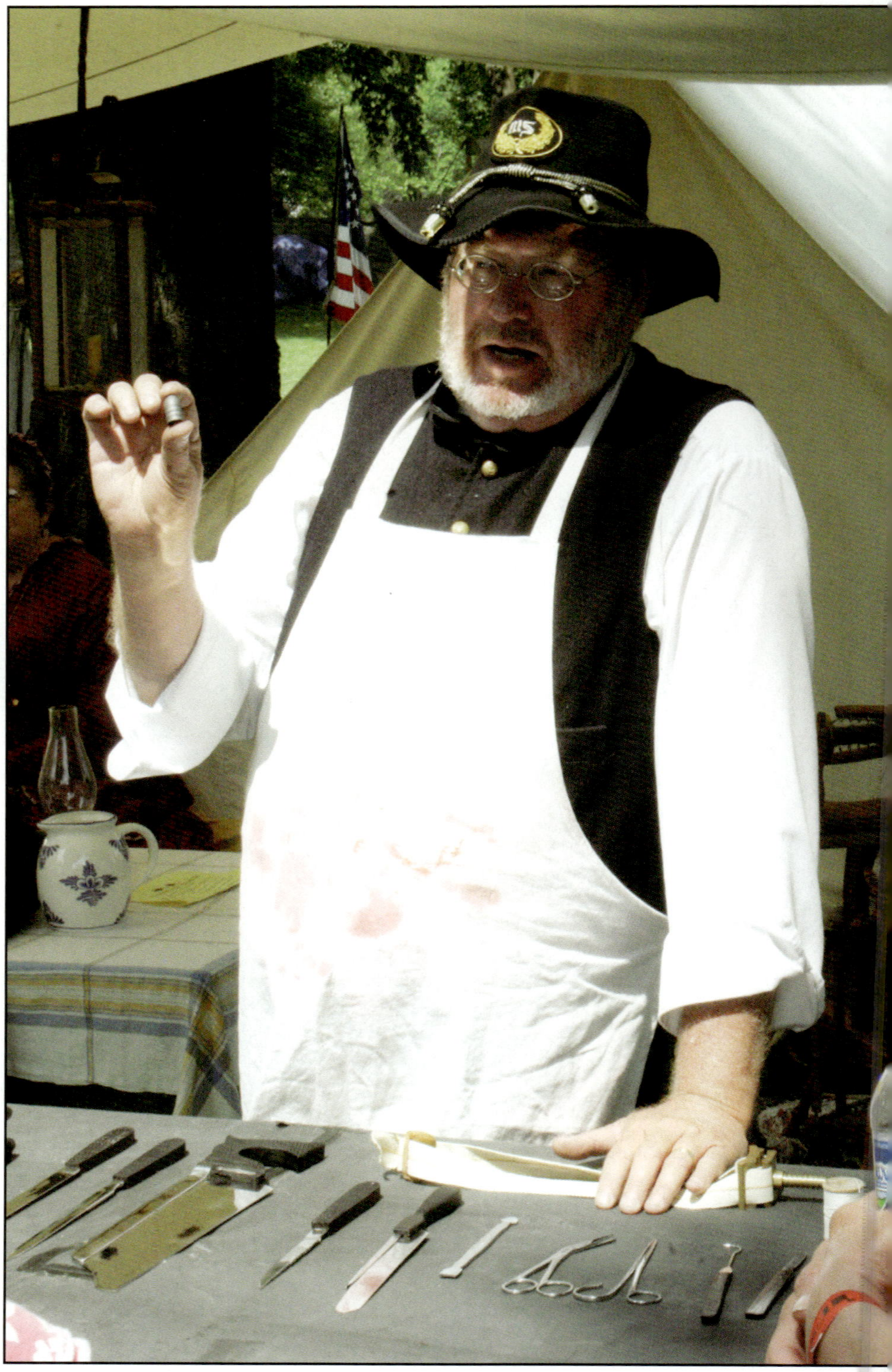

ABOVE: Union soldier re-enactor Dave Walker of Van Wirt, Ohio, teaches Jack Dryden of Madison how to march.

RIGHT: Field surgeon re-enactor Lee Downey of Angola, Ind., explains to visitors how medical care was administered on the Civil War battlefield.

BELOW RIGHT: Jim Coon of Indianapolis demonstrates the Civil War-era weapons used by Confederate soldiers.

BELOW LEFT: Patrick Thevenow of Madison builds and repairs traditional muzzleloading firearms using original craftsmanship.

Photos by Don Ward

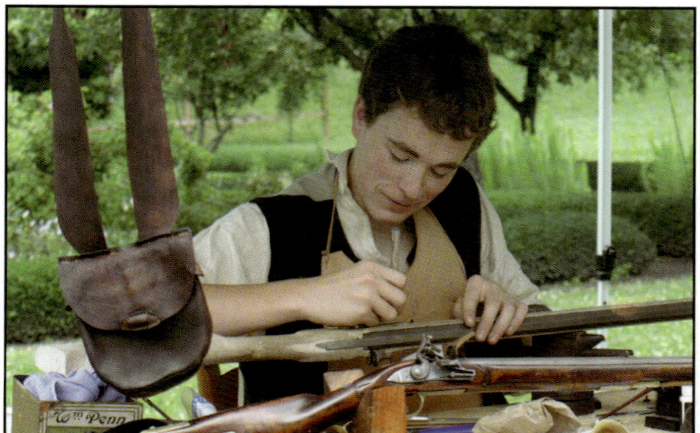

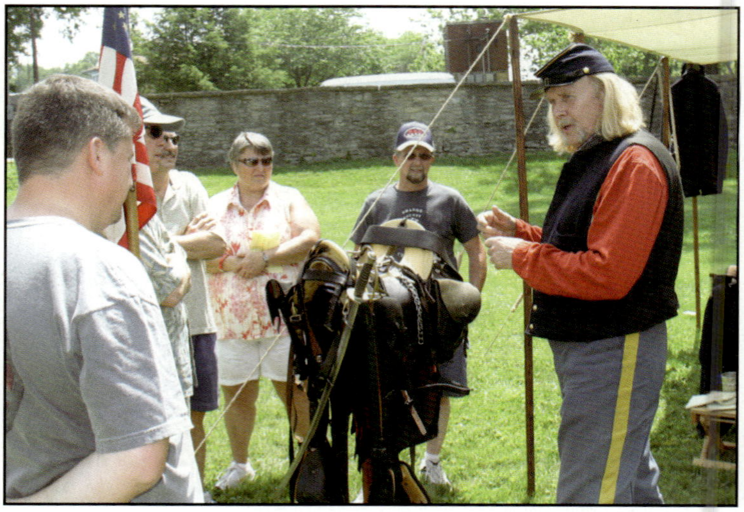

Music at Rucker Complex

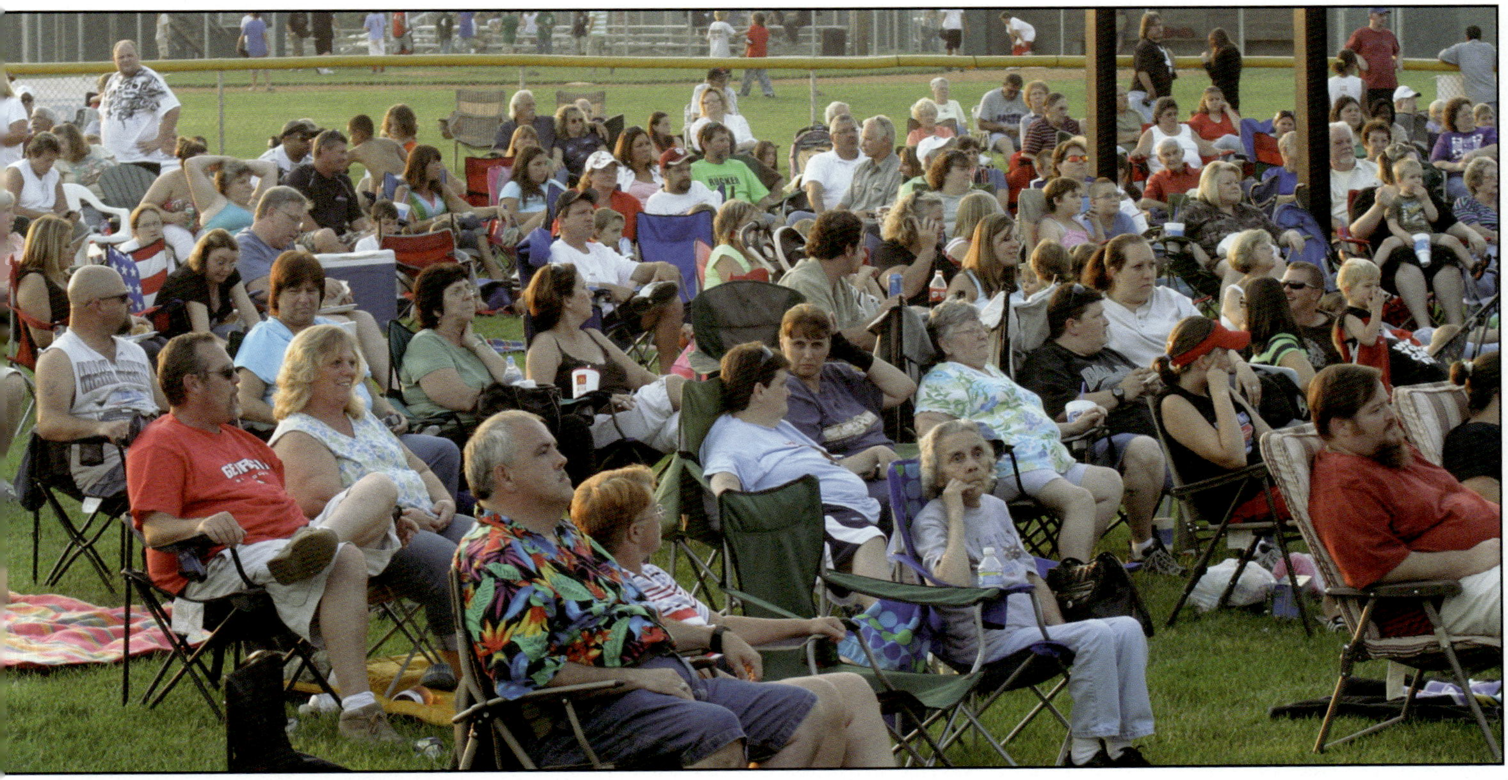

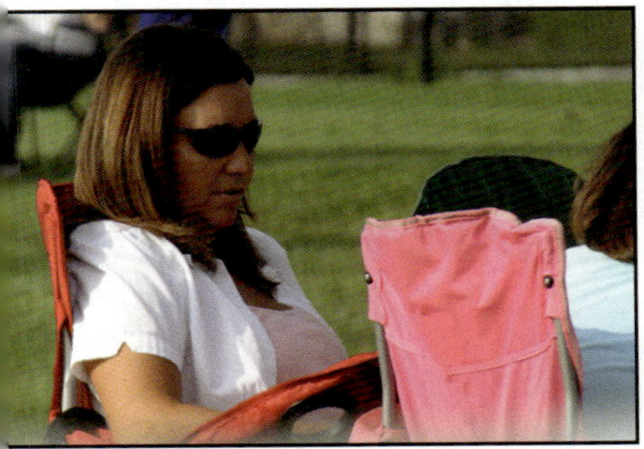

Cookie Binzer

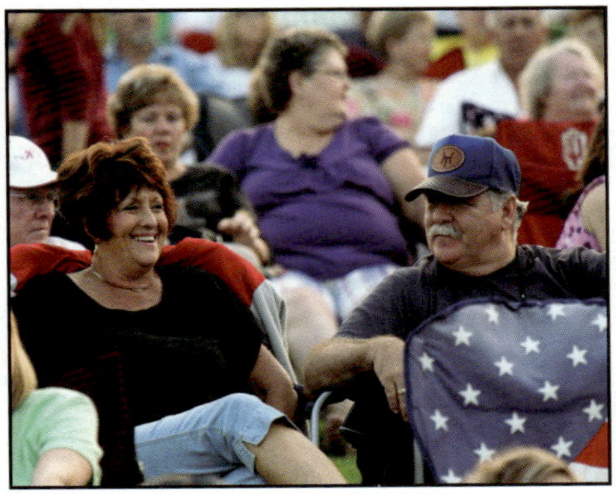

Above, a large crowd attends the June 13 concert at Rucker Complex.

Top and far left photos by Don Ward

Left, Padgett and Mike Taylor enjoy the concert.

Below, Kenny Guthrie (left) and Brook Reindollar perform as The Blues Devils.

Photos by Kathy Chandler

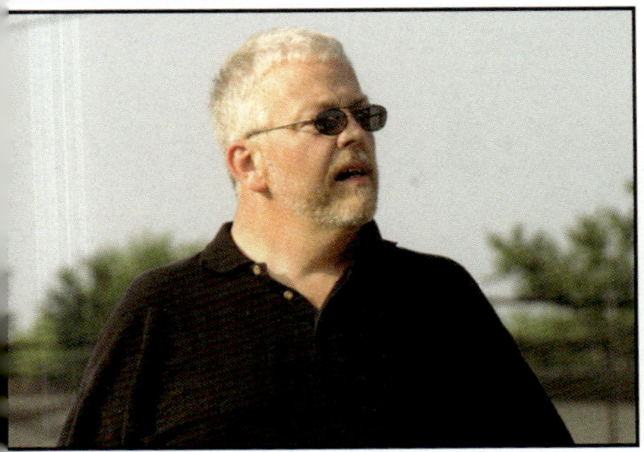

Scott Bate

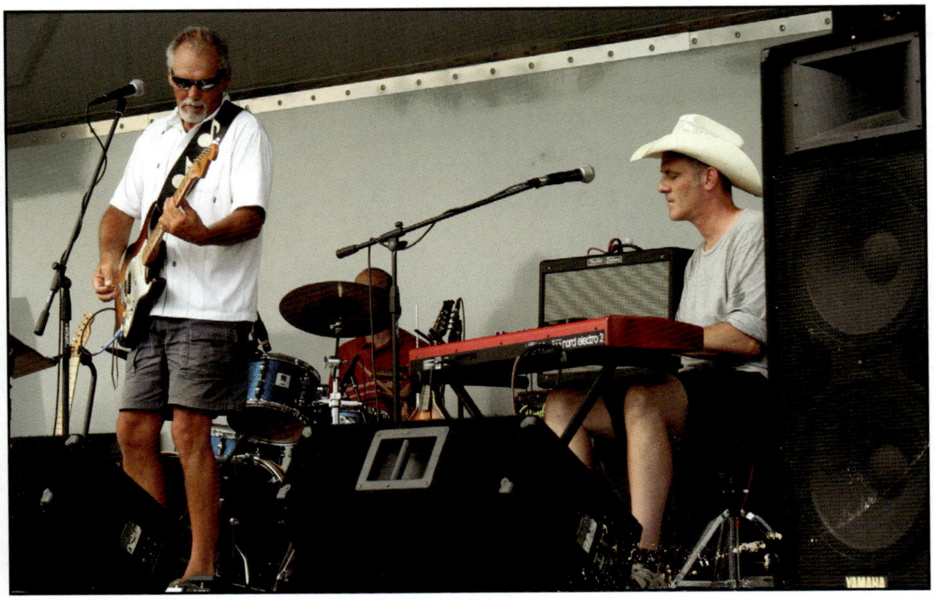

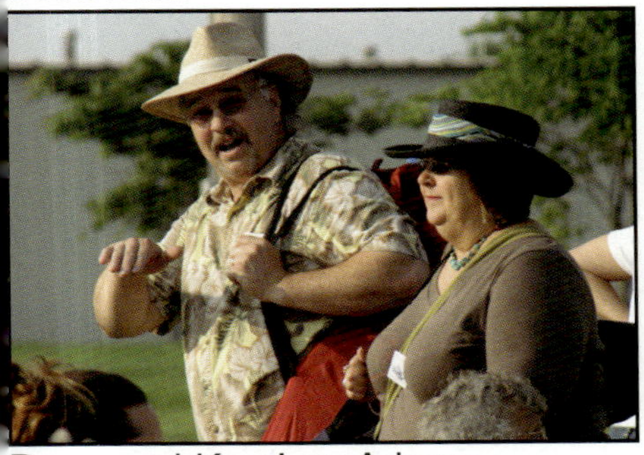

Dave and Kay Lou Adams

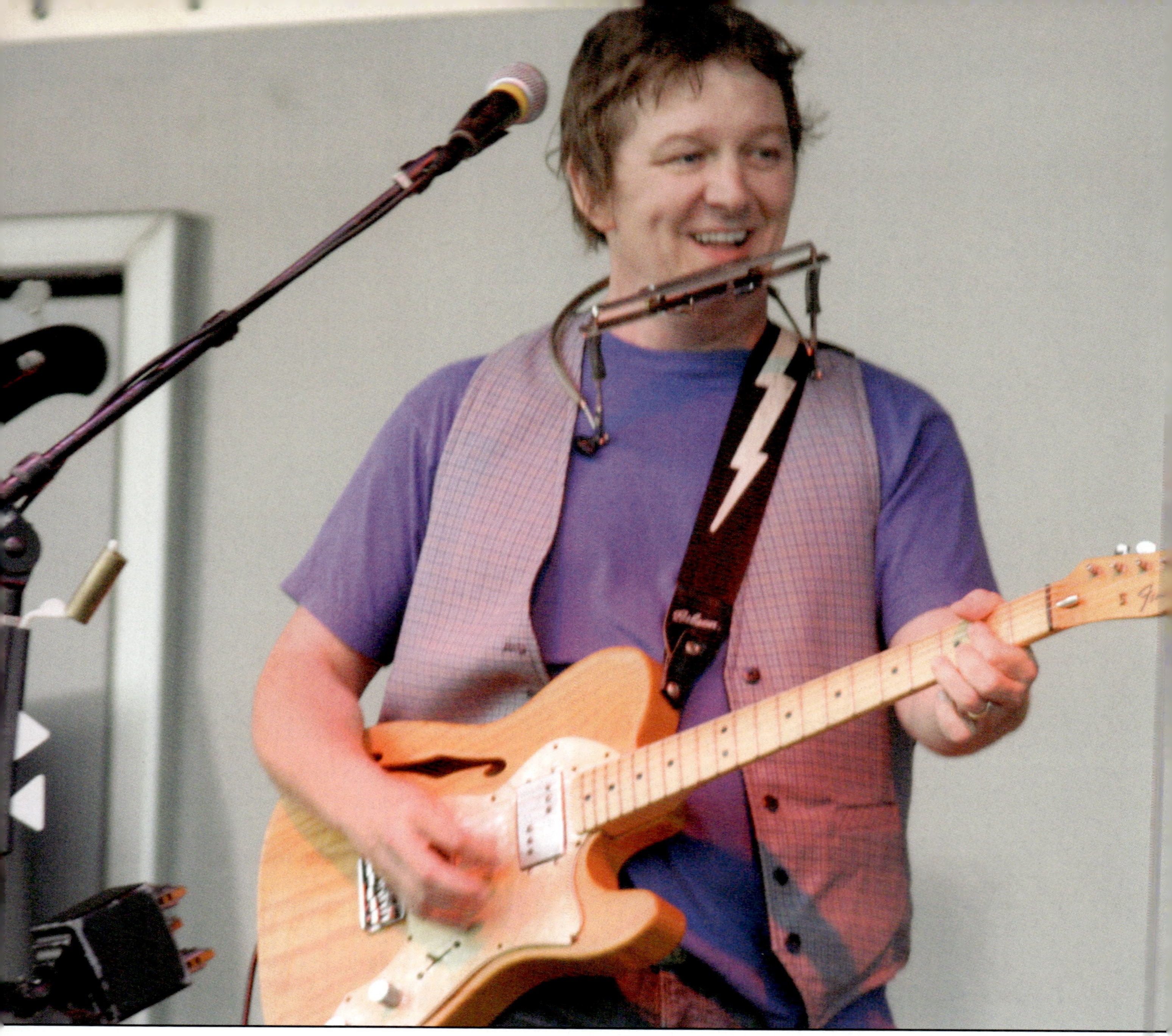

RIGHT: Drummer Chris Croxton, who finished third in the "Madison's Got Talent" contest, performs for the Rucker Sports Complex crowd.

SECOND PHOTO AT RIGHT: Drew Geerts, who won the "Madison's Got Talent" contest, performs at Rucker Sports Complex.

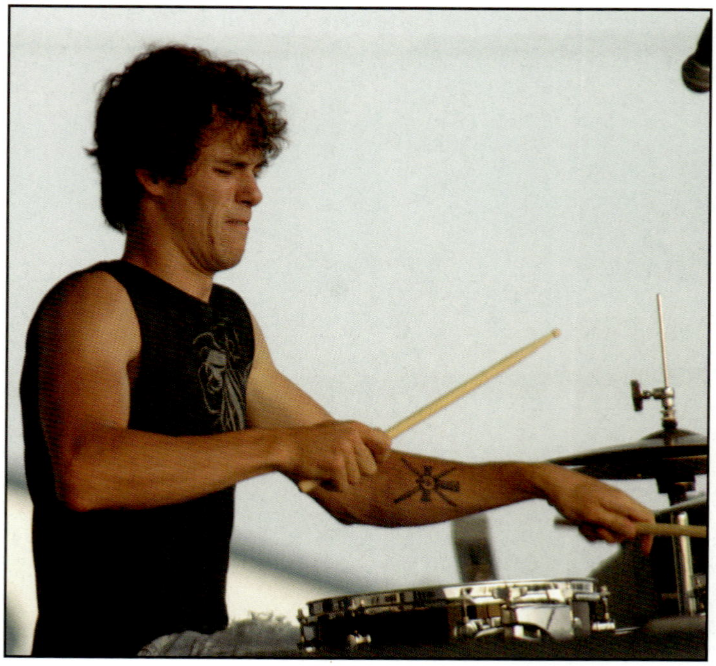

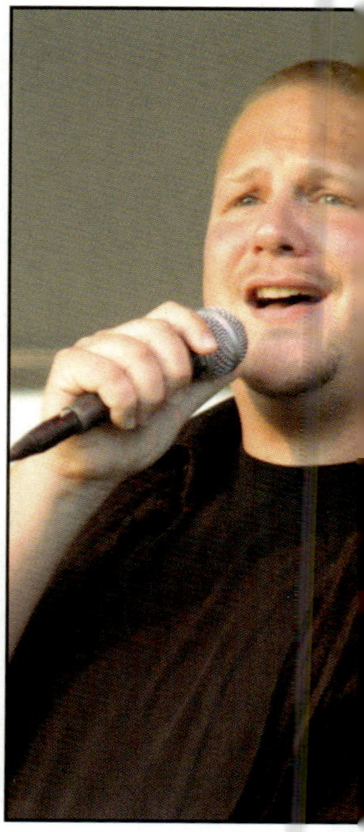

Music, Laser Light Show

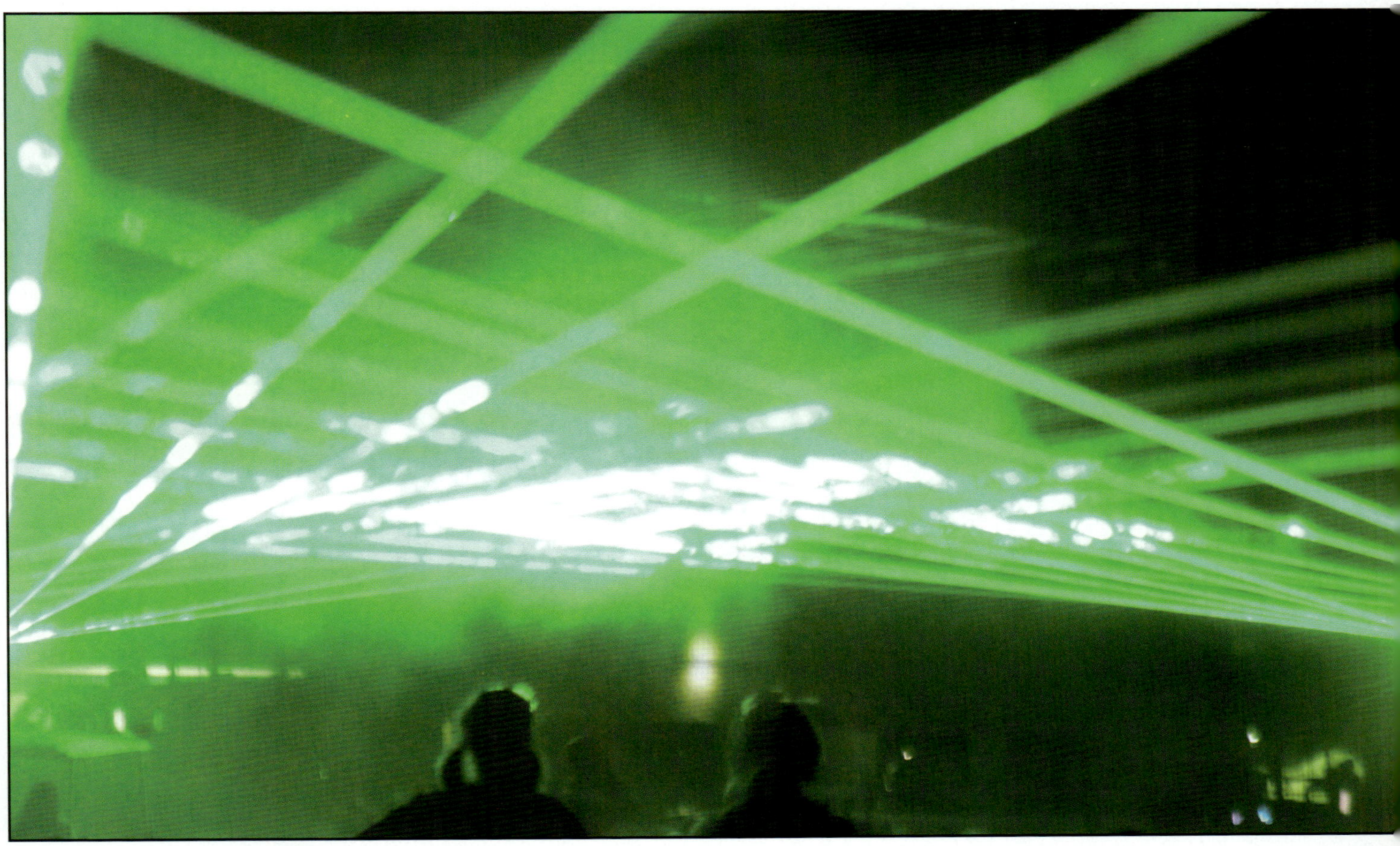

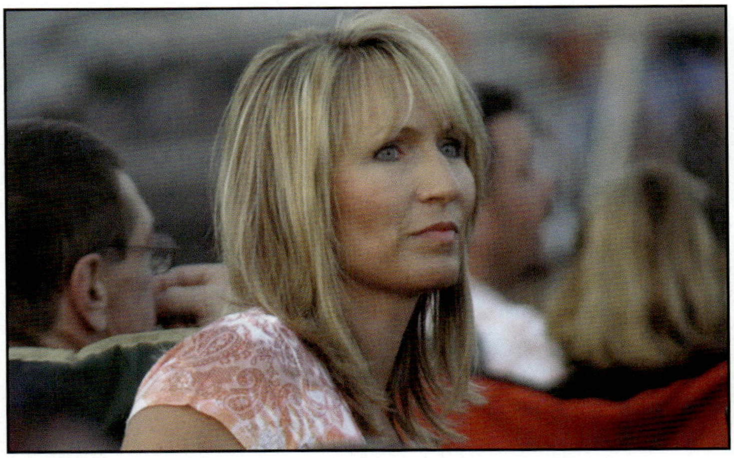

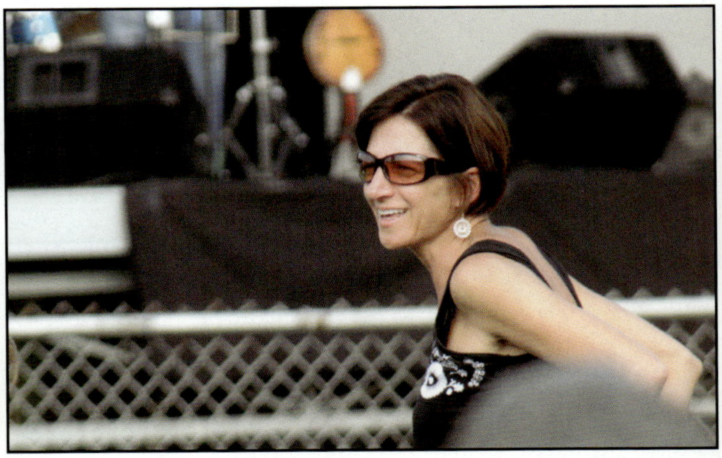

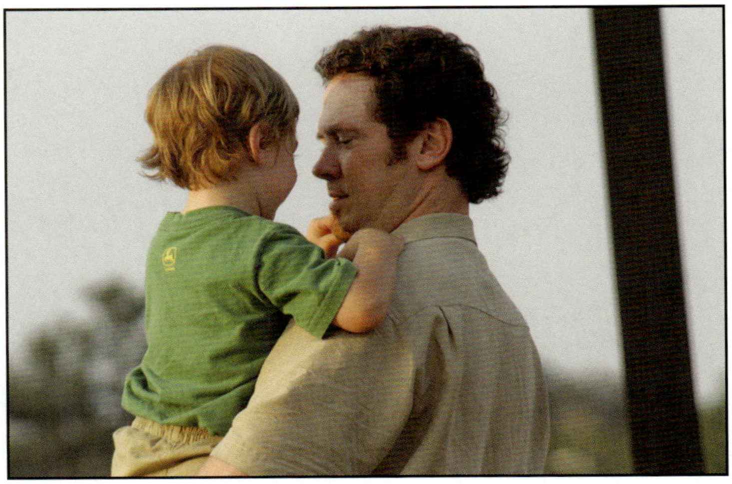

TOP LEFT: Singer Rusty Bladen entertains the crowd prior to the Laser Light Show (top right) and fireworks June 13 at Rucker Sports Complex.

ABOVE LEFT: Lisa Croxton of Madison.

ABOVE RIGHT: Sandi Bruns of Madison.

LEFT: Trevor Lytle and son, Roman, 3, of Madison at the concert.

Photos by Don Ward

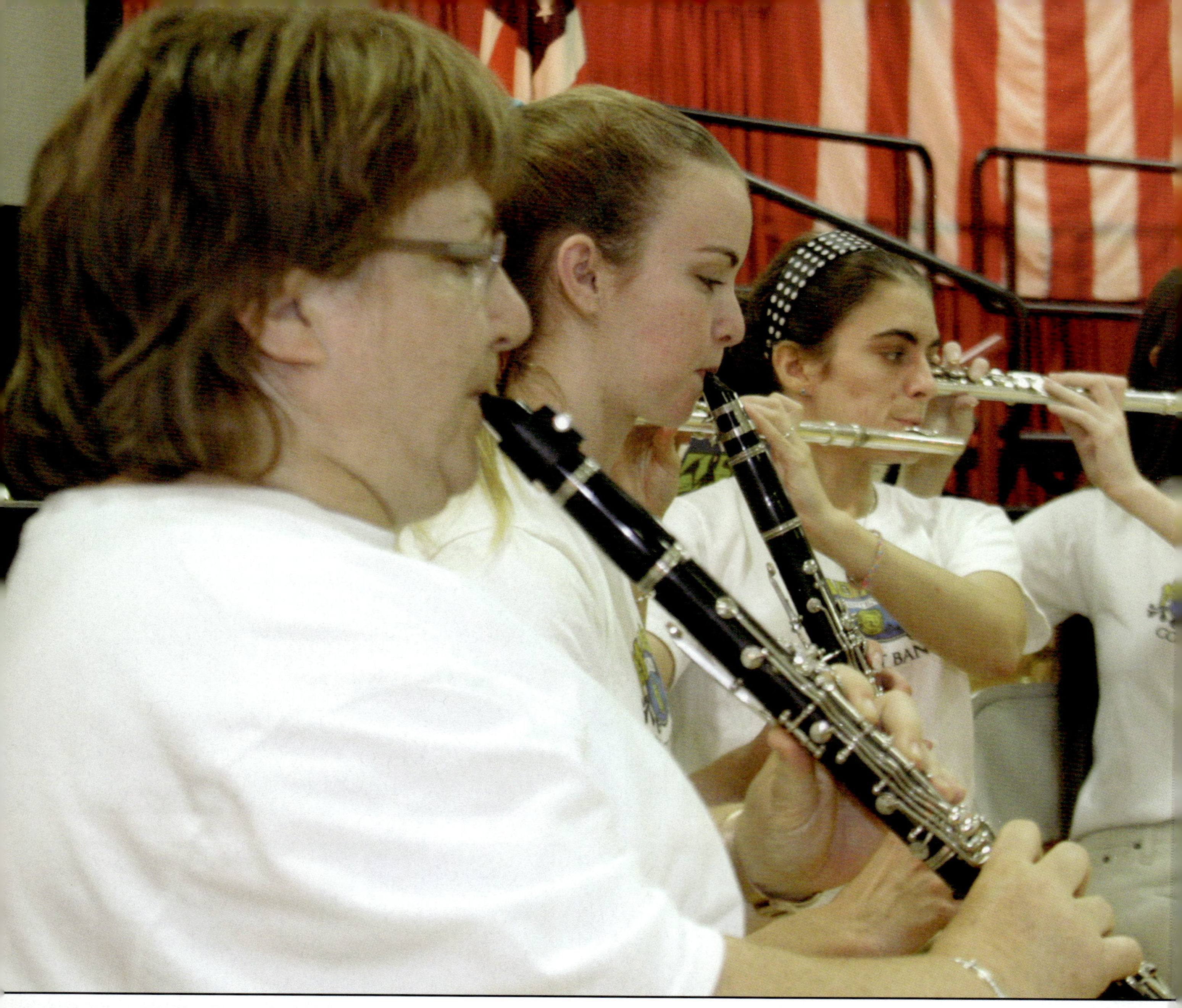

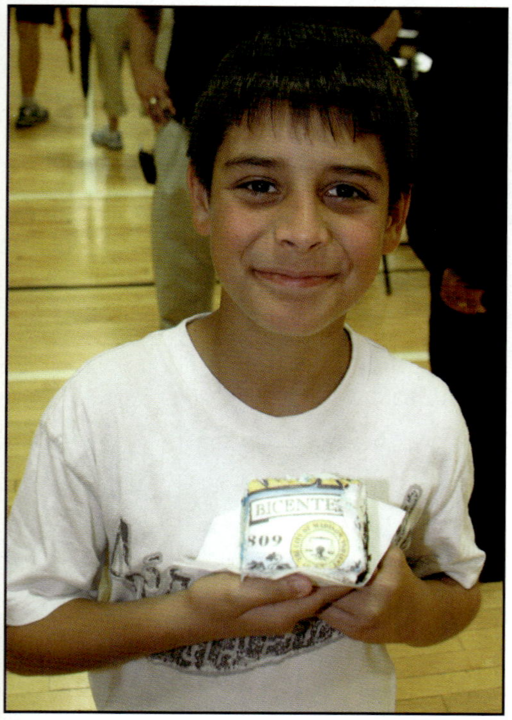

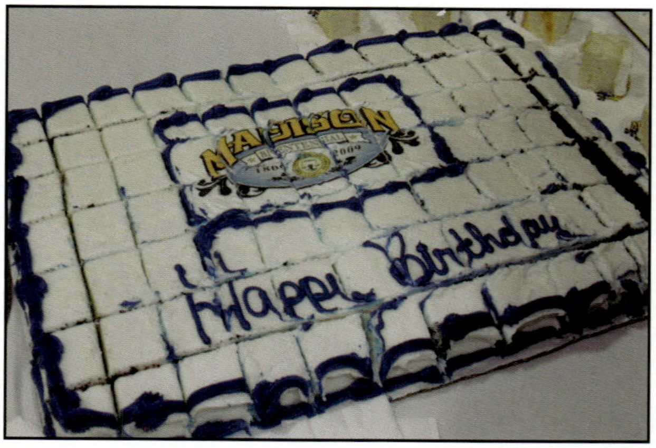

Grant Ward (left) prepares to eat what he calls "the best piece" of a Bicentennial Birthday Cake (above).

A young girl (right) receives a piece of Birthday Cake as anxious children await their turns.

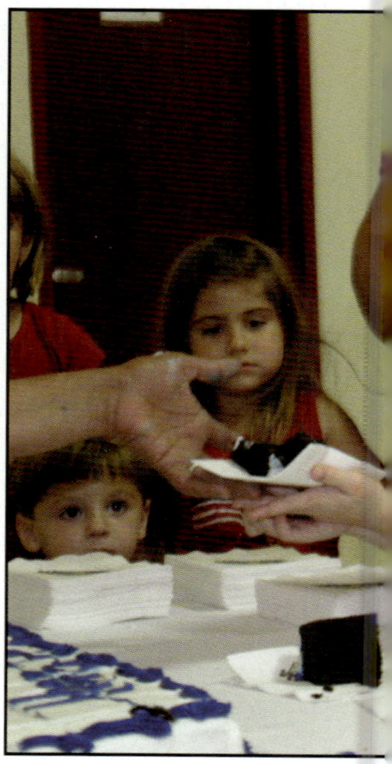

Closing Ceremony

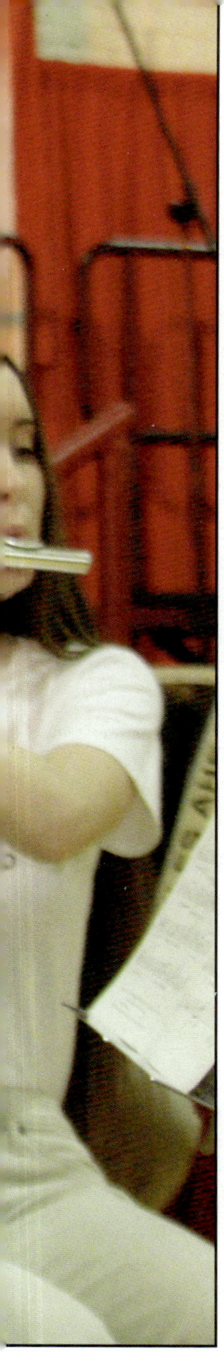

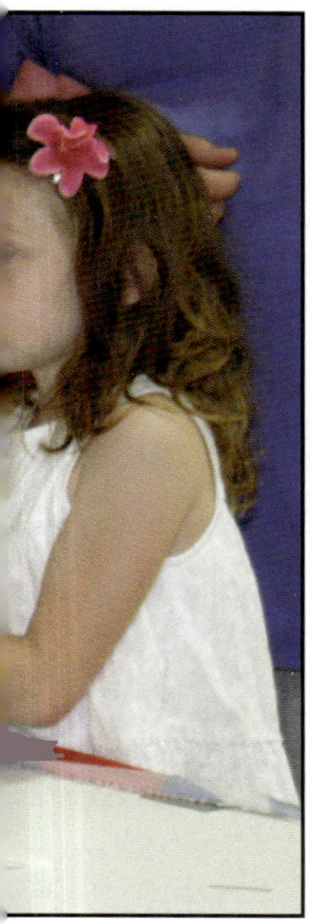

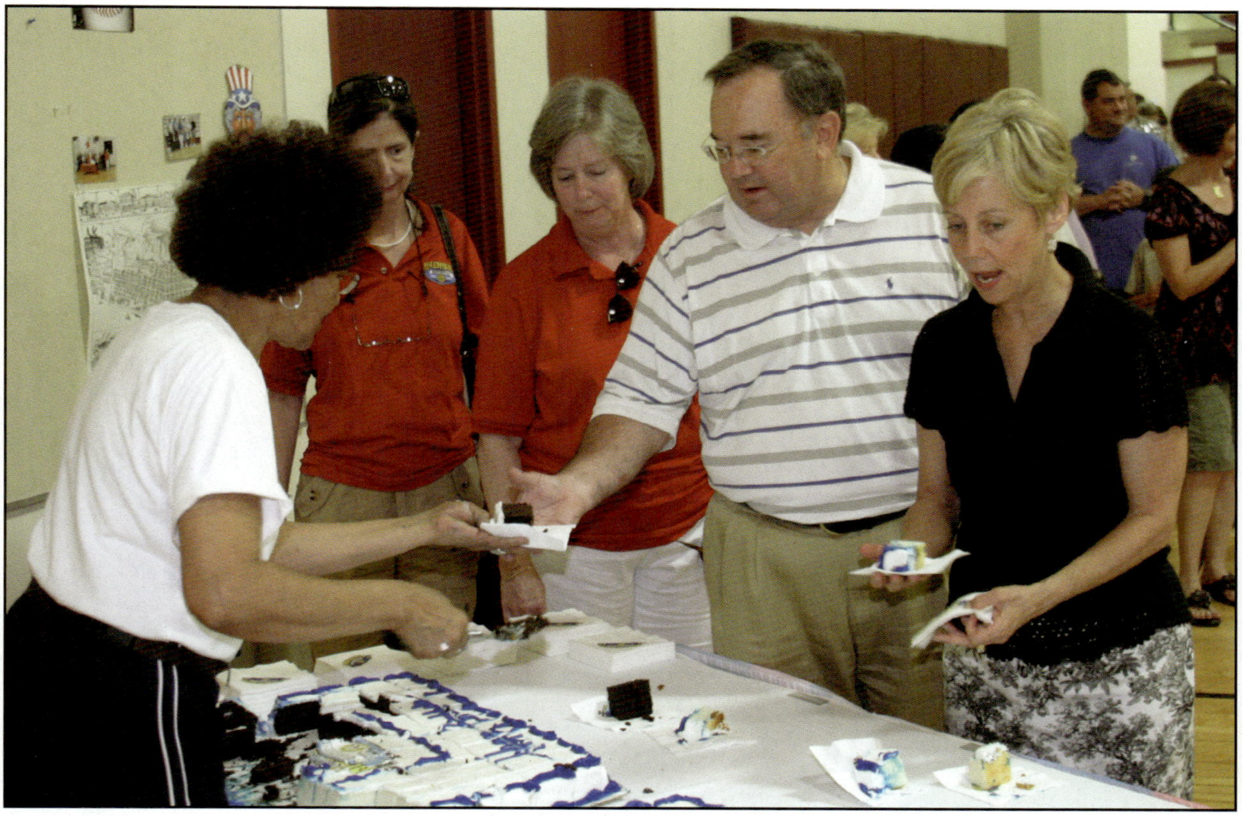

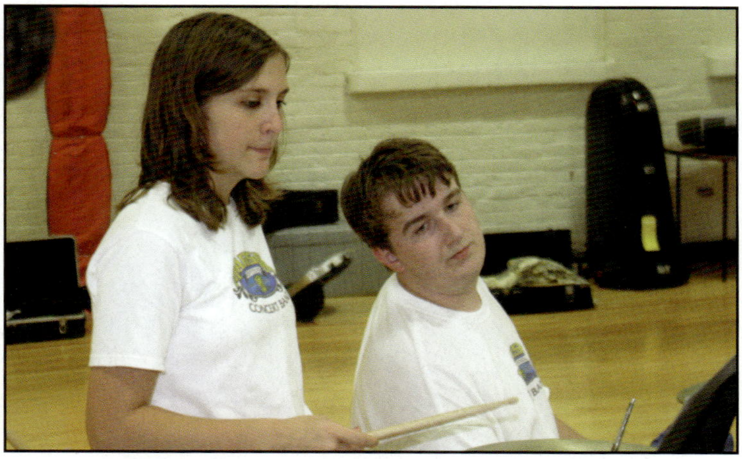

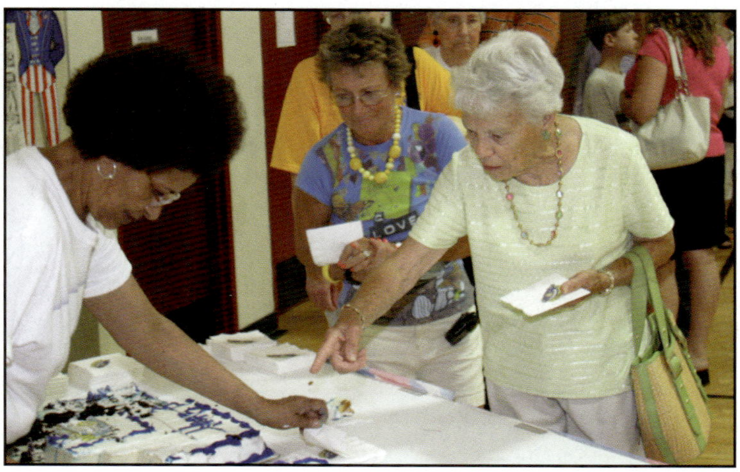

TOP LEFT: Members of the Bicentennial Band perform June 14 at the Closing Ceremony inside the Brown Gym.

ABOVE: (From left) Jane Michelle Kelly, Georgie Kelly and Rob and Michelle Barlow line up for a piece of Bicentennial Birthday Cake from server Iraci Rowlett.

LEFT: Members of the Bicentennial Band percussion section perform.

BELOW LEFT: These ladies line up for cake, selecting a piece of either vanilla or chocolate flavored Birthday Cake.

Photos by Don Ward

Jim Grant (right) poses in one of his many costumes June 14 at the conclusion of the Closing Ceremony. At far right, Madison Mayor Tim Armstrong makes his closing remarks of the Bicentennial. Below, (from left) Rory Fulk, Mason and Isabella May await their turn for a piece of Birthday Cake

Photos by Don Ward

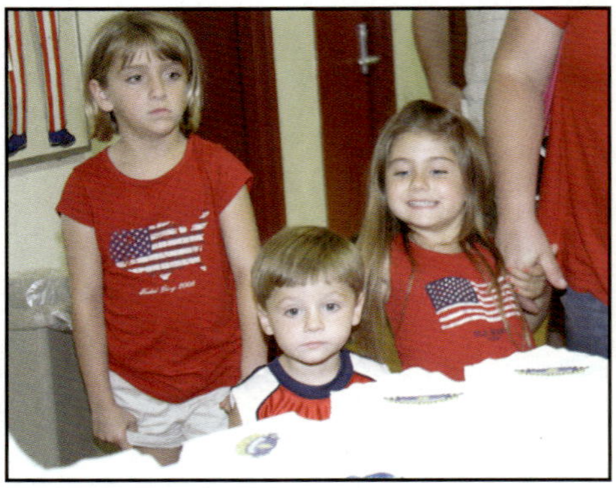

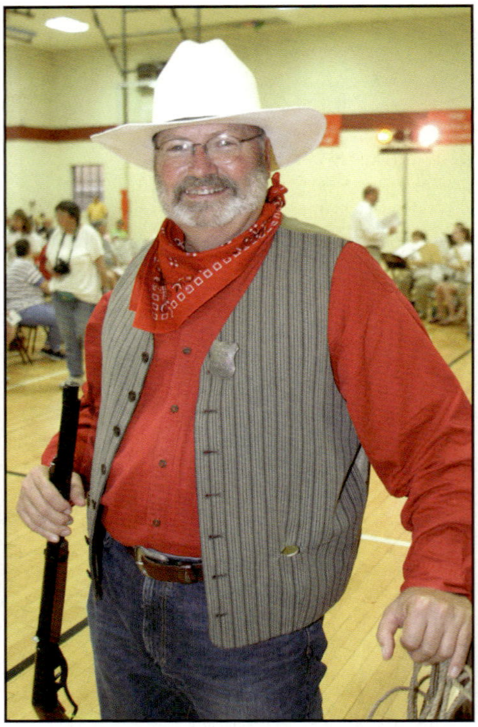

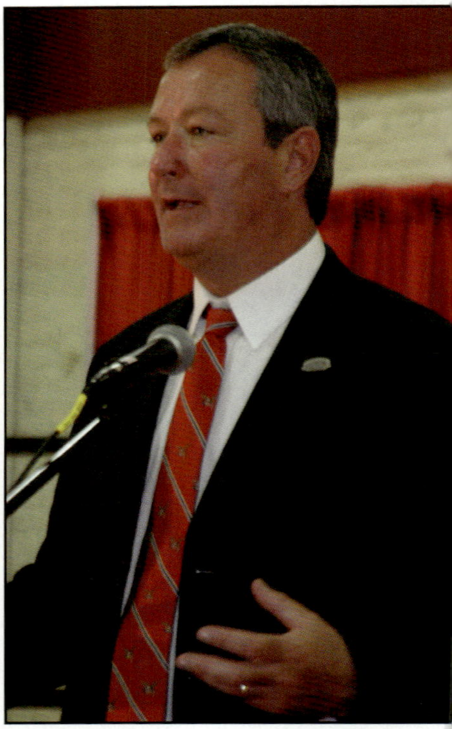

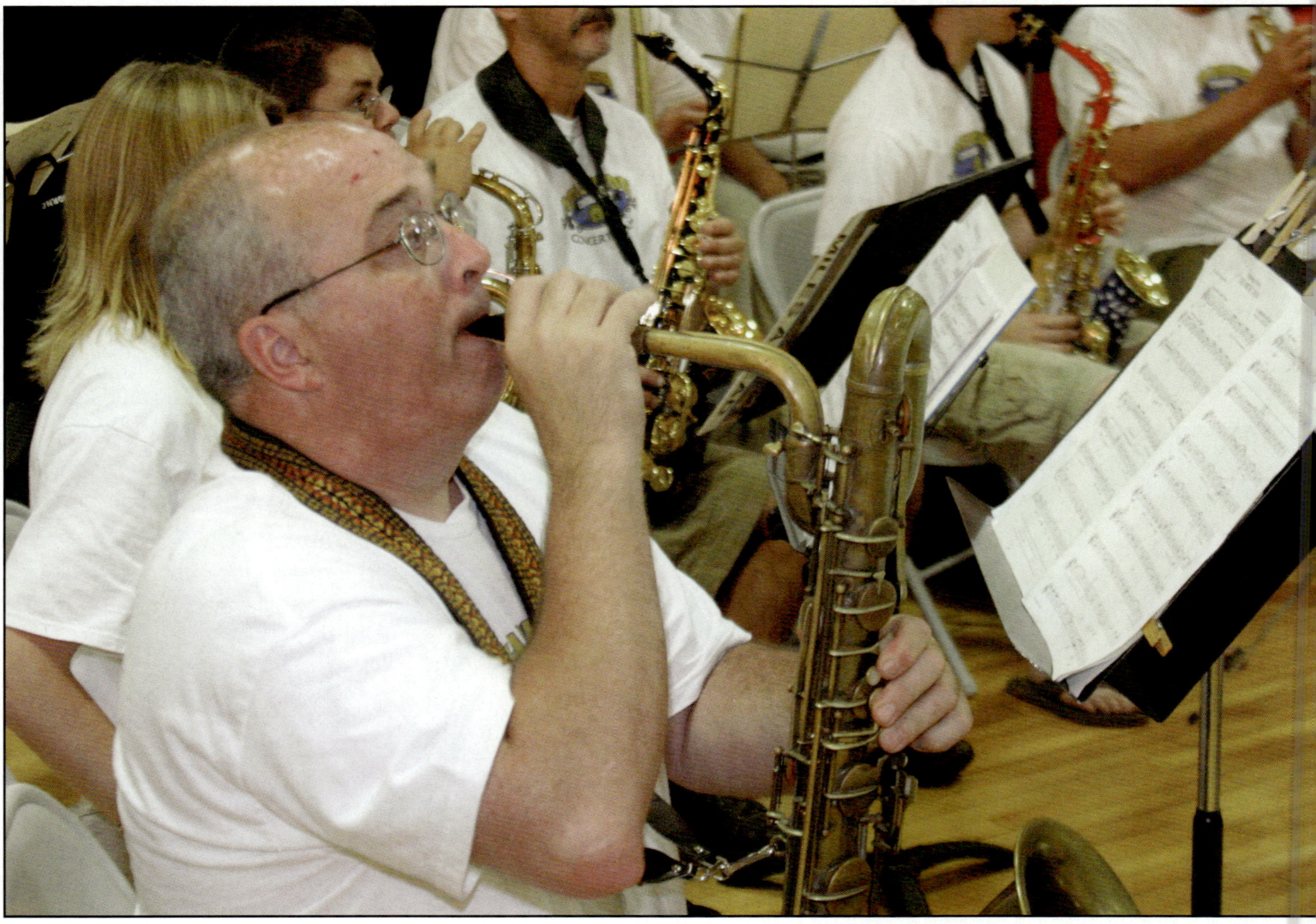

Scott Davis of the Bicentennial Band adjusts his saxophone reed as the band played at the Closing Ceremony.

Bicentennial Community Photo

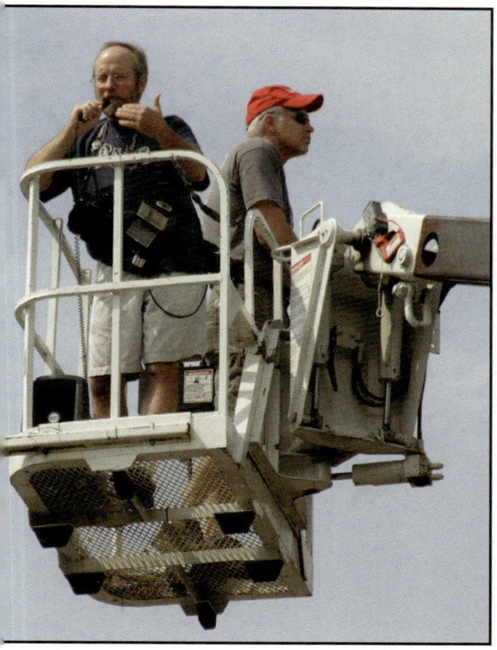

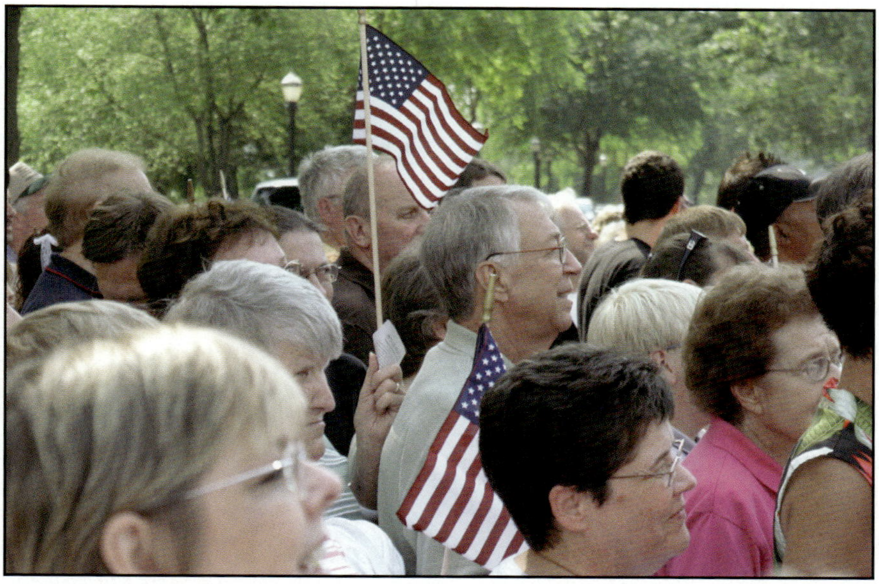

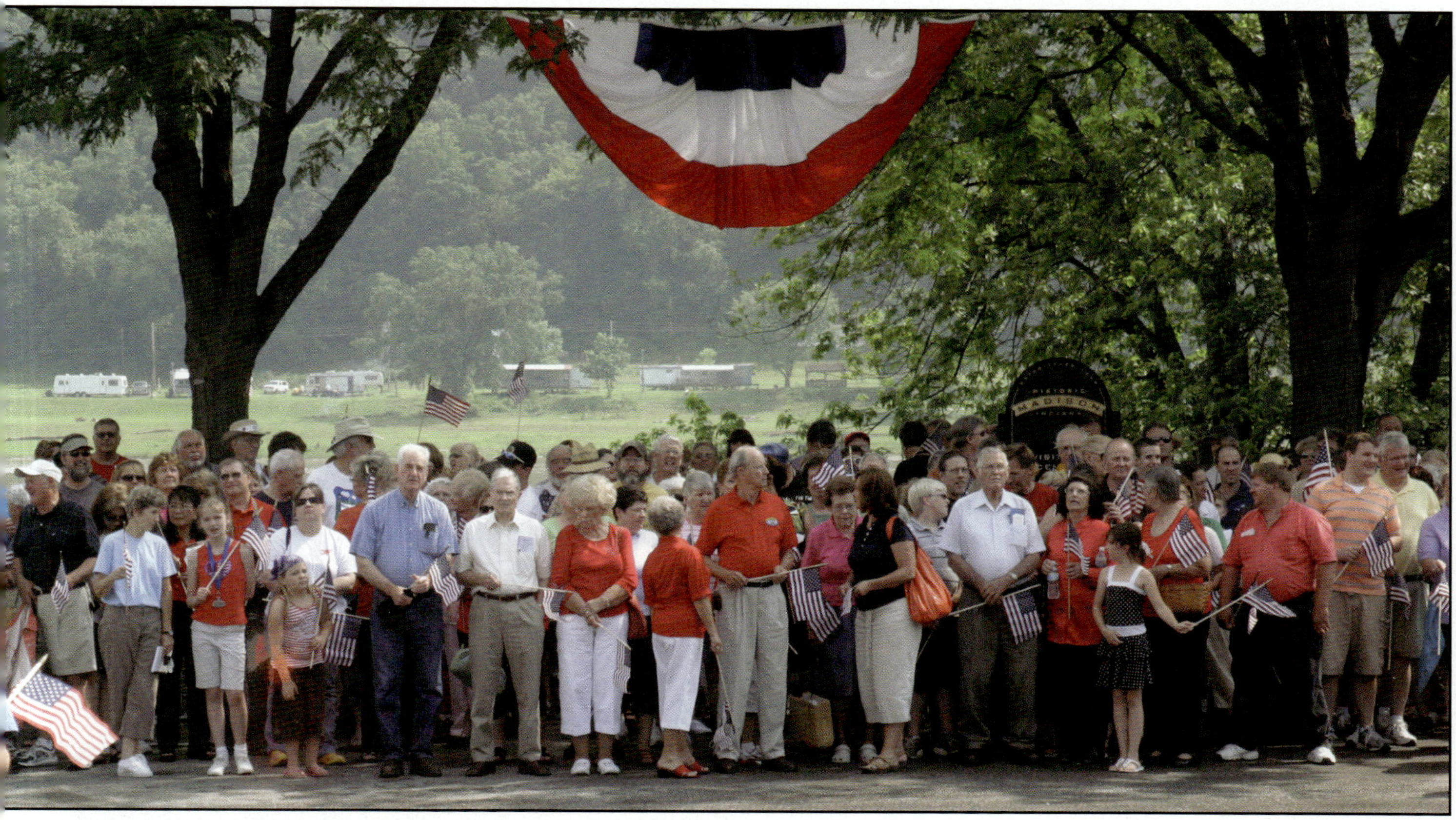

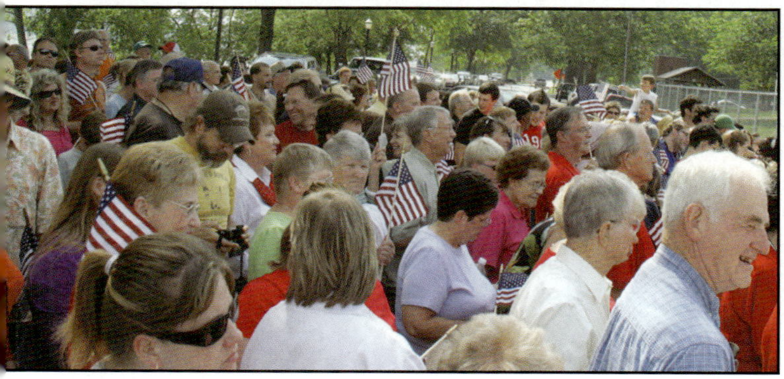

Pat Heitz (top left photo) of Heitz Sign Co. controls the bucket lift June 14, guiding photographer Michael Heitz (with microphone) into place for a Bicentennial Community Photo. The photo (Pages 124-125) was taken at Broadway Street and Vaughn Drive following the Closing Ceremony at the Brown Gym. It concluded the nine-day celebration that marked Madison's 200 years.

Photos by Don Ward

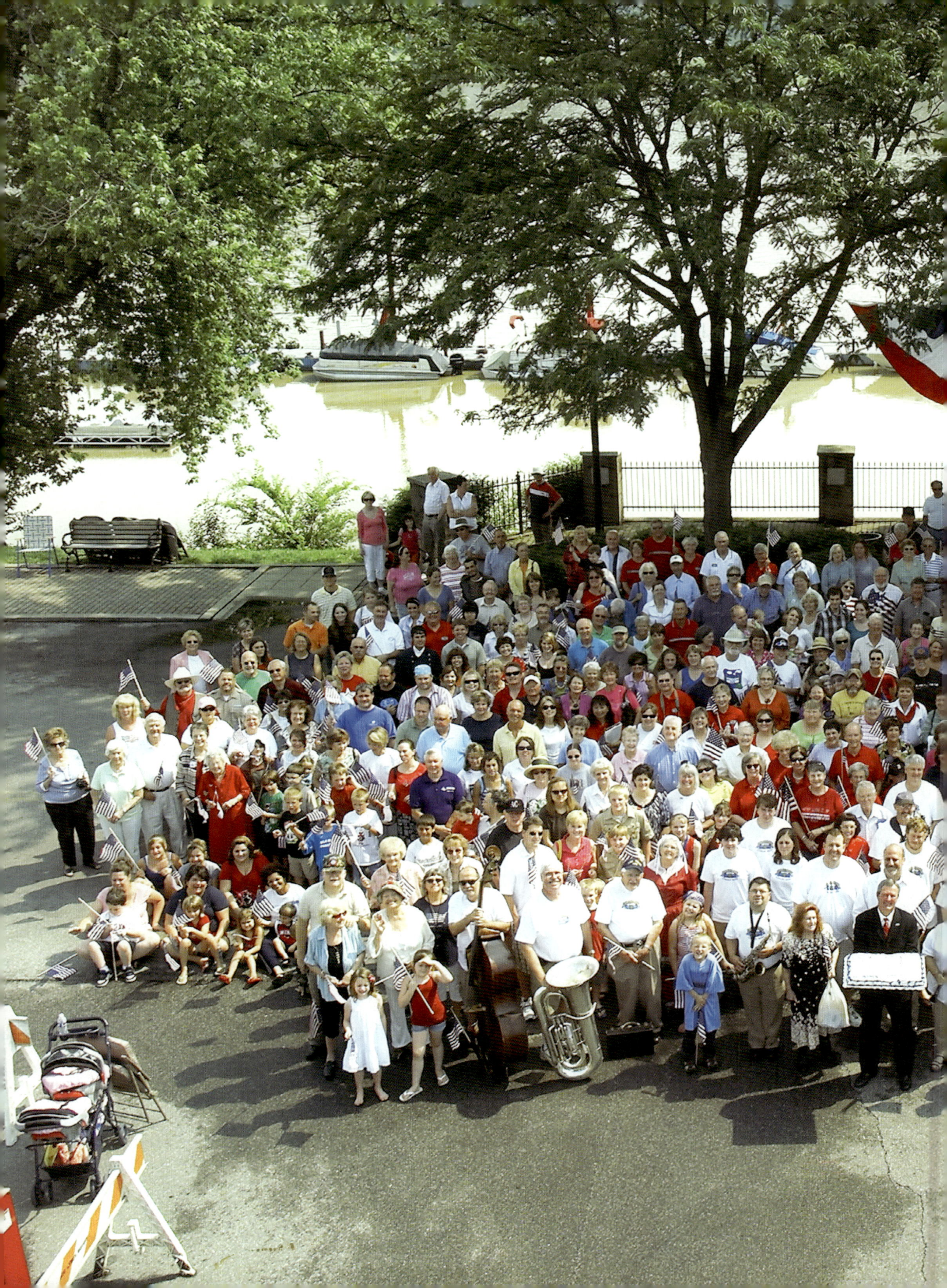

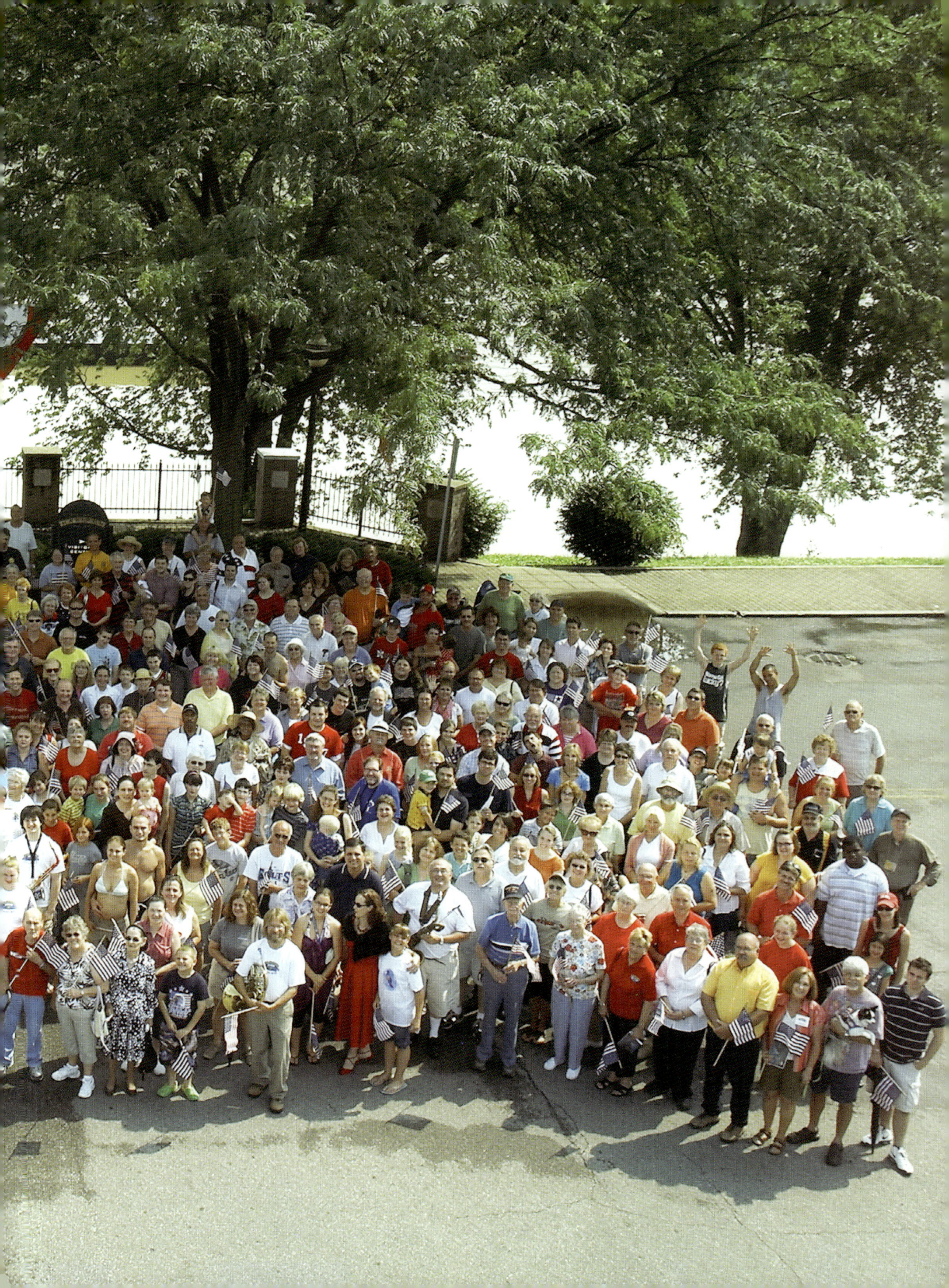

Party Planners

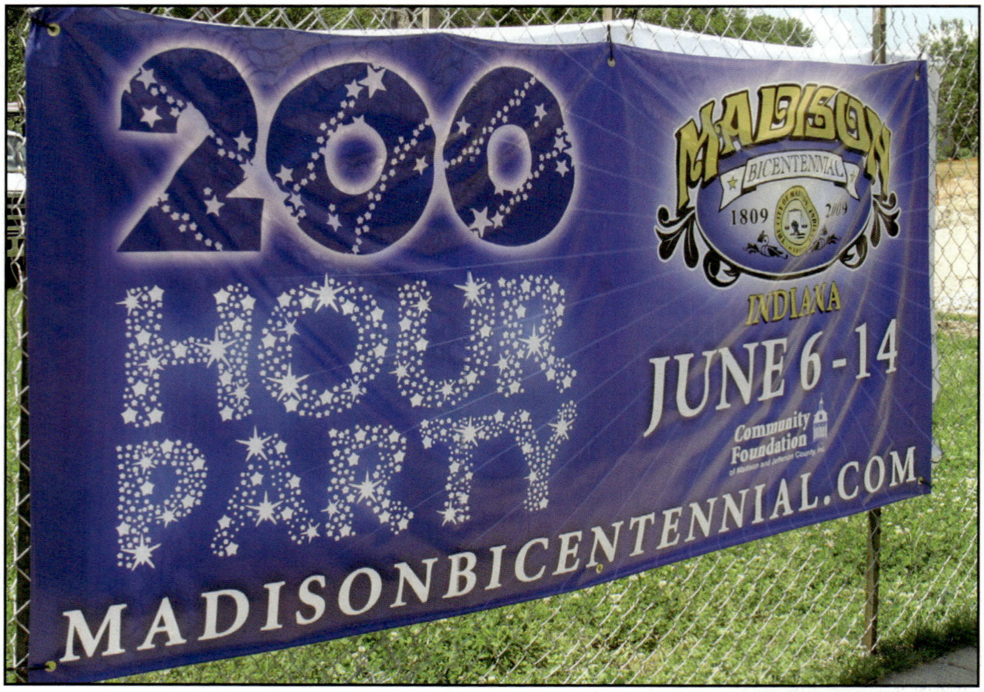

Photo by Don Ward

The Madison Bicentennial Banner hangs on a fence near the riverfront.

200-Hour Party Committee Chairs, Volunteers and Supporters

Committee Chairs

Margaret Seifert and Rotary Club, Founder's Parade
Jenny Eggenspiller, 5K and Opening Ceremony
Frank Taff, Fire Muster
Fire Captains, fire station open houses
Michael Heitz and Rivercrest Marina, Lighted Boat Parade
Gerry Reilly, Cincinnati Orchestra and Lanier Days
Jennifer Grove and Nancy Gruner, 1920s-1930s Gala Cocktail Party
Leticia Bajuyo, Arts Day
Kevin Snyder, Community Picnic and Events at Clifty Falls State Park
Joe Carr, Historic Sites Day Events
Ann Fairchild and Kevin Snyder, Geocaching
Juanita DeWeese, Pie-Baking Contest
Maddie Gray and Senior Center, Euchre Tournament
Susan Brewer, Historic Characters
Stephanie Hellmann, Trinity United Methodist Church Ice Cream Social
Alva Tripp and Madison Performing Arts, Heritage in Music Concert
Laura Hodges and Madison Area Chamber of Commerce, Cruisin' Clifty
Laura & Tony Ratcliff and Ohio Theatre, Film Festival and Talent Show
Lynn Maricle and Nancy Gruner, Madison's Got Talent Show
Steve Dattilo, Block Party
Chip Binzer and Joe DeVito, Music
Laura Morris and Madison Precision Products, Concert and Laser Light Show
Lisa Smitley, Old Fashioned Chautauqua
Jill Keller, Vintage Baseball
Linda Phillips, Spelling Bee
Al Huntington, Madison Memorabilia Exhibit
Rhonda Deeg, Historic Trades Fair
Marylin McQueen, Living Stories Videos
Terri Waller and Tanya Besse, Hospitality
Bill Welch, 1809 Service Praise Concert
Bill and Jennifer Maginn, Patriotic Concert
Elizabeth Thomas, Closing Ceremony

Other Key People:

PeeWee Lakeman, Madison City Parks Dept.
Chief John Wallace, Madison City Police Dept.
Chief Steve Horton, Madison City Fire Dept.
Burke Jones, Doug Vest and Kenny Washer, Madison City Street Dept.

Also Thanks to These People:

Bobbie Wooldridge, Laura Macon (counselors) and the ladies from the **G.R.I.P. Therapeutic Community** at the Indiana Department of Corrections for making all the bunting and street banners.
Meese, Orbitron & Dunne for putting in all the grommets to be able to hang them.
Michael Heitz Studio and Heitz Sign Co. for providing the photograph at the closing ceremony.
Wal-Mart, Kroger and Horst's Bakery for donating the cakes at the closing.
Anne Saxe for the Bicentennial Recipe Book
Larry Wickersham for the Bicentennial "Churches of Madison" music CD
Camille Fife and Ron Grimes for the Bicentennial History Book
Don Ward and RoundAbout Madison for the Bicentennial Photography Contest and this "Faces of Madison" Commemorative Photo Journal Book
Vivian Shatley for the Bicentennial Quilt

$500-$5,000 Sponsors:

MainSource Bank; Farmers Bank of Milton; Centra Credit Union; Meese, Obitron, Dunne; Kroger; Lee Rogers Fund; Neida Rogers Fund; Lanier Mansion Foundation; Indiana Arts Commission; Indiana Humanities Council; Beam, Longest & Neff; Bernadin, Lockmueller & Associates; Bingham McHale Attorneys at Law; Crowe Horath LLC, Culotta & Culotta, Attorneys; Energy Systems Group; FPBH Engineers & Surveyors.

Note: See list of $10,000-$100,000 Primary Sponsors, Page 13.

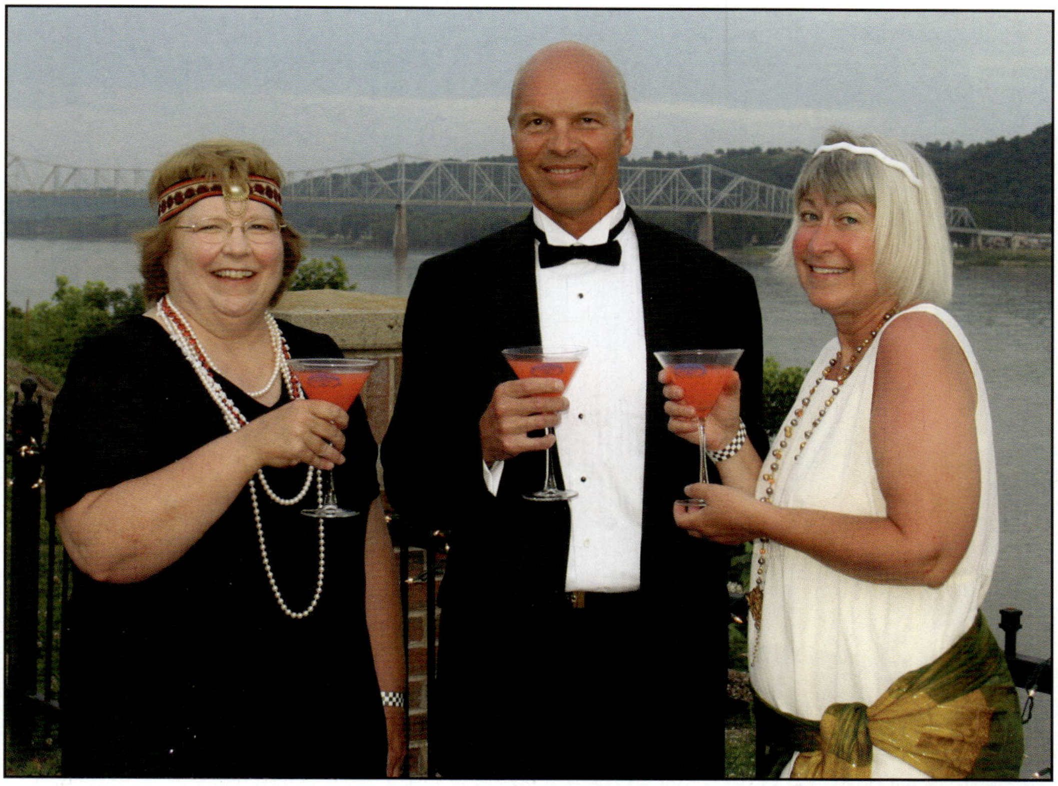

Photo by Randy Porter

From left, Madison Bicentennial Marketing Chair Laura Hodges, RoundAbout Madison Editor and Publisher Donald L. Ward, and Bicentennial Chairwoman Jan Vetrhus on June 7 toast the success of the weeklong event with a "Bicentini" at the 1920s-1930s Gala Cocktail Party, held at the Madison riverfront.

A toast to the Madison Bicentennial!

Thanks to everyone who participated in the Madison Bicentennial celebration and for making this such a special event for the entire community.

This photo journal book was conceived and produced to help commemorate and preserve the images of this 200-Hour Party, June 6-14, 2009.

I would like to especially thank Jan Vetrhus and Laura Hodges for their help and support in producing this book. Truly, their dedication to the Madison, Ind., community is immeasurable and will be remembered for years to come.

– Donald L. Ward
Editor, Publisher, Owner,
RoundAbout Madison

Index

Guide to Photographs

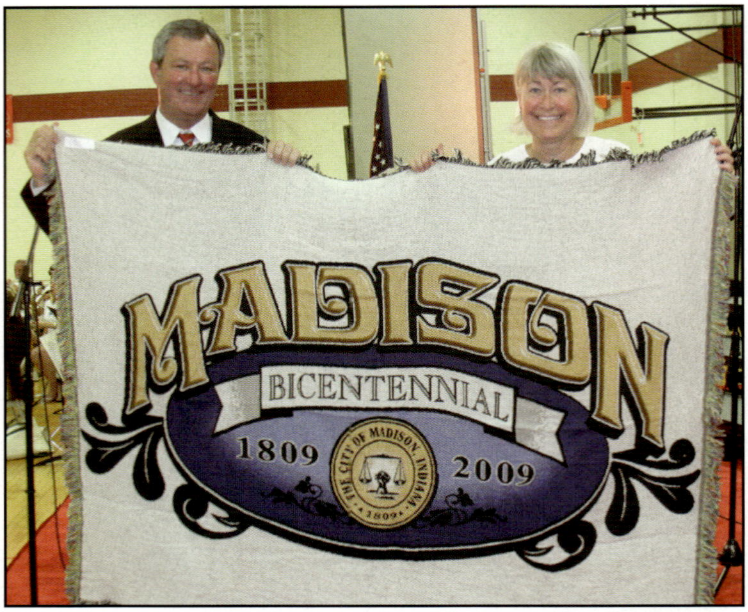

Photo by Don Ward

Madison Mayor Tim Armstrong and Bicentennial Chairwoman Jan Vetrhus display a Bicentennial afghan that was given away as part of a series of prize drawings held June 14 at the Closing Ceremony. The afghans are for sale at various area retailers, along with several other Bicentennial souvenirs.

1– Rick Berry, Bob Schoenstein, Pete Backus, Tom Patterson, Tim Armstrong, Laura Hodges.
2 – Tim Armstrong, Jim Lewis.
3 – Dave Cheatham, Jan Vethrus.
5 – Joyce Randles, Connie Partington, Sandie Gooden, Ashley Roberts, Stephanie Hellmann, Emily Roberts, Bryce Worrell, Brianna Worrell, Brandilyn Worrell, Margo Watkins, Wayne Engle, Jan Vetrhus, Bob Fourhman, Betsey Vonderheide, Bill Demaree.
7 – Margaret Seifert, Tim Armstrong.
8 – Brick Boldery, Arial Hall, Brienna Miller, Tucker Adams, Vance Neace, Caitlyn Brooks, Lesley Reverman, Kristen Garrett, Mary Elizabeth Goldsmith, Vivian Shatley, Louise Anthony, Anna Bell.
10 – Jordyn Bilz, Jamie Smith, LeAnn Fox, Lydia Arney, Matthew Sedam, Katie Hartman.
11 – Tim Armstrong, Riley Chisholm, Brianna Humphrey, Tatiana Buckner, Vy Huynn, Dalton Bowen, Aaron Blades, Amanda Asher, Zeb O'Neal, Gavin Wendel, Abby Hanson, Gracie True.
12 – Charles Moman, Sadie Courtney, Nichole Waldon, Kate McKay, Mike Bowen.
13 – Mathys Cutter, Stephanie Hellmann, Janice Barnes, Carolyn Stutler, Lisa Smitley, Laura Hodges, Rusty Bladen, Charlotte Hubbs, Rhonda Deeg, Jan Vetrhus, Amy Christner, Laura Ratcliff, Kevin Snyder, Nancy Gruner, Camille Fife, Harold Lakeman, Margaret Seifert, Susan Ohlendorf, Terrie Waller, Frank Taff, Matt Forrester, Alva Tripp, Chip Binzer, Jim Grant, Gerry Reilly, Anne Saxe, Janice Barnes, Camille Fife-Salmon, Ron Grimes, Bob Thomas.
14 – Drew Geerts, Samantha Buchanan.
15 – Kyle Clerkin, Kate McKay, Chris Croxton.
16 – Betsey Vonderheide, Bill Demaree, Bob Fourhman, Bryce Worrell.
17 – Connie Partington, Dorothy Jones, Joyce Randles, Jan Vetrhus.
18 – Stephanie Hellmann, Margo Watkins, Sue Livers, Wayne Engle.
19 – Bryce Worrell, Joyce Randles, Bob Fourhman, Wayne Engle.
21 – Chad Schafer, Dave and Nina Campbell.
25 – Andrew Forrester.
26 – Julie Berry, Tom Pietrykowski.
28 – Heather Atkinson, Tim Armstrong, Catharine Graham, Lisa Konkle, Gina Center, Jenny Eggenspiller, Linda Zapp, Jeff Melton, Tammy Courtney, John and Patti Wallace.
29 – Jim Cole, Tim Armstrong, Leslie Cutshaw, Zack Hawkins, Kim Cieslinski, Chris and Trace Strouse, Tonya Schmidt.
30 – Jenny Straub Youngblood, Patty Cooper Wells, Lou Knoble, Bob Saueressig, Bill Borden, Sally McWilliams.
31 – Chris Heitz, Marguerite Ligon, Lou Knoble, Lillie Wingham, Bob Saueressig, Barbara Walters-Dixon, Jenny Straub Youngblood, Kevin Carlson, Patty Cooper Wells, Hal Davis, Jane Devito, Teresa Waller, Bill Borden, Larry Rudolech, Tim Armstrong, Georgie Kelly.
32 – Wayne Engle, Camille Fife, Connie Partington, Bryce Worrell, Baron and Betty Hill, Tim Armstrong, Al Huntington.
33 – Joyce Wells, Betsey Vonderheide, Susan Ohlendorf, Dorothy Jones.
35 – Baron and Betty Hill, Dave Cheatham Al Huntington, Janice Hardy Stanley.
38 – Corey and Evan Murphy, Erin Laufer, Lauren Cieslinski, Tom Armstrong, Markt Lytle, Al Huntington, Morris Wooden, Donald Vaughn.
39 – Karen Buchanan, Kenton Mahoney, Addie Turner, Don Cochran, Larry Wickersham.
40 – Al Huntington, Ray Wilson, Jane Jacobs, Mary Goode Wallis, Debbie and Kristen Snodgrass.
41 – Sue Livers, Tim Armstrong, Jan Vetrhus, Laura Hodges.
42 – Tommy McQueary, Taylor Starks, Justin McQueary, Adam Stewart, Ronald Barnes, Mike Snell, Frank Taff
43 – Carl Morgan, Tim Monoghan.
45 – Jimmy Davis, Rick Bennett, Brook Reindollar, Jenna Watkins.
46 – Pamela Stockard, Matthew Williams.
47 – Pam Quick, Sarah Adams.
48 – Ava Rowland, Vince Lee, Lauren Ringel.
49 – Frank and Carolyn Gunter.
50 – Erin, Gavin and Gabriel McMahon, Alex Ratcliff.
51 – Bryce Worrell, Gina Center, Tammy Boldery.
52 – Kathie Petkovic, Kate McKay, Nichole Waldon, Sadie Courtney, Elizabeth Hayes.
53 – Jim Grant, Kevin and Margo Watkins, Eric and Kelly Rector.
54 – Candi Miller, Charlie and Kathy Rohlfing, Tom and Mary Davee, Nancy Gruner, Erik and Jennifer Grove, Bill and Whitney Settles.
55 – Sandra Straub, Sarah Marshall, Jill Turner, Holly Robinson, Rhonda Deeg, Jack Patchin, Kelly Rector, Camille Fife, Jane Devito.
56 – Amy Vaughn, Sean Cleary, Dan and Laura Hodges, Nichole Waldon, Kate McKay, Sadie Courtney, Jennifer Wright.
57 – Debbie Armstrong, Jenny Eggenspiller, Camille Fife, Elizabeth Sorba, Miranda Jackson, Tristen Walters, Catherine Lesaux, Meredith Terrell, Chris Heitz.
58 – Tiffany Black.
60 – Kevin, Emma and Kayla Snyde Trey Ashby, Owen Altermatt.
61 – Randie and Tasha Carson, Annalisa Strickland.
62 – Tiffany Black, Kay Stokes.
63 – Carson Denton.
64 – Bob and Heidi Saueressig, Sus Brewer.
65 – Greg Ziesemer, Kriss Luckett.
66 – June Ritchie, Janet Furnish.
67 – Juanita DeWeese, Janet Faubush, Roselle Schmabel, Sara Mir
68 – Dean Jackson, Monty Geisler, John Staicer.
69 – Dave Butler, Brook Reindollar, J Polley, Jack Martindale, Charlie Schnabel.
70 – Stephanie Hellmann, Bill and Mary Lou Hill.
71 – Bill and Stasia Wiseman.
72 – Chip and Aiden Binzer.
73 – Amiah Rae Owen, Bruce Hagga
74 – Skyla Judkins.
75 – Conner Brough, Matt Marsh.
76 – Andrew Forrester, Fred Koehle
77 – Lewis and Betty Stoner.
78 – Howard and Elaine Long, Chris and Janice Rider.
79 – Bob Schafer.
80 – Ron Young, Louis Munier.
81 – John Wallace, Jeff Frazier, Bill Andrews, Don Ward, John Staicer.
83 – Paul Kelly.
84 – Brooke and Hailey Bayless, Pa and Caroline Grote.
85 – Bernard Kelley, Tim Armstrong, Whit, Jack and Christopher Grote, Maria Stoner, Elsa Conboy, Rick Holl and Kyle Barton.
86 – John Adkins, Leticia Bajuyo, David Jenkins.
87 – Chris Jesse, Joe Devito.
88 – Lindsae Recknor, Michael Totte Kathy, Bethany, Brystol, Kimberly and Emery Recknor.
89 – Terry Wullenweber.
90 – Macy Reno, Jim Coon, Jim Kin John, Sara and Jack Dryden.
91 – Stephen Bowman, Sonya Hoffman, Susan Walters, Dennis Jorgensen, John and Daniel Krantz, Dennis Vermillion.
92 – Dave Walker, Jack Dryden, Lee Downey, Patrick Thevenow, Jim Coo
93 – Mike and Padgett Taylor, Cooki Binzer, Scott Bate, Dave and Kay Lo Adams, Kenny Guthrie, Brook Reindoll
94 – Rusty Bladen, Chris Croxton, Drew Geerts.
95 – Lisa Croxton, Sandy Bruns, Trevor and Roman Lytle.
96 – Grant Ward.
97 – Rob and Michelle Barlow, Georgie Kelly, Jane Michelle Kelly, Ir Rowlett.
98 – Jim Grant, Tim Armstrong, Rory Fulk, Mason and Isabella May, Scott Davis.
99 – Michael Heitz, Pat Heitz.
103 – Laura Hodges, Don Ward, Jan Vetrhus.
104 – Tim Armstrong, Jan Vethrus.